Learning, Education and Games
Volume One: Curricular and Design Considerations

Edited by Karen Schrier

Written by members of the Learning, Education and Games (LEG) Special Interest Group (SIG) of the International Game Developers Association (IGDA)

Learning, Education and Games
Volume One: Curricular and Design Considerations

Learning, Education and Games
Volume One: Curricular and Design Considerations

Edited by Karen Schrier

*Written by members of the Learning, Education and Games (LEG) Special Interest Group (SIG)
of the International Game Developers Association (IGDA)*

Table of Contents

SECTION I—Curricular Considerations

SECTION II—Design Considerations

Introduction

Karen Schrier
Kschrier@gmail.com

I am thrilled to introduce this brand new book series, *Learning, Education and Games*, which examines the latest research and design techniques for creating and using games for learning. This is the first book in a two-book series, which was written, edited, and reviewed by members of the Learning, Education and Games (LEG) Special Interest Group (SIG), a subset of the International Game Developers Association (IGDA).

But first, let us take a step back. Is there even a connection between games and learning? Popular opinion and mainstream media seem to suggest that games, if anything, are the antithesis to learning. On the other hand, my experiences during the past decade have repeatedly reminded me how much learning and games are interconnected. I observed how the power of play helps us experiment with new identities, safely explore choices and consequences, and push the boundaries of a system. I experienced how games provide access to new worlds and alternate systems of values, past moments of history, and social interaction with people from diverse cultures, perspectives, and experiences. I saw how games could situate learning in authentic contexts, such as environmental disaster zones for science learning, physical battle sites for history learning, foreign countries for language learning, or even in real texts for literature and literacy learning. Essential skills—from math facts acquisition to vocabulary building to civic literacy—could be taught through games, if the games were properly designed. The potential for teaching complex thinking skills—such as creativity and innovation, ethical thinking, design and problem solving, systems thinking, and computational understanding—also seem to be suggested by burgeoning research.

On the flip side, we know there are limits to what any game can do, just like any educational program, process, or activity. One game may fit a particular pedagogical need, audience, and set of goals and constraints, while the same game could be inappropriate in a different context. One game may support certain learning styles or skill needs, but not others. Just as the potentials of games for learning have been suggested, the limits also need to be identified. We need to not only understand whether a game can teach, but the conditions under which it can (or cannot) help someone learn.

Assessing the efficacy of games in support of the acquisition and long-term practice of skills and concepts in games has shown to be challenging. While assessing other types of educational interventions and programs is often tricky, games—and their many factors, ecologies, and contexts—may confound us even further. Despite these challenges, in the past decade or so, the attention to and research of games and learning has blossomed exponentially.

Likewise, there has been an increase in the creation and use of learning games in classrooms and informal education sites (e.g., afterschool, libraries, home), as well as a growth in the number of websites, applications, and other media devoted to educational games. With the advent of more accessible and open game tools, engines, and platforms, there is also an emerging indie scene of educational game makers.

Games and gaming for learning have also crept into unexpected corners—from the government to the workplace, hospitals and doctor's offices, and the military. Although the term gamification has been bandied about more recently to discuss games being used in not-typically-game contexts, people have been trying to design powerful and engaging experiences using good games for years. While espousing the pros and cons of "gamification" is not the focus of this book series, the fact that the use of this term has increased so rapidly (though perhaps in misaligned contexts), further suggests a need to reevaluate the intersection of games and learning.

Despite all of the technological, social, and economic innovations that have allowed us to create, play, iterate on, replicate, and research digital games, we also cannot overlook the many forms games can take. Games—whether digital, hybrid, virtual, analog, online, offline, console, web-based, text-based, graphics-intensive, or mobile—are, at their core, games. Human beings have been playing games, and learning from games, since the start of humankind. We cannot forget that games are, at their essence, about sharing and communicating truths about ourselves. And, if you play a game, no matter what you have learned *something*—which is, at the very least, how to play the game.

For these reasons, it is an appropriate juncture to pause and consider the state of learning, education and games. The mission of this book series is to articulate the limits and potentials of games for learning, to identify the best practices, exemplars, and case studies, and to explore what remains to be examined. Educators, school policymakers, parents, and designers struggle to understand better ways to develop and use games for learning and education. With this book, we seek to empower these audiences to understand the primary theories, latest research findings, and best practices, and use this knowledge to better design and integrate games into their homes, classrooms, districts, libraries, afterschool centers, day cares, workplaces, and museums.

Please note that this book series will describe the potential and limits of games to foster learning—but will not examine whether games are inherently good or bad, nor will it consider popularly discussed issues that could be counter to learning, such as game addiction, violence, or diminished physical activity. This book seeks to be a thoughtful and conversational approach to a burgeoning and complex field, so as to inform future design, policies, standards, curricula, and products. Additionally, we will try to steer away from defining games for learning and education with a snazzy term or acronym, such as those used in the past (e.g., edutainment, edugames). Instead, we will make the assumption that this book covers any game that is primarily designed or used for learning and education—even if it is (as it should be) also designed for fun, engagement, meaningfulness and/or entertainment.

Finally, this book will also cover games whose primary use is not that of learning. For example, mainstream, commercial off-the-shelf games (even controversial ones such as the *Grand Theft Auto* or *Call of Duty* series) can potentially be modified, altered, recontextualized, or reflected upon for educational purposes. That said, we agree that there are a ton of poorly designed and inadequately implemented educational games out there (and there are also bad games of all ilk and purpose). Instead of merely critiquing their existence, we hope that the theories, practices, and approaches described in this book will help to constructively change their use and design.

How To Use This Book

This first volume of this series on learning, education and games is divided into two main sections. The first section focuses on curricular considerations and dives into a number of disciplines and relevant design and research frameworks, techniques, and practices. This section includes chapters on STEM (science, technology, engineering and mathematics), computational thinking, history and social studies, literacy, music, physical education, emotional health, ethics, and 21st century skills. While these are not the only topics covered in school and informal educational outlets, they are an initial stab at unraveling the intricacies of teaching particular skill sets and themes through games.

The second section covers primary design and assessment considerations, and concentrates on illustrating game design techniques in relation to educational needs. While designing games is always a complex process, designing for educational purposes adds another layer of complexity, which we try to tease out in this section. In particular, we provide an overview of the methods of designing educational games, as well as narrow in on a few relevant topics such as defining goals and targeting an audience. We also cover techniques for playtesting and iterative design, as well as education assessment methodologies and practices as applied to games and game design.

Each individual chapter is divided into a number of segments, including the:

1. **Introduction**, which covers the major questions and terms related to the topic;
2. **Key Frameworks**, which introduces the primary theoretical frameworks for the use, design and evaluation of games for learning;
3. **Key Findings**, which relays the major recent findings in the field;
4. **Assessment Considerations**, which discusses specific assessment challenges or opportunities;
5. **Future Needs**, which lays out the open questions and gaps in research or application;
6. **Best Practices**, which summarizes the key takeaways and most effective techniques and findings.

Each chapter also includes two to four **case studies** to illustrate the theories and findings in practice. You can read the case studies individually or in the context of the chapter. Every chapter also provides a list of useful **resources** and relevant further reading (and gaming!).

In the next volume, we will focus on classroom, audience, and other contextual considerations as they relate to designing, using, and evaluating learning, education and games.

Acknowledgements

Many people helped out in the preparation of this first book in the series. I want to thank the authors: Katrin Becker, Elena Bertozzi, Meagan Bromley, Shannon Campe, Lucas Crispen, Sabrina Haskell Culyba, Paul Darvasi, Jill Denner, Ira Fay, Rick Ferdig, Owen Gottlieb, Ethan Hein, Bruce Homer, Liz Jasko, Randy Kulman, Elizabeth LaPensée, Jakob Leyrer, Robin Mellecker, Jim Parker, Kristine Pytash, Gabriela Richard, Roy Seitsinger, David Simkins, Teresa Slobuski, Manuel Sprung, Ralph Vacca, Charlotte Weitze, Linda Werner, Lisa Witherspoon, and Stephen Yang.

I want to thank the founding director and president of the Learning, Education and Games (LEG) SIG, Stephen Jacobs, and the LEG SIG steering committee members. I want to thank Katherine Ponds for her editorial and organizational assistance. In addition, Mark Chen provided valuable input into the creation of a database of platforms and game creation tools.

I want to thank the hardworking peer reviewers: Courtney Aiello, Elena Bertozzi, Mark Chen, Pierre Depaz, Brock Dubbels, Allan Fowler, Joseph France, Randall Fujimoto, Lisi Gopin Geffen, Jessica Hammer, Jenna Hoffstein, Liz Jasko, Elyssebeth Leigh, Anna Loparev, Matthea Marquart, Keiju Matsunaga, Robin Mellecker, Gabriel Recchia, Peter Shea, Ryan Sittler, Teresa Slobuski, Deborah Solomon, Moses Wolfenstein, and Nicole Zdeb. I also want to thank those people who helped with copyediting the manuscript, including Robert Dran Jr. I want to thank Drew Davidson and the ETC Press for their support and guidance in publishing this book series.

Finally, I want to thank my family, including my husband, David Shaenfield and my daughter, Alyssa, who was born during the writing and editing of this book.

Karen Schrier, Editor

Author Bios

Katrin Becker

President, Mink Hollow Media and Adjunct Professor, Mount Royal University, Calgary, Alberta, Canada, www.minkhollow.ca/becker, becker.minkhollow@gmail.com

Katrin Becker is an internationally known expert in the design and analysis of Serious Games. She holds two degrees in computer science and a Ph.D. in Educational Technology with a focus on instructional game design. She has over 30 years of teaching experience in science, engineering, education, and art, and she has taught computer science, video game design, digital game-based learning, and technical writing. Her teaching innovations have been internationally recognized and she is widely published in the areas of computer science education, educational technology, and digital game based learning. She designs and develops eLearning in all sectors, and has consulted for various organizations on the use of digital games for instructional purposes. She has designed and developed several educational and advertising games. She is also the author of a book on the technical aspects of simulations and games written for non-technical people. Finally, perhaps as counterpoint to her work in and with digital technology, she runs a small farm where she has been raising waterfowl and other animals for over twenty years. This farm forms the basis for her "Ducks in the Classroom" program, which has been providing eggs for hatching in classrooms locally since 1988, and information on school hatching projects globally since 2001.

Elena Bertozzi

Associate Professor, Game Design & Development, Quinnipiac University, Hamden, Connecticut, U.S., http://engendergamesgroup.com, elena.bertozzi@quinnipiac.edu

Elena Bertozzi has developed curricula and game design programs at Indiana University, Bloomington, University of Wisconsin, Whitewater and LIU. She founded the Engender Games Group Lab to facilitate partnerships between the public and private sectors. Her team of student artists, programmers, and interface designers has worked on a wide range of projects ranging from frog identification to helping women make decisions about birth control. She is currently involved in efforts to increase the quality of game proposals submitted for federal funding, and she is working on a serious game to promote safe sex practices funded by a Gates Foundation Global Challenge grant.

Meagan Bromley

Doctoral Student at New York University, New York, New York, U.S., meagan.kathleen@gmail.com

Meagan Bromley is a current doctoral student in New York University's Educational Communication and Technology program and a Research Assistant at CREATE lab, a member of the Games for Learning Institute. Her research interests include family learning, literacy learning in digital environments, interaction design for gestural interfaces, and the role of media in the development of cognitive skills like executive functions. Meagan's background working in media has included film development and production in the entertainment industry, field research with Sesame Workshop's Education, Research and Outreach Group and the Joan Ganz Cooney Center, and collaborations with companies including Microsoft Studios, Nokia Research, E-Line Media, IDEO, the New York Hall of Science and faculty at NYU, University of Vienna and LIFE Center. In that time, she contributed to studies in television and game-based digital media, investigating the assessment of learning and usability on interactive media designed for the web, handheld mobile devices and tablets, as well as the Nintendo Wii and Microsoft Kinect. She has also worked as a game designer and project manager on numerous projects. Meagan holds a Bachelor's degree in Film Studies from UC Berkeley, and a Master's degree in Digital Media Design for Learning from New York University.

Shannon Campe

Research Associate, ETR (Education, Training, Research), Scotts Valley, California, U.S., http://www.etr.org/, shannonc@etr.org

Shannon Campe is a Research Associate and Project Coordinator at Education, Training, Research (ETR). Her work focuses on bridging research and practice in K-12 education, with a focus on youth and technology. Current and recent projects include a study of how computational thinking develops in middle school students when they program computer games and a synthesis of research on children programming games. Her understanding of both educational practice and computer programming has led to presentations and publications in the fields of education and computer science education.

Shannon's other contributions include assisting with writing grant proposals, and coordinating large, multi-site research projects. Her skills include teaching, working with teachers and schools to bridge research and practice and to monitor fidelity of implementation, data collection and management, data analysis, and curriculum design. Shannon enjoys working in all areas of education with the focus on coordinating all parts and team members of a project, while staying connected to the students and teachers involved in the work.

Lucas Crispen

Instructor, Pixel Arts Game Development Education, Portland, Oregon, U.S., lucas.crispen@gmail.com

Lucas Crispen is an independent game developer and instructor for Pixel Arts Game Development Education in Portland, Oregon. He holds a degree in computer science and mathematics. He has worked with Buzz Monkey Software, where he contributed to multiple titles, including two games in the *Tomb Raider* series. He is currently working on an unannounced game while teaching and writing a curriculum for game programming courses at Self Enhancement, Inc., a non-profit organization that provides educational opportunities to disadvantaged middle school and high school youth.

Sabrina Haskell Culyba

Senior Game Designer, Schell Games, Pittsburgh, Pennsylvania, U.S.,
www.schellgames.com, sabrina@schellgames.com

Sabrina Haskell Culyba is a Senior Game Designer at Schell Games. Her design work in the game industry includes Disney's *Toy Story Midway Mania* ride, Disney's *Pixie Hollow Online* MMO, SeaWorld's *Race for the Beach* interactive exhibit, and several transformational games. She co-founded Interbots (interbots.com), where her work includes several high-end animatronic characters, as well as several mobile applications for young children with Autism. Sabrina received her B.S. in computer science and her Master's in entertainment technology from Carnegie Mellon University.

Paul Darvasi

High School Media Studies and English Teacher and Co-Director, Toronto Student Film Festival, Toronto, Canada, www.ludiclearning.org, pauldarvasi@yahoo.ca

Paul Darvasi teaches high school English and media studies in Toronto, Canada, and is co-director of the Toronto Student Film Festival. He earned an English literature degree from McGill University, a Master of Educational Technology from the University of British Columbia and is a Ph.D. candidate in York University's Language, Culture, and Teaching program. He designed *The Ward Game*, a pervasive game to teach high school seniors *One Flew Over the Cuckoo's Nest*, and he is co-designing *Blind Protocol*, an inter-school Alternate Reality Game (ARG) that instructs on privacy and surveillance. Paul has lived and worked in South America, Africa and some remote communities in northern Canada. He spent many years working in Antarctic and expedition tourism, including leading trips to Machu Picchu and the Galapagos Islands. He has optioned a feature film screenplay, and worked as freelance journalist and translator in Santiago, Chile. His current work explores the instructional possibilities offered by the intersection of narrative, games and literature.

Jill Denner

Senior Research Scientist, ETR (Education, Training, Research), Scotts Valley, California, U.S., http://www.etr.org/, jilld@etr.org

Dr. Jill Denner is a Senior Research Scientist at Education, Training, Research (ETR), a non-profit organization in California. She does applied research in K-12 settings, with a focus on increasing the number of women and Latino/a students in computer science and information technology. Her current focus is on how middle school students learn while creating computer games, the role of peers and families in children's educational pathways, and increasing diversity in community college computer science classes. Dr. Denner has been a Principal Investigator (PI) on several NSF grants, published numerous peer-reviewed articles, and co-edited two books: *Beyond Barbie and Mortal Kombat: New Perspectives on Gender and Gaming,* published by MIT Press in 2008, and *Latina Girls: Voices of Adolescent Strength in the U.S.,* published by NYU Press in 2006. Dr. Denner has a Ph.D. in developmental psychology from Teachers College, Columbia University.

Ira Fay

Assistant Professor of Computer Science and Game Design at Hampshire College and CEO of Fay Games, Amherst, Massachusetts, U.S., http://irafay.com, ira@irafay.com

Ira Fay is an Assistant Professor of Computer Science and Game Design at Hampshire College and is the CEO of Fay Games, a studio primarily focused on games for educational impact. He previously co-founded the Game Design and Development program at Quinnipiac University, where he was an Assistant Professor of Game Design and Development. Before beginning his academic career, Ira was a Senior Game Designer at Electronic Arts (Pogo.com), where he led Pogo iPhone game development and released several top web games. Prior to Pogo, Fay worked at Z-Axis (Activision) on *X-Men 3*, at Maxis on *The Sims 2,* and at Walt Disney Imagineering on *ToonTown Online.* Fay graduated from Carnegie Mellon University with a bachelor's degree in computer science and master's degrees in information systems management and entertainment technology. He is also a published board game designer.

Richard E. Ferdig

Summit Professor of Learning Technologies, Professor, Instructional Technology, Kent State University, Kent, Ohio, U.S., http://www.ferdig.com, rferdig@gmail.com

Richard E. Ferdig is the Summit Professor of Learning Technologies and Professor of Instructional Technology at Kent State University. He works within the Research Center for Educational Technology and also the School of Lifespan Development and Educational Sciences. He earned his Ph.D. in Educational Psychology from Michigan State University. He has served as researcher and instructor at Michigan State University, the University of Florida, the Wyzsza Szkola Pedagogiczna (Krakow, Poland), and the Università degli studi di Modena e Reggio Emilia (Italy). At Kent State University, his research, teaching, and service focus on combining cutting-edge technologies with current pedagogic theory to create innovative learning environments. His research interests include online education, educational games and simulations, the role of faith in technology, and what he labels a deeper psychology of technology. In addition to publishing and presenting nationally and internationally, Ferdig has also been funded to study the impact of emerging technologies such as K-12 Virtual Schools. Rick was the founding Editor-in-Chief of the *International Journal of Gaming and Computer Mediated Simulations,* is the current Associate Editor-in-Chief of the *Journal of Technology and Teacher Education*, and also serves as a Consulting Editor for the Development Editorial Board of *Educational Technology Research and Development* and on the Review Panel of the *British Journal of Educational Technology.*

Owen Gottlieb

Jim Joseph Fellow and Ph.D. Candidate in Education and Jewish Studies at New York University, New York, New York, U.S., http://www.converjent.org, owen@converjent.org

Owen Gottlieb is a Jim Joseph Fellow and Ph.D. Candidate in Education and Jewish Studies at the NYU Steinhardt School of Culture, Education, and Human Development. He specializes in Digital Media and Games for Learning. Gottlieb is the founder and director of ConverJent: Jewish Games for Learning (www.converjent.org). His mobile GPS augmented reality game, *Jewish Time Jump: New York* was nominated for Most Innovative Game by the 2013 Games for Change Festival. Gottlieb's eclectic background includes project management for Internet software development, screen and television writing for Paramount and Universal, and rabbinic ordination (Reform). Gottlieb's work crosses the fields of Jewish education, the learning sciences, the digital humanities, media studies, cultural anthropology, and social studies education. He holds a bachelor's degree from Dartmouth College, master's degrees from the University of Southern California School of Cinematic Arts and Hebrew Union College-Jewish Institute of Religion. He is a member of the Writers Guild of America, West; the Central Conference of American Rabbis; and the International Game Developers Association.

Ethan Hein

Adjunct professor of Music Technology and Music Education at New York University, New York, New York, U.S., http://ethanhein.com/, ethan@ethanhein.com

Ethan Hein teaches music tech to future music teachers at NYU and Montclair State University. A graduate of NYU's Music Technology program, Ethan has spent fifteen years performing, teaching, composing, and writing about music. He is a co-developer of Play With Your Music, a MOOC (Massively Open Online Course) that introduces audio production concepts and techniques, developed in collaboration with NYU, the MIT Media Lab, P2PU, and Peter Gabriel. He works with the NYU Steinhardt Music Experience Design Lab, developing new software and physical interfaces for music learning, engagement and creativity.

Bruce Homer

Associate Professor, The Graduate Center at City University of New York, New York, New York, U.S., BHomer@gc.cuny.edu

Dr. Bruce D. Homer is an Associate Professor of Educational Psychology in the Learning, Development and Instruction subprogram at the Graduate Center, City University of New York. He is the director of the Child Interactive Learning and Development (CHILD) Lab there, and co-Director of the CREATE lab at New York University. His research examines how children acquire and use "cultural tools" to store and transmit knowledge (e.g., language, literacy, and information technologies), and how these tools transform developmental and learning processes. He and his colleagues have been investigating how different design patterns in games affect student learning and motivation, as well as ways of embedding assessment into educational games to provide to students and educators. This line of work has included examinations of emotional design for improved learning outcomes in video games, and recently involved research on the potential of video games to assess and train executive functions in children. Dr. Homer holds an MA in Applied Cognitive Science and a Ph.D. in Human Development and Applied Psychology from the University of Toronto.

Liz Jasko

UX Designer, The Lathe, New York, New York, U.S., www.lizjasko.com, ljasko@gmail.com

Liz Jasko is a UX designer specialized in purposeful technology. She has guided user experiences in educational media, games and mobile apps including work for Discovery Kids and Bayer Pharmaceuticals. She is the co-organizer of the Game-Based Learning NYC Meetup group, and a member of the IGDA. Jasko holds a B.A. in Communications & Media Arts for Interactive Media/Game Studies from Marist College. Her article "How Video Games Can Revolutionize the Static Classroom" was published in the *Fox Forum* academic discourse journal of Marist College, and she was awarded by the School of Communications and the Arts for "Outstanding Achievement in Interactive Media/ Game Studies." After a semester studying abroad in Italy, Jasko took a special interest in researching and designing language-learning games.

Randy Kulman

Founder and President, LearningWorks for Kids, PeaceDale, Rhode Island, U.S., http://www.learningworksforkids.com/, randy@learningworksforkids.com

Randy Kulman, Ph.D. is the Founder and President of LearningWorks for Kids, an educational technology company that specializes in using video games and interactive digital media to teach executive-functioning and academic skills. For the past 25 years Dr. Kulman has also been the Clinical Director and President of South County Child and Family Consultants, a multidisciplinary group of private practitioners that specializes in assessment and interventions for children with learning disorders and attention difficulties. Additionally, Dr. Kulman is the author of numerous essays on the use of digital technologies for improving executive-functioning skills in children in which he has developed concepts such as "play diets" and "engamement" to help parents and teachers understand the impact of digital technologies on children. He is the author of *Train Your Brain for Success: A Teenager's Guide to Executive Functions* and the co-author of a chapter in the book *Designing Games for Ethics: Models, Techniques, and Frameworks* published in 2011 by IGI Global. He is also the author of the forthcoming 2014 book *LearningWorks for Kids: Playing Smarter in the Digital World*.

Elizabeth LaPensée

Game Researcher, Designer, and Writer, Portland, Oregon, U.S., elizabethlapensee@gmail.com

Elizabeth LaPensée, Ph.D., specializes in Indigenous determination in game development, including research, design, writing for games and participating in game development education for Indigenous youth. She contributed writing and consultation for the transmedia property *Animism* (2011). She has consulted and written for games such as Andy Schatz's *Venture Arctic* (2007). Currently, she is designing a board game about Northwest Native traditional foods with the Northwest Indian College as well as co-designing a suite of Tulalip traditional foods games for the Oregon Museum of Science and Industry. She is passionate about living by example as well as passing on skills and providing access to technology to empower the next generations to determine their own representations in games.

Jakob Leyrer

Doctoral Student, Psychology, University of Vienna, and Research Assistant at Games4Resilience Lab, Vienna, Austria, jakob.leyrer@univie.ac.at

Jakob Leyrer is a current doctoral student in the Department of Psychology at the University of Vienna, and a Research Assistant at the Games4Resilience Lab. His research centers around the development of games to train emotional understanding and executive functioning in children. As a project manager on the game *EmoJump*, he has assembled groups of graduate students, artists and programmers to design and build a research prototype. On *Space Ranger Alien Quest* he has worked in collaboration with teams from New York University, the Graduate Center at City University of New York, and programmers from the University of Applied Sciences Technikum Wien to build a game engine and lead playtesting and research studies in local schools with Austrian children. He has presented his research findings throughout Europe at both academic and game industry events.

Robin Mellecker

Post Doctorate Fellow, Institute of Human Performance, The University of Hong Kong, Hong Kong, robmel@hku.hk

Dr. Robin Mellecker received her Ph.D. at the University of Hong Kong and is currently a Post Doctorate Fellow in the Institute of Human Performance at the University of Hong Kong. Robin is a passionate researcher who examines ways in which modern computer gaming technology can be used to encourage children to participate in physical activity and to learn academically. Robin has published and presented her research findings and has won awards for her research locally and internationally. Her aim is to engage multiple stakeholders in planning, implementation, and evaluation of physical activity and learning intervention strategies and to enhance the likelihood that innovative technologies will be incorporated into activity and learning programs that are sustainable and can be replicated in schools and community settings.

Jim Parker

Professor of Art at the University of Calgary and Principal Designer at MinkHollow Media Ltd, Alberta, Canada, www.ucalgary.ca/~jparker, parker@minkhollow.ca

Jim Parker is a full Professor in the Department of Art at the University of Calgary, teaching game design and media art, and before that he taught Computer Science at the same school for 26 years (image processing, game development) and Drama for two years. He is the author of six books, the latest being, *Game Development Using Processing.* He has most recently has been conducting research in virtual theatre and in computer games, especially serious games. Jim is also the principal designer at MinkHollow Media Ltd, a serious game developer in Canada.

Kristine E. Pytash

Assistant Professor, Literacy Education, Teaching, Learning and Curricular Studies, Kent State University, Kent, Ohio, U.S., http://www.literacyspaces.com/, kpytash@kent.edu

Kristine E. Pytash is an assistant professor in Teaching, Learning and Curriculum Studies at Kent State University's College of Education, Health, and Human Services, where she co-directs the secondary Integrated Language Arts teacher preparation program. She was a former high school English teacher. Her research focuses on disciplinary writing, writing instruction in juvenile detention facilities and the literacy practices of youth in alternative schools and juvenile detention facilities. Her recent work has appeared in the *Journal of Adolescent & Adult Literacy, English Journal, Voices from the Middle,* and *Middle School Journal.*

Gabriela T. Richard

Postdoctoral Research Fellow for Academic Diversity, Graduate School of Education, University of Pennsylvania, Philadelphia, Pennsylvania, U.S., http://www.gabrielarichard.com, gric@upenn.edu

Gabriela T. Richard is a Postdoctoral Research Fellow for Academic Diversity at the University of Pennsylvania in the Graduate School of Education. She is a National Science Foundation (NSF) and AAUW-funded scholar, whose research speaks more broadly to issues important to media designed for formal and informal education. Specifically, her research focuses on how to design and implement educational media and technology that is inclusive and sensitive to how social realities can disproportionately affect identification and achievement (particularly across sociocultural experiences, including gender, ethnicity, and sexuality). She has worked as an interactive designer, and taught instructional design and educational games courses at New York University, CUNY, and University of Pennsylvania. Before starting her Ph.D., she developed an innovative outreach program, which taught New York City public school students and teachers how to develop tangible media with physical computing, which received grant funding from the NSF. For over ten years, she has taught youth how to develop interactive and tangible media, including digital games. She has presented widely on why diversity matters in media design, as connected to her research findings of marginalizing practices in game culture and their relationship to social identities and stereotype threat. She received her master's degree from the Interactive Telecommunication Program at New York University, and her Ph.D. from the Educational Communication and Technology Program at New York University.

Karen Schrier

Assistant Professor of Media Arts, Marist College and Director, Play Innovation Lab, Marist College, Poughkeepsie, New York, U.S., www.playinnovationlab.com, kschrier@gmail.com

Dr. Karen Schrier is an Assistant Professor of Media Arts at Marist College, where she leads the concentration in Interactive Media/Game Design. She also directs the Play Innovation Lab (www.playinnovationlab.com), which researches and creates games and media for education and social change. Prior to Marist, she designed and produced websites, apps, and games at Scholastic, BrainPOP, Nickelodeon and ESI Design. She is the editor of this book series on games and learning, and has previously edited two books on games and ethics: *Designing Games for Ethics* and *Teaching Values through Play*. Dr. Schrier is also currently writing a book on games and social change (Johns Hopkins University Press, 2015). She is a member of the steering committee of the IGDA Learning, Education, and Games (LEG) SIG—the group that collaborated to write, review and edit this book. She holds a doctorate from Columbia University, master's degree from Massachusetts Institute of Technology, and a bachelor's degree from Amherst College.

Roy M. Seitsinger, Jr.

Superintendent of Schools, Westerly Public Schools, Westerly, Rhode Island, U.S., http://westerly.k12.ri.us, rseitsinger@westerly.k12.ri.us

Roy Seitsinger, Ph.D., has held the full range of educational leadership and learning positions since he began his career as a Title I literacy teacher for grade two in 1977. He is a former superintendent, assistant superintendent, middle school principal, middle school assistant principal, elementary school principal, and classroom teacher. He has led classrooms from kindergarten through high school in New England and grade four at an international school in London. Dr. Seitsinger has been the Superintendent of Schools in Westerly, Rhode Island since August 2010. During his tenure he has amassed a set of innovations that has gained statewide attention, not the least of which is his innovative partnership with the Town of Westerly in the creation of a joint Finance Director. Dr. Seitsinger was the Director of Middle School and High School Reform for the Rhode Island Department of Education from 2006 to 2010. As a community member Dr. Seitsinger continues to read to children, is a member of several professional organizations, and serves on the board of the local Supper Table, an organization dedicated to bring healthy meals to the less fortunate.

David Simkins

Assistant Professor, Rochester Institute of Technology, Rochester, New York, U.S., www.davidsimkins.org, dwsimkins@gmail.com

David Simkins is an assistant professor at the Rochester Institute of Technology where he is engaged in the assessment of games for learning for the National Science Foundation (NSF) and Department of Education (DoE) funded projects. In addition to work in learning assessment, he is a designer and a qualitative and mixed methods researcher of role-play in face-to-face and video game contexts. His Ph.D. is from University of Wisconsin-Madison Department of Curriculum and Instruction. Dr. Simkins is a founding member of the Games, Learning, and Society group at the University of Wisconsin-Madison.

Teresa Slobuski

Liaison Librarian for Elementary Education, Special Education, and Social Work at San Jose State University, San Jose, California, U.S., http://instantiatethis.com, teresa.slobuski@sjsu.edu

Teresa Slobuski, MLIS, is the liaison librarian for elementary education, special education, and social work at San Jose State University. She also serves as the librarian for San Jose State's nascent Learning and Games Education Initiative and manages International Games Day at the Library on campus. As the elementary education liaison she oversees collections of current and historical California textbooks for kindergarten through eighth grade. Slobuski completed her master's degree in library and information science at Rutgers University in her home state of New Jersey. She received her undergraduate degree in English from St. Mary's College of Maryland. She conducts research on a variety of topics such as the impact of non-text media on information retrieval, children's literature, and educational technology topics, especially the use of games as educational tools. In her free time, she spends as much time playing games as reason allows. She resides in San Jose, California and loves the sunny weather.

Manuel Sprung

Professor of Clinical Child and Adolescent Psychology, University of Vienna and
Founding Director of the Games4Resilience Lab, University of Vienna, Vienna, Austria,
www.manuelsprung.at, manuel.sprung@univie.ac.at

Dr. Manuel Sprung is a Professor of Clinical Child and Adolescent Psychology in the Department of Psychology at the University of Vienna, and founding director of the Games4Resilience Lab in the division of Clinical Child and Adolescent Psychology at the University of Vienna. Dr. Sprung has held academic and research positions at various universities in Europe and the U.S., including a position at Harvard University. His research interests are at the intersection of traditional areas of psychology and bridge with other academic disciplines, such as informatics, and exercise and sports science. He conducts transnational research on the efficacy and transportability of evidence-based child and adolescent mental health services. Research in the Games4Resilience Lab is aimed at developing innovative ways to disseminate effective interventions and to prevent child and adolescents mental health problems, to help fill the current treatment gap in mental health care.

Ralph Vacca

Doctoral student at New York University, New York, New York, U.S., ralph.vacca@nyu.edu

Ralph Vacca is a doctoral student in New York University's Educational Communication and Technology program and researcher at dolcelab. His research focuses on the use of technology to promote personal wellness for social wellness, specifically promoting empathy, compassion, emotion regulation, and civic engagement. Ralph's background includes design of award-winning commercial games and simulations in the area of mental health, the design of social change games, and exploring social entrepreneurship as vehicle for serving at-risk populations. Ralph holds a bachelor's degree in entrepreneurship from City University of New York, and master's degree in educational leadership from NYU.

Charlotte Lærke Weitze

Doctoral student, Learning and Philosophy Department and ILD-lab at Aalborg University,
Copenhagen, Denmark, http://personprofil.aau.dk/126686, cw@learning.aau.dk

Chartlotte Weitze was trained as a pianist at The Royal Danish Conservatory of Music and earned a M.SC. from the IT University of Copenhagen, focusing on digital design and communication. In her master's thesis, she developed a model of how to develop motivating and engaging learning game as well as a concept for a music learning game, which she has described in the article, *The Smiley model—*

Concept Model for Designing Engaging and Motivating Games for Learning. She is interested in design of learning games—both professional design of learning games, as well as learners' design of games as a way to become subject experts. In addition, she is interested in methods for competence development of teachers when they need to be innovative in respect to the use of IT in teaching. She is also interested in the development and measurement of students' and teachers' motivation and engagement in learning situations. She is a Ph.D. student in the Department of Learning and Philosophy and ILD-lab: IT and learning design at Aalborg University in Copenhagen.

Linda Werner

Adjunct Professor of Computer Science, Baskin School of Engineering, University of California, Santa Cruz, California, U.S., http://www.soe.ucsc.edu/people/linda, linda@soe.ucsc.edu

Dr. Linda Werner is an Adjunct Professor of Computer Science (CS) at the University of California, Santa Cruz. She has experience as an educator and researcher at the university, community college, high school, and junior high levels. Dr. Werner was the Primary Investigator (PI) on an NSF-funded study of the retention of female CS students, the results from which provide convincing evidence for using pair programming in introductory CS courses. She has been invited to share her research on pair programming at the university and middle school levels in international settings, as well as NSF and ACM JETT/TECS sponsored workshops. In addition, she has many years of experience as a software engineer. She has consulted on an NSF-funded study to design, implement and conduct research on game design as a strategy for increasing girls' interest, skills, and confidence in technology. She was also the co-PI of an NSF-funded study of middle school students, computer game design, and computational thinking. She is a co-PI of an NSF-funded study of community college CS students looking at the role of motivation, family support and prior computer use, particularly digital gaming. Linda Werner has a Ph.D. in CS from the University of California, San Diego.

Lisa Witherspoon

Assistant Professor, The University of South Florida, The School of Physical Education and Exercise Science, Tampa, Florida, U.S., Withersp@usf.edu

Lisa Witherspoon, Ph.D. is an Assistant Professor at The University of South Florida in the School of Physical Education and Exercise Science. She received her academic qualifications in Early Childhood Education, curriculum and instruction, with a cognate in Physical Education. Dr. Witherspoon serves as the Co-Director of the USF Active Gaming Research Laboratories. Her research focuses on understanding the effects of active gaming technologies on physical activity and improvements in lifelong physical activity behaviors. Dr. Witherspoon is also an established business advisor, author and presenter at International and National conferences and events related to the field of active gaming. In addition, she serves on National committees and Advisory Boards related to physical education, active gaming, sports and fitness concepts. Dr. Witherspoon's most recent achievement has landed her a role as PE Central Active Gaming Managing Editor. She has been elected as an Inaugural iTeach Fellow at the University of South Florida to assist future teachers and current faculty in using technology in the classroom. In addition, Dr. Witherspoon has served as a consultant for national and global organizations as well as many corporations in writing curriculum and conducting presentations.

Stephen Yang

Assistant Professor, Health Promotion & Wellness, at SUNY Oswego,
Oswego, New York, U.S., exergamelab@gmail.com

Stephen P. Yang, Ph.D. is a Lecturer and Research Associate in the Center for Obesity Research (CORE) at SUNY Cortland. Dr. Yang actively pursued technologically innovative methods to promote physical activity in his role as a former high school teacher. Dr. Yang researches the effectiveness of using exergames (active video games) and technologies for children, adolescents, and adults with and without disabilities. His innovative approach to facilitate learning involved technology and problem-based learning principles. He has been actively involved in promoting the field of exergaming since its infancy and has published and presented internationally and nationally. As a contributor with the Games for Health (GFH) Project, Dr. Yang consults with video game developers, toy and technology firms, and exergaming companies on products and services. In recognition of his expertise, he was appointed to the Board of Advisors of Exergame Fitness and has been interviewed for several national news services. Throughout all his research and collaborations, Dr. Yang wishes to examine the effectiveness of using exergames as a gateway to inspire people to be more active and healthy over their lifetime.

Curricular Considerations

CHAPTER 1

Science, Technology, Engineering, and Mathematics (STEM)

Using Games to Teach, Practice, and Encourage Interest in STEM Subjects

Elena Bertozzi, *Quinnipiac University, Hamden, Connecticut, U.S., elena.bertozzi@quinnipiac.edu*

Key Summary Points

 Many games purport to teach, practice, or encourage interest in STEM subjects; however, many fail to do so in ways that can be statistically shown to be effective. The potential benefits of such games are often overstated. All parties should be more cognizant of realistically achievable outcomes.

 Designers and educators should establish parameters to determine what constitutes a successful game experience and design usability tests that measure the degree of improvement in students' aptitude and performance following engagement with STEM games.

 Progress is being made both in building STEM games and assessing their effects. Analysis of some successful games is helpful in determining how to include games in curricula and demonstrating how they support educational goals.

Key Terms

STEM
Self-efficacy
Technological literacy
Scientific method
Intrinsically motivating
Game physics
Playful learning

Introduction

Educators, politicians, and businesspeople are among the many parties concerned about the decline of STEM (science, technology, engineering, and mathematics) competency in the United States. Other countries such as China and the Nordic countries are doing a much better job of preparing citizens for a highly technological and scientifically complex world (OECD, 2013). A scientifically informed and competent workforce is essential for success in an increasingly technological world. Regardless of what kinds of work students eventually go into, understanding the scientific process, fostering a sense of wonder about the world around us and the bodies we inhabit, and encouraging engagement with math and computer programming will enrich their lives and help them make informed decisions as an electorate.

Concurrently, we have seen enormous growth and development in the computer, mobile and casual game markets, along with hardware development that has enabled a range of new ways to interface with computer games on multiple platforms. As a result, academics, funding organizations, and developers have fostered interest in the potential use of games on multiple platforms to help encourage, teach, and practice STEM competencies. Many games, such as *MathBlaster*, which claim to accomplish these goals have been produced and successfully marketed despite the fact that there is little proof of their effectiveness (Greer, 2013). Games that have actually demonstrated measurable success (e.g., *Wuzzit Trouble* in improving math understanding (Beveridge, 2013)) are rarer.

One reason for the difficulty in suggesting that games are more effective at motivating and teaching students than traditional methods is that STEM subjects are complex and difficult, and achieving competency in these areas typically requires long periods of focused practice. Games can be very helpful in exposing children to scientific concepts and demonstrating how fascinating they are, but creating games that successfully teach how to calculate statistics or the properties of different chemical reactions, for example, has proven to be much more challenging. Progress is being made as developers and researchers determine what works best and how to deploy such games in educational environments (Clark, Tanner-Smith, Killingsworth, & Bellamy, 2013).

The profitability of the game industry over the past decade has led to innovation and rapid development of large-scale world simulations, such as *World of Warcraft* and *Eve Online*, which are populated by millions of players. At the moment, these environments are used primarily for entertainment purposes; however, they are now being explored for their educational potential as well. Such worlds can allow students to virtually experience and inhabit worlds different from the one in which they live. For example, researchers at San Francisco State University have created a game entitled *World of Balance* where players can manipulate the presence and growth of the flora and fauna native to a habitat and attempt to organize multiple interacting ecological systems to increase the health of the biome (http://smurf.sfsu.edu/~debugger/wb/). Games such as these demonstrate how complex systems are structured by allowing students to see and change them. Massively multiplayer online (MMOs) worlds can also expose students to economic principles such as currency and exchange rates, or the way incremental increases in technology can favor one side over another in a conflict, and the importance of forming and maintaining alliances. Games can also reduce the tedium of practice by creating environments with achievable goals and intrinsic rewards so that students will be motivated to continue seeking to overcome challenges.

It is important that both developers and educators realistically assess both the potential and limitations of such games so that they can be usefully deployed in learning environments. For example, 3D game environments are much costlier than simpler 2D games with less complex graphics, and are not necessarily more effective at communicating STEM concepts. The previously mentioned game *Math Blaster* allows the players to navigate 3D environments, but the 2D *Wuzzit Trouble* game does a better job of teaching math. New tools are being developed to help educators assess different games to determine what works best in any given environment. Common Sense Media created an online tool (http://www. commonsensemedia.org/app-reviews) where teachers and parents can share their experiences with and assessments of new applications and educational products. Serious game conferences, such as the Serious Play conference, now routinely include panels on outcomes measurement and assessment. The National Science Foundation (NSF) created a track specifically to fund educational STEM games, and academics and game developers are establishing more rigorous standards for demonstrating efficacy.

Students often avoid STEM subjects because they are difficult. Learning calculus and physics, for example, requires complex thinking, hours of repeated practice, and self-discipline. Games may be an important impetus for exposing students to practical uses of STEM and fostering an interest in being able to do it themselves. Simply playing with technology and managing the interfaces through which it is accessed is not enough, however. This chapter seeks to explore how games can be used to help students really go "under the hood" and understand how technology and science operate at a much more fundamental level. Some games create environments that allow players to see and manipulate items, such as molecules, which are very small in the real world so that students can learn how the building blocks of life combine. Other games provide players with actual blocks and give them a sandbox in which to use them to create any kind of structure with a variety of materials. Another strategy is to create a series of scenarios that present the player with complex problems and provide the tools to solve them. The player is given a goal and encouraged to explore.

Academics in the developing field of game studies are working to determine whether STEM-related games actually succeed in helping students engage with and succeed in STEM subjects when they are not playing. This chapter will discuss examples of games that are currently being used successfully to promote scientific thinking and practice. Additionally, we will explore some of the challenges of building such games and list best practices for ways that educators can deploy such games and monitor results.

Key Frameworks

The act of playing games on machines is in and of itself practice with technology (Bertozzi & Lee, 2007). Many intelligent living beings use play as a way to become familiar with and adept at manipulating the tools required for success in specific ecosystems (Heinrich, 1999). Human beings living in technologically complex worlds have an advantage if they have acquired the high-level skills necessary to create and manipulate the technologies that make our world work. Students who play a lot of games on computers, tablets, and phones may experience pleasure from this activity. If the pleasure is interrupted, they are strongly motivated to return to it. Thus, such children are more likely to learn how the technology works so that they can fix it if it is broken and therefore have a better understanding of how it works. The V-chip, which was meant to protect children from adult content, is an excellent example. Many parents were unable to make it work by themselves and had to call their children to figure out how to use and remove it because the children understood the control system better than the parents did (Hazlett, 2004).

Children who play video games are much more likely to want to learn software engineering and computer programming than children who do not (Egenfeldt-Nielsen, 2006; Overmars, 2004). The recent creation and expansion of game design and development programs on college campuses is an international phenomenon that both recognizes the economic importance of the business of selling games (and thus the flourishing job market for developers) and the presence of strongly motivated students who want to be able to earn a living creating a medium that they love.

Researchers have determined that playing science-based games (forensic science mystery solving, for example) both increases fact retention and the likelihood that students will report motivation to pursue science-based careers (Miller, Chang, Wang, Beier, & Klisch, 2011). More longitudinal studies will be required to see if players actually do pursue such careers. Klopfer (2008) has worked extensively on integrating mobile technologies such as phones and tablets into science education by putting students in environments and asking them to solve problems using participatory simulations and play (Klopfer, 2008). Like the forensic science game mentioned above, the idea is to make the learning of science more similar to the practice of science (Rosenbaum, Klopfer, & Perry, 2007). Now that the viability of science games is better established, more specific studies seek to determine which deployments of games are more effective. For example, one study tested to see if is it better to let students play games freely or interrupt the play experience to introduce traditional learning experiences and found no difference in learning outcomes between the two methods (Koops & Hoevenaar, 2013). Other studies are focused on isolating which elements of gameplay are most important to successful learning outcomes. Pavlas et al., found that video game self-efficacy (experience with and comfort level with games as a technology) and achieving a state of flow were the most significant predictors of learning success (Pavlas, Heyne, Bedwell, Lazzara, & Salas, 2010).

Good educational games tend to rest on similar frameworks. Norman (1994), defined some useful parameters for relaying information through games. Games meant to teach should:

1. **Provide a high intensity of interaction and feedback:** As mentioned above, games need to be fun and immersive so that students are engaged and receptive to learning.
2. **Have specific goals and established procedures:** Narrowly-focused games with specific outcomes (as discussed in the case studies) allow educators to assess how gameplay impacts knowledge retention.
3. **Motivate:** Good games have in-game incentives such as scores, badges, leveling up and rewards for victors.
4. **Challenge:** Provide a continual feeling of challenge that is neither so difficult as to create a sense of hopelessness and frustration, nor so easy as to produce boredom.
5. **Direct engagement:** Provide a sense of direct engagement, producing the feeling of directly experiencing the environment, directly working on the task.

There have been shifts in frameworks as more research is done in the field. In the past, games were implemented in the classroom with an "instructionist" perspective (making instructional materials looks like games). A more successful strategy appears to be a constructionist perspective (making games that embed learning) (Kafai, 2006). Early games for learning often seemed merely to be quizzes or flashcards that had been made digital and interactive, but lacked intrinsic motivation (they were not fun in and of themselves). Now it is understood that games have to be fun to play in addition to implementing their educational goals.

Case Study: Crowdsourcing Science (*Foldit* and *EyeWire*)

An important development is the creation and use of games that crowdsource tasks and problem solving. Such games not only help researchers advance their goals, but also allow the general public to view, educate themselves about and play with complex physical phenomenon that they would otherwise be unlikely to be involved with (Good & Su, 2011).

For example, *Foldit* was created because scientists had been unable to resolve certain biomechanical functions without an understanding of how complex proteins were folded. A group of researchers at the University of Washington decided to use crowdsourcing as a way of addressing the problem (Game Science at University of Washington & University of Washington Department of Biochemistry, 2012). They created a series of game environments, allowed anyone to log into the system, and gave players the proteins as puzzles to solve. The environment was competitive and rewarded players both through scoring and through the good feeling that they were helping researchers solve important problems related to human health.

Eyewire (eyewire.org) is another example of making science problems available to the general public. The goal of Eyewire is to map the neurons in the human retina. The game takes a large number of high-resolution images of the brain and asks players to help identify which structures in the images are neurons and which are not. Players are initially trained in this identification through a tutorial and then encouraged to compete with other players to see how quickly and accurately they can identify the greatest number of neurons. As with the *Foldit* game, *Eyewire* allows access to highly detailed and specific scientific information to anyone who wants to login. The images are aesthetically interesting and the challenge is intellectually satisfying.

Both of these games could be used in school environments to show students the complex and fascinating structures that make up the human body and to provide contemporary examples of the ways that science can manipulate them to improve health. Given their narrow focus, clearly defined tasks, demonstrably successful motivational incentives and explicit parameters for success, they serve as examples of the aforementioned attributes of successful educational games. Additionally, the games demonstrate how much time and painstaking attention to detail are necessary to make significant discoveries. Games of this type are not appropriate for all age levels, but they can serve as examples of how complex scientific information can be presented and explained to the public through play. It is important that educational games both demonstrate the potential of science and how difficult (and satisfying) it can be to make progress. Recent studies of the effects of playing these and similar games demonstrate that they do in fact improve cognition (Latham, Patston, & Tippett, 2013).

Key Findings

Although a great deal more work needs to be done to determine how games that effectively and playfully communicate STEM information can be constructed and deployed, there is some existing research documenting such effectiveness.

One major finding is that good games motivate players and can broaden their interests (Egenfeldt-Nielsen, 2006). Games can introduce players to the idea of environments as constructions— assemblages of parts that can be wondered at, explored, taken apart, studied, and rebuilt. Games such as *Neverwinter Nights* not only allow players to play in the world, but also provide players with the opportunity to "mod" the world. They can create their own modifications of the play environment and then publish them so that others can play their new version of the game (Kaplan-Rakowski & Loh, 2010). Play worlds can expose students to specific systems and networks of systems to help them see the way that things are connected and how their actions can affect individual parts. These concepts are fundamental to the sparking of curiosity about science, math, and engineering, which are based on our desire to understand ourselves, the world around us, and how everything works.

Minecraft, for example, is now one of the most played games in the world (22 million players) and is being used in both high school and college classrooms because the development team has specifically sought collaborations with educators to both implement the game in educational environments and study its effects (http://minecraftedu.com). *Minecraft* is a massively multiplayer online role-playing game (MMPORG) where players can construct structures out of a variety of different materials and then navigate through the worlds that they and others have built to accomplish a variety of different tasks. This game has been used successfully to further STEM education in multiple settings (Short, 2012) (see more in Case Study Two).

Another finding is that games can provide players with the opportunity to learn mathematical and scientific concepts intuitively rather than symbolically in the same way that a person can learn to play the piano without knowing how to read music (Devlin, 2013). Many schools begin teaching with the symbolic representation—numbers and graphs, for example—rather than introducing the concepts first and the symbolic representation afterward. Singapore math is taught according to the latter system (Hoven & Garelick, 2007). Games work similarly in that players can see the importance of understanding how the physical environment works to succeed in the game. In *Angry Birds*, for example, players have to intuitively figure out what kind of projectile to use and the angle and amount of force with which to launch it. These considerations involve thinking scientifically. Some educators have capitalized on this and are using the game in the classroom to teach how objects move through space and the math and science needed to calculate trajectories (Crecente, 2011).

Other findings include the proven effectiveness of using games for motivating and reinforcing the repeated practice necessary to become adept at the kinds of complex skills required in many STEM fields. Educators and developers are collaborating to build games specifically to introduce students to subjects in a way that makes repeated practice intrinsically motivating. Universities have started game development degree programs on their campuses that allow faculty to work together with students in STEM subjects to create games that reinforce specific skill sets such as mechanical engineering (Coller & Scott, 2009). Games are also increasingly being used in healthcare. *Atendiendo el Parto en Casa* (Bertozzi et al., 2013), for example, is being used to train midwives in developing countries how to deal with potentially fatal complications. Another game, *Underground*, creates an environment in which doctors, aspiring doctors and anyone who is interested can learn the motor skills required for laparoscopic surgery (Grendel Games, 2013) (see Case Study Three).

Case Study: Scenario-Based Games for Science (*Plague.Inc* and *Underground*)

Some developers have created scenario-based games for communicating science knowledge. These games immerse the player in an environment in which they must learn about a specific problem and acquire a specific skill set to survive in the game. *Plague.Inc*, for example, is a top-rated game for the Android platform. The premise of the game is that the player wants to infect all human beings and thereby eliminate humankind from the Earth. In the course of doing so, players learn a great deal about infectious diseases, how they spread, and how to infect (and also protect) populations. Through the play of the game, players also have to learn geography and demographics, how viruses mutate, and how to make a virus maximally virulent. By providing a goal that is the opposite of what might be expected—destroying fellow human beings rather than saving them—players can not only enjoy the gameplay, but also enjoy the thrill of breaking taboos, which can significantly add to a game's appeal (Bertozzi, 2008).

Other games can be more straightforward in their approach. Bertozzi's Engender Games Group lab, for example, has created a game aimed at educating midwives in developing countries (Bertozzi et al., 2013). Traditionally-trained midwives can make errors, which result in the death of the mother or the neonate during labor and delivery. In the developing world, midwives are often not literate, which further complicates training them. Using a scenario-based video game, midwives can play through the results of different actions and see how outcomes can improve using alternative methods (Cohen, Cragin, Wong, & Walker, 2012; Cragin, DeMaria, Campero, & Walker, 2007).

The Grendel team in Holland released a game, *Underground*, aimed at teaching surgeons (and prospective surgeons) how to acquire the physical coordination necessary to be skillful at laparoscopic surgery (Grendel Games, 2013). A local hospital discovered that the enormous amount of money that they had invested in a lab where physicians could practice their skills went to waste because physicians found the exercises in that lab to be extremely boring. Grendel's scenario-based game, with its compelling story and credible goals, which required players to become adept at using certain manual skills, was a much more successful method of encouraging physicians to exercise their skills in this area (GoogleTechTalks, 2012).

Assessment Considerations

There are now a plethora of games purporting to teach STEM subjects and it is very difficult to determine which ones are most effective for which contexts or learners. Given that there are not yet any professional rating or ranking systems to inform educators about which games are most effective in reaching specific teaching goals, the following questions can help an educator determine if a game is worth using for STEM learning. These questions are drawn from Norman's previously mentioned framework (1994) and from usability studies on interactive applications in general (Nielsen, 2000).

1. **Does the game have a narrow, specific, measurable outcome?** Look for games that have smaller and thus more achievable parameters for success.
2. **How long is the game?** Consider how long students will be playing the game and look for games that realistically promise what can be practiced or communicated in that amount of time.
3. **Is the interface clear and understandable for the target audience?** Many games present the player with challenges, but the user interface is not clear. When players get stuck, they may not be able to figure out how to get out of the situation. Good games include tutorials that walk players through gameplay or offer help sections.
4. **Has the game been run through cycles of usability and outcomes testing to ensure that stated goals are being met?** For example, if the game says that it is going to teach students to memorize and implement the multiplication tables, the company website should have usability and outcomes testing data to demonstrate effectiveness.
5. **Reputable third party assessment and endorsement of games can also help.** Ratings may or may not be useful. Games may be highly rated because they are fun to play; it is more difficult to find ratings assessing effectiveness.
6. **Does the game have internal means of measurement and reward that encourage players and promote continued engagement?** Players love to be given feedback. Scoreboards, badges, positive and negative sounds that respond to player behavior are all means by which games can keep players informed about how they are doing. Good educational games can integrate this assessment with the learning goals of the game. It is helpful for teachers if in-game assessments can support external assessment.
7. **Does the game provide educators with access points so that it can be integrated into existing classroom activities?** It is important to remember that games do not need to stand alone as learning tools. Teachers must integrate them into their own specific classroom environments in the same way other media are utilized. Thus, educator input into the development process is very useful. Game developers need to hear from educators about how this aspect of games can be improved.

Future Needs

Given the fact that using video games in the classroom is a relatively new phenomenon, educators currently have little guidance about how to use them effectively. Many schools now provide students with tablets (such as iPads) and encourage educators to integrate them into classroom activities. These efforts have coincided with an increased push for core competencies and outcomes assessment from the government and other agencies. It is essential that schools, educators and developers work together to find a way to develop and deploy games that foster an interest in and practice competencies in STEM subjects. Teachers cannot be expected to be able to review games and determine what will and will not work in the classroom without formal structures to assist them.

Case Study: Modding an Existing MMORPG with *Minecraft*

Rather than creating an entirely new game, educators can use existing games for educational purposes. The benefit of doing this is that the challenge of creating a compelling and fun experience has already been accomplished; now the game just needs to be implemented in a new setting. *Minecraft* is a sandbox game that provides players with a wide range of materials and tools and a great deal of freedom to do whatever they want inside the game space. The passage of time is simulated in the gamespace; day occurs and then night falls. During the day, players can accumulate materials and build things with them. At night, enemies emerge and it is important to have created structures that protect players from harm, otherwise death and destruction ensues. The game simulates the challenges living beings face in a natural environment and therefore many aspects of gameplay can be related to myriad scientific fields. To play the game, players must intuitively grapple with the principles of physics and architecture to put together structures that can protect them from enemies. They have to learn and use economic principles to acquire goods, resources, and capital so that they have the means to construct adequate protection. Many players create elaborate versions of structures that exist in the real world (e.g., the Taj Mahal) or in fictitious worlds (e.g., the Starship Enterprise). Educators are currently using this game to introduce and practice a range of engineering and science concepts (Short, 2012; West & Bleiberg, 2013), such as Bob Kahn's implementation in Brentwood Middle School (2013). There are many resources for educators at minecraftedu.com, including a wiki to help teachers and players answer questions and develop innovative ways to use the game.

Some games allow players to modify the game (known as "modding") by giving them access to the source code and encouraging them to come up with their own content. There are many games that leverage player interest to create new content in existing game worlds. Such games open their worlds to modifications by players who are able to build new sections of the game and then see what happens when players play inside of them (Soflano, 2011). *Minecraft* encourages modding and this aspect of the game has been utilized to teach and practice coding of artificial intelligence agents in game worlds (Bayliss, 2012). As both developers and educators come to recognize the potential benefits of games for education, we will see more targeted examples of gameplay that teach specific concepts.

Best Practices

Educators seeking games that will encourage, educate, and promote practice with STEM subjects should be aware of the fact that many games claiming to do so fail to meet the criteria for effective learning tools. This will change as the industry matures and educators and developers create and test new products and develop means for measuring effectiveness. At the moment, there are few directories or other tools for educators to use to find games that have proven effective. Educators should seek out games with a narrow focus with goals that appear reasonable and achievable. They should look for games that have been tested and can present evidence of outcomes assessment and usability analysis. Most importantly, games should be fun. Otherwise, they are simply interactive training environments masquerading as games. A good game motivates players to want to engage with it. STEM games should foster a sense of wonder and appreciation of the challenges involved in learning complex natural phenomena. Given the increased focus on the potential of games for educational motivation and achievement, games are attracting more funding (DeLoura & Metz, 2013) and more rigorous forms of assessment (Clark et al., 2013). This will certainly result in the development of better games and the means to integrate them into curricula.

Resources

Games

3rd World Farmer
Angry Birds
Big Seed
FoldIt
Extrasolar
EyeWire
Minecraft
Motion Math games
Newton's Playground
Plague.Inc
Rube Works: The Official Rube Goldberg Invention Game
Save the Seas
Sid's Science Fair
World of Balance (http://smurf.sfsu.edu/~debugger/wb/)
Wuzzit Trouble

Books

Baek, Y.K. (Ed.), *Gaming for Classroom-Based Learning: Digital Role Playing as a Motivator of Study*. Hershey, PA: IGI-Global.

Devlin, K. *Mathematics Education for a New Era. Video Games as a Medium for Learning*

Gee, J. *What Video Games Have to Teach Us About Learning and Literacy (Second Edition)*. New York, NY: Palgrave Macmillan.

Ifenthaler, D., Eseryel, D & Ge, X. (Eds). *Assessment in Game-Based Learning: Foundations, Innovations, and Perspectives.* New York, NY: Springer

Klopfer, E. *Augmented Learning: Research and Design of Mobile Educational Games*

Squire, K. *Video Games and Learning: Teaching and Participatory Culture in the Digital Age*

Websites

MinecraftEdu: Bringing Minecraft to the Classroom (http://Minecraftedu.com)

Educade (http://Educade.org)

Common Sense Media (http://www.commonsensemedia.org (see sections for STEM games)

Consortia & Labs

STEM Education Coalition (http://www.stemedcoalition.org/)

The New Media Consortium (http://www.nmc.org/news/get-technology-outlook-stem-education-2013-2018)

VirginaTech School of Education STEM Education Collaboratory (http://www.soe.vt.edu/STEM/collaboratory.html)

The Institute for Advanced Learning and Research STEM Internships (http://www.ialr.org/index.php/advanced-learning/k-12-programs/stem-internships)

References

Bayliss, J. D. (2012, 7-9 Sept. 2012). *Teaching game AI through* Minecraft *mods.* Paper presented at the Games Innovation Conference (IGIC), 2012 IEEE International.

Bertozzi, E. (2008). "I Am Shocked, Shocked!" Explorations of taboos in digital gameplay. *Loading...The Canadian Journal of Game Studies, 1*(3), online.

Bertozzi, E., & Lee, S. (2007). Not just fun and games: Attitudes towards technology and gameplay. *Women's Studies in Communication.*

Bertozzi, E., Walker, D., Rouse, C., Nguyen, N., Cooper, M., & Cooper, N. (2013). Atendiendo El Parto En Casa Retrieved January 21, 2013, from http://ardeaarts.org/atendiendo/

Beveridge, C. (2013). Review: *Wuzzit* Trouble. *Aperiodical.* Retrieved from aperiodical.com website: http://aperiodical.com/2013/09/review-wuzzit-trouble/

Clark, D., Tanner-Smith, E., Killingsworth, S., & Bellamy, S. (2013). Digital games for learning: A systematic review and meta-analysis (executive summary). Menlo Park, CA.

Cohen, S. R., Cragin, L., Wong, B., & Walker, D. M. (2012). Self-efficacy change with low-tech, high-fidelity obstetric simulation training for midwives and nurses in Mexico. *Clinical Simulation in Nursing, 8*(1), e15-e24. doi: http://dx.doi.org/10.1016/j.ecns.2010.05.004

Coller, B. D., & Scott, M. J. (2009). Effectiveness of using a video game to teach a course in mechanical engineering. *Computers & Education, 53*(3), 900-912. doi: http://dx.doi.org/10.1016/j.compedu.2009.05.012

Cragin, L., DeMaria, L. M., Campero, L., & Walker, D. M. (2007). Educating skilled birth attendants in Mexico: Do the curricula meet international confederation of midwives standards? *Reproductive Health Matters, 15*(30), 50-60. doi: http://dx.doi.org/10.1016/S0968-8080(07)30332-7

Crecente, B. (2011). *Angry Birds,* happy physicists. Retrieved June 10, 2013, from http://kotaku.com/5815767/angry-birds-happy-physicists

DeLoura, M., & Metz, E. (2013). Games win big in education grants competiton. Retrieved August 18, 2013, from http://www.ed.gov/blog/2013/05/games-win-big-in-education-grants-competition/

Devlin, K. (2013). The music of math games. *American Scientist*, 101, 87.

Egenfeldt-Nielsen, S. (2006). Overview of research on the educational use of video games. *Nordic Journal of Digital Literacy, 3.* Retrieved from http://www.idunn.no/ts/dk/2006/03/overview_of_research_on_the_educationaluseof_video_games

Game Science at University of Washington & University of Washington Department of Biochemistry. (2012). The science behind *Foldit.* Retrieved June 10, 2013, from http://fold.it/portal/info/about

Good, B., & Su, A. (2011). Games with a scientific purpose. *Genome Biology*, 12(12), 135.

GoogleTechTalks (Producer). (2013). *Playing Surgery:* A laparoscopy game for surgeons. Retrieved from http://www.youtube.com/watch?v=rpSvDvYvJGk

Greer, T. (2013). Mobile learning to reach $2.1 billion in North America by 2017. *Internet Learning Technology Research.* Retrieved August 17, 2013, from http://www.ambientinsight.com/News/Ambient-Insight-2012-2017-North-America-Mobile-Learning-Market.aspx

Grendel Games. (2013). *Underground.* Retrieved June 11, 2013, from http://www.grendel-games.com/index.php/products/serious-games/32-Underground

Hazlett, T. (2004). Requiem for the V-Chip. *Slate.* Retrieved from http://www.slate.com/articles/arts/gizmos/2004/02/requiem_for_the_vchip.html

Heinrich, B. (1999). *Mind of the raven: Investigations and adventures with wolf-birds* (1st ed.). New York: Cliff Street Books.

Hoven, J., & Garelick, B. (2007). Singapore math: Simple or complex? *Educational Leadership, 65*(3), 21-38.

Kafai, Y. B. (2006). Playing and making games for learning: Instructionist and constructionist perspectives for game studies. *Games and Culture, 1*(1), 36-40. doi: 10.1177/1555412005281767

Kahn, B. (2013). Middleschool *Minecraft.* Retrieved January 8, 2014, from http://www.middleschoolminecraft.com/

Kaplan-Rakowski, R., & Loh, C. S. (2010). Modding and rezzing in games and virtual environments for education. In Y. K. Baek (Ed.), *Gaming for Classroom-Based Learning: Digital Role Playing as a Motivator of Study* (pp. 205-219). Hershey, PA: IGI-Global.

Klopfer, E., & ebrary Inc. (2008). Augmented learning research and design of mobile educational games (pp. xvii, 251 p.). Retrieved from http://site.ebrary.com/lib/yale/Doc?id=10223881

Koops, M., & Hoevenaar, M. (2013). Conceptual change during a serious game: Using a Lemniscate Model to compare strategies in a physics game. *Simulation & Gaming, 44*(4), 544-561. doi: 10.1177/1046878112459261

Latham, A. J., Patston, L. L. M., & Tippett, L. J. (2013). The virtual brain: 30 years of video-game play and cognitive abilities. [Review]. *Frontiers in Psychology, 4.* doi: 10.3389/fpsyg.2013.00629

Miller, L. M., Chang, C.-I., Wang, S., Beier, M. E., & Klisch, Y. (2011). Learning and motivational impacts of a multimedia science game. *Computers & Education, 57*(1), 1425-1433. doi: http://dx.doi.org/10.1016/j.compedu.2011.01.016

Nielsen, J. (2000). *Designing Web usability.* Indianapolis, Ind.: New Riders.

Norman, D. A. (1994). *Things that make us smart : defending human attributes in the age of the machine.* Reading, Mass.: Addison-Wesley Pub. Co.

OECD. (2013). PISA 2012 results: What students know and can do. Retrieved December 23, 2013, from http://www.oecd.org/pisa/keyfindings/pisa-2012-results.htm

Overmars, M. (2004). Teaching computer science through game design. *Computer, 37*(4), 81-83. doi: 10.1109/mc.2004.1297314

Pavlas, D., Heyne, K., Bedwell, W., Lazzara, E., & Salas, E. (2010). Game-based learning: The impact of flow state and videogame self-efficacy. *Proceedings of the Human Factors and Ergonomics Society Annual Meeting, 54*(28), 2398-2402. doi: 10.1177/154193121005402808

Rosenbaum, E., Klopfer, E., & Perry, J. (2007). On location learning: Authentic applied science with networked augmented realities. *Journal of Science Education and Technology, 16*(1), 31-45. doi: 10.1007/s10956-006-9036-0

Short, D. (2012). Teaching scientific concepts using a virtual world—*Minecraft*. Teaching Science, 58(3), 55-58.

Soflano, M. (2011). Modding in serious games: Teaching Structured Query Language (SQL) using NeverWinter Nights. In M. Ma, A. Oikonomou & L. C. Jain (Eds.), *Serious Games and Edutainment Applications* (pp. 347-368): Springer London.

West, D. M., & Bleiberg, J. (2013). Education technology success stories. *Issues in Governance Studies,* from http://www.insidepolitics.org/brookingsreports/education_technology_success_stories.pdf

CHAPTER 2

Computational Thinking

Using Computer Game Programming to Teach Computational Thinking Skills

Linda Werner, *University of California, Santa Cruz, California, U.S., linda@soe.ucsc.edu*
Jill Denner, *ETR, Scotts Valley, California, U.S., jilld@etr.org*
Shannon Campe, *ETR, Scotts Valley, California, U.S., shannonc@etr.org*

Key Summary Points

1 Computer game programming can be used to engage middle school students in the development of computational thinking skills.

2 This paper describes a framework, Game Computational Sophistication, which is used to evaluate students' games regarding their computational sophistication.

3 Best practices include suggested assessment strategies, and ways that teachers can use computer game programming to maximize computational thinking.

Key Terms

Computer game programming
Computational thinking
Metrics for operationalization of computational thinking
Computational sophistication
Programming construct
Pattern
Game mechanic
Middle school

Introduction

A good way for teachers to motivate students to work on computational thinking (CT) skills is by bringing computer game programming into the K-12 classroom. CT is described as a set of skills that includes formulating problems, logically organizing and analyzing data, representing data through abstractions, and automating solutions (Barr & Stephenson, 2011). Selby (2013) proposes a definition of CT focusing on the activities that develop acquisition and provides evidence of CT skills. These include the ability to think in abstractions, generalizations, algorithmically, and in terms of decomposition and evaluation.

Wing (2006) explains that "(c)omputational thinking will be a fundamental skill used by everyone in the world by the middle of the 21st century." The Computer Science Teachers Association (CSTA) has included elements of CT in its "K-12 Computer Science Standards," such as problem solving, algorithms, data representation, modeling and simulation, and abstraction (CSTA Standards Task Force, 2011). These standards also identify a developmental progression in these skills. For example, a middle school level understanding of abstraction involves being able to decompose a problem into sub-parts, whereas a high school level understanding of abstraction involves using procedural abstraction, object-oriented design, and functional design to decompose a large-scale computational problem.

While most agree that CT is a set of important skills to develop, there is little guidance on how to teach them. Lee et al. (2011) describe an instructional progression that includes the steps that teachers can take to engage students in CT and involves creating models and simulations, as well as designing and programming computer games. Selby (2013) suggests that the following activities can lead to the development of CT skills: problem solving, systems design, automation, modeling, simulation, and visualization. Our own and others' research suggests that the design and building of computer games, if done with appropriate guidance and appropriate game development tools, leads children to develop and show evidence of the use of CT skills (Denner & Werner, 2011; Denner, Werner, & Ortiz, 2012; Werner, Denner, Campe & Kawamoto, 2012; Werner et al., 2012; Repenning, Webb, & Ioannidou, 2010; Resnick et al., 2009).

In this chapter, we describe how making a computer game can engage middle school students in CT. We offer a framework that we developed to evaluate students' games for CT, and include examples of how to identify different aspects of CT in specific games, such as problem solving, algorithms, modeling, and abstraction. Finally, we describe best practices that instructors can use to increase the likelihood that computer game programming will involve CT.

Key Frameworks

The research in this chapter builds on prior studies in the areas of complex problem solving and novice programming. The creation of computer games can be a complex problem solving activity and one that young students are capable of doing. Designing and programming a game is what Jonassen (2000) has described as a "design problem" that is ill-structured, requiring the student to define the goal, the solution path, and how to evaluate the solution. For example, most games include the key features of complex problem solving that were identified by Quesada, Kintsch, & Gomez (2005). These include tasks that are: 1) dynamic (each action changes the environment), 2) time dependent, and 3) complex (requires a collection of decisions that determine later ones). To study these features, research must look at how students attempt to solve problems—what they do when they are faced with situations that are dynamic (each action changes the environment), time dependent (use timers to enhance the gameplay experience) and complex (decisions made early in the game determine later decisions).

Historically, the first programs students create are not considered complex systems since they are not dynamic, not time dependent, and not complex. These first programs typically do not focus on the user of the program. Instead, these programs implement small, but highly constrained, computational tasks, such as adding integers or displaying the words "Hello World." With the advent of powerful, yet simple-to-use, novice programming environments such as *Alice and Scratch*, young students can create their own dynamic systems—computer games—and in doing so, the students focus on the user or game player, of their creations.

Our effort to understand what children learn by programming games is based on decades of studies. For example, research on the development of programming knowledge has described developmental progressions. Both Linn (1985), with her "chain of accomplishments" example, and Robins, Rountree, & Rountree (2003) describe three dimensions that can be used to distinguish between effective and ineffective computer programming novices:

1. **Knowledge:** The knowledge of design, language, and debugging tools;
2. **Strategies:** The strategies for design, implementing the program using a programming language, and debugging; and
3. **Models:** The mental models of the problem domain, the desired program, and the actual program.

These three dimensions—knowledge, strategies, and models—provide a useful framework for identifying the types of thinking that a student engages in while programming. While these dimensions sometimes overlap, Robins et al. (2003) suggest thinking of them as stages in the process of acquiring programming skills, and within each stage, students progress through the phases of designing, generating, and evaluating their program.

Research on children programming games and digital stories has focused less on progressions and more on the computer programs the children create. These efforts typically focus on the use of programming constructs, which are one of the fundamental computer science building blocks that are accessible to students in novice programming environments (Denner & Werner, 2011; Brennan & Resnick, 2012). Most of these studies have summarized which programming constructs appear in students' final programs, but do not distinguish between programming constructs that have been successfully or unsuccessfully used. The analysis of computer programs created by children done by Werner, Campe, & Denner (2012) is important because it relies not only on the presence of a programming construct, but also analyzes its use. This analysis determines whether the programming construct is reachable along some program path and whether the construct, when executed, causes abnormal program execution.

We propose a new framework for analyzing how children develop CT skills during computer game programming called "Game Computational Sophistication" that has been informed by the work by Jonassen (2000), Quesada et al. (2005), Linn (1985) and Robins et al. (2003). This framework emerged from our analysis of student games, and accounts for multiple levels of complexity that go beyond programming constructs to look at whether game programmers are creating complex systems. At the simplest level of the framework, are the elementary code pieces of students' games or programming constructs. These include a programming language's instruction set, and what are typically described in studies of how computer game programming can teach students higher order thinking.

At the next level of computational sophistication, students put together multiple programming constructs to create instances of "patterns," which are higher order computer science building blocks that use combinations of programming constructs. Patterns create additional program functionality but may or may not be contiguous segments of code. Expert programmers have libraries of these patterns, sometimes called "plans," from which to build their programs (Brooks, 1977; Pea & Kurland, 1984; Jeffries et al., 1981; Ehrlich & Soloway, 1984). Software engineers call these plans "design patterns," based on the work by Alexander (1997) who writes they "provide a common vocabulary for design, they reduce system complexity by naming and defining abstractions, they constitute a base of experience for building reusable software, and they act as building blocks from which more complex designs can be built (Gamma et al., 1993)." It is suggested by Kreimeier (2002) that game developers "make a sustained, conscious effort to define and describe the recurring elements of their daily work … so we can begin to create software tools made or adapted specifically for game design purposes." The identification of game design patterns creates a common language for both designing and analyzing games (Holopainen & Bj⊠rk, 2003). Repenning and his colleagues describe patterns at the level of phenomena (e.g., collision, transport, and diffusion), and they explore whether students can transfer the use of those patterns to other applications (Ioannidou, Bennett, Repenning, Koh, & Basawapatna, 2011). While these authors have advanced our understanding of how to think about and identify patterns, studies examining the incomplete, successful, and unsuccessful patterns used to create games developed by middle school youth are nonexistent.

At the highest level, the game computational sophistication includes "game mechanics," which are a combination of programming constructs and patterns. They are used to make the game fun to play and to challenge the player. Game mechanics are the actions, behaviors, and control mechanisms that are available to the player (Hunicke, LeBlanc, & Zubeck, 2004) and provide the kinds of actions that the player must take to move gameplay along. Sicart (2008) provides a definition of game mechanics that is useful for game analysis: "methods invoked by agents, designed for interaction with the game state… something that connects players' actions with the purpose of the game and its main challenges." In other words, the game designer must engage in complex problem solving to create rules, interactions between the rules, and the mechanics (the game pieces that provide the interactivity for the player) to address a challenge or set of challenges within the game. We know of no studies of games that identify game mechanics in games developed by youth. Discussions with game design experts and researchers have advanced our understanding of how to think about and identify game mechanics. Similar to the research on programming constructs and patterns, we are not familiar with any research that has examined the properties of incomplete, successful, and unsuccessful game mechanics in games developed by youth.

Key Findings

In this section, we describe how we used the Computational Sophistication framework to understand how computer game programming can teach children computational thinking skills. To assess the computational sophistication of the students' games, we first identified the programming constructs, patterns, and game mechanics that are possible given the programming environment used, and then analyzed the games' program codes for instantiations of these three types of computer game building blocks. The differences lie in the number and computational sophistication of the programming constructs and patterns used, the number of mechanics, as well as the complexity of the integration of constructs into patterns, patterns into mechanics, and the integration between the mechanics.

The study took place in technology elective classes during or after school at seven public schools in California. Three hundred and sixty-five middle school students using the *Alice* programming environment made the games. Over a two-year period, we offered our entire *Alice* curriculum 16 different times, each over a semester. Classes were randomly assigned for students to work on their games in a pair or by themselves. Students spent approximately ten hours learning to use *Alice* by following worksheets with step-by-step instructions to introduce programming constructs, and another ten hours programming their games. Students chose the content of their games with the limitations being that the content is appropriate for school, as defined by their teacher; that the game is interactive, has a player outcome, and includes player instructions. A total of 231 games were created.

The games were analyzed for the following *Alice* programming constructs, presented in order from least to most sophisticated: *do in order* statement, *do together* statement, simple event handlers, built-in functions, *set* statement, more sophisticated event handlers, student-created methods, student-created and non-list variables, *if/else* statement, *loop* statement, *while* statement, student-created parameters, student-created functions, student-created list variables, *for all in order* statement, *for all together* statement, nested *if/else* statement.

For patterns, we identified the following 15 patterns in the student-created games, again listed from least to most sophisticated (see Table 1). The last column shows the percentage of the 231 games that included each pattern.

Table 1. Patterns

Pattern	Pattern Description	%
Parameters	Setting parameters such as font size, as seen by (but not duration) available for all built-in methods	35.5%
Sound	Use of audio sounds not built into Alice methods	13.9%
Movement	Controlling object or camera movement with key or mouse	19.5%
Manipulating subparts	Programming subparts of an object to change during the game (e.g., arm of one character hits another and just their head falls off)	25.5%
Instructions	Instructions are programmed via 3D text, methods	71.9%
Phantom objects	Using not-in-view objects to move and position other objects	4.3%
Embedded methods	Student-created method that is embedded within another method	27.3%
Dialog box	Player is asked for input, input is read in, and program uses the input	15.6%
Vehicles	Vehicle property is used so that when the vehicle object moves, an attached object moves in unison with it	21.2%
Collision	There is a program action depending on the distance one object is from another	21.2%
Camera control	Changing the view according to movement or player input within one scene	39.4%
Scene change	Programming movement to and from different scenes	12.6%
Counters	Integer variable created and initialized, variable's value incremented or decremented, and threshold value of variable triggers additional action	7.8%
Timers	Integer variable created and initialized, variable's value changed as time passes, and threshold value of variable triggers additional action	9.5%
List processing	List variables are created and used with For all in order or For all together	2%

We identified the following 11 game mechanics in the student-created games (see Table 2) based on discussions with game design experts and researchers (A. Sullivan, G. Smith, T. Fristoe & L. McBron, 2011) and by analyzing the students' games. We have found that there was a range of computational sophistication, based on programming constructs and patterns used, to build each of these game mechanics. The last column shows the percentage of games that included each game mechanic.

Table 2. Game mechanics

Game Mechanic	Game Mechanic Description	%
Collecting	Player attempts to accumulate objects to advance in game.	19.9%
Timed Challenge	Player is given a time limit to complete game task.	11.3%
Exploration	Player moves an object or the camera to find objects beyond player's initial range of view. Movement is not restricted to occur along a designated path.	13.0%
Shooting	Player shoots at object; actual projectile must be present.	2.6%
Racing	Player moves object across a finish line within time limit or moves an object in competition with other objects.	3.9%
Guessing	Player answers questions via clicking, typing, or moving an object.	22.9%
Hidden Objects	Player searches for an object that is hidden either beyond view or "hidden in plain sight."	6.1%
Navigation	Player moves object and/or camera from one location to another known location often on a designated path.	16.5%
Levels	Player moves between at least 2 stages by gathering points or fulfilling a challenge.	2.2%
Avoidance	Player moves object to avoid either stationary or moving obstacle based on player proximity to obstacle. Feedback to proximity is required.	3.5%
Hitting Moving Objects	Player attempts to click on moving object or moves something (character, object, camera) closer to a moving target to prompt another action.	5.6%

To illustrate what our Computational Sophistication Framework looks like when applied to games, specifically to illustrate a range of sophistication in what these patterns and mechanics look like, we have included two case studies (see case study section).

Case Study: *M808 Super Battle Tank*

One of the more computationally sophisticated games created by the middle school students in our study was made by a pair of boys, titled *M808 Super Battle Tank*. The students use eight unique patterns to implement three different game mechanics (Collecting, Timed Challenge, and Exploration). The student programmers use two additional patterns to enhance the visual aspects of the game. The game instructs the player to drive a tank around a city (the Exploration game mechanic) to find and destroy seven cars by clicking on them to start fires (the Collection game mechanic) within a particular time limit (the Timed Challenge game mechanic). A "win" message appears if the player destroys seven cars within the allotted time; a "lose" message appears if the time runs out and seven cars are not destroyed.

In Table 3 are listed each of the patterns used to implement each of the game mechanics found in *M808 Super Battle Tank*. To demonstrate the detail collected during our analysis, Table 3 also includes the more sophisticated programming constructs that students used to implement patterns for their Collecting game mechanic. The programming constructs have been italicized in the Collecting Game Mechanic column.

The "Instructions" pattern is part of this game's three game mechanics since the instructions are needed to inform the game player what items to collect (part of the Collecting game mechanic), inform the game player that only three minutes are given to complete the collecting (part of the Time Challenge game mechanic), and inform the game player to move around the scene to find the cars (part of the Exploration game mechanic).

Table 3. The integration of patterns and mechanics in *M808 Super Battle Tank*

Pattern	Collecting Game Mechanic	Timed Challenge Game Mechanic	Exploration Game Mechanic
Instructions	Destroy 7 cars	Destroy 7 cars within 3 minutes	Move around city to see cars
Vehicles			Camera using tank as vehicle
Camera Control			Player seeing back of tank while moving around game scene
Embedded methods	Blow up cars, counting, etc.	Check count of how many cars are blown up, win and lose messages, etc.	
Phantom objects	Placement of instructions	Placement of instructions	Placement of instructions
Timer		Destroy 7 cars within time limit	Move around to destroy 7 cars
Counter	Count the number of cars collected (i.e., clicked on) as you move through scene. *Uses variables, student-created methods, simple and more sophisticated event handlers, set statement, and built-in functions.*	Destroy 7 cars within time limit.	
Parameters	Car blowing up style is abrupt; for look and feel		
Manipulating subparts	Tank's turret is turned; for look and feel		
Key/mouse control	Tank's turret is moved. *Uses simple event handlers.*		

Case Study: *Fishy Attack*

Fishy Attack, made by a girl working alone, is a game showing a mid-range level of computational sophistication. It has two game mechanics, "Collecting" and "Timed Challenge," which the student implemented using four distinct patterns (see Table 4). The student programmed the Timed Challenge mechanic using only the Instructions pattern. The student programmed a monkey to give instructions using the *say* built-in method call and modified the duration parameter's default value of the say to keep the instructions on the screen for five seconds giving the player more time to read each of the instructions. The student also programmed a *print* programming construct that persistently displays "click on all the fishy..." below the game scene. It is important to note that the student used simple event handler programming constructs to make the fish invisible when collected. The use of simple event programming to accomplish this collecting does not constitute the use of a pattern.

Table 4. The integration of patterns and mechanics in *Fishy Attack*

Pattern	Collecting Mechanic	Timed Challenge Mechanic
Instructions	Click on all fish. Uses simple event handlers.	Click on all fish within 40 seconds.
Embedded methods	All remaining fish sink underwater.	
Timer	Click on all fish within 40 seconds.	
List processing	All remaining fish sink underwater in unison.	

The opening screen shot for *Fishy Attack* is shown in Figure 1. After the monkey on the island says, "Can you please help me get off this island," the player is instructed to "click on all the fishy" (the Collecting game mechanic) before they drown (the Timed Challenge game mechanic). As the player clicks on fish, they disappear and are saved. Unfortunately, there is no code for one of the fish to disappear when the player clicks on it; therefore, there is no way to *win* by saving all the fish from drowning. It is unclear if this was the intent of the student. When the time runs out and the player has not succeeded in saving all of the fish from drowning, all the unsaved fish *sink* underwater.

Figure 1. Opening screen shot for Fishy Attack

Assessment Considerations

Game-based assessment techniques such as we have described with our game computational sophistication framework provide only one strategy for measuring computational thinking skills. Their contribution is that they allow a quantifiable measure of definable aspects of CT, and we can say with reasonable confidence that the students engaged in those aspects. The games themselves cannot tell us how deeply the students engaged in those aspects of CT, however, or why the students included or did not include certain features—whether it was due to the complexity of the programming construct or pattern, or to a lack of interest in having that particular feature in their game. A more comprehensive picture of CT skills requires additional assessments, such as a test of students' knowledge transfer, or the collection of more in-depth, qualitative data from both students and teachers.

For example, Werner et al. (2012) measured transference of CT skills with the Fairy Assessment, which is an *Alice* game that students play solving increasingly more sophisticated CT problems by adding, debugging, and modifying the *Alice* programming code. More than 300 middle school students' solutions were scored resulting in a range of CT skills. Administration of the assessment was not costly; however, scoring of the solutions was time-consuming. Burke & Kafai (2012) analyzed *Scratch* programs created by ten inner city middle school youth enrolled in a digital storytelling class. Regarding CT skills, they found widespread use of concepts such as loops and event handling but only limited use of the more sophisticated programming concepts such as conditionals, Boolean logic, and variables. Limitations include concerns about what students were able to do on their own without help from others. Additionally, their study involves only a small number of students.

In another example, Repenning et al. (2010) have begun the analysis of games students have created using *AgentSheets* looking for the presence of CT skills. Middle and high school teachers involved in their projects report high student engagement. Limitations include whether demonstrated CT skills are transferable. The researchers have identified next steps such as to show that the students' game building skills are transferable to other areas of STEM education. The researchers have built an inventory of higher-level CT patterns used in game development. Their next step is to show use of these patterns in computational biology and chemistry simulations and robotics applications.

Brennan & Resnick (2012) have developed the most comprehensive assessment package for *Scratch* projects. This consists of three parts: 1) Automated project portfolio analysis, 2) Interviews about artifacts created, and 3) Design scenario-based testing. These researchers have identified limitations of this assessment package, repeating concerns of what students are able to do on their own when looking at the results of the automated project portfolio analysis. They reported the interview portion of the assessment is time-consuming, taking one to two hours per interview. Additionally, the researchers believe this portion of the assessment package would benefit from multiple interviews per student occurring progressively during the project development period. The design scenario part of the assessment package, similar to the Fairy Assessment described above, is time-consuming in delivery.

Future Needs

Computer game programming can teach CT skills, and we have begun to identify the kinds of computational thinking that middle school students engage in while making their personal choice of games with the *Alice* programming environment. There are limitations to our work, such as:

1. The Computational Sophistication Framework was developed by analyzing games created in Alice and needs to be tested on games created with other tools to see if the distinction between constructs-patterns-mechanics makes sense and to see if other patterns or mechanics emerge.

2. The findings need to be compared against other measures of CT collected from the same students to ensure their reliability.

3. The findings do not contribute to efforts to understand CT learning progressions, and further work is needed to determine whether certain patterns (or mechanics) are more sophisticated than other patterns (or mechanics) and whether there is a range of sophistication in how patterns or mechanics are used.

4. For this approach to be used by teachers, the assessment and analysis needs to be automated.

Case Study: *Scratch* as a Path to Programming
(written by Lucas Crispen and Elizabeth LaPensée)

Scratch (scratch.mit.edu/) is a graphical programming language and development environment that is an accessible, effective, and engaging way to teach coding. It has been particularly accessible for middle school and high school students at the Self-Enhancement Academy Inc. (SEI), a non-profit organization supporting disadvantaged youth through a full-time middle school and after-school program. This case study describes the application of *Scratch* in a programming class at SEI taught alongside a partnership with Pixel Arts Game Education (www.gameeducationpdx.com/), a non-profit dedicated to reducing the barriers of access to game development technology and education. Experiences with Scratch are based on three middle school classes and one high school class taught across Fall 2013, Winter 2014, and Spring 2014 with individual class sizes ranging between five and fifteen youth.

Initially, Lucas Crispen—a game programmer with professional industry experience and academic experience in teaching and developing curriculum for weekend and summer classes and camps in digital media and game programming—was brought in to teach a general coding class. SEI selected Code Academy (www.codeacademy.org) due to its robust curriculum, and while it is excellent overall for teaching Javascript and web design, it failed to meet the needs of SEI's youth. Foremost, youth faced a learning curve since they had little to no prior programming experience, brought on by limited computer access outside of SEI classrooms. Many youth were intimidated by screens of code and self-defeating when encountering issues.

Based on these concerns, as well as a desire to better engage youth in an after-school programming class with no mandatory attendance or grade system, Crispen developed a curriculum around the visual programming environments *Scratch* and *SNAP* (a visual drag-and-drop programming language, snap.berkeley.edu). He noticed an immediate improvement in the engagement level of youth as well as the speed with which they were able to pick up basic programming concepts.

The curriculum involves nine weeks of two one-hour sessions each week, beginning with open-ended discussions about programming and simple exercises in *SNAP* and *Scratch*. In Weeks two and three, youth learn how to manipulate sprites, learn about the 2D coordinate system by drawing shapes and patterns with the pen tool, and engage in simple conditionals and loops while making a simple line-based *Snake*-like game with user input. Week 4 invites experimentation and excites youth by encouraging "hacking." The students play games from the *Scratch* community, identify how these games function based on previous lessons, and then "hack" the code of these games to adjust the difficulty level and/or change graphics or sound, which is well-supported by Scratch's "Remix" functionality.

The remainder of the curriculum reinforces core concepts including compound logic, multi-case conditionals, and conditional loops as youth make their own maze games and elevate to making their own versions of *Flappy Bird*, through cycles of development, playtesting, and iteration with other youth in the class. Youth were especially engaged by contributing to the *Flappy Bird* "clone" community and reinforced skills established earlier.

When using *Scratch* in programming curriculum, there is room for improvement in terms of performance. *Scratch* has performance issues on older computers, which is a concern for institutions and organizations with restricted technology funding. The browser version of *Scratch* also requires reliable Internet connections and speed. This can result in frustration for youth and for instructors working within limited class time.

Overall, *Scratch* is successful in achieving STEM outreach by establishing concepts and enthusiasm reinforced by integrating popular games throughout curriculum. *Scratch*'s visual nature avoids many of the language difficulties associated with learning traditional programming and allows students to focus on developing computational thinking skills and understanding core concepts. From a game development perspective, it provides an easy introduction to handling keyboard and mouse inputs, as well as a simple sprite-based system for drawing objects on the screen.

Since *Scratch* does not currently convert visual programming to existing programming language, it is best implemented as a path to understanding foundations that can be followed-up by a tool like *Stencyl* (www.stencyl.com/), which is currently used in the game development classes by Pixel Arts Game Education. Youth in the programming classes are able to directly correlate their experience designing a game with the classic *Snake* mechanic, a maze game, and a *Flappy Bird* clone to more advanced steps for designing their own self-determined games.

Best Practices

Based on our findings (Campe, Denner, & Werner, 2013), the following principles should guide teachers on how to use computer game programming to develop and engage students in computational thinking skills:

1. **Curriculum:** Schedule technology modules into your class. The entire *Alice* curriculum fits well into one semester's schedule of four hours of class meetings per week.
2. **Technology:** Choose one of the novice programming environments (Kelleher & Pausch, 2005). *Alice* and *Scratch* are the most popular and the CSTA publishes lists of resources for both of these programming environments for teachers to use in their K-12 classrooms.
3. **Teacher Prep:** Understand the range of computational sophistication involved in making different types of games using tables such as those we have given in this chapter for patterns. Understand the types of games that same-age students are interested in making to assist students in determining personal interest (Denner, Ortiz, Campe, & Werner, 2014).
4. **Pedagogy:** Guide the students to make the more sophisticated types of games. For example:
   a. Provide examples of more sophisticated games made by same-age students.
   b. Provide scaffolding to students for learning the novice programming environment and learning key constructs and patterns for game design and creation (Campe et al., 2013; Campe, Werner & Denner, 2012; Webb & Rossen, 2013).
   c. Guide students to design and create a practice game first. This activity motivates students to learn more sophisticated programming constructs, patterns, and game mechanics.
   d. Include student, teacher, and peer review activities of students' games to provide feedback highlighting game functionality and usability issues (such as that seen in the second case study with a "no win" situation). These can be done as group, pair, or individual activities and can be done at various points during the game development process.

Resources

Websites and Reports

National Research Council. *Report of a Workshop on the Scope and Nature of Computational Thinking.* Washington, DC: The National Academies Press, 2010.

National Research Council. *Report of a Workshop on the Pedagogical Aspects of Computational Thinking.* Washington, DC: The National Academies Press, 2011.

CSTA/ISTE CT resources (https://csta.acm.org/Curriculum/sub/CompThinking.html)

Alice website (http://www.alice.org/)

Scratch website (http://scratch.mit.edu/)

SNAP website (http://snap.berkeley.edu/)

References

Alexander, C. (1979). *The timeless way of building* (Vol. 1). Oxford University Press.

Barr, V., & Stephenson, C. (2011). Bringing computational thinking to K-12: what is involved and what is the role of the computer science education community? *ACM Inroads, 2*(1), 48-54.

Brennan, K., & Resnick, M. (2012). New frameworks for studying and assessing the development of computational thinking. In *Proceedings of the 2012 annual meeting of the American Educational Research Association,* Vancouver, Canada.

Brooks, R. (1977). Towards a theory of the cognitive processes in computer programming. *International Journal of Man-Machine Studies, 9*(6), 737-751.

Burke, Q., & Kafai, Y. B. (2012, February). The writers' workshop for youth programmers: digital storytelling with scratch in middle school classrooms. In *Proceedings of the 43rd ACM technical symposium on Computer Science Education* (pp. 433-438). ACM.

Campe, S., Denner, J., & Werner, L. (2013). Intentional computing: Getting the results you want from game programming classes. *In Journal for Computing Teachers.* Retrieved on September 8, 2013 from http://www.iste.org/store/product?ID=2850

Campe, S., Werner, L., & Denner, J. (2012). Game programming with *Alice:* A series of graduated challenges. In P. Phillips (Ed.), *Special Issue Computer Science K-8: Building a Strong Foundation.* Computer Science Teachers Association.

CSTA Standards Task Force. (2011). K-12 computer science standards. Retrieved on January 5, 2014 from http://csta.acm.org/Curriculum/sub/CurrFiles/CSTA_D-12_CSS.pdf.

Denner, J., Ortiz, E., Campe, S., & Werner, L. (2014). Beyond stereotypes of gender and gaming: Video games made by middle school students. In H. Agius & M. Angelides (Eds.), *Handbook of Digital Games.* Institute of Electrical and Electronic Engineers.

Denner, J., & Werner, L. (2011, April). Measuring computational thinking in middle school using game programming. *Annual Meeting of the American Educational Research Association.* New Orleans, LA.

Denner, J., Werner, L., & Ortiz, E. (2012). Computer games created by middle school girls: Can they be used to measure understanding of computer science concepts? *Computers & Education, 58*(1), 240-249.

Ehrlich, K. & Soloway, E. (1984). An empirical investigation of the tacit plan knowledge in programming. *Human Factors in Computer Systems.* Norwood, NJ: Ablex Publishing Co.

Game mechanics (n.d.). Retrieved on June 25, 2013 from the Wikipedia Web site: http://en.wikipedia.org/wiki/Game_mechanics.

Game Mechanics (n.d.). Retrieved on June 25, 2013 from the Gamification Wiki: http://gamification.org/wiki/game_Mechanics.

Gamma, E., Helm, R., Johnson, R., & Vlissides, J. (1993). *Design patterns: Abstraction and reuse of object-oriented design.* Springer Berlin Heidelberg.

Holopainen, J., & Björk, S. (2003). Game design patterns. *Lecture Notes for GDC.*

Hunicke, R., LeBlanc, M., & Zubek, R. (2004, July). MDA: A formal approach to game design and game research. *In Proceedings of the AAAI Workshop on Challenges in Game AI.*

Ioannidou, A., Bennett, V., Repenning, A., Koh, K.H., & Basawapatna, A. (2011). Computational thinking patterns. *American Educational Research Association* conference, New Orleans.

Jeffries, Robin, Turner, A., Polson, P., & Atwood, M. (1981). The processes involved in designing software. In J.R. Anderson (Ed.),. In *Cognitive skills and their acquisition* (pp. 255-283). Hillsdale, NJ: Erlbaum.

Jonassen, D. H. (2000). Toward a design theory of problem solving. *Educational technology research and development, 48*(4), 63-85.

Kelleher, C. & Pausch, R. (2005). Lowering the barriers to programming: A taxonomy of programming environments and languages for novice programmers. *ACM Computing Surveys (CSUR), 37*(2), 83-137.

Kreimeier, B. (2002). The case for game design patterns. Retrieved on March 16, 2011 from http://www.gamasutra. com/view/feature/132649/the_case_for_game_design_patterns.php?print=1.

Lee, I., Martin, F., Denner, J., Coulter, B., Allan, W., Erickson, J., Malyn-Smith, J., & Werner, L. (2011). Computational thinking for youth in practice. *ACM Inroads, 2*(1), 32-37.

Linn, M. C. (1985). The cognitive consequences of programming instruction in classrooms. *Educational Researcher, 14*(5), 14-29.

Pea, R. D., & Kurland, D. M. (1984). On the cognitive effects of learning computer programming. *New Ideas in Psychology, 2*(2), 137-168.

Quesada, J., Kintsch, W., & Gomez, E. (2005). Complex problem-solving: a field in search of a definition?. *Theoretical Issues in Ergonomics Science, 6*(1), 5-33.

Repenning, A., Webb, D., & Ioannidou, A. (2010). Scalable game design and the development of a checklist for getting computational thinking into public schools. In *Proceedings of the 41st ACM technical symposium on Computer science education* (pp. 265-269). ACM.

Resnick, M., Maloney, J., Monroy-Hernández, A., Rusk, N., Eastmond, E., Brennan, K., Millner, A., Rosenbaum, J., Silverman, B., & Kafai, Y. (2009). Scratch: programming for all. *Communications of the ACM, 52*(11), 60-67.

Robins, A., Rountree, J., & Rountree, N. (2003). Learning and teaching programming: A review. *Computer Science Education, 13*(2), 137-172.

Selby, C. (2013). Computational thinking: the developing definition. (Submitted). In, *The 18th Annual Conference on Innovation and Technology in Computer Science Education*, Canterbury, GB, 01-03 Jul 2013

Sicart, M. (2008). Defining game mechanics. *Game Studies, 8*(2).

Soloway, E. (1986, September). Learning to program = learning to construct mechanisms and explanations. *Communications of the ACM 9*, 850-858.

Webb, H., & Rosson, M. B. (2013, March). Using scaffolded examples to teach computational thinking concepts. In *Proceedings of the 44th ACM technical symposium on Computer science education* (pp. 95-100). ACM.

Werner, L., Campe, S., & Denner, J. (2012). Children learning computer science concepts via Alice game-programming. In *Proceedings of the 43rd. ACM conference on Computer Science Education (SIGCSE 2012)*. Feb. 29-Mar. 3, Raleigh, N. Carolina, USA.

Werner, L., Denner, J., Campe, S. & Kawamoto, D.C. (2012). The Fairy Performance Assessment: Measuring computational thinking in middle school. In *Proceedings of the 43rd. ACM conference on Computer Science Education (SIGCSE 2012)*. Feb. 29- Mar. 3, Raleigh, N. Carolina, USA.

Wing, J. M. (2006). Computational thinking. *Communications of the ACM, 49*(3), 33-35.

Acknowledgments

Our thanks go to the teachers and administrators at our seven schools, specifically Anne Guerrero, Shelly Laschkewitsch, Don Jacobs, Sue Seibolt, Karen Snedeker, Susan Rivas, and Katie Ziparo. Thanks also to teaching assistants, Will Park, Chizu Kawamoto, and Joanne Sanchez; and to Pat Rex and Eloy Ortiz, for instructional materials design and technology support. Thanks to Dominic Arcamone, Stephen Butkus, Melanie Dickinson, Anthony Lim, and Kimberly Shannon for their game analysis work. Thanks to all of the students who participated. This research is funded by a grant from NSF 0909733 "The Development of Computational Thinking among Middle School Students Creating Computer Games." Any opinions, findings, conclusions or recommendations expressed in this material are those of the authors and do not necessarily reflect the views of the National Science Foundation.

CHAPTER 3

Literacy

Using Video Games for Literacy Acquisition and Studying Literate Practices

Richard E. Ferdig, *Kent State University, Kent, Ohio, U.S., rferdig@gmail.com*
Kristine E. Pytash, *Kent State University, Kent, Ohio, U.S., kpytash@kent.edu*

Key Summary Points

 There are four areas typically addressed within the broader concept of literacy and games: (1) educational games to teach reading and writing; (2) commercial, non-educational games that instructors use for literacy acquisition; (3) commercial, non-educational games that unintentionally provide literacy practice; and (4) educational and non-educational video games as literate practices.

 Research provides evidence that both educational and non-educational video games can be used for literacy acquisition and instruction.

 Literacy researchers view media such as video games as literate practices worthy of their own study.

Key Terms

Literacy
Reading
Writing
Literacy practices
Literacy acquisition
Educational video games
Commercial video games

Introduction

Since the mid- to late-1980s, there have been video games created with the sole intent of improving the literacy acquisition of its users. Literacy acquisition here refers to early acquisition (e.g., phonemic awareness, an understanding of spoken language), advanced practices (e.g., formal writing), and even second language acquisition. Gee (2003) provided perhaps the strongest impetus for educators to explore the connection between video games and literacy. He developed principles associated with video games that could be applied to students' literacy learning, such as active engagement, motivation in literacy tasks, and exploration of discourse and affinity groups. For Gee, these principles existed in video game use and could also be applied in rethinking literacy acquisition and instruction.

Since then, a number of educators have begun to explore how video games can be used in the literacy classroom. There are four main ways to understand the relationship between video games and literacy. The first way is through literacy acquisition. Educators and video game designers have developed video games directly aimed at teaching students to read. These games, such as *Reader Rabbit* (1986) or *Smarty Ants* (2012) are specifically built to teach core reading concepts and developing reading skills in early readers. Concepts such as phonemic awareness, vocabulary, fluency, and comprehension are usually emphasized.

Second, educators have explored how concepts in commercial video games could be used to teach literacy concepts. The uses of commercial games here are pedagogically intentional with literacy teachers having specific rationales for using these particular video games in literacy classrooms. While these video games were not created solely for educational purposes, educators can conceptualize how the principles associated with video games are related to literacy acts. Literacy teachers view these games as a way to engage students in literacy practices while teaching specific concepts central to reading and writing. An example would include students creating characters in *The Sims* (2000) and then writing about those characters.

A third connection also relates to commercial games. The focus here, however, is not pedagogical. Researchers want to study commercial games for the purpose of understanding literacy outcomes without intentionally assigning the games in a learning environment. For instance, educators and researchers might be interested in how players in *World of Warcraft* (2004) are using reading, writing, and communication skills to interact with other players. Researchers and educators in these cases are simply interested in what is being gained by players who play without a pedagogical set of instructions surrounding the gameplay (Steinkuehler, 2008).

A fourth relationship between literacy and video games relates to an exploration of video games as literacy practices. Walsh (2010) acknowledges that researchers have used terms, such as "procedural literacy" (Bogost, 2007), "gaming literacies" (Salen, 2007), and "gaming literacy" (Zimmerman, 2008); however, Walsh uses the term, "systems-based literacy practices" defined as "an understanding of how to configure the machine or device the digital game is played on, in addition to knowing how to play the game and having the knowledge of where to find information that allows a better understanding of the system (game, program, virtual world, etc.) itself" (p. 27).

It is important for anyone exploring the notion of video games and literacy to first understand the purpose of the examination. These four relationships are summarized in Table 1 and provide an examination of the specific conditions necessary for literacy learning through video games. These relationships also provide insight into how researchers define literacy: whether it is viewed as a skill-set or a broader view of literacy as multimodal practice.

Table 1. The relationship between video games and literacy

Relationship between Video games and Literacy	Example
1. The pedagogical use of literacy games to improve reading, writing and speaking skills.	A teacher uses Reader Rabbit to attempt to improve reading scores.
2. The pedagogical use of non-literacy games to improve reading, writing, and speaking skills.	A teacher uses *The Sims* (2000) to have students write fan fiction.
3. Studying the existing use of non-literacy games to explore literacy practices of users.	An educator or researcher studies writing abilities and/or changes over time of *World of Warcraft* players.
4. Studying video game use and design as literate practices.	Researchers and educators explore tutorial gameplay within *Lego Star Wars: The Video Game* (2005) as negotiations of existing novice and expert practices.

Case Study One: *Writing Pal*

Writing Pal, an intelligent tutoring system, is directed by Danielle McNamara at Arizona State University's Learning Science Institute. This system explores how students acquire and develop writing skills. *Writing Pal* uses videos to introduce students to various writing strategies that facilitate learning across the writing process (e.g., brainstorming, drafting, revising). Students can engage in eight writing strategy modules, which have puzzles and competitive elements, as well as narrative elements, such as role-playing. *Writing Pal* also has options for students to engage in game-based strategy practice of their rhetorical writing skills. The essay tools provide automatic feedback and students' scores. For example, one of the games included in *Writing Pal* is *Adventurer's Loot*, which helps students practice paraphrasing strategies by examining word choice, combining sentences and fixing run-on sentences (Roscoe, Brandon, Snow, & McNamara, 2013). Students become a treasure hunter and are given clues to decipher. Students earn treasures if they answer correctly, whereas a monster appears if they answer incorrectly.

Roscoe et al. (2013) explored the influence of *Writing Pal* on adolescents' persuasive writing. Of the 65 students involved in the study, 33 engaged in *Writing Pal* and 32 students were in the condition group, which only had students interact with the essay and feedback tools within the game.

Writing strategies, such as how to write an introduction, body paragraphs, concluding paragraphs, and revision strategies were embedded within the game. Students' knowledge was measured through a pre-post writing strategy open-ended questionnaire, measures of writing, reading comprehension, vocabulary, and attitudes toward writing. Students who participated in the *Writing Pal* condition accumulated a greater number of new strategy concepts. Students also expressed enjoying the games, finding the games helpful, and rated the graphics as appealing. Overall, Roscoe et al. (2013) found that *Writing Pal* provided students with clear goals for their writing and motivation to achieve these goals. Students playing *Writing Pal* also learned more new writing strategies than those adolescents who wrote and revised their essays with feedback only.

While this study took place on a university campus in a laboratory setting, Roscoe et al. (2013) note that further research will take place in high school English language arts classrooms and will be used for longer periods of times, over the course of semesters or entire school years. Exploring student interactions with games in authentic classroom settings is important to understanding how educational games could benefit teaching and learning. Roscoe et al. (2013) contend that future research should continue to explore the many potential advantages of designing educational games to motivate and engage students in learning content, specifically writing. The authors also state that future research could examine how an increase in graphics, music, and other features might further engage students in educational games. This study is an example of an educational game created with the sole intent of improving literacy scores.

Key Frameworks

There are two key theoretical perspectives that deserve attention: new literacies and Gee's conceptions of cognitive learning with video games. Historically, literacy was defined as the acts of reading and writing and the cognitive processes that followed. New technologies have redefined literacy practices, however. Leu, Kinzer, Coiro, & Cammack (2004), defined new literacies for the 21st century as:

> The skills, strategies, and dispositions necessary to successfully use and adapt to the rapidly changing information and communication technologies and contexts that continuously emerge in our world and influence all areas of our personal and professional lives. These new literacies allow us to use the Internet and other ICTs to identify important questions, locate information, critically evaluate the usefulness of that information, synthesize information to answer those questions, and then communicate the answers to others.
> (Leu et al., 2004, p. 1572)

The concept of new literacies broadens our perspectives and definitions of literacy. In turn, it helps us explore technologies such as video games for multiple purposes. At the basic level, it is possible to understand video games for using and potentially improving core literacy skills like reading, writing and communicating. At a more enhanced level, we can also begin to explore video games as literate practices in and of themselves. We can begin to ask questions about the literacy practices of novice vs. expert gamers, and we can also explore transfer among multiple literate environments (e.g., games, work, home, classroom).

A second important framework comes from Gee's work on games. In his *What Video Games Have to Teach Us About Learning and Literacy* (2003), Gee explored the cognitive learning that occurs during video games and then explored how 36 learning principles could be applied to the learning of reading and writing. He specifically explores principles such as:

1. **Semiotic domains:** Gee makes the case for games and places where learning occurs. He contends that video games are semiotic domains, much like other activities in life (and as argued by those interested in new literacies).
2. **Learning and identity:** Identity here relates to the fact that games allow the development of an identity, but that games also allow you to identify with the game environment.
3. **Situated meaning and learning:** Like real life, games allow an exploration of a world. You can learn things about your world as you interact with it and the characters it contains.
4. **Telling and doing:** As pedagogical research has demonstrated, giving users opportunities to learn by doing, including making mistakes, provides more enhanced learning then just talking or discussion.
5. **Cultural models:** Games have implicit and explicit models and views of the world. They can embed cultural practices and norms as well as question those practices.

6. **The social mind:** The focus here is on the value of multiplayer and peer learning environments. Unlike many of our school practices, which are individualistic, these literacy practices are social connected and networked.

The theoretical perspectives presented here make a strong case that literacy acquisition, albeit intentional or unintentional and through educational or commercial games, can occur through video gameplay and video gameplay itself is a literate practice that is worth of study.

Case Study Two: MMORPGs for Language Learning

Kongmee et al. (2011) conducted a study of massive multiplayer online role-playing games (MMORPGs) and their potential for language learning. The multiplayer games selected by the authors for evaluation and those chosen by students were all commercial off-the-shelf games, or were intended for entertainment rather than solely for educational purposes. "Three MMORPGs were used in the study: *Godswar Online* (GO), *Hello Kitty Online* (HKO), and *Asda Story* (AS)" (p. 4).

The authors selected MMORPGs as a subject of study because they hypothesized that Internet-based games, such as MMORPGs, offered an opportunity to provide alternative social interaction to support language learning. These games provided tasks for players, which by their very nature, required interaction with others. Finally, because the objectives and challenges within a game are often repetitive, they believed the games would provide repeated practice on tasks within a motivating environment.

The researchers invited eight undergraduate students in a Thai university to participate. They introduced the MMORPGs and then watched the students' progress through both recorded sessions and by playing along with the character in the virtual worlds. The participants were then given various tests before, during, and after the MMORPG experiences.

The authors provided evidence in their study that learners who participated in a game-based environment produced positive achievements in reading, vocabulary, conversational relevance, writing, and public speaking. This was documented through a virtual ethnography measured with the support of screen recorders; however, participants also grew in their pre- and post-test scores on an *ELLIS Placement Test.* The authors conclude:

> The findings demonstrate that MMORPGs can successfully support language
> learning as illustrated by the improvements in the standard language tests and the
> participation and progression in the game itself. The students became more active in
> using English, showing greater patience in reading, being more motivated to write
> and also to produce dialogue when speaking and chatting.
> (Kongmee et al., 2011, p. 10.)

The authors attribute this growth to the authentic game environment and its ability to motivate players. This is not to suggest this literacy achievement could only be accomplished through MMORPGs. The fact that learning occurred naturally in an enjoyable situation, however, provided an impetus for continued participation from the students. This study is an example of how commercial games, which were not created with the sole intent of improving literacy scores, could be used pedagogically to achieve desired outcomes.

Key Findings

This section reports researchers' findings as they explore the links between video games and literacy. The findings below represent the four ways in which literacy and games intertwine:

1. The use of educational games for literacy acquisition;
2. The intentional use of commercial games for literacy acquisition;
3. The study of unintended literacy practices in commercial games; and
4. Games as literate practices.

Educational games created to teach literacy

There are researchers and educators committed to creating video games specifically to advance students' reading and writing knowledge. These games are created for educational has suggested that educational games can improve literacy achievement (Calfee, Pearson, & Callahan, 2012; Rosas et al., 2003).

For example, *Smarty Ants* (Calfee et al., 2012) was created to engage elementary-aged students in effective reading instruction, incorporating the National Reading Panel's defined components of reading instruction including, phonemic awareness, phonics, vocabulary, fluency, and reading comprehension. In this video game, students' literacy skills are initially assessed. Students then engage in series of activities based on phonological awareness and literacy acquisition skills. In the preliminary data analysis, researchers found kindergarten students' engaged in *Smarty Ants* had higher gain in reading achievement scores on the CORE Phonics survey than students in control classrooms. In addition, the teachers reported *Smarty Ants* was successfully implemented into their literacy instruction. They noted that the program allowed their literacy instruction to be personalized and targeted, as students could work at their own pace. Teachers self-reported that it seemed students were motivated and engaged in the video game.

Similarly, Rosas et al. (2003) examined five research designed educational video games using the platform of Nintendo's Gameboy in the context of economically disadvantaged schools in Chile. The five video games were *Magalu, Hermes, Tiki-Tiki, Roli, and Hangman*. A total of 1274 students were placed in an experimental group, an internal control group, or an external control group. Students in the experimental groups played video games over a three-month period for an average of 30 hours, the students in the internal control group were in the same school as the experiment group, but did not play video games, and the external control group was in schools without any access to the experiment. Rosas et al. (2003) found significant differences between the experimental groups and internal controls groups in terms of reading comprehension, as compared to the external control groups. Researchers reported that students were motivated and wanted to play the video games not only during class, but also during free time during the day. Also, both the teachers and students had a quick appropriation of the video game, so it was easily incorporated in the classroom. These factors could have contributed to the finding.

These studies suggest that students' literacy skills increase when engaged with the specific educational video games employed. While there are significant numbers and varieties of educational games that aim to support literacy learning, there is still research needed that explicitly shows the benefits to students using these games for literacy skills acquisition.

Commercial games to intentionally teach literacy

Educators have begun exploring how commercial video games could be used to teach reading and writing. In the studies featured in this section, the intended design of the video game was for entertainment and commercial purposes. Educational researchers have documented how students' engagement in games—whether playing them in their personal lives or in the classroom—can be used as a scaffold for developing writing practices. For example, through playing and referencing commercial games, teachers can help students connect their knowledge of games to new knowledge about reading and writing. deWinter & Vie (2008) highlight how *Second Life* can be used in composition courses to explore narrative writing through creating avatars and interacting with others in a virtual world. Through these experiences students can consider the complexities of the term "identity," including what it means to have a writerly or literate identity. deWinter & Vie (2008) also contend that *Second Life* provides composition teachers with opportunities to engage students in discussions about ethics, power, and critical media literacy.

Similarly, Gerber & Price (2011) explored how games could serve as a platform for writing instruction in a variety of genres. The authors link traditional print-based genres to concepts in video games. For example, Gerber & Price argue that "walk-throughs" in video games are actually expository texts; therefore, students could learn the features of expository writing by composing their own walkthroughs for their favorite video games.

The key findings from these studies suggest that educators can use commercial games to teach particular literacy skills. Specifically, researchers have explored how video games can serve as a catalyst for writing instruction, particularly narrative writing. Video games are often based on fictional worlds and characters players design, a creative process that is similar with aspects narrative writing.

Unintended literacy outcomes of commercial game use

A third realm focuses on the examination of literacy practices within gameplay where no pedagogical instruction is provided. One of the main outcomes in this area is that game players will engage in literate practices on their own without the need for instruction to do so. Gumulak & Webber (2011) interviewed 28 young adults (24 males and four females) who regularly play video games such as *Grand Theft Auto, Call of Duty,* and *Resident Evil.* While players reported a number of benefits, such as awareness of problem-solving skills, they also noted that they were engaged in the paratexts, or supporting materials, which surround the game. Gumulak & Webber found that 80% of the young adults read reviews about the games. Young adults also reported a connection between books they enjoy reading and the games they enjoy playing. For instance, one of the participants self-reported that his reading skills increased because of his use of video games; however, this claim was not further measured or validated by the investigators.

Studies like this suggest that the act of playing a video game engages students in literacy practices and may influence their literacy habits even if the game was not played in an educational setting or with the specific intent of literacy acquisition.

Video games as literate practices

Finally, researchers have begun to explore how video games can be conceptualized as literate practices. Steinkuehler (2007) argues that video games "are not replaying literacy activities but rather are literacy activities" (p. 298). She surveyed the literacy practices associated with Massively Multiplayer Online (MMO) games and the paratexts that support players. Steinkuehler examined two notions of literacy: first, as a set of cognitive processes and skills and second, as more contemporary definitions of literacy being plural, situated, meaning-making activities. From both of these stances, Steinkuehler argued that MMOs are very much literacy practices. Players must read significant amounts of texts in the video game, as well as engage in blogs, websites, fan fiction, fan websites, and discussion boards.

In the classroom, Beavis & O'Mara (2010) presented case studies of two teachers who conceptualized literacy units with video games. The first teacher engaged students in close readings of images from video games, such as *Grand Theft Auto,* to conduct critical analyses. Their analyses led to the creation of multimodal compositions focused on an awareness of the games they play and their engagement with these games. The researchers found students

> frequently demonstrated their mastery of the review genre both in writing and
> in online multimodal form, a deep knowledge of specific games and the gaming
> environment, and the capacity to anticipate what new players would need to know,
> while also assuming a shared degree of internet savviness and knowledge.
> (Beavis & O'Mara, 2010, p. 67)

The second teacher, featured in Beavis & O'Mara's (2010) article, had students create games using *GameMaker*. Students relied on genre knowledge and narrative plotlines to design and construct video games. Students then engaged in peer-review to provide each other with feedback about their games. The two case studies revealed that the analysis of video games and engagement in the creation of video games allowed students to practice metacognitive tasks related to how video games are conceptualized and their personal engagement in video games. Teachers can draw on students' current knowledge about video games to help them connect to knowledge about writing. These case studies also represent examples of how video games become their own literate practices worthy of study. Video games have an entire literate practice that surrounds them as many players read and write paratexts, such as reviews, websites, cheats, walk-throughs, and discussion forums. Players are not just engaging with those pieces of texts, but also thinking deeply about how that information influences their future gameplay.

Case Study Three: *World of Warcraft*

Steinkuehler & Duncan's (2008) study documents and assesses the specific literacy practices within *World of Warcraft* by analyzing a random sample of approximately two thousand discussion posts on the "priest forum" on the official website. Specifically assessing "scientific habits of mind" (Steinkeuhler & Duncan, 2008, p. 532) the researchers used benchmarks from the American Association for the Advancement of Science (1993), Chinn & Malhotra's (2002) theoretical framework for evaluating inquiry tasks, and Kuhn's (1992) epistemological framework.

Steinkuehler & Duncan found that participants who play *World of Warcraft* and engage on discussion forums participate in social knowledge construction and argumentation. When analyzing the discussion forums, 86% of the "talk" could be considered social knowledge construction in that participants were sharing knowledge and discussing to solve problems. Participants also engaged in scientific argumentation by proposing theories and engage in a questioning and response type discussion. The authors also found that 58% of the *World of Warcraft* forum posts also displayed systems-based reasoning, while one-tenth of forum posts revealed model-based reasoning. The study found, "forms of inquiry within play contexts such as these are authentic although synthetic: even though the worlds themselves are fantasy, the knowledge building communities around them are quite real" (Steinkeuler & Duncan, 2008, p. 541).

Steinkuehler & Duncan have three implications for their work. First, they acknowledge that certain schools or educators might not see the benefits of games and the gaming culture. They hope research of this type might begin to break down those barriers. Second, they ask, who are the people engaged in this play and what resources do they have? Steinkuehler & Duncan emphasize that the digital divide might not be solely between the "have and have-nots," but the "do and do-nots" (542). This means that the digital divide might not only be between people who have access to technology and those who do not, but also those people who have access to technology, yet do not play video games. Finally, they acknowledge that exploring video games as literate practices can bridge spaces between home and school practices. Engaging in video games at home, as well as school, might not only provide access to technology some may not have, but it also might encourage those who might not normally play video games to play them.

This study is an example of two uses of commercial video games. First, it is an examination of the use of a commercial game that has produced literate outcomes without direct pedagogical intervention. Second, it is an example of a commercial game whose play itself becomes a literate practice worthy of study.

Assessment

What does it mean to assess video games as literate practices? Theoretical perspectives can help researchers examine how video games are constructed and how players enact literacy practices through engagement in video games. Educators can also assess video games and literacy by exploring how certain principles innate to games can be applied to reading and writing practice. There are four main ways to assess the connection between video games and literacy:

1. Assess how video games, produced specifically for educational purposes, advance students' learning of reading and writing; pre- and post-test measures can examine students' before and after participating in video games.
    2. Assess how literacy educators are integrating video games into reading and writing classrooms; focus on examining the differences in outcomes based on games created for educational purposes and games created for commercial use, but used in an educational setting; examine the conditions necessary for literacy learning through playing video games.
3. Assess the intended and unintended consequences of engaging students in video games in literacy classrooms; focus on the contexts in which games are played and how playing games outside of the classroom might engage students in meaningful literacy practices; this would also include examining how the curriculum might bridge students' in-school and out-of-school literacy practices.
4. Assess the impact of commercial video game use on traditional literacy outcomes and any literate practices of users who play in out-of-school settings (such as at home).

Future Directions

Advances in technological tools are changing the nature of reading and writing. Young adult literature is moving from solely print-based books to multiplatform books encompassing images, videos, and audio. Digital writing and multimodal composition are changing how we understand and define writing. These advances have led educators to conceptualize and recognize video games as literary practices and have led to discussions about how the principles associated with video games could be applied to reading and writing instruction. As educators consider and redefine the notions of what it means to be a "reader" and "writer," they will need to learn effective instructional approaches for incorporating video games into the literacy curriculum. Researchers can continue to explore teachers' instructional decision-making regarding using video games in the classroom. Future work could explore how teachers decide the appropriate game to include in the curriculum and the question of whether video games should be implemented in ways that just replace traditional print-based activities, and the extent to which they are transforming educational practices. For example, how do video games create opportunities for cooperative and collaborative literacy learning, which traditional methods may not do as effectively, or may do differently?

The inclusion of video games into the classroom also brings up questions of access and power. More research is needed on the affordances, limitations, potentials, and constraints of using video games in reading and writing classrooms. Who are the teachers implementing video games in their classrooms and what are the challenges they face? Educators can explore the effect of parents and administrator's support or lack of support when in using video games for instructional purposes. Finally, as technological tools, such as haptics or tools applying motion or vibrations to engage participants' sense of touch, are becoming more advanced, educators will also have to consider how technology associated with video games might influence the ways we teach students to read and write.

Case Study Four: Understanding the Potential of Language-Learning with Mentira (written by Liz Jasko)

Today's language-learning games cover a diverse range of purposes, scopes, and applications. This holds especially true in the mobile sphere, where highly accessible casual mobile games such as *MindSnacks, Rosetta Stone Arcade Academy,* and *Duolingo* offer interactive, autonomous learning experiences to help any average person pursue a variety of language choices. These games tend to primarily focus on vocabulary and basic sentence structure, utilizing engaging ways to effectively achieve interest and retention. While the presence of such commercial games continues to grow, second language acquisition (SLA) researchers and teachers seek more complex, sophisticated ways to elevate foreign language classroom instruction through the use of games.

Chris Holden and Julia Sykes are among the pioneering effort behind *Mentira*—a place-based mobile language-learning game. The game was designed locally at the University of New Mexico, Albuquerque to be constructively integrated with a Spanish 202 course over a period of four weeks. This story-driven game presents a murder mystery plot that requires players to identify with a virtual family identity, seek clues through dialogue with non-playing characters (NPCs), and collaborate with other students to solve a mystery. The story unfolds in a real, nearby Spanish-speaking neighborhood, requiring both interacting in Spanish and physically visiting the town to find clues. Students are first introduced to it in the classroom, and are either provided phones or use their own devices to collaboratively advance through the story in the classroom, at home, and ultimately in the town where the story takes place (Holden & Skyes, 2011a). It was built with the ARIS engine—a technology that uses GPS to create a hybrid world of virtual interactive characters, items, and media placed in physical space (Holden & Skyes, 2011b).

Over several years of designing, iterating, and evaluating *Mentira* based on its experimental use as a real component of classroom curriculum, Holden & Skyes emphasize the following goals and outcomes in their publication, *Prototyping Language-Based Locative Gameplay* (Holden & Skyes, 2011a).

1. **Situated language learning** extends the subject of Spanish out of the classroom and into a nearby Spanish-speaking community, accomplishing the notion that "since knowledge occurs in conjunction with context, the learning process should be tied to a meaningful situation" (Schrier, 2005). Holden & Skyes (2011a) found this to be true, since the most well received aspect of the game integration was at the end, when students took a field trip to finally use the augmented reality game in the actual town.

2. **Narrative** created a higher-level connection to the content. Holden & Skyes (2011a) formatted the game into a murder mystery based on historical fiction because it created authenticity and a real-world connection that still allowed them flexibility to create the simple and direct goal of the game, which was solving a murder.

3. **Pragmatics-approach** attempts to address language learning in the context of "critical learning"—when learning is not just limited to understanding meaning in a particular realm, but also invites the reproduction and active use of the learning (Gee, 2003). Holden & Skyes explain, "Instead of revolving around the assimilation of vocabulary, the conversations work in terms of pragmatics: knowing the social setting and acting appropriately" (2011a, p. 119). They accomplish this by integrating a fair amount of vocabulary unfamiliar to the students, and by structuring the conversations of different NPC family identities to require specific ways of social interaction, such as programming NPCs to withhold important information for advancing through the murder mystery if the student speaks to them in a rude tone. Where the game falls short is the way in which these dialogues take place through *Mass Effect* style textual multiple-choice responses. Instead, the use of voice, audio, and language construction could potentially be used, such as the voice communication with real players that drives Babbel's mobile language learning game, *PlaySay*.

4. **Task-based language teaching (TBLT) approach** also focuses the content predominantly on meaning and secondarily on form, as outlined by Purushotma, Thorne and Wheatley (Purushotma et al., 2009; Reinders, 2012). Ellis (2003) identifies the key components of TBLT as perspective, authenticity, language skill, cognitive processes and outcome— which are propelled in *Mentira* through the first three points. Rather than designing a game to learn things about a language, a game is designed to use a language as a means to achieving a goal.

5. **Collaborative play** is also executed through what Holden & Skyes (2011a) refer to as "jigsaws." The family identities assigned to each student behaved as a crucial constraint in the game, because no player was able to access the entirety of information. To move forward through the story, students had to collaborate to piece together the clues. Holden & Skyes (2011a) found, however, that the actual collaboration between students in the classroom was not naturally instigated and that it usually required the direct intervention of the teacher.

In addition to these key points, Holden & Skyes (2011a) emphasize:

1. The importance of iterating the design based on student feedback.
2. Maintaining continuity by using the mobile game over time and outside the classroom.
3. Promoting risk-taking by bringing students in a real-world setting to practice language.
4. Recognizing how the execution of the game matters and not just the vision.

Overall, they found that the behaviors they wanted *Mentira* to provoke, "playfulness, inventiveness, collaboration and risk-taking—the behaviors that did not manifest in the classroom—emerged spontaneously in surprising ways during the field trip portions of the game" (Holden & Skyes, 2011a, p. 125). Holden and Skyes continue to push the boundaries, incorporating the positive takeaways and addressing the weaker areas. While the scope of this experiment was limited in regards to platform and distribution, the potential for future development based around this concept is immense.

Resources

Articles

Alberti, J. (2008). The game of reading and writing: How video games reframe our understanding of literacy. *Computers & Composition, 25*(3), 258-269.

Apperley, T. (2010). What game studies can teach us about video games in the English and literacy classroom. *Australian Journal of Language & Literacy, 33*(1), 12-23.

Bradford, C. (2010). Looking for my corpse: Video games and player positioning. *Australian Journal of Language & Literacy, 33*(1), 54-64.

Gee, J., Levine, M. H. (2009). Welcome to our virtual worlds. *Educational Leadership, 66*(6), 48-52.

Gumulak, S. & Webber, S. (2011). Playing video games: learning and information literacy. Aslib Proceedings: *New Information, 63*(2/3), 241-255.

Hui-Yin H. & Shiang-Kwei, W. (2010). Using gaming literacies to cultivate new literacies. *Simulation & Gaming, 41*(3), 400-417.

Hunter, R. (2011). Erasing "property lines": A collaborative notion of authorship and textual ownership on a fan wiki. *Computers & Composition, 28*(1), 40-56.

Leonard A., Meng-Tzu, C. Holmes, S. (2010). Assessing twenty-first century skills through a teacher created video game for high school biology students. *Research in Science & Technological Education, 28*(2), 101-114.

Meyers, E. M. (2009). Tip of the iceberg: Meaning, identity, and literacy in preteen virtual worlds. *Journal of Education for Library & Information Science, 50*(4), 226-236.

Miller, M. & Hegelheimer, V. (2006). The SIMs meet ESL: Incorporating authentic computer simulation games into the language classroom. Interactive Technology and Smart Education, (2006), 311-328.

Ranalli, J. (2008). Learning English with The Sims: Exploiting authentic computer simulation games for L2 learning. *Computer Assisted Language Learning, 21*(5), 441-455.

Robison, A J. (2008). The Design is the game: Writing games, teaching writing. *Computers & Composition, 25*(3), 359-370.

Schrader, P. & McCreery, M. (2008). The acquisition of skill and expertise in massively multiplayer online games. *Educational Technology Research & Development, 56*(5/6), 557-574.

Sewell, W. & Denton, S. (2011). Multimodal literacies in the secondary English classroom. *English Journal, 100* (5) 61-65.

Smith, G. G., Li, M., Drobisz, J., Park, H. R., Kim, D., & Smith, S. D. (2013). Play games or study? Computer games in eBooks to learn English vocabulary. *Computers & Education, 69,* 274-286.

Steinkuehler, C. (2010). Video games and digital literacies. *Journal of Adolescent & Adult Literacy, 54*(1) 61-63.

Steinkuehler, C. & Duncan, S. (2008). Scientific habits of mind in virtual worlds. *Journal of Science Education Technology, 17*(6), 530-543.

Thorne, S. L., Fischer, I., & Lu, X. (2012). The semiotic ecology and linguistic complexity of an online game world. *ReCALL, 24*(3), 279-301.

Wohlwend, K. E. (2009). Early adopters: Playing new literacies and pretending new technologies in print-centric classrooms. *Journal of Early Childhood Literacy, 9* (2), 117-140.

Games/Simulations

Book Worm (https://www.nintendo.com/games/detail/PPPdYw-fw9kLv55iYhT5Llgo6XxFQRGQ)

Grand Theft Auto (http://www.rockstargames.com/grandtheftauto/)

Mentira (http://www.mentira.org/)

Playtime Theatre (https://itunes.apple.com/us/app/playtime-theater/id411289693?mt=8)

SimCity (https://www.facebook.com/SimCity)

Smarty Ants (http://www.smartyants.com/)

Storybook Workshop (https://www.nintendo.com/games/detail/8P8tfzT9FHjnkyhfreEvpnnKpxtngOvO)

World of Warcraft (http://us.battle.net/wow/en/)

Writing Pal (http://129.219.222.66/Publish/projectsitewpal.html)

Websites

ABCya (http://www.abcya.com/)

ICT Games (http://www.ictgames.com/literacy.html)

Literacy Sites Literacy Games (http://www.literacysites.com/litgames.htm)

PBS Kids Reading Games (http://pbskids.org/games/reading/)

The Dictionary Project (http://www.dictionaryproject.org/resources/word-games-puzzles-and-interactive-literacy-games)

References

Beavis, C. & O'Mara, J. (2010). Computer games—pushing at the boundaries of literacy. *Australian Journal of Language & Literacy, 33*(1), 65-76.

Bogost, I. (2007). Persuasive games: *The expressive power of digital games.* Cambridge: MIT Press.

Brake, D. (2008). Shaping the 'me' in *MySpace*: The framing of profiles on a social network site. In K. Lundby (Ed.), *Digital Storytelling, Mediatized Stories: Self-Representations in New Media* (pp. 285–300). New York: Peter Lang Publishing.

Calfee, R., Pearson, P.D. & Callahan, M. (2012). *Smarty Ants.* Retrieved from, http://www.smartyants.com/research/research-reports

deWinter, J., & Vie, S. (2008). Press enter to "say": Using *Second Life* to teach critical media literacy. *Computers & Composition, 25*(3) 313-322.

Eleá, I. (2011). Fanfiction and webnovelas: The digital reading and writing of Brazilian Adolescent girls. *The Handbook of Gender, Sex and Media, 24*, 71-87.

Ellis, Rod. (2003). *Task-based Language Learning and Teaching.* Oxford: Oxford University Press.

Gee, J. P. (2003). *What video games have to teach us about learning and literacy.* New York: Palgrave Macmillan.

Gerber, H., & Price, D. (2011). Twenty-first century adolescents, writing, and new media: Meeting the challenge with game controllers and laptops. *English Journal, 101* (2), 68-73.

Holden, C, & Sykes, J. (2011a). *Mentira*: Prototyping language-based locative gameplay. S. Dikkers, J. Martin, & B. Coulter. (Eds.) *Mobile Media Learning: Amazing Uses of Mobile Devices for Learning.* Pittsburgh, PA: ETC Press, 112-129.

Holden, C., & Sykes, J. (2011b). Leveraging mobile games for place-based language learning. University of New Mexico, ARIS Games, 1-22. Accessed at: http://arisgames.org/wp-content/uploads/2011/04/Holden_Sykes_PROOF.pdf.

Kongmee, I., Strachan, R., Montgomery, C., & Pickard, A. (2011). Using massively multiplayer online role playing games (MMORPGs) to support second language learning: Action research in the real and virtual world. In: *2nd Annual IVERG Conference: Immersive technologies for Learning: virtual implementation, real outcomes, 27-28 June 2011.* Middlesborough, UK.

Leu, D. J., Kinzer, C. K., Coiro, J. L., & Cammack, D. W. (2004). Toward a theory of new literacies emerging from the Internet and other information and communication technologies. In R. B. Ruddell & N. J. Unrau (Eds.), *Theoretical Models and Processes of Reading* (5th ed.), pg. 1570. Newark, DE: International Reading Association.

Purushotma, R., Thorne, S., & Wheatley, J. (2009). "10 Key Principles for Designing Video Games for Foreign Language Learning."

Reinders, Hayo, ed. (2012), *Digital Games in Language-Learning and Teaching.* Houndsmills: Palgrave Macmillan.

Roscoe, R., Russell, B., Snow, E., & McNamara, D. (2013). Game-based writing strategy practice with the *Writing Pal.* In K.E. Pytash & R.E. Ferdig (Eds) *Exploring Technology for Writing and Writing Instruction.* IGI-Global; Hershey, PA.

Salen, K. (2007). Gaming literacies: A game study design in action. *Journal of Educational Multimedia and Hypermedia, 16*(3), 301-322.

Schrier, Karen. (2005). Revolutionizing history education: Using augmented reality games to teach histories. MIT Thesis, Accessed at: http://karenschrier.wordpress.com/publications/cms.mit.edu/research/theses/KarenSchrier2005.pdf

Steinkuehler, C. A. (2008). Cognition and literacy in massively multiplayer online games. *Handbook of research on new literacies. Mahwah NJ: Erlbaum*, 1-38.

Walsh, C. (2010). Systems-based literacy practices: Digital games research, gameplay and design. *Australian Journal of Language & Literacy, 33*(1), 24-40.

Zimmerman, E. (2008). *Gaming literacy: Design as a model for literacy in the 21st century.* Retrieved from http://ericzimmerman.com/files/texts/Chap_1_Zimmerman.pdf.

CHAPTER 4

History and Social Studies

Using Digital Games to Teach History and Historical Thinking

Karen Schrier, *Marist College, Poughkeepsie, New York, U.S., Kschrier@gmail.com*

Key Summary Points

 Consider your pedagogical goals when designing games for history—whether you are focused more on teaching facts and data, concepts and themes, and/or decision-making and resource management.

 Carefully consider the balance between maintaining historical accuracy and fun and engaging gameplay and actions.

 Well-designed games can provide effective learning opportunities for students to develop historical thinking and historical empathy skills.

Key Terms

Historiography
Historical thinking
Historical empathy
Situated cognition
Social studies games
History games
Communities of practice
Constructivism
Constructionism

Introduction

How do we define a game as being a history game? Would games from the *Civilization, Sim City,* or *Assassins Creed* series count as history games? Uricchio argues that, "historical simulations that are based upon manipulation of quantities of things like economic production, religious intensity, foreign trade, bureaucratic development, and literacy indeed fall more into the realm of sociology or anthropology than history" (Uricchio, 2005, p. 331). In this chapter, we will consider social studies games as those games that directly deal with history topics, and also those games related to politics, economics, resource management, and civics, as well. For the purposes of this chapter, I will mainly focus on the history/historical aspects of social studies games. In addition, while this chapter will focus on designing and using digital games for educational purposes, there are a number of analog games, including card, board, and role-playing games that may be relevant to history education. (A few analog examples are included in the Resources section).

There are three main types of social studies/history (digital) games. These include games that focus on the:

1. **Representation of the past.** This type of game enables the player to interact with a game representation of a particular historic or economic moment. This moment is recreated in the game and an aspect of this moment is re-performed by the player through the game. Typically, these games encourage "the player to engage in a speculative or "what if" encounter with a particular past...efforts are usually taken to maximize the accuracy of historical detail, allowing the setting and conditions to constrain and shape game play" (Uricchio, 2005, p. 328). Two examples are Muzzy Lane's *Making History* series and Channel 13/WNET's *Mission US*, a series of game modules that take players through different moments in history, such as during the Underground Railroad or the events leading up to the Revolutionary War in Boston (see Case Study One). In *Mission US*, for example, middle school players play as Nat, a printer's apprentice, and relive the Boston Massacre incident from a unique perspective.

2. **Interaction with historic themes, concepts, choices, or resources.** This type of game deals with social studies in a more abstract way, where the player may be working within historic themes, decisions, or resource deliberations, and acting like "a godlike player [who] makes strategic decisions and learns to cope with the consequences, freed from the constraints of historically specific conditions" (Uricchio, 2005, p. 328). This second type of game is typically less focused on maintaining the historical accuracy of moments or time periods, but more focused on allowing access to relevant historic questions, causes and effects, and/or systematic issues. For example, consider the *Civilization* series by Sid Meier, or *The Redistricting Game*, a game that enables players to "redistrict" based on voter constraints to understand the consequences of gerrymandering.

3. **Play within a historical or history-related setting.** This type of game may have elements of the other types of history games, but is less focused on maintaining historical accuracy or immersing players in specific historical moments or decisions. This type of game features a quasi-historical setting or themes, which may or may not be based on research or reality, and could involve alternative histories, alternative "presents," or an incorrect juxtaposition of historical events. Examples of this include the commercial off-the-shelf series *Assassins Creed* games, which features historic settings such as Italy and the Revolutionary War-era colonies. Even games such as Rockstar's *Grand Theft Auto* series and L.A. Noire could be seen as historical artifacts, in a sense. The game designers spent such attention to detail when recreating the cities represented in the games, such as Los Angeles in the 1940s, or New York City in the 2000s, that through playing the game you can, in essence, experience the city with the flavor of that time period (albeit still from the designers' perspectives).

There is an underlying question in history games as to what extent do they represent history accurately. This is a key tension when designing and using history games, as there is always a tradeoff between maintaining accuracy and representing details, and simulating themes, questions, and consequences, while also ensuring a fun, engaging experience. This tension in how to appropriately represent history in a game parallels some of the key tensions in history education.

One of the driving questions in history education is what types of content, skills, and practices it should include. On the one hand, there are a number of history teachers, researchers, and practitioners that feel that learning history facts—such as the dates of battles, the order of events in a war, or the major figures in a movement—is a solid foundation for history education. These teachers feel that learning these facts first will ground students in the topic so that they could then approach the broader themes. They view these facts as not debatable and "free from social context" (Squire & Barab, 2004, p. 506). Likewise, some social studies educators teach history as unmovable—in other words, history is not open to interpretation, but rather, there is an acceptable understanding of the past that should be provided to students. Students, in essence, are a blank slate who need learn the "better story" or the most appropriate and dominant narrative of the past (Downey & Levstick, 1991; Squire & Barab, 2004; Seixas, 2000).

On the other hand, Squire & Barab (2004) and Seixas (2000) argue that focusing only on facts and master narratives may be more akin to myth telling or heritage education than actual critical historiography (the practice of history). Rather than cultivating a love of history, these tactics may decrease students' overall interest in history and lead to misconceptions about how history is typically practiced (Seixas, 2000; Wineburg, 2001; Squire & Barab, 2004).

For these reasons and others, some history teachers, theorists, and practitioners, believe that it is more important for students to learn how to think like a historian—to sift through evidence, identify biases, and interpret perspectives—than it is to learn a litany of facts and figures.

> Whereas students read textbooks, memorize facts, and recite "ready-made"
> knowledge, academics, curators, journalists, and social activists do a lot more: They
> consider research topics of theoretical and/or practical importance, consult original
> sources, produce arguments, interpret data in dialogue with existing theory, and
> negotiate findings within social contexts.
> (Squire & Barab, 2004, pp. 505-6).

These educators argue history is open to interpretation, and is, at its core, a representation of the past, but not the past itself. They believe students who grapple with past moments, trends, or eras, should keep in mind that it is just one possible interpretation, and there may be many other ways to view the past. These educators encourage students to question not only other's interpretations of the past, but also how current issues and events are presented, whether in the media, via friends, or by teachers. In the history classroom, students can potentially rewrite or resist master narratives and reconcile their own or their community's interpretations with dominant interpretations, while also exploring their own identity in relation to history (Barnett et al., 2000; Squire & Barab, 2004).

There are many other pedagogical styles and strategies history educators use to express the past. Some history educators privilege the "people" part of history, such as the personal struggles, perspectives, and obstacles; whereas others emphasize how limited resources, geographies, or technologies interact, or how cultures collide, for example. Moreover, some history educators feel that to truly understand history, one needs to be in the shoes of its inhabitants, and empathize with the issues, problems, goals, trends, and perspectives of the time. They might argue that interpreting a historic moment with a more modern mindset could render any consideration of past events invalid. Or, they believe that at the very least, one's current biases should be reflected on when re-interpreting the past. These educators may be proponents of practicing historical empathy, which is the process of taking on another's perspective and cultural and social context so as to more properly understand his or her attitudes, feelings, actions, and decisions in the past.

Thus, there are many styles and approaches that history educators grapple with when deciding how to teach history. These lead to further questions when making history games. How much should the game incorporate alternative perspectives, such as from other cultures, countries, races, ethnicities or genders? How does a game explain human atrocities, such as genocide or slavery, in terms students will understand? Can place and location affect the player's understanding of history? Should the game focus mainly on historical and human crises, or should it also include role models, heroes/heroines, and positive advancements, which might be more inspiring to students? These are also the types of questions game designers regularly ask themselves as they design games for history education.

Another key question any game designer or game player should ask is the differences between playing a history digital game, versus experiencing history through another medium, such as a documentary video or textbook. Schut (2007) discusses the key differences. For example, history in games is played, rather than just presented or questioned. While other media can help people ask "what if" questions, games allow players to run with those questions and see varying outcomes (2007).

> This results in a very open-ended picture of history....In a book, history is
> completed; the future work of the historian may change history, of course, but
> not the specific history that the reader is currently engaging. ... In a digital game,
> however, history is never set: The player always has the ability to redo history. ...
> Although the player has freedom to change the course of history, it is only to the
> degree that the game system allows.
> (Schut, 2007, p. 230)

As a result, games may not offer a clear and linear narrative of history, but instead typically center around historical systems and places (Schut, 2007), or through their play, question the standard versions of the past.

In the next sections, I will describe and annotate a few different learning and history education theories that may be useful to employ when designing and using games in history education. I will also present findings and best practices.

Case Study One: Mission US

Mission US is a series of free online browser-based adventure games that cover specific moments in United States history (such as the Boston Massacre/events leading up to the Revolutionary War in Boston, the Cheyenne Indians in the 1860s, and the Underground Railroad in 1848), and is geared toward middle school students. *Mission US* is in the process of being developed by WNET/Channel 13 (PBS) and Electric Funstuff, a game company, with content expertise from CUNY historians and assessment directed by Education Development Center (EDC). The game is funded by the Corporation for Public Broadcasting's "American History and Civics Initiative."

The goal of *Mission US* is to teach historical thinking skills and historical empathy, using as a backdrop specific moments from history. For example, module one, "For Crown or Colony," takes participants back in time to play as fictional Nathaniel Wheeler, a printer's apprentice, during the time of the American Revolution and Boston Massacre. In the 2014-released module three, "A Cheyenne Odyssey," players play as Little Fox, a boy living in the Northern Cheyenne tribe in 1866. The game is a point-and-click adventure game with a strong story foundation. Players are able to participate in tasks, such as helping Paul Revere (in module one), and making alliances with various NPCs (non-playing characters), who may be devoted to Loyalist or Patriot causes. One of the pivotal moments is when the player, as Nat, watches the Boston Massacre, and then makes decisions about what was seen. Each player gets a slightly different set of perspectives on the Massacre based on a randomized series of vignettes drawn from a database of possible perspectives on the Massacre (e.g., British soldiers wielding guns or colonists throwing snowballs). Students in a class are invited to deliberate what they saw, and to consider why each person saw the Massacre slightly differently. As a result of one's dialogue choices related to their interpretations of the Massacre, one's game ending and alliances may end up slightly differently.

As mentioned earlier, the team creating *Mission US* consisted of historians from CUNY, game designers (Electric Funstuff) and producers from PBS/Channel 13. History educators were also brought in as user testers. Each of these groups had different goals, needs, and requirements. The game designers wanted to make an effective, fun, engaging, and compelling game that also fit into any technological constraints; the historians wanted to maintain historical accuracy and represent the American Revolution appropriately; the history educators wanted an experience that fits into their classrooms, curriculum, and teaching style, which also meets core standards. To move forward in designing and executing the game, this meant that the team had to collectively balance these needs, address competing concerns, appropriately represent history for the target demographic, and still maintain an engaging and economically feasible game. The team regularly reflected on their decisions, and tested their assumptions with their users, which helped to create a more successful and effective game experience, as well as helped them to identify any problems with the game.

Key Frameworks

There are a few different theories of history and history education that can inform our design and use of games for social studies learning. While there are many possible theories, I have chosen to describe two different frameworks of history education, including Seixas's three history education frameworks, and Munslow's three approaches to historiography. I have also selected two frameworks specifically focused on designing games for history: McCall's five principles for designing history games and the History Multimedia Interactive Educational Game (HMIEG) framework. In addition, I chose four learning theories and concepts that may be useful to those creating games for history, including situated cognition, communities of practice, historical thinking, and historical empathy, and I briefly mention constructionism and constructivism.

Frameworks: History education

Seixas (2000) outlines three possible options for history education. This includes:

1. The **"Best Possible Story" model:** Seixas (2000) explains that the aim of history education in the "Best Possible Story" model is to share the single most agreed-upon narrative of history. The purpose of this model is to enable a unified and collective view of history (Kee, 2011). Limits of this model are that there is a lack of agreement of what really happened in the past, making this type of "best fit" model practically impossible (Kee, 2011; Seixas, 2000; Lowenthal, 1996). It may also be difficult to use this approach when making a history game, because it may be hard to ensure all players receive the same, standardized narrative of the past.

2. **"Disciplinary History" model:** The "Disciplinary History" Model gives students the opportunity to weigh different perspectives on the past, which simulates more closely the typical practice of history by historians (Lowenthal, 1996; Kee, 2011).

3. **"Postmodern History" model:** The "Postmodern History" model questions whether historians can construct the past without subjectivity, and encourages the analysis of historical arguments, as well as reflection on the historian's own biases or choices (Jenkins, 2003; Kee, 2011). "Whereas History simulation games may give the player the impression that he or she has an accurate portrait of the past, in all of its complexity, …. [this model] highlights our distance from the past and the difficulty of reconstructing an 'accurate' picture of what has gone on before" (Kee, 2011, pp. 434-5).

Munslow (1997) breaks down three other frameworks for historiography in *Deconstructing History* (Munslow, 1997). The three approaches to how historians can represent the past are as follows:

1. **Reconstructionist history,** in which historians discover facts through empirical methods. This is similar to how a scientist might conduct science—historians would collect evidence, analyze it and uncover what really happened in the past (Schrier, 2005; Munslow, 1997).

2. **Constructionist history,** in which the historian incorporates his/her own present and past experiences when judging the past. This approach contends that one's own sociocultural frames and personal values can affect interpretations of the past (Schrier, 2005; Munslow, 1997).

3. **Deconstructionist history.** The third approach is Deconstructionist, which is not focused on empiricism but considers how information is interpreted, and seeks to put the personal back into history. In this approach, all evidence, such as transcripts, diaries, amateur videos, notes, images, or films are considered texts and are interpretable (Schrier, 2005; Munslow, 1997). These documents are a "representation of the past rather than the objective access to the reality of the past" (Munslow, 1997, pp. 17-35). How we revise and rewrite the past is influenced by our present position, and all interpretations are relative and individual.

Frameworks: History game design, use, and evaluation

One possible framework for using and evaluating games for history education is by McCall (2011), who lists five driving principles in his book, *Gaming the Past.*

1. **Principle I, "Introduce the Purpose of Simulation Gaming and the Characteristics of the Medium"** (McCall, 2011, p. 24) involves introducing students to the critical analysis of games, and help them consider the limits and potentials of the medium, while also helping them think through how history is constructed, rather than set in stone.

2. **Principle II, "Play Reflectively and Attentively; Observe and Engage in the Problem Space"** (McCall, 2011, p. 24) explains that students should first play the game without having to engage in higher-level history analysis. Students should have opportunities to closely attend to the game's goals, choices, and consequences, as well as any biases embedded in the game.

3. **Principle III, "Study Independent Historical Evidence on the Historical Problem Space"** (McCall, 2011, p. 24) suggests that designers, educators and their students should spend time with primary and secondary sources on the historical topic, and use this to help question assumptions in the game, and within the historical evidence.

4. **Principle IV, "Discuss, Debrief, Evaluate, Extend"** (McCall, 2011, p. 24) explains that time should be spent deliberating how the game was designed to support a possible version of the past, and to compare it to available evidence. He explains that educators should encourage the analysis of how and why the game presents the historical issues as it does, and the extent to which the choices available in the game mimicked the available choices historically.

5. **Finally, Principle V, "Critique, Critique, Critique"** (McCall, 2011, p. 25) encourages educators to question the validity of the game, while trying to avoid comparisons to "reality" or "how it really was" (McCall, 2011, p. 25).

Another possible framework to use for evaluating and designing history games is called the History Multimedia Interactive Educational Game (HMIEG), which is a "design model for teaching history" (Zin, Yue, & Azizah, 2009) and drawn from their interpretation of research on learning and game design. There are eight features in the pedagogical component of HMIEG, including "engagement, learning goal determination, motivation, critical thinking, psychological needs, explorations, challenge and competition" (Zin et al., 2009). According to Zin et al. (2009), these eight features specifically help support the learning goals (2009). "Constructivism theory, information processing model and Tolman Learning Theory are used in HMIEG design to enable students to remember historical facts and thus enhance learning" (Zin et al., 2009). There are 15 features in the game design component of HMIEG, or "feedback, fantasy, fun, rules, security, entertainment, immersive, active participation, control path, track and manage progress, interaction, task, narrative, control and imagination" (Zin et al., 2009). While Zin et al. (2009) have some useful observations and have connected research to their design principles, it is unclear the extent to which each of these principles directly affects history learning, as their model as a whole, and as components, has not been tested empirically.

Finally, while this is not a framework, per se, the *Mission US* team (Schrier & Channel 13, 2009) made the following specific design choices, which they explain contributed to the effectiveness of designing and using *Mission US* to meet specific pedagogical goals. These include:

1. **Simplification of animation:** The team simplified the animation so they did not distract the player from any text or audio happening concurrently.
2. **Modular play:** They developed short segments (25-45 minutes long) that could be integrated into a classroom class period.
3. **Balanced control and freedom:** They allowed for a number of mini-tasks and mini-decisions (such as choosing among dialogue choices), but also had enough constraints in the narrative as well.
4. **Goals and mini-tasks:** They designed a clear, overall goal to follow, and also designed a number of mini-tasks to complete in the game.
5. **Integration in curricula and standards:** The game included many points where a teacher could connect it to different social studies curricula, and it was tied to state and national history standards.
6. **Pivotal climax and resolution:** The game builds toward a climax (the Boston Massacre), which everyone experiences slightly differently. The deposition scene also shows the possible consequences to one's interpretations.

Frameworks: Related learning theories and concepts

There are also a number of more general learning theories that can help us consider how to better use games to support history learning and historical thinking, specifically.

One theory is situated cognition. In this approach, "context and learning, knowing and doing, are seen as intertwined and interdependent" (Schrier, 2006). The authentic tools and resources, as well as problems, situations, and contexts needed to complete an activity are mixed with the thinking, learning, and necessary actions (Klopfer et al., 2003; Brown, Collins, & Duguid, 1989; Dede et al., 2002). The learners' environment, context, and situation are seen as essential to the learning process (Schrier, 2006). In other words, learners wanting to understand history could practice authentic historic problems and goals within a relevant context, using realistic tools, data, texts, evidence or people. For example, a game based on this framework might situate authentic historical evidence, such as first-person testimonials, in a virtual version of a historic site or location. For example, one game, *Reliving the Revolution*, situates historic evidence, testimonials of the Battle of Lexington, within in a real and authentic location, the site of the Battle or Lexington, Massachusetts (See Case Study Two).

Bruner's (2009) work on situated cultural contexts also may be useful when designing games, as he argues that learning is additionally situated in a cultural context "learning and thinking are always situated in a cultural setting and always dependent upon the utilization of cultural resources" (Bruner, 2009, p. 162). A related concept is the "Community of practice," (Lave & Wenger, 1991) where learners collaborate to apply knowledge to solve authentic problems, while learning the vocabulary, taxonomies, epistemic frames, and rules of a specific community, vocation, or culture (Shaffer, 2005). A community of learners could be online, in an environment such as *iCivics* (see Case Study Three) or in person with a shared activity, game, or virtual experience, such as in the case of Mission US (see Case Study One).

Finally, historical empathy and historical thinking are also compelling concepts. Historical thinking is "History as a way of knowing" (Schrier et al., 2010, p. 258) and involves mimicking the activities of actual historians (e.g., analysis of evidence, interpreting causality, explaining change, bias identification, reflecting on one's role in the narrative formation) (Lee, 1983; Seixas, 1996, 2006; Wineburg, 2001). One major component of this is called historical empathy, which is defined as "…where we get to when we have successfully reconstructed other people's beliefs, values, goals, and attendant feelings" (Ashby & Lee, 1987, p. 63). Oftentimes students may judge the past in light of present-day norms and values, rather than activating prior factors, frames, and points of view (Wineburg, 1991, 2001; Schrier et al., 2010). Instead of deciding that other's perspectives are the "result of ignorance, stupidity, or delusion" (Barton & Levstik, 2004, pg. 211), we need to consider whether they make sense in the context of past moral codes or social values. In other words, attaining historical empathy "suggests that one can contextualize these perspectives from within a historical frame of reference or put oneself in the mindset of someone in history" (Schrier et al., 2010, p. 258). A game that helps students try on someone else's perspective and understand their cultural context, mindset, and obstacles, may be able to help them better interpret the past.

Other relevant frameworks are constructivism and constructionism, as well as social learning theory. Piaget's theory of constructivism focuses on how people learn through actively constructing ideas and knowledge. Constructionism, developed by Papert (1980) builds on this theory in *Mindstorms: Children, Computers, and Powerful Ideas,* and focuses on learning by making or constructing, particularly with others. For example, a game that enables participants to collaboratively construct historic artifacts using authentic materials may be useful for understanding how materials may have contributed to its look, feel, and function.

Finally, briefly, social learning theory suggests that people learn from observing other people's experiences, rather than needing to experience something directly (Bandura, 1977). This theory supports learning from games where the player may observe an avatar's or NPC's experience with an event, but may not directly interact with the historic incident.

Case Study Two: *Reliving the Revolution*

Schrier designed one of the first location-based games to teach children about history and to practice historical thinking skills. The game, *Reliving the Revolution (RtR)* (2005), invited participants to explore the physical location of the Battle of Lexington (Lexington, Massachusetts) and access virtual information about the Battle using GPS-enabled Palm Pilots (this was before iphones existed and GPS was integrated into phones). The game was tailored to students in middle and high school, and provided numerous mini-narratives based on first-person testimonials written by minutemen soldiers, British (regular) soldiers, local loyalists, and other townspeople, which would automatically appear on the players' phones depending on where they were standing at the physical Battle of Lexington site. To complete the game, students needed to interpret and weave together the first-person narratives about the historic moment of the Battle and create a meta-narrative about who fired the first shot at the Battle.

During the game, students worked together in pairs and played as a specific role based on a real historic figure (e.g., a minuteman solider, a female loyalist). Each role received slightly different information; for example, if a player was playing as a minuteman soldier and "talking" to a British Regular, they may have been receiving false or biased information. If they were "talking" to Paul Revere, the information might have been more accurate. This necessarily affected their reading of the evidence, and they needed to interpret and use the evidence they found accordingly. This also meant that they needed to compare evidence found with the evidence received by players in other roles to see where there were differences, if any.

RtR was tested with three separate groups of students, including college students and middle school/ high school students. RtR was suggested to support and motivate historical thinking, 21st century skills, such as collaboration and media fluency, as well as civic literacy. While the game itself was engaging because of its story, its encouragement of physical exploration of a site, and its use of technology, the experience was also effective because of the factors outside of the game. For example, a guide/mentor posed questions during the student deliberations, encouraged students to consider other perspectives, and provided necessary context to the history mission.

Key Findings

There are few empirical studies that have investigated the use of history games in classroom and informal settings. In this section I will consider some recent studies and their limitations.

Squire & Barab (2004) describe the use of *Civilization III* to explore the potential of using games to teach history by modifying the game and testing it with kids in social studies classrooms. They explain how "world history and geography became tools for playing [*Civilization III*] a stark contrast to how history is frequently taught. Failure to understand basic facts (such as where the Celts originated) drove them to Learn" (Squire & Barab, 2004, p. 512). Their study suggests that students did develop "systemic-level understandings" (Squire & Barab, 2004, p. 512) of history, through their gameplay, whereas incorporating more "historical texts as resources" (Squire & Barab, 2004, p. 512) might have further connected the game to history, such that the students were effectively replaying history and not just gaming the system (Squire & Barab, 2004, p. 512; Durga & Squire, 2008). One possible limitation of the study is that so much of the students' involvement and engagement with the game, and understanding of its connection to history, may be predicated on the teacher/mentor role. (For more about this research, see Squire's (2005) dissertation.)

Corbeil & Laveault (2011) tested a simulation game in a History of International Relations course. They found that those in the experimental group (those who received a game) had higher comprehension on a history test. Those students who were able to more formally reason (based on a Piagetian framework, and tested prior to the study) were able to attain significantly higher scores on the exam (Corbeil & Laveault, 2011).

> [They] also noted a favorable reaction to the game of those students preferring more social styles of learning… active involvement was the only affective factor significantly linked to learning. We might generalize this by saying that simulation games can help motivate social-minded students…. We must try to give students mobile and tactile instruments, which they can manipulate themselves as tools to study and understand ideas and abstract concepts. Games must also allow participants to discuss among themselves hypotheses, methods, and lines of approach in terms of situation analysis and choice of strategy. A game with predetermined results and behavior is no longer, in our sense, a game.
> (Corbeil & Laveault, 2011, p. 474)

One possible limitation of this study is that it seemed the students' prior knowledge, personality, learning style, and ability may have affected their comprehension as a result of the game intervention. While this would be expected, it makes it difficult to narrow down what exactly the game helps do to support comprehension.

Schrier (2005, 2006) created a location-based GPS-enabled game, *Reliving the Revolution (RtR)* to teach and motivate historical thinking, historical empathy, and the critical thinking of history (Schrier, 2005, 2006). The game takes place in the historic site of the Battle of Lexington, an event during the (American) Revolutionary War. In the game, participants needed to explore the Lexington battle site and access historical testimonials about the Battle, which were triggered to appear on a Palm Pilot mobile device, depending on where the participant was located in the town. The goal of the game was to try to understand who fired the first shot at Lexington, based on the interpretations of the evidence, a history mystery that is still unsolved. A pilot study of the game, using middle and high school students, suggested that the participants employed a variety of skills through the playing of the game, such as problem solving, community and global awareness skills, and the consideration of multiple perspectives (Schrier, 2005, 2006) (See more in Case Study Two). Limitations of this study include no empirically testing, no control group, and a limited sample size. The study was ethnographic, descriptive, and anecdotal, rather than tested using experimental conditions.

Anecdotal results on two other location-based experiences, *Jewish Time Jump* and *Dow Day*, have suggested they are effective in helping participants relive a historic moment. *Dow Day* is a situated documentary created using ARIS, a platform, which helps participants relive the moment of the 1967 Dow Chemical Corporation protest on the University of Madison-Wisconsin campus. For more about *Jewish Time Jump*, see Chapter 11, Case Study Two.

Assessment Considerations

To properly design or use (and then assess) the efficacy of a game for history education, one must be very clear as to the approach and learning goals. It follows that if the goal is to teach battle facts about the Civil War, then it would be more useful to have a pre- and post-game assessment that addresses students about these facts. Likewise, if the game focuses on teaching students historical empathy, a pre- and post-game task should help the educator assess whether historical empathy skills are being employed differently before, during and/or after the intervention. For example, with *Mission US*, students were invited to investigate a photo of the Boston Massacre before and after the game. Based on their evaluations, questions, and interpretations of this photo, they were rated in their practice of historical empathy.

The game itself should also be considered as a potential site of effective assessment, rather than having assessments that are only external to the game experience. In other words, assessment should be built into the game, and integrated in a way that it does not feel arduous or separate, but that part and parcel of the gameplay is achieving something or performing something that in and of itself shows that the player has learned what they need to learn, and also reveals what the player still needs to learn.

Moreover, the actual design of the game should be tested and re-tested throughout the process, such that the educational and design goals are being met. In *Mission US*, there were a number of design principles implemented to guide the creation of the game. These included using an authentic context and content, social context and collaboration, and engaging story, building an avatar/player relationship, and scaffolding vocabulary acquisition. These principles were tested (in terms of their efficacy in supporting the goals for the target audience, and also in their presence in the design) informally during playtesting, as well as through formative and summative assessments, throughout the design and implementation process. Testing should be built into the entire process as an integral part of design and assessment (see more in Case Study One).

Future Needs

There are many tensions and questions in how to better articulate history and social studies concepts and ideas through a game system. Empirical analysis, coupled with descriptive and ethnographic accounts, could support the endeavors of those educators, designers, and developers looking to make games for social studies learning. In addition, we should search for new techniques and assessment tools that can help us understand what students are actually learning and doing in these games and outside of the games in the long term, and which game elements or external elements are supporting it. We should also consider the teacher's role in supporting these games and any learning, and we should be open to considering alternative views of history pedagogy and practice.

Case Study Three: iCivics

iCivics.org is online education project with a suite of games related to civics, social studies, government, and justice. It is managed by iCivics, a non-profit organization that was started by Justice Sandra Day O'Connor, who observed that students did not understand even the basic civics concepts, such as the answer to "Which are the branches of government?" but they knew who the judges were on *American Idol,* for instance. The website includes lesson plans for educators and a teacher guide, along with dozens of games aimed to teach a variety of government and civics concepts.

In the mini-game, *Argument Wars,* created by Filament Games, you play as a lawyer who is arguing a case that is being presented to the Supreme Court. The player, playing as a lawyer avatar, argues real historic cases, such as *Brown vs. Board of Education.* The game uses clever mechanics to support argument formulation. For example, at one point in the game, the player can choose from a set of cards to "pitch" an argument. The opponent then chooses cards to "pitch" his or her own argument and the player can choose to object to any of the opponent's statements, mimicking lawyers in a courtroom. The judge has a limited number of "ruling points" that s/he can disperse depending on the validity of either side's arguments. The winning side is the one who has the most points at the end of the mini-game. At the end of the case, the game also explains which side actually won when the real case went to trial.

Other mini-games include *Branches of Power,* where the player can manage and balance the three branches of government, while trying to pass new laws, and *Do I Have a Right,* where the player runs a law firm that specializes in constitutional law and needs to judge whether possible clients "have a right" based on authentic constitutional rights.

The iCivics games also provide different achievements based on progress. For example, the "Rain Maker" achievement is for players who finish a game and do not lose any cases. iCivics also has weekly and monthly leaderboards. The website explains that three million students play the iCivics games each year and is used by over 40,000 educators. iCivics games have been evaluated in a number of studies, including LeCompte et al. (2011) and Kawashima & Ginsburg (2012). For example, LeCompte et al. (2011) researched students who played any iCivics games for one hour per week for six weeks and found a 19% increase in test scores on a pre- to post-test on civic knowledge. Qualitatively, they also found that the students seemed highly motivated to play the game and seemed to look forward to their social studies classes.

Best Practices

There are a number of best practices that have emerged in designing and using digital games for social studies and history education.

1. **Clearly identify your pedagogical approach.** When designing or using a game to teach history, questions of pedagogical and historiographic approach should be answered as quickly as possible and communicated effectively within the team. The questions and tensions listed in this chapter—whether to maintain the highest accuracy to details or to focus on broader trends, whether to highlight personal obstacles or macro-level scale economic issues, or whether to include uncomfortable issues like the Holocaust, human trafficking, or slavery—are all present as well when designing history education games. It is problematic when designers and educators do not, up front, define their pedagogical approach and the skills and practices they want the game to enable, as well as reflect on the implications of these choices. Instead, many designers and educators try to make a one-size-fits all solution, which ends up being overwhelming or confusing; or, they use an off-the-shelf game without considering its implications.

2. **Understand the limits and potentials of games.** Games should not just be used to further engage students in the boring topic of history. Rather, each individual game's what potentials and limits should be considered, as well as the factors under which the game will be used and the curricular goals.

3. **Understand the values and biases embedded in the game's design and performance.** As such, and with any representation of the past, games can therefore embed a number of biases and oversimplifications (McCall, 2011). No piece of media, whether a game or a different medium, can fully represent history and all of its complexity. "No imaginable set of "historical" representations can do justice to the fullness of "history" as past" (Uricchio, 2005, p. 331). Moreover, Schut argues that "history games are predisposed toward presentations of history that are stereotypically masculine, highly systematic, and focused on spatially oriented interactivity" (Schut, 2007, pg. 230). This often requires a teacher or other educator to be involved in supporting, critiquing, reflecting, and questioning of the

designers' choices and decisions in how they represented the past, its people, systems, and places, its boundaries and constraints, and the choices it allows or disallows, as well as what it did not represent. After all, there may have been infinite other ways a game could have been designed.

4. **Consider the role of the teacher, guide, or mentor.** The teacher or guide is an integral part of the *Reliving the Revolution (RtR)* experience, and research has shown that this role is essential (McCall, 2011; Schrier et al., 2010). *RtR* itself was just one part of the learning experience. Other aspects of the curriculum, such as worksheets, in-class debates around the game, reflection exercises, diaries, and dramatic tasks, were related to the game but not the game itself. Designing not only the game, but the curriculum and mentorship around the game, seemed to add up to a more holistic educational experience for the players, which was anecdotally effective. More research should consider the extent to which the activities and guidance around the game contribute to its educational efficacy.

5. **Consider the differences between games and other media.** It is also important to consider the differences between how history is presented in other media, versus how it can be presented in games.

Table 1 may be useful as initial questions to ask when designing a game for history/social studies learning.

Table 1. Initial questions to consider when designing and using games for history education

Initial Questions to Consider When Designing and Using Games for History Education
1. What is the approach to history education—are skills such as inquiry, bias identification, or perspective-taking more important, or is memorizing facts and figures more essential?
2. To what extent does the historical place, people, and items need to be accurate and what does "accuracy" mean in the context of the game?
3. What are the learning goals and how will those be communicated and achieved through the game?
4. Are students experiencing alternate approaches to a historical moment, or even interpreting it themselves, or are they learning how others have interpreted it and then applying that to new situations?
5. Are students playing the game immersing themselves in a historical figure's shoes, or are they playing as themselves and thinking about differences between today and yesterday?
6. If you are using an off-the-shelf game, look under the hood and consider the designers' perspectives and biases—how are their approaches to history or values integrated into the game's design and how will this affect any learning that results?

Resources

Books and publications

Akkerman, S., Admiraal, W., & Huizenga, J. (2009). Storification in history education: A mobile game in and about medieval Amsterdam. *Computers & Education*. 52(2): 449-459.

López, J.M.C. & Cáceres, M.J.M. (2010). Virtual games in social science education. *Computers & Education*. 55(3): 1336-1345.

McCall, J. (2011). *Gaming the Past*. New York, NY: Routledge.

Shaffer, D. (2006). *How Computer Games Help Children Learn*. New York, NY: Palgrave MacMillan.

Squire, K. (2004). *Replaying History: Learning World History through Playing Civilization III*. Doctoral Dissertation. (http://website.education.wisc.edu/kdsquire/dissertation.html)

Stearns, P., Seixas, P., & Wineburg, S. (Eds). (2000) *Knowing Teaching & Learning History*. New York: New York University Press.

Vansledright, B. (1997/8). "On the importance of historical positionality to thinking about and teaching history." *The International Journal of Social Education*. 12(2), 1-18.

Games and websites

ARIS (http://arisgames.org/)

Assassins Creed

Axis and Allies

Battle of Lexington Reenactment
(every Patriot's Day morning in Lexington, Massachusetts) (http://www.battleroad.org/)

Carcassonne

Civilization

Cruel Necessity: The English Civil Wars, 1640-1653

Democracy 3

Diplomacy

Dow Day

Frequentie 1550 (<http://freq1550.waag.or)

Gaming the Past blog (http://gamingthepast.net/)

Grand Theft Auto

Historical board games
(https://www.facebook.com/HistoricalBoardGames and http://en.wikipedia.org/wiki/Category:Historical_board_games)

History Channel games (http://www.history.com/games/)

Historypin (http://www.historypin.com)

iCivics (www.icivics.org)

Jewish Time Jump

LA Noire

Making History

Mission US (www.mission-us.org)

Muzzy Lane (http://muzzylane.com/project/making_history/edu)

National Council for the Social Studies (NCSS) (http://www.socialstudies.org/standards)

Play it Again Project (history of games) (http://playitagainproject.org/)

Play the Past (http://www.playthepast.org/)

Puerto Rico

Red Dead Redemption

Redistricting Game (http://www.redistrictinggame.org/)

Reliving the Revolution

Revolutions

Risk

River City

SimCityEdu (www.simcityedu.org)

Smart History (http://www.yourcommonwealth.org/)

The Migrant Trail (http://theundocumented.com/)

The Republica Times

Tiki-Toki (http://www.tiki-toki.com/)

Your Commonwealth (http://www.yourcommonwealth.org/)

References

Ashby, R. and Lee, P. (1987). Children's concepts of empathy and understanding in history. In C. Portal (Ed.), *The history curriculum for teachers (62-88)*. London, UK: Falmer.

Bandura, A. (1977). *Social learning theory*. Englewood Cliffs, NJ: Prentice Hall.

Barnett, M., Barab, S., Schatz, S., Warren S. (2000). Designing a community of inquiry in an undergraduate history course: A clash of cultures. Paper presented at the 2000 Annual Meeting of the American Educational Research Association. New Orleans, LA.

Barton, K. C. and Levstik, L. S. (2004). *Teaching history for the common good*. Mahwah, N.J.: Lawrence Erlbaum Associates.

Brown, J., Collins, A., and Dugid, P. (1989). Situated cognition and the culture of learning, *Educational Researcher, 18*, 32-42.

Bruner, J. (2009). Culture, Mind, and Education. In K. Illeris (Ed.), *Contemporary theories of learning*. New York, NY: Routledge.

Corbeil, P. and Laveault, D. (2011). Validity of a simulation game as a method for history teaching. *Simulation and Gaming, 42*(4), 462-475.

Dede, C., Whitehouse, P., & Brown-L'Bahy, T. (2002) Designing and studying learning experiences that use multiple interactive media to bridge distance and time. In C. Vrasidas & G. Glass (Eds.), *Current perspectives on applied information technologies. Vol. 1: Distance education,* (1-30). Greenwich, CN: Information Age Press.

Downey, M., Levstik, L. (1991). Teaching and learning history. In J. Shaver (Ed.), *Handbook of research on social studies teaching and learning,* (400-410). New York: Macmillan Publishing Company.

Jenkins, K. (2003). *Rethinking history*. New York: Routledge.

Kee, K. (2011). Computerized history games: Narrative options. *Simulation & Gaming, 4*, 423-440.

Klopfer, E., Squire, K., & Jenkins, H. (2003). Augmented reality simulations on handheld computers. Paper presented at the American Educational Research Association Conference, Chicago, IL.

Klopfer, E., Squire, K. & Jenkins, H. (2002). Environmental detectives: PDAs as a window into a virtual simulated world: Wireless and mobile technologies in Education. *Proceedings of the IEEE international workshop,* (95-98).

Lave, J. & Wenger, E. (1991). *Situated learning: Legitimate peripheral participation*. Cambridge, UK: Cambridge University Press.

Lee, P. (1983). History teaching and philosophy of history. *History and Theory, 22*(4), 19-49.

Lee, P. & Ashby, R. (2000). Empathy, perspective taking, and rational understanding. In edited J. O. L. Davis, E. A. Yeager & S. J. Foster. *Historical Empathy and Perspective Taking in the Social Studies*, (21-50). Maryland: Rowman & Littlefield Publishers, Inc.

Lowenthal, D. (1996) *Possessed by the past: The heritage crusade and the spoils of history*. New York: Free Press.

McCall, J. (2011). *Gaming the Past*. New York, NY: Routledge.

Munslow, A. (1997). *Deconstructing history*. New York, NY: Routledge.

Papert, S. (1980). *Mindstorms: Children, computers, and powerful ideas*. New York, NY: Basic Books.

Piaget, J. (1926). *The language and thought of the child*. London: Routledge & Kegan.

Schrier, K. (2005). Revolutionizing history education: Using augmented reality games to teach histories. (Master's thesis, Massachusetts Institute of Technology, 2005).

Schrier, K. (2006). Using augmented reality games to teach 21st century skills. *Proceedings of ACM siggraph 2006 educators program*. Boston, MA.

Schrier, K., & Channel 13. (2009). *The research-informed game design approach to Mission US*. Unpublished whitepaper.

Schrier, K., Diamond, J., and Langendoen, D. (2010). Using *Mission US*: For crown or colony? to develop historical empathy and nurture ethical thinking. In K. Schrier & D. Gibson (Eds.), *Ethics and game design: Teaching values through play*, (239-261). Hershey, PA: IGI.

Schut, K. (2007) Strategic simulations and our past: The bias of computer games in the presentation of history. *Games and Culture. 2*(3), 213-235.

Seixas, P. (1996). Conceptualizing growth in historical understanding. In D. Olson & N. Torrance (Eds.) *Education and human development*. London: Blackwell.

Seixas, P. (2000). Schweigen! die kinder! or, does postmodern history have a place in the schools? In Stearns, P., Seixas, P., & Wineburg, S. (Eds.) *Knowing teaching & learning history: National and international perspectives*. New York, NY: New York University Press.

Squire, K., & Durga, S. (2006). Productive gaming: The case for historiographic game play. To appear in R. Ferdig (Ed.) The handbook of educational gaming. Hershey, PA: Information Science Reference.

Squire, K., & Barab, S. (2004). Replaying history: Engaging urban underserved students in learning world history through computer simulation games. *Sixth international conference of the learning sciences*. Santa Monica, United States: Lawrence Erlbaum Associates.

Uricchio, W. (2005). Simulation, history and computer games. In J. Goldstein and J. Raessans. (Eds.) *Handbook of Computer Game Studies*, 327-338. Cambridge, MA: MIT Press.

Wineburg, S. (2001). *Historical thinking and other unnatural acts: Charting the future of teaching the past*. Philadelphia: Temple University Press.

Wineburg, S. S. (1991). Historical problem solving: A study of the cognitive processes used in the evaluation of documentary and pictorial evidence. *Journal of Educational Psychology, 83*, 73-87.

Zin, N., Yue, W., and J. Azizah. (2009). Digital game-based learning (DGBL) model and development methodology for teaching history. WSEAS Transactions on Computers, 8(2): 22-333.

CHAPTER 5

Music

Music Games in Education

Ethan Hein, *New York University, New York, New York, U.S., ethan@ethanhein.com*

Key Summary Points

 The greatest challenge music educators face is to translate young people's innate enjoyment of music into sustained interest and focus in the classroom. Even when students are fortunate enough to have access to music education, many disengage, and many abandon formal musical study entirely (Mota, 2013).

 Common reasons for children and teens to become discouraged by music classes or lessons include a steep technical barrier to entry requiring many hours of practice to overcome, the fact that classroom music is typically socially or culturally inauthentic and unfamiliar, and the stress and anxiety of performance.

 There are three major types of music games: drill-and-skill, rhythm games, and music toys. Each has its pros and cons for learning music.

Key Terms

DAW
Electronic music
Generative music
MIDI
Notation software
Remix
Sequencer
Win condition

Introduction

Games hold promise for the teaching of music due to their accessibility and ability to engage the player. It remains to be seen how much of this promise will be realized. Koops & Taggart (2011) define "work" as a means toward accomplishment, and "play" as a means toward personal physical, emotional, or cognitive well-being. It is no accident games and music share the verb "to play." Work is necessary to master the basic skills that enable musical play, as it is in any creative undertaking. Music games show their strongest educational potential when they make the work feel like play as well (Dillon, 2007).

Among American high school students who have access to elective music classes, only five percent choose to take them (Lowe, 2012). Nearly all young people like music, so why do they abandon its study in such overwhelming numbers?

Harwood & Marsh (2012) observe that traditional music education asks students to perform two challenging learning tasks at the same time: 1) they must learn unfamiliar repertoire, and 2) they must do so using unfamiliar tools and techniques. The technical and notational barriers to entry discourage some beginners. Others find it difficult to relate to the music they are learning. Still others are stymied by the combination of both factors.

Music games can ease some of the pedagogical burden, both in their content and their delivery methods. The game format is generally familiar and appealing to young people. Commercial games such as the *Rock Band* series use recognizable pop and rock songs—material students are more likely to find personally meaningful (see Case Study One). Games can give even novice players a taste of the excitement of performing, a feeling that is normally only available only to very adept musicians.

Beginner-level music students must simultaneously learn (1) music concepts, (2) the notation system encoding those concepts, and (3) the instrumental or vocal techniques necessary to translate the symbols into sound. How useful are games for each of these three tasks?

Most games explicitly aimed at the educational market, so-called "drill-and-skill" games, recreate traditional classroom activities in the computer: reading and writing notation, identifying intervals and scales, and the like. Such tasks are extrinsically motivated, since students typically play the games at the behest of a teacher or parent, and/or as part of or in addition to structured music lessons. Drill-and-skill games have a significant advantage over pencil-and-paper methods because they offer instant feedback, both sonic and visual. Rather than having to wait for a teacher to correct the assignment, students find out instantly whether they have marked a note correctly. Furthermore, students can match notation to sounds without having to simultaneously struggle with instrument mechanics.

Games can help with the learning of music concepts through the use of novel interactive visualization systems. Wilkie, Holland, & Mulholland (2010) demonstrate that the most effective metaphors for aiding in musical understanding are tangible and bodily. Chords and keys are "containers" for notes. Repetitive patterns are cycles. Pitch is a vertical ladder. A consonant note is "in the center," while a dissonant one is "at the periphery." A song is a narrative, beginning at a "source," moving along a "path" toward a "goal." The best music games use such metaphors to create intuitive mappings between sound and image. For example, the *Rock Band* series represents musical time as a road or track, along which you travel in the first person. Such visualizations can create an intuitive musical understanding that paves the way for learning traditional notation and instrumental skills.

Most games do not teach instrumental or vocal techniques directly. Instrument simulation games such as the *Rock Band* and *Guitar Hero* series are roundly criticized for simplifying and misrepresenting real instruments, and their players are derided as not being "real musicians" (Miller, 2009). *Rock Band 3* is a rare exception in that it attempts to teach actual instrument technique (see Case Study One).

Most mainstream commercial music games center around rhythm, rather than pitch, timbre, or other aspects of music. In rhythm games, you move or press controls in sync to a song, following onscreen notation, often using a specialized controller. Rhythm games fall into several subgenres:

1. **Dance games:** *Dance Dance Revolution, Let's Dance*
2. **Instrument simulations:** *Rock Band, Guitar Hero, Donkey Konga*
3. **Singing games:** *Karaoke Revolution, SingStar*
4. **More abstract games:** *FreQuency, VibRibbon, Rez*

There is a category of experimental music games that are more properly called "music toys," open-ended generative systems in which the player interacts improvisationally with a semi-autonomous synthesis system. Examples include *SimTunes, Electroplankton, Wii Music, Nodebeat*, and *Bloom*. The iPad and iPhone are particularly congenial platforms for music toys. While these programs superficially resemble games in their presentation, they generally do not have a competitive aspect *per se*, and are more like musical instruments.

Case Study One: Rock Band 3

Rock Band 3 was released in 2010 by Harmonix Music Systems for the Xbox 360, PlayStation 3, Wii, and Nintendo DS. As with previous titles in the series, *Rock Band 3* enables you to "play" rock and pop songs while using special controllers mimicking guitar, bass, and drums. Unlike the previous two games, *Rock Band 3* includes a keyboard controller. Players can also sing three-part vocal harmonies. The game includes thousands of songs and can be played by up to seven people at a time.

Critics of rhythm games complain that players are not learning actual, transferable music skills. Harmonix addressed that criticism with *Rock Band 3*'s novel Pro Mode. In place of the usual simplified abstractions, Pro Mode aims to teach players the actual instrumental parts on more realistic controllers. For example, Fender sells a real guitar with custom electronics to use with Pro Mode—not only is it a fully functional MIDI controller, but it can sense the location of the player's fingers to give nuanced feedback. Pro Mode has an easy level that offers simplified versions of songs, similar to the abstractions in previous *Guitar Hero* titles. As the player advances, the complexity increases and the transcriptions become more complete.

Rock Band 3 also includes tutorials on technique and music theory developed by experts from the Berklee College of Music, though these are somewhat perfunctory. More intriguing is Practice Mode, which slows down songs and allows the player to loop specific sections. The game's designers needed a notation system that anyone could learn to sight-read. Their solution is what they describe as "a Montessori approach," a graphical tablature showing chord fingerings as modular shapes. This enables the game to teach actual songs first, introducing theory only optionally, if at all—a strategy used by many self-taught guitarists (Booth & Dubrofsky, 2011).

There is not much data on the effectiveness of *Rock Band 3* in the music classroom. Cassidy & Paisley (2013) found that the game promotes flow and invites disciplined and constructive engagement. They did not explicitly measure gains in musical skill, however. Peppler, Downton, Lindsay & Hay (2011) conducted a study of 26 children in an afterschool club, with a hypothesis that the subjects would measurably improve their music skills. The authors' argument in favor of *Rock Band 3* as a teaching tool centers not on Pro Mode, but on the in-game notation system. They see the game's value not in its teaching of instrument mechanics, but in its interactive visualization of music theory and song structure. The results of their study were inconclusive, but did show some improvement in participants' rhythm and reading skills.

Schultz (2008) observes that, like the MIDI piano roll, rhythm games are interactive graphical scores. They connect visual abstractions to sound in an intuitive way, showing particular ingenuity in the Z-axis "driving mode" representation of musical time. Furthermore, rhythm games give crucial real-time feedback: failing to hit a note correctly both sets off an animated visual response and causes the player's instrument to temporarily drop out of the mix. Peppler et al. (2011) observe that, "This dynamic feedback is rarely afforded to musicians outside of gameplay, who must be told by someone with more experience (usually a parent, bandmate or teacher) if what they played was contrary to what was written on the page" (p. 6).

Rhythm game notation shares some key features with traditional music notation, including models of metric hierarchy, subdivision, measurement and pattern identification. The beginner-level notation shows only the most structurally important events in each phrase, using an abstraction system similar to the reductions performed by music theorists when analyzing a piece. In spite of its simplicity, the notation still retains the song's overall melodic contour.

Rock Band benefits music students by enabling them to study culturally authentic material directly from recordings, as popular musicians do in actual practice. The visual notation adds considerable value to such aural learning: "[E]ven those trained in formal notational systems report hearing new elements in the music through this activity than from score-reading or listening, alone" (Peppler et al., 2011, p. 5). Furthermore, every Rock Band session is a performance. In this sense, it may be a more "realistic" music experience than the decontextualized pieces and exercises in music class. Much more research is needed on whether the pleasure of *Rock Band 3* translates to the learning of transferable musical skills.

Key Frameworks

Games can address several of the obstacles to music learning listed above in the introduction. Students' frustration with too-difficult or too-simple tasks can be addressed with multiple difficulty levels and self-pacing. Well-designed games offer individually calibrated challenges, carefully matching the player's ability to steadily escalating challenges. While failure in music performance is embarrassing and frustrating, Tobias (2012) observes that, in games, "Failure is designed to encourage players to determine better solutions to a given problem and allows for multiple opportunities to reach a particular goal" (p. 5).

Performance anxiety is a powerful obstacle to music learning. Games can assuage this anxiety by providing opportunities for private virtual performance. Students who are too shy to perform for peers can engage with music in the safety of their bedrooms or headphones.

Most overtly educational music games use the same sorts of artificial melodies found in traditional teaching materials. By contrast, pop-oriented commercial games use material that young people are familiar with and enjoy. More importantly, the games enable players to learn aurally from recordings as well as from notation. Recordings can act as expert peers or virtual master teachers. A desire to imitate pop stars can motivate young people, particularly teenagers, to perform disciplined study.

Ideally, music class should be a genuine community of learning that speaks to students' musical selves. Students often express social solidarity with each other by resisting music class, whereas social solidarity could, instead, encourage other's to further engage with music class. Green (2002) argues that the Eurocentric basis of traditional music education is incompatible with students' enculturation. She proposes integrating the following informal, pop-oriented pedagogical practices into formal music education for young students:

1. Allowing learners to choose the music.
2. Learning by listening to and copying recordings.
3. Learning in friendship groups with minimal adult guidance.
4. Learning in personal, haphazard ways.
5. Integrating listening, playing, singing, improvising, and composing.

Music games support these practices to varying extents.

Well-designed games create engagement by promoting a flow state, a total absorption that makes the player gratifyingly oblivious to anything else. Good musical experiences also involve flow states, and music classes are most effective when they foster flow. There are five elements necessary to bring about flow states (Csíkszentmihályi, 2009):

1. Immediate feedback contributing to a balance between skill and challenge;
2. Merged action and awareness, completely occupying students' attention;
3. Deep, sustained concentration;
4. Control of the situation, and the freedom to generate possibilities; and
5. Loss of self-consciousness.

The single strongest rationale for including games in the music classroom is their self-motivating, flow-promoting quality. Ideally, a student who experiences flow brought on by self-motivated disciplined practice in the game context will be inspired to pursue the same state in other contexts (Dillon, 2007). Challenge is a strong motivation for learning when the student has a commensurate skill level. Well-designed games promote flow by continually adjusting their difficulty level to meet the player's present state of understanding. Rhythm games have an additional quality that strongly promotes flow, which is that they involve physical activity (Custodero, 2002).

Music games have a major limitation in their flow-inducing capabilities: they typically give the player little control over the music being produced. Music toys are the exception; their purpose is to foster expressiveness, and they enable even complete novices to exercise control and implement their own ideas.

Case Study Two: *iGotGame*

The major shortcoming of both drill-and-skill games and rhythm games is the absence of improvisation. The player moves through the song like a train on a track, and the games penalize any variation from the prescribed notes. Not all real-life music is improvisational either, but there is usually some element of personal expressiveness. Not so in music games—mimicry is the only way to play. Rosenstock (2010) recognized this shortcoming, and devised a game to try to address it. Working with students at the Worcester Polytechnic Institute, he developed *iGotBand*, an experimental rhythm game that incorporates improvisation. While the basic gameplay follows the *Rock Band* model, you need not reproduce the given note sequences exactly; you are free to use any rhythm and you can interject notes of your choosing.

Rosenstock's game is an admirable attempt at incorporating improvisation into a music game, but he fails to address some basic problems. The improvisation in *iGotGame* has no bearing on the player's success or failure. This makes it a nice but meaningless feature. Rosenstock readily admits this to be a problem, and his discussion of the issue is enlightening. Games and music share the verb "to play," but in both domains, the word has several distinct meanings. Rosenstock introduces the term *paidia*, meaning childlike play: spontaneous and unruly. The musical equivalent would be freeform jazz, or generative music toys. By contrast, there is play as *ludus*: games with ordered rules and a win condition, such as chess or basketball (and indeed, nearly all video games.) The musical equivalent of *ludus* is classical composition and more formally-bound jazz styles such as bebop.

Like most other rhythm games, *iGotBand* is an example of *ludus*. The improvisational aspect is a dash of *paidia*, but it has no bearing on the win condition, and therefore is not intrinsic to the experience. In fairness to Rosenstock, it is difficult to imagine how one could possibly devise an unambiguous system of rules for judging improvisation. Rosenstock attempts to address this problem by suggesting that players vote on the quality of others' improvisation. This merely defers the issue, however; there is still no rule-based system for making judgments beyond whatever arbitrary criteria players would use for voting.

Improvisation might superficially resemble a game, but Rosenstock inadvertently demonstrates how fundamentally incompatible it is with a win condition. Music toys with game-like interfaces can potentially serve the goal of expressiveness much better than perhaps games can; more research should be conducted to tease out this relationship.

Key Findings

Ruthmann (2006) lists three goals that music education technology should meet. They include:

1. Broadening participation;
2. Enabling greater musical creativity through improvisation; and
3. The widespread teaching of music composition.

Rhythm games have been shown to inspire broader participation in "real music" (Miller, 2009; Peppler et al., 2011). Some games offer composition tools, though these are usually limited. Most games actively work against improvisation (see Case Study Two).

Egenfeldt-Nielsen (2007) uses the term "edutainment" to describe games explicitly designed for educational use, with *Math Blaster!* as his canonical example. He takes a dim view of such titles, for two reasons: the educational content is frequently disconnected from the game elements, and the in-game learning is typically rote, resulting in weak skill transfer. A meta-study of the effectiveness of such edutainment titles showed that while they do work, there is no reliable evidence they perform better (or worse) than any other learning method (Egenfeldt-Nielsen, 2007). Nevertheless, music teachers and parents have embraced drill-and-skill games, perhaps because of their similarity to traditional curriculum materials.

Commercial rhythm games such as *Rock Band* and *Guitar Hero* are the source of considerable controversy. These games certainly require (and inspire) a great deal of disciplined practice. But are players really learning music? Ruthmann (2006) argues that the best curriculum activities derive from real-world activities, ideally retaining the essential values of the original. The objects and operations of the adapted activity should be genuine instances of the original activity, however simplified. By this logic, rhythm games should be very valuable for educators. Many musicians and teachers, however, criticize simplified game controllers that do not realistically represent actual instruments. For example, while the drum kits in *Rock Band* and *Guitar Hero* games correspond somewhat closely to real drum kits, the pads are simply on-off controllers with no dynamics or expression.

As of this writing, there has been little research on how well rhythm games teach traditional music skills and theory. Some early research points to the games' effectiveness (Peppler et al., 2011). Other studies, however, show improvement only in tracking the kinds of visual prompts used in the game notation. Richardson & Kim (2011) explain: "Repeated play of these games may create some form of musical rehearsal, but their non-literal and varying performance mappings are arguably removed from or even counter-productive to both the rehearsal of the specific music approximated and the general practices of traditional music education" (p. 278).

On the other hand, Richardson & Kim's study of student experience of rhythm games includes some anecdotes that reveal the games' unexpected educational benefits. For example, one of their subjects cites the games' power to reduce anxiety: "I have never sung in front of anyone before, but this was the best way to do it, I guess, because everyone was watching the screen" (Richardson & Kim, 2011, p. 288). The games also encourage close and active listening. Another participant comments, "I'd never listened to music in layers like that" (Richardson & Kim, 2011, p. 288). Such close study of "real-world" recordings is invaluable for situating the notes on the page in a meaningful context (Green, 2002).

In their analysis of the *Rock Band* series and *SingStar*, Gower & McDowall (2012) observe that these games have a major advantage over traditional music education for teaching pitch and rhythm: the games give real-time auditory and visual feedback. Each note played or sung prompts an immediate graphical and sonic event informing the player whether it was right or wrong. Such continual and granular performance assessment would be difficult to deliver any other way. Even in one-on-one private instruction, a teacher cannot readily react to every individual note in the moment.

Beyond their musical value, the aforementioned popular music games are also excellent tools for engaging with the cultural history of popular music (Gower & McDowall, 2012). For example, the *Rock Band* series' library comprises of thousands of songs spanning five decades. Furthermore, the games themselves are potential objects of rich study. The graphical avatars can provoke conversation about gender and cultural stereotypes in music and its pop cultural presentation (Tobias, 2012). The games can also act as a springboard for a more general philosophical discussion of the nature of music performance and authenticity in virtual contexts (Miller, 2009).

Smith (2004) observes that "playing [rhythm] games can feel like a genuinely musical experience: the controller is no longer a trigger but a percussion instrument, and the player stops thinking in terms of locking on targets and instead tries to feel the groove" (p. 65). Smith (2004), however, is concerned that players have little agency in the game, since they are restricted to preprogrammed button presses triggering preprogrammed sounds: "The pleasure of agency in electronic environments is often confused with the mere ability to move a joystick or click on a mouse. But activity alone is not agency" (p. 61). The *Rock Band* and *Guitar Hero* games do have special modes allowing remixing of their content or the creation of new playable songs. These systems are more limited than full-blown music production software, but for that reason, they are also more accessible to novices.

Creativity has entered one music game through an unexpected vector. *Dance Dance Revolution (DDR)* was born in the arcades of Japan and from its inception was a spectator sport or a performance for a real-world audience. The performance aspect of *DDR* has taken on a life of its own with the practice of "freestyling"—dancing while facing away from the screen and toward the crowd, incorporating upper-body moves that have no bearing on the game (Smith, 2004). To pull this off, freestylers must memorize the steps to songs and then how to do them backward so that they can turn and face the crowd. The home version of *DDR* subsequently turned freestyling into an official game feature by adding a mirror mode that turns the steps backward.

Assessment Considerations

Drill-and-skill games aim to transfer concrete musical skills like notation, ear training, and transcription. It is a straightforward matter to assess student progress in this context: either they do the exercises correctly or they do not. By contrast, student work with music toys defies easy assessment. These titles are intrinsically open-ended and expressive, so there is no obvious way to gauge "successful" or "unsuccessful" usage. It is better to consider music games as new instruments, rather than as exercises or games, per se. We can judge a music toy based on how discoverable its rules are, and by the depth and quality of its generative output.

Rhythm games pose the greatest challenges for assessment. On the one hand, they have clear win conditions and internal scoring systems. On the other hand, the game objectives may not map onto the curriculum easily, or at all. One approach to assessment is to evaluate players' expressiveness within the games, as we would with music toys. We might also examine players' mastery of skills and knowledge that generalize into other musical settings.

Future Needs

Teachers may well appreciate the engaging, flow-promoting qualities of rhythm games, but wish that they included other forms of music. Smith (2004) cites one of the rare classical music rhythm games, *Mad Maestro*, first released in 2001 for the PlayStation 2. The gameplay follows the *Rock Band* model, but with the player "conducting" an orchestra playing the classical greatest hits: *The Marriage of Figaro, Swan Lake, Pictures at an Exhibition*, and so on.

We might imagine *Conductor Hero,* in which you use a motion controller to conduct different world-class ensembles, starting with small chamber works and progressing through large-scale symphonies. Such a game, however, is not likely to emerge from the marketplace anytime soon. A satirical article in *The Onion* (2007) illustrates the challenges:

Activision Reports Sluggish Sales For Sousaphone Hero

> In the wake of *Guitar Hero*'s success, we thought the public was more than ready for
> additional popular American musical genres in a simulated-performance format,
> but people don't seem to be responding to marches as well as we had hoped…If you
> score enough points, you can unlock the ultimate level: playing in the John Philip
> Sousa–led Marine Band at Grover Cleveland's inauguration.
> (p. 1)

Educational and government organizations that wish to produce non-pop rhythm games with the level of polish and engagement found in commercial titles face two major obstacles: the considerable expense of developing complex multimedia software and custom controllers, and the expense and logistical complexity of licensing the music and musician likenesses.

Aside from the music toys, music games permit little or no creativity on the player's part. There are a few exceptions, however. Later titles in the Guitar Hero series have included GH Mix, a composition tool that enables you to create original music in the game environment. The controllers act as primitive MIDI instruments for sequencing notes into the game's "piano roll." Players can also record your own vocals. Songs created this way are fully playable within the game and can be shared with other players via the game's online network.

Harmonix has also created the *Rock Band Network,* a platform for translating original recordings into playable *Rock Band* songs using the audio editing software *Reaper* along with a special plug-in. These recordings need not be rock or pop songs. Tobias (2012) suggests that music teachers take advantage of this feature to expand the musical possibilities of the rhythm game format:

> Opportunities for students, whether in rock bands creating original music or brass quintets performing baroque works, to have their music played with controllers in a video game environment offer varied entry points into these musics and raise compelling questions about what it means to create, listen to, and perform music in this context. Whether deciding how to distribute brass quintet parts across the game controllers or visualizing the rhythms of an original riff, students' use of video games in the music classroom affords new ways of interacting with music from multiple viewpoints. The implications of creating, arranging, and playing Gabrieli on a plastic guitar controller or samba on rubber drums are yet to be seen. (p. 15)

Rather than waiting for *Conductor Hero* to be released, educators may be well advised to follow Tobias' suggestion to repurpose existing titles for their own purposes.

Case Study Three: *My Note Games!*

There are many drill-and-skill music games on the market. The state of the art is well represented by *My Note Games!*, released by Appatta Ltd for iOS in 2011. This app comprises several distinct games. The most basic and introductory exercises are free, and you can purchase upgrades to the full games within the app. Your score across all exercises is kept in the form of "Aural IQ," and the app uses this measure to calibrate difficulty levels. The games include:

1. ***Hear It, Note It!*** A transcription game: You hear a melody and use the game's notation editor to transcribe it. You can listen any number of times until you enter your first note, at which point you must write from memory. If the transcription is incorrect, the melody plays again and you can make corrections.

2. ***Tap That Note:*** You are shown a simple melody with a row of note names below it. You must tap the note names in the sequence they are written on the score. The game can be played in treble, bass, alto, or tenor clef. It tracks your timing as well as your note choices, though not very precisely. You have approximately one second per note, for an implicit minimum tempo of 60 beats per minute.

3. ***Play That Note:*** This game tests sight-reading ability. You play a short melody on your instrument into the built-in mic, and the game tracks your accuracy note-by-note. A variety of instruments are supported, and there is beta support for singing and whistling as well, though the pitch-tracking for the latter two works unevenly at best. The game requires you to keep your instrument in tune, and to that end, supplies a built-in tuner. Here, again, note durations are not very important, so long as you play faster than about 60 beats per minute.

4. ***Play-A-Day:*** This game involves a more demanding sight-reading exercise, which requires more exact timing. You are given eight melodies, and when you can play all of them correctly, you advance to the next eight. The melodies are generated randomly and are not exceptionally musical, which raises the issue of cultural authenticity.

As a delivery system for traditional classroom and homework exercises, *My Note Games!* are well-designed. The immediate feedback is gratifying, the self-pacing and automatic difficulty adjustments are conducive to learning, and the graphics are cheerful and colorful. As a game, however, the app leaves much to be desired. The musical content is dry and artificial, and any motivation is largely extrinsic. Appatta's website copy for *Play-A-Day* sums it up well: "Play it every day and show your teacher how fast you are progressing!" In other words, pleasing your teacher is your reason for playing, not the satisfaction of the game itself. Will students who do not already respond to traditional music pedagogy fare any better when the same content comes in the form of an iOS app? So far, there have been no rigorous empirical studies providing a satisfactory answer to this question (Egenfeldt-Nielsen, 2007).

Best Practices

1. **Encourage interaction with generative music systems.**
   a. Burnard (2012) encourages us to take a broad view of musical creativity in digital contexts. Games that are not centered on music can still offer opportunities for engagement and invention. As game soundtracks become more sophisticated and generative, players inadvertently collaborate with the composer and sound designer to produce the actual music coming out of the speakers.
   b. Burnard also praises the level creation system in *LittleBigPlanet*, which allows player/designers to add interactive music elements to their levels in the form of cartoon boomboxes. Electronic music blurs the line between sound design and composition, and interactive audio environments such as *LittleBigPlanet* give future musicians a taste of both practices.

2. **Avoid the blank canvas.**
   a. Ruthmann (2012) observers that traditional music creation software uses the metaphor of a blank canvas or void. It is intimidating for novices to have to fill an empty screen with notes, samples and loops. Music toys such as the networked collaborative performance program *jam2jam* (http://www.savetodisc.net/jam2jam/) start the user off with pre-existing sound and images to be manipulated.
   b. Even when music toys start with a blank canvas, they present a much lower barrier to entry than an empty *Garageband* session or Sibelius score. Apps such as *Bloom* or *Nodebeat* begin to produce musical sound in response to the most tentative or random user actions. With the music underway immediately, the user can then explore the parameters of the system through playful improvisation.

3. **Encourage play with non-game music tools.**
   a. The music toy *Singing Fingers* records and plays back sound through the visual metaphor of finger painting. You sing or make sounds while drawing on the screen, creating colorful lines. Once your drawing is complete, you can play back your sounds by retracing your lines. The sound is arrayed over the length of the line and can be scrubbed forward or backward at any speed. Ruthmann (2012) suggests drawing a staircase while singing a scale, so that each step of the staircase displays as a different color. Then students can recreate a melody by touching steps on the staircase, giving them a visceral connection between the sound and visual representation of pitches.
   b. Tools such as *Garageband* and *Sibelius* can be made more like music toys simply by pre-filling them with musical material. Rather than giving students an empty session or document, you might give them a dense block of existing music and challenge them to create something new through subtraction only.

c. Ruthmann (2012) suggests a playful use of *Google Translate:* making the software beatbox. By setting both the "From" and "To" languages to German, you can enter consonant groupings that the software speaks in a manner similar to beatbox sounds. Many adolescents love beatboxing, but they can be reluctant to do so in front of their peers, especially in a classroom setting. Letting *Google Translate* do the initial performing gives them a safe space to work out ideas, and even create full-fledged rhythm tracks.

4. **Motivate the creation of music games.**

   a. The most ambitious music educators can use the *Scratch* visual programming environment (http://scratch.mit.edu) to enable their students to create new music and multimedia, and even to generate your own music games. The *Scratch* companion site for teachers (http://scratched.media.mit.edu) offers free lesson plans and project ideas, including working code.

Resources

Book

McPherson, G. and Welch, G. (Eds.). *The Oxford Handbook of Music Education*. Oxford: Oxford University Press.

Games and Tools

There is a growing body of full-fledged music games and tools that run entirely within the web browser, with no additional software or hardware needed. Prominent examples include:

Soundation (http://soundation.com/) is not a game, but rather a digital audio workstation similar to *Garageband*. It is particularly useful for Windows-based environments.

jam2jam (http://www.jam2jam.com/) is a collaborative media performance tool that enables music and video remixing in real time over the internet.

PBS maintains a collection of browser games for children of preschool age (http://pbskids.org/games/music.html).

Websites

Dr. Alex Ruthmann's website (http://www.alexruthmann.com/blog1/): Collects a variety of resources, including several mentioned in the previous section.

The Experiencing Audio Research Group at NYU (http://experiencingaudio.org/): Studies and creates technologies and experiences for music making, learning, and engagement. They "collaborate with technology developers, educational agencies, teachers, students and musicians in the creation of solutions to real world music education challenges."

The *Rock Band 3* Pro Mode design process: Game designers may find inspiration here (http://www.rockbandaide.com/wp-content/uploads/2011/03/Jason_Booth_Sylvain_Dubrofsky_Design_Prototype_Through_Production.ppt).

The Everyday Play cluster on The New Everyday blog (http://mediacommons.futureofthebook.org/tne/pieces/everyday-play): Curated by Sam Tobin, this a collection of mostly personal reflections on the role of play in daily life.

Scratch (http://scratch.mit.edu): A programming language for creating interactive music, multimedia and games. The website includes curriculum ideas and code examples.

Scratch lesson plans (http://scratched.media.mit.edu)

http://www.savetodisc.net/jam2jam/

Events

Music education hack days: Gatherings that bring together programmers, educators and musicians to quickly produce and present new projects in a casual environment. Past events have taken place in New York (http://musiceducationhack.splashthat.com/) and London (http://www.meetup.com/The-London-Educational-Games-Meetup-Group/).

References

Booth, J. & Dubrofsky, S. (2011). *Rock Band 3:* Prototype through production [PowerPoint slides]. Retrieved from 2011 Game Developers Conference: http://www.rockbandaide.com/wp-content/uploads/2011/03/Jason_Booth_Sylvain_Dubrofsky_Design_Prototype_Through_Production.ppt

Burnard, P. (2012). *Musical creativities in practice.* Oxford University Press.

Cassidy, G. and Paisley, A. (2013). Music-games: A case study of their impact. *Research Studies in Music Education,* 35: 119.

Custodero, L. (2002). Seeking challenge, finding skill: Flow experience in music education. *Arts Education and Policy Review,* 103(3), p. 3–9.

Csíkszentmihályi, M. (2009). *Flow: The psychology of optimal experience.* New York: Harper Perennial Modern Classics.

Dillon, S. (2007). *Music, meaning and transformation: Meaningful music making for life.* Cambridge Scholars Publishing.

Egenfeldt-Nielsen, S. (2007). Third generation educational use of computer games. *Journal of Educational Multimedia and Hypermedia,* 16(3), p. 263-281.

Finney, J. (2007). Music education as identity project in a world of electronic desires. *Music Education with Digital Technology* (p. 18–73). Continuum International Publishing Group.

Gower, L. & McDowall, J. (2012). Interactive music video games and children's musical development. *British Journal of Music Education,* Volume 29, Issue 1, p. 91-105.

Green, L. (2002). *How popular musicians learn: A way ahead for music education.* Surrey: Ashgate Publishing Group.

Harwood, E. and Marsh, K. (2012). Children's ways of learning inside and outside the classroom. In McPherson, G. and Welch, G. (Eds.). *The Oxford Handbook of Music Education.* Oxford: Oxford University Press.

Hassenzahl, M. (2010). Experience design: Technology for all the right reasons. Synthesis Lectures on Human-Centered Informatics. Morgan Claypool.

Koops, L. & Taggart, C. (2011). Learning through play: Extending an early childhood music education approach to undergraduate and graduate music education. *Journal of Music Teacher Education,* 20: 55.

Lowe, G. (2012). Lessons for teachers: What lower secondary school students tell us about learning a musical instrument. *International Journal of Music Education,* 30: 227.

Miller, K. (2009). Schizophonic performance: *Guitar Hero, Rock Band,* and *Virtual Virtuosity. Journal of the Society for American Music,* 3(4), p. 395–429.

Miller, K. (2012). *Playing Along: Digital games, YouTube, and virtual performance.* Oxford: Oxford University Press.

Mota, G. (2013). Young children's motivation in the context of classroom music: An exploratory study. *Bulletin of the Council for Research in Music Education,* (141).

Peppler, K., Downton, M., Lindsay, E., and Hay, K. (2011). The Nirvana effect: Tapping video games to mediate music learning and interest. *International Journal of Learning and Media,* 3(1), p. 41–59.

Peppler, K. (2013). Opportunities for interest-driven new arts learning in a digital age. Retrieved from the Wallace Foundation: http://www.wallacefoundation.org/knowledge-center/arts-education/key-research/Documents/New-Opportunities-for-Interest-Driven-Arts-Learning-in-a-Digital-Age.pdf

Renwick, J. & Reeve, J. (2012). Supporting motivation in music education. In McPherson, G. and Welch, G. (Eds.). *The Oxford Handbook of Music Education.* Oxford: Oxford University Press.

Richardson, P. & Kim, Y. (2011). Beyond fun and games: A framework for quantifying music skill developments from video game play. *Journal of New Music Research,* Vol. 40, No. 4, p. 277–291.

Rosenstock, J. (2010). Free play meets gameplay: *iGotBand,* a video game for improvisers. *Leonardo Music Journal,* Vol. 20, p. 11–15.

Ruddock, E., & Leong, S. (2005). "I am unmusical!": the verdict of self-judgment. *International Journal of Music Education,* 23(1), p. 9–22.

Ruthmann, A. (2006). Negotiating learning and teaching in a music technology lab: Curricular, pedagogical, and ecological issues. PhD dissertation, Oakland University, Rochester, Michigan. (2012). Engaging adolescents with music and technology. In Burton, S. (Ed.). *Engaging Musical Practices: A Sourcebook for Middle School General Music.* Lanham, MD: R&L Education. (2013). Exploring new media musically and creatively. In Burnard, P. & Murphy, R. (Eds.). *Teaching Music 20 Creatively. Learning to Teach in the Primary School Series.* London: Routledge.

Schultz, P. (2008). Music theory in music games. In Collins, K. (Ed.) *From Pac-Man to Pop Music: Interactive Audio in Games and New Media.* Surrey: Ashgate Publishing Group.

Smith, J. (2004). I can see tomorrow in your dance: A study of *Dance Dance Revolution* and music video games. *Journal of Popular Music Studies,* Volume 16, Issue 1, p. 58–84.

Tobias, E. (2012). Let's play! Learning music through video games and virtual worlds. In McPherson, G. and Welch, G. (Eds.). *The Oxford Handbook of Music Education.* Oxford: Oxford University Press.

Wilkie, K.; Holland, S.; & Mulholland, P. (2010). What can the language of musicians tell us about music interaction design? *Computer Music Journal,* Vol. 34, No. 4, p. 34-48.

CHAPTER 6

Physical Health

Combining Physical Activity with Learning: An Interactive Approach

Robin Mellecker, *The University of Hong Kong, Hong Kong, China, robmel@hku.hk*
Lisa Witherspoon, *University of South Florida, Tampa, Florida, U.S., withersp@usf.edu*
Stephen Yang, *SUNY Oswego, Oswego, New York, U.S., exergamelab@gmail.com*

Key Summary Points

This chapter introduces the potential of pairing physical activity with video game technology that has the potential to foster learning.

The chapter reviews the possible mediating factors that facilitate learning and outcomes through physical interactions with video game technology.

Key Terms

Exergaming
Activegaming
Active Learning
ActivLearning
Exercise
Physical gaming

Introduction

An educational tool that is engaging, enjoyable, improves educational outcomes, and increases physical activity levels would appear to be unlikely. Yet current advances in interactive technologies include three key components—physical activity, video gaming, and educational content—have the potential to be valuable complements to traditional forms of educational instruction (Shayne, Fogel, Miltenberger, & Koehler, 2012). The use of physical activity game-based learning or active learning games, which will be referred to as "Active Learning" throughout the chapter is characterized by the interplay of the three key components and has recently been used as a successful physical activity and e-learning alternative (Fogel, Miltenberger, Graves, & Koehler, 2010; Mellecker, Witherspoon, & Watterson, 2013). Incorporating Active Learning into physical education lessons has shown to improve physical activity levels in inactive children and provides an active alternative that is enjoyable, improves skills that are necessary for physical movement, and increases physical activity levels (Fogel et al., 2010; Maeda & Randall, 2003). Using Active Learning inside the classroom has also resulted in promising learning outcomes, teacher acceptance, and student enjoyment (Mellecker et al., 2013).

Proponents of traditional physical education (PE) programs that focus primarily on sport and exercise regimes may be reluctant to embrace Active Learning into physical education lessons. Removed from many curriculums or cancelled due to increased focus on national and state mandated testing, physical education is slowly being eliminated from the school day (National Association for Sport and Physical Education & American Heart Association, 2012). Inclement weather conditions or lack of space also limit the amount and level of physical activity participation. For students beginning an exercise regime for the first time or for those students ridiculed due to their lack of skill or success in sport and exercise, Active Learning may prove to be an attractive alternate physical activity as most games are easy to play and can be individualized for a participants' skill level. Individualized and graded challenges (competence) and self-selected levels (autonomy) in video games allow the user to participate at a pace that suits one's skill-level and understanding, and this promotes engagement and sustainability in an activity (Sheldon & Filak, 2008). This is particularly relevant in active video gameplay, as it requires players to meet the cognitive demands, as well as the physical effort of each level in the game, but also allows players to determine the speed at which they perform a task or move to the next level. The "play at your own pace" feature in Active Learning could also instill the confidence needed to engage in physical activity. When addressing the lack of interest or unwillingness to participate in physical activity and when considering the positive attributes associated with Active Learning, there is a potential advantage to using Active Learning as a physical activity and learning alternative, which should be studied further.

Case Study One: *Learn-Pads*

Researchers at the Multimedia Communication Research Laboratory University of Ottawa designed *Learn-Pads*, a math Active Learning system. The team has piloted the program to determine whether children enjoyed their experience when playing with the *Learn-Pad* system as well as the social component of playing with others (Karime, Al Osman, Gueaieb, Aljaam, & El Saddik, 2011), both important variables for initiation and long-term adherence to learning programs and physical activity. When using the *Learn-Pads* children are given a mathematical equation, including multiplication, addition or both (e.g., (8+3) x 2). To solve the math problem, children jump and jog over the Learn-Pads within a set time. When the children are moving over the *Learn-Pads*, verbal spelling of the number that has been reached and whether the child is reaching the correct answer accompany the movement pattern. The difficult level in the *Learn-Pads* system is customized to ensure the game is suitable for various cognitive abilities. In the first pilot study, children were asked to assess the difficulty of the math, enjoyment and whether they would recommend the *Learn-Pads* game to their friends. Subjective feedback from the children suggests that the children enjoyed playing the game. In addition, math difficulty level was determined by age and observation of the children indicates that *Learn-Pads* promote social interaction. Although it appears that the main objective of the *Learn-Pads* is to address learning math and social bonding, this first pilot study did not assess step counts or physical activity increases from stepping on the *Learn-Pads*. The authors report that this game will continue to revise the system to include more topics such as shapes, vocabulary, and letters as well as a heart rate monitor and vibrating pads. It also appears that physical activity was simply a condition for the learning to occur and for this reason it would be interesting for future research to address the benefits from the physical activity component used in the *Learn-Pad* system.

Key Frameworks

Active Learning includes physical activity and video game technology, with the added value of knowledge transfer capabilities. This is a novel and innovative approach to learning that has yet to be assigned a specific framework. Recent suggestions to create a framework for active video games that incorporates theories of play and fun include the Design, Play, and Experience (DPE) Framework (Mellecker, Lyons, & Baranowski, 2013). The expanded Design, Play and Experience (DPE) Framework suggest that bodily movements consistent when children are engaged in active video gaming evoke a sense of play. The embedded "play" in video game technology is a key component of the DPE Framework and is influenced by the learning subcomponent. The learning subcomponent in the DPE Framework drives content and pedagogy design, as well as the type of teaching that may lead to self-directed learning. This self-directed approach is also prevalent in play scenarios as children readily engage in free play and learn as a result of independently directed play. Although not specifically designed or expanded to include Active Learning, the DPE Framework includes the constructs of play as well as the subcomponents of physical activity, teaching, and learning, and therefore may help to further advance Active Learning as a tool for use in the classroom.

Key Findings

The educational benefits of combining physical activity with video games appear to be abundant. Both video gaming and physical activity increase blood flow to the brain. This response triggers numerous physiological responses, such as a catecholamine release (Koepp et al., 1998). These responses have been linked to emotions that are important for learning. Enjoyment is an important component for initiating and adhering to educational activities, as well as physical activity.

Evidence indicating positive learning outcomes from playing video games have emerged highlighting increased physical benefits (Barnett, Hinkley, Okely, Hesketh, & Salmon, 2012; Vernadkis, Gioftsidou, Antoniou, Ioannidis, & Giannous, 2012) cognitive outcomes (Chuang & Chen, 2009) and social interactions (Chou & Tsai, 2007). Functional motor skill proficiency, including object control skill, has been achieved with games designed to engage individuals in physically active gameplay (Barnett et al., 2012). Video game technology has also been useful in improving analytical skills and recall processing (Chuang & Chen, 2009). Student reports suggest that gameplay may influence relationships with friends and promote social interaction (Chou & Tsai, 2007).

To educators and parents already focused on student performance, standardized tests, and the recently added Common Core Standards (CSS), incorporating video games and more physical activity into the curriculum may seem time-consuming and counterintuitive. In reality, if physical activity is incorporated into the learning experience using a holistic approach, the potential to accomplish specific learning outcomes could surpass expectations using traditional teaching strategies (Prensky, 2001). Improvements in cognitive development and academic achievement have been reported as a result of regular participation in physical activity (Tomporowsk, Davis, Miller, & Naglieri, 2008). Physically active children have higher executive functioning (e.g., cerebral processing involved in goal directed behavior) and when compared with sedentary peers perform better academically (Best, 2010; Davis et al., 2011). When children are physically active during the school day, on-task behavior improves (Mahar et al., 2006) and emerging evidence indicates that physical activity improves behavior and cognitive performance in children with ADHD (Gapin, Labban, & Etnier, 2011) Moreover, children who engage in regular physical activity are more likely to live healthier lives, avoiding the diseases associated with an inactive lifestyle (LeMasurier & Corbin, 2006). In addition to the known physical health benefits, regular participation in physical activity also results in social competence or a willingness to interact with peers (Centers for Disease Control and Prevention, 2010) as well as positive psychological well-being, such as improved self-esteem (Nieman, 2002). Fusing physical activity into educational content and video gameplay has considerable potential in obtaining learning outcomes. Learning benefits may be possible with even short bursts of activity that are synonymous with child activity patterns (Bailey et al., 1995).

Recently, educators have implemented physically active video gaming or active video gaming in physical education classes, increasing the opportunity for students to engage in physical activity while participating in an enjoyable activity (Maloney, Stempel, Wood, Patraitis, & Beaudoin, 2012).

Although newly introduced, active video gaming has been shown to increase motor skills (Barnett et al., 2012), balance (Sheehan & Katz, 2013), executive function skills (Staiano, Abraham, & Calvert, 2012), and knowledge about healthy nutritional habits (Mellecker et al., 2013). Considerable evidence is mounting on the benefits of using technology in educational settings and video games offer the type of experience that students have come to expect in their classrooms. Combining the two components, physical activity and video gaming (Active Learning) will provide the educational tool educators can use as they look to improve learning environments and connect with the students in their classrooms.

In the classroom?

Children confined to a classroom environment for long periods during the day lose concentration, which is counterproductive to learning and may ultimately result in an ineffective learning environment (Pellgrini & Davis, 1993). The use of alternatives activities to alter undesirable behavior is of increasing interest to policymakers eager to improve school based physical activity and academic performance (Centers for Disease Control and Prevention, 2010). Adjusting to a curriculum that appears to be stretched and ridden with time constraints has left teachers searching for physical activity alternatives to address these constraints (Ward et al., 2006). Improvements in academic performance and behavior are being realized from participation in physical activity, dispelling the belief that physical activity reduces the amount of time for academic related activities and is counterproductive to learning (Bartholomew & Jowers, 2011; Trost & van der Mars, 2010). To address this issue and to promote physical activity participation, physical activity programs have been introduced into the classroom environment to promote learning (Bartholomew & Jowers, 2011; Mahar et al., 2006). Physically active academic lessons incorporated into classroom lessons improve on task-behavior (Mahar et al., 2006) and are showing promising learning outcomes (Bartholomew & Jowers, 2011). Teachers engaging children in physical activity in the classroom environment are able to increase their productivity and subsequently spend more time engaging children in learning activities (Maeda & Randall, 2003).

Changes in learning and behavior typically require children to participate in physical activity for as little as five to ten minutes (Centers for Disease Control and Prevention, 2010). Increased concentration (Caterino & Polak, 1999), as well as improvements in on-task behavior is suggested to occur when using short duration physically active "brain breaks" (short breaks between lessons that include body movements) led by teachers in the classroom (Mahar et al., 2006). The learning effects occur in response to the brain derived neurotropic factor (BDNF), a protein responsible for growth and development of neurons and connections in the brain and has been associated with improvements in learning following short bouts of activity (Winter et al., 2007). This approach to learning has also resulted in increased daily in-school physical activity levels that are synonymous with public health guidelines (Bartholomew & Jowers, 2011; Mahar et al., 2006).

Case Study Two: Active Learning in Schools

George Velarde at Siesta Vista Junior High School in California has created a physical education program by including Active Learning as a valuable aspect in the physical education program. Mr. Velarde's program includes technology for learning such as *HopSports, Nintendo Wii*, virtual bikes, and *Dance Dance Revolution*. The "new" Physical Education (PE) program is based on teaching fitness, health and wellness rather than traditional team sports and skills that has been the focus of traditional physical education. Sierra Vista transformed their PE program into a personalized physical education curriculum that utilizes technology to engage children in physical activity and maintain interest throughout junior high school. Students are engaged in enjoyable and challenging activities that enable them to learn knowledge, attitudes, and behaviors related to functional motor skills, physiological responses to exercise, and even core vocabulary words printed on the backs of the PE uniforms. During PE lessons, use heart rate monitors to track their workout intensity and to learn about the cardiovascular efforts associated with physical activity. The *Polar Cardio GX* heart rate monitoring system allows the students to view their heart rate in real-time on a screen while they are exercising thus providing a valuable feedback and learning tool. Other physiological parameters, such as heart rate, step counts, and calories burned, are also tracked in some of the game based technology systems that are used in the program. Physical education lessons are all encompassing and interdisciplinary. One of the more interesting components of the program includes lessons that incorporate traditional exercise with game based technology. Physical education at Sierra Vista has moved into the classrooms with "brain breaks" during classroom time. Children are encouraged to get out of their seats and exercise during a five-minute break and are often asked to lead the activity breaks. The students are also given the opportunity to use the *Gamebikes* in math classes. Once a month the school opens it doors to the community and invites parents and children to come to the school to experience the joy of using the active game-based technology and learn how exercise impacts learning as well as health and fitness. Mr. Velarde's PE program is well received by the students, parents, and fellow teachers and was recently recognized by Michelle Obama's *Lets Move!* Active Schools program as a model "Active School." This program is a testament to the possibilities afforded by Active Learning alternatives in school PE programs.

Assessment Considerations

Determining the outcomes from Active Learning introduces a degree of complexity. As mentioned throughout the chapter, activity game-based learning is inclusive of three diverse components (physical activity, educational content and video gaming) and therefore is capable of producing numerous outcomes. To add to the complexity, existing literature on assessment of learning outcomes when using activity Active Learning is scant. Furthermore, numerous devices are used to measure physical activity preventing comparisons across video games and studies. The two most popular forms of technology driven physical activity assessment tools, the pedometer and accelerometer have been introduced into mobile devices and more recently been developed with video game technology. Pedometers are used to track number of steps while the accelerometer is used to assess velocity of movement. The pedometer is an inexpensive tool and can be used to assess physical activity patterns of large groups of people whereas the accelerometer is more expensive but has a much higher degree of accuracy than the pedometer. *Zamzee*, a social networking game-based activity monitor has recently introduced an inexpensive triaxial accelerometer that has proven to be useful with young children by providing a reward system for being physical active. Accelerometers are now common in mobile devices and can be used with mobile-based apps to assess physical activity. Both of these devices are also used in research to understand the amount and intensity of physical activity when children play physically active technology driven games.

Future Needs

Technological changes occur at speeds unseen in any other form of learning application. For these reasons, there is an urgent need to learn more about how these systems can be used in the academic classroom and other environments that promote learning. Establishing and implementing best practice evidenced-based models will be crucial if we are to maximize the full potential of Active Learning technology in the academic or the physical education classroom. With this in mind, there is a need to understand long-term sustainability and attempt to understand the correlates that produce interest and engagement to achieve best practice approaches to implementing successful game based e-learning physical activity programs. It would also be interesting to learn how Active Learning approaches differ from traditional forms of teaching and which form of teaching students prefer.

The key to the success of Active Learning is based on the educators and the educational system. Many teachers currently in the classroom are digital immigrants and lack the confidence to embark on a new teaching regime especially when it includes technology-based learning. An understanding of teacher attitudes and experiences when implementing Active Learning into the classroom environment is necessary for successful implementation. In addition, adequate training and continued professional development will be required to encourage and develop physically active educational tools.

Furthermore, continuous assessment is needed to ensure that learning goals are being achieved and physical activity guidelines are being met when children engage in Active Learning. Similar to other forms of assessment, test anxiety will surely be apparent if children are aware of pending assessments. Embedding relevant content and assessing any changes to student attitudes, behaviors, or knowledge using Active Learning is one of the benefits of using technology (Shute, 2011). Little is known about this seemingly valuable attribute or whether embedded assessment can be used with success when implementing Active Learning. Finally, establishing specific guidelines, safety precautions and privacy policies for school-aged students will be necessary prior to implementing these technologies.

Case Study Three: Two Research Laboratories

Two labs are directed by Lisa Witherspoon, an Assistant Professor at the University of South Florida (USF) and focus on Active Learning, which the labs call "ActivLearning." One lab is located in an elementary school and the second lab is located in the Physical Education and Exercise Science building on the USF campus. The university aims to understand the effects of ActivLearning products when children engage in physical education. The "living" laboratory located in the elementary school is used for physical education programs that are implemented into the PE curriculum. Research studies are used to determine the efficacy and to provide an evidence base for physical education. Specific emphasis is placed on learning objectives that are based on evidenced based research and best practices approaches to learning. Whereas the research laboratory located in the USF Campus focuses specifically on research. Learning more about how different populations appreciate the games as well as learn through the games is the main focus. The labs house fully functioning active gaming rooms equipped with numerous ActivLearning products. The labs focus on understanding the effects of active gaming on various populations (specifically children) including behavior, academic performance, product preference assessment, skill development, physiological performance and physical education outcomes. A recent program introduced by the USF active gaming research labs discovered that ActivLearning activities provide children with a cognitive benefit related to nutrition and science academic content. The students involved in these pilot studies were asked to play online video games involving nutrition and science principles whilst stepping on Footgaming pads and the *Gamercize* stepper, respectively. Students in these pilot studies achieved academic success, elevated heart rates and reported high levels of enjoyment. ActivLearning research is ongoing at USF as the topic is insufficiently researched and may provide educators important information on effective and efficient methods for teaching and implementing ActivLearning programs. Currently, USF is investigating the use of "brain breaks" throughout the school day to understand the consistency of physical activity breaks and effects of "brain breaks" on behavior and learning. Additionally, researchers are exploring the use of a multiplayer system by Konami, *DanceDanceRevolution-Classroom Edition (DDR-CE)*, to learn about the physiological and cognitive effects of the product on middle school students.

Best Practices

Some key factors are emphasized to realize the full learning potential of Active Learning in the classroom:

1. To ensure that skill levels are appropriately set and to avoid frustration for the children the Active Learning games should be age and topic appropriate. Allowing or including students to choose games and or levels can empower them, give them greater feelings of autonomy, increased enjoyment and perhaps motivate them to continue playing.

2. The learning outcomes and physical activity objectives should be combined into the playing of the games. By blending the physical activity and learning content into a game the teacher has an opportunity to assess students with less test anxiety.

3. The games should be set at a level that provides physical and cognitive challenges but does not overwhelm the student. Teachers and or the games/technology should provide meaningful and appropriate constructive feedback to their students to further enhance feelings of competence and self-efficacy. Teachers should also be able to adapt or change games according to student skill levels. This scaffolding approach may lead to a more appropriate (and less frustrating) experience.

4. The intensity level of the activity should be kept within a range that corresponds to physical activity guidelines or health outcomes. Current physical activity recommendations suggest that children should be participating in 60 minutes of physical activity that makes them sweat and breath hard referred to as moderate to vigorous intensity physical activity. Students performing activities below these thresholds may still improve skills, increase their confidence and receive health benefits; and should be encouraged to continue participating at their skill and fitness level.

5. Learning and health benefits may occur within a short duration of activity and this type of activity is consistent with activity patterns during childhood. Implementing Active Learning in the classroom in short intermittent bouts offers children an activity they enjoy and provides the teacher with a transition activity that has proven to be beneficial for students.

6. Teachers should be well acquainted with the Active Learning games and should be trained to use the system prior to implementing programs into the classroom or learning environments. Many schools also have student leaders within each class that are able to assist teachers (especially substitute teachers) in using the equipment and teaching others (including parents during an open house or parent/teacher conference). These opportunities should be seized upon as these helping hands can be well-versed in technology and a valuable resource for students and teachers.

Educators are instrumental in facilitating and implementing activity game-based learning into the educational environment. Determining the most suitable system, platform, and game requires the educator to consider the user, the physical activity, and learning outcomes. Currently, there are a number of popular commercially available active game-based learning systems that can be used to promote physical activity and learning (e.g., functional motor skills), including *Dance Dance Revolution (DDR), Microsoft Kinect, Nintendo Wii,* and *XaviX* (see Table 1 for more details). Similar to other teaching applications, it is essential for the teacher to not just provide the game, but to pair the lesson plan with the technology and desired learning outcomes. To assist teachers and to provide possible Active Learning alternatives specific game platforms and software, targeted learning outcomes, and the body movements required to play each of the games are highlighted in Table 1.

Resources

Table 1.

Comparisons of Active Learning systems and games, targeted learning outcomes, and body movement required for gameplay

Categories	Games	Targeted learning outcomes	Physical activity
Rhythmic Dance			
DDR Classroom Edition iDance Nintendo Wii XBOX Kinect	Pump it Up, iDance, Just Dance Kids, Dance Central	**Math:** pattern recognition **P**hysical: motor skills, rhythm, timing, syncopation	Stepping, jumping, dancing, twisting
Sensor-Based			
Microsoft Kinect Nyoyn Wild Planet XaviX Vtech Vmotion Zippity Swinxs	Animal Scramble, Brain and Body, Sesame Street: Once Upon a Monster, Nebula/ Strip, Soundsteps, Animal Scramble, Hyper Jump, Ask, Listen, Learn: Kids and Alcohol Don't Mix™, Jackie Chan Challenge	**Math skills:** logic, executive control, numbers & counting, spatial awareness, sequencing, pattern and object recognition **Physical:** eye-hand coordination, agility, balance **Science:** Science: species recognition, ecosystem, food chain energy cycle, mapping skills, animal behavior **Social responsibility:** caring for the environment, recycling, caring for others **Spelling** **Other:** recognizing musical notes and color, sound and visual recognition, health nutrition behaviors	Stepping, jumping, kicking, waving, rolling, running, sliding, touching, sweeping, standing up, hand and arm gesturing
Virtual Bikes			
BrainBike Fisher-Price Smart Cycle Racer Expresso HD Youth Exercise Bike	Neuroactive, Math Mountain, Shape Lake, Number Fields, Letter Creek	**Math:** logic, pattern recognition, visual acuity, alphabet, shapes **Physical:** eye-hand coordination, motor skills,	Bicycling: steering, pedaling

Books and Articles

Bartholomew, J.B., & Jowers, E.M. (2011). Physically active academic lessons in elementary children. *Preventive Medicine, 52*, S51-S54.

Bogost, I. (2011). *How to Do Things with Videogames.* Minneapolis: University of Minnesota Press.

Papastergiou, M., (2009). Exploring the potential of computer and video games for health and physical education: A literature review. *Computers and Education, 53*, 603-622.

Ratey, J. (2008). *Spark: The Revolutionary New Science of Exercise and the Brain.* New York, Hachette Book Group USA.

Staiano, A.E., & Calvert, S.L. (2011). Exergames for physical education courses: Physical, social, and cognitive benefits. Child Development Perspectives, 5(2), 93–98.

Zemliansky, W. (2010). *Design and Implementation of Educational Video Games.* IGI Global. Hershey, PA.

Websites

Action Based learning (http://abllab.com/)

ActiveLearning Blog (http://activlearninggames.blogspot.com/)

Machine Dance Report (iDANCE in Norway) (http://www.positivegaming.com/benefits/machine-dance-research-projects/stokke-machine-dance-project-report)

Microsoft Kinect School Activity Plans
(http://www.microsoft.com/education/en-us/products/Pages/kinect.aspx#3)

Exergames Unlocked (http://exergamesunlocked.org/)

PE Central (http://www.pecentral.org)

Researchers

Tom Baranowski, Ph.D. (http://www.bcm.edu/cnrc/faculty/baranowskit.htm)

Barbara Chamberlain, Ph.D. (http://aces.nmsu.edu/mediaproductions/)

Ann Maloney, M.D. (http://www.umassmed.edu/Content.aspx?id=92224)

Floyd Mueller, Ph.D. (http://exertiongameslab.org/)

Adam Noah. Ph.D (http://mediaartsliu.com/faculty_top.html)

Amanda Staiano, Ph.D. (http://www.pbrc.edu/research-and-faculty/postdocs/)

Josh Trout, Ph.D. (http://www.csuchico.edu/kine/faculty_staff/index.shtml)

Lisa Witherspoon, Ph.D (http://www.coedu.usf.edu/main/index.html)

Stephen Yang, Ph.D (http://www.linkedin.com/in/stephenpyang)

Stephan Göbel, Ph.D (Stefan.Goebel@hom.tu.darmstadt.de)

Labs and Projects

Canadian Exergaming Research Center (www.ucalgary.ca/exergaming)

Exercise4Learning (http://www.exercise4learning.com/)

Exergame Lab (www.exergamelab.org)

Gateway Unified School District (Matt Diskin) (http://www.californiaprojectlean.org/doc.asp?id=249)

Learning Readiness PE, Naperville, IL (http://learningreadinesspe.com/)

Sierra Vista Jr. High PE (George Velarde) (http://www.hartdistrict.org/sierra/pe/)

Active Gaming Research Laboratory University of South Florida
(http://www.coedu.usf.edu/main/departments/physed/labs/xrkLab.html)

References

Bailey, R. C., Olson, J., Pepper, S. L., Porszasz, J., Barstow, T. J., & Cooper, D. M. (1995). The level and tempo of children's physical activities: an observational study. *Medicine and Science in Sports and Exercise, 27*(7), 1033-1041.

Barnett, L. M., Hinkley, T., Okely, A. D., Hesketh, K., & Salmon, J. (2012). Use of electronic games by young children and fundamental movement skills? *Perceptual and Motor Skills, 114*(3), 1023-1034.

Bartholomew, J. B., & Jowers, E. M. (2011). Physically active academic lessons in elementary children. *Preventive Medicine, 52,* S51-S54.

Best, J. R. (2010). Effects of physical activity on children's executive function: Contributions of experimental research on aerobic exercise. *Developmental Review, 30,* 331-351.

Caterino, M. C., & Polak, E. D. (1999). Effects of two types of activity on the performance of second-, third-, and fourth-grade students on a test of concentration. *Perceptual Motor Skills, 89*(1), 245-248.

Centers for Disease Control and Prevention. (2010). *The association between school-based physical activity, including physical education and academic performance.* Atlanta, GA.

Chou, C., & Tsai, M. J. (2007). Gender differences in Taiwan high school students' computer game playing. *Computers in Human Behavior, 23,* 812-824.

Chuang, T. Y., & Chen, W. F. (2009). Effect of computer-based video games on children: An experimental study. *Educational Technology & Society, 12*(2), 1-10.

Davis, C. L., Tomporowski, P. D., McDowell, J. E., Austin, B. P., Miller, P. H., Yanasak, N. E., .Naglieri, J. A. (2011). Exercise improves executive function and achievement and alters brain activation in overweight children: A randomized controlled trial. *Health Psychology, 30*(1), 91-98.

Fogel, V. A., Miltenberger, R. G., Graves, R., & Koehler, S. (2010). The effects of exergaming on physical activity among inactive children in a physical education classroom. *Journal of Applied Behavior Analysis, 43,* 591-600.

Gapin, J. I., Labban, J. D., & Etnier, J. L. (2011). The effects of physical activity on attention deficit hyperactivity disorder symptoms: the evidence. *Preventive Medicine, 52 Suppl 1,* S70-74. doi: 10.1016/j.ypmed.2011.01.022.

Koepp, M. J., Gunn, R. N., Lawrence, A. D., Cunningham, V. J., Dagher, A., Jones, T., Grasby, P. M. (1998). Evidence for striatal dopamine release during a video game. *Nature, 393*(6682), 266-268.

LeMasurier, G., & Corbin, C. B. (2006). Top 10 reasons for quality physical education. *Journal of Physical Education Recreation and Dance, 77*(6), 44-53.

Maeda, J. K., & Randall, L. M. (2003). Can academic success come from five minutes of physical activity. *Brock Education, 13*(1), 14-22.

Mahar, M. T., Murphy, S. K., Rowe, D. A., Golden, J., Shields, A. T., & Raedeke, T. (2006). Effects of a classroom-based program on physical activity and on-task behavior. *Medicine and Science in Sports and Exercise, 38*(12), 2086-2094.

Maloney, A. E., Stempel, A., Wood, M. E., Patraitis, C., & Beaudoin, C. (2012). Can dance exergames boost physical activity as a school-based intervention? *Games Health Journal, 1*(6), 416–421.

Mellecker, R. R., Witherspoon, L., & Watterson, T. (2013). Active learning: Educational experiences enhanced through technology-driven active game play. *The Journal of Educational Research.* doi: 10.1080/00220671.2012.736429.

Mellecker, R.R., Lyons, E.J., & Baranowski, T. (2013). Disentangling fun and enjoyment in exergames using an expanded design, play, expereince framework: A narrative review. *Games for Health Journal: Research, Development and Clincal Applications.* 2(4):183-190.

National Association for Sport and Physical Education, & American Heart Association. (2012). 2012 Shape of the Nation Report: Status of Physical Education in the USA. Reston, VA: American Alliance for Health, Physical Education, Recreation and Dance. Retrieved from http://www.heart.org/idc/groups/heart-public/@wcm/@adv/documents/downloadable/ucm_308261.pdf.

Nieman, P. (2002). Psychosocial aspects of physical activity. *Paediatr Child Health, 7*(5), 309-312.

Pellgrini, A. D., & Davis, P. D. (1993). Relations between children's playground and classroom behavior. *British Journal of Educational Psychology, 63,* 88-95.

Prensky, M. (2001). *Digital game-based learning.* New York, NY: McGraw Hill.

Shayne, R. K., Fogel, V. A., Miltenberger, R. G., & Koehler, S. (2012). The effects of exergaming on physical activity in a third-grade physical education class. *Journal of Applied Behavioral Analysis, 45*(1), 211-215.

Sheehan, D. P., & Katz, L. (2013). The effects of a daily, 6-week exergaming curriculum on balance in fourth grade children. *Journal of Sport and Health Science, 2*(3), 131-137.

Sheldon, K. M., & Filak, V. (2008). Manipulating autonomy, competence, and relatedness support in a game-learning context: New evidence that all three needs matter. *British Journal of Social Psychology, 47*, 267-283.

Shute, V. J. (2011). Stealth assessment in computer-based games to support learning. In S. Tobias & J. D. Fletcher (Eds.), *Computer Games and Instruction* (pp. 503-523). Charlotte, NC: Information Age Publishing.

Staiano, A. E., Abraham, A. A., & Calvert, S. L. (2012). Competitive versus cooperative exergame play for African American adolescents' executive function skills: short-term effects in a long-term training intervention. *Dev Psychol, 48*(2), 337-342.

Tomporowsk, P. D., Davis, C. L., Miller, P. H., & Naglieri, J. A. (2008). Exercise and children's intelligence, cognition and academic achievement. *Educational Psychology Review, 20*(2), 111-131.

Trost, S. G., & van der Mars, H. (2010). Why we should not cut P.E. Health and Learning, 67(4), 60-65.

Vernadkis, N., Gioftsidou, A., Antoniou, P., Ioannidis, D., & Giannous, i. M. (2012). The impact of Nintendo Wii to physical education students' balance compared to the traditional approaches. *Computers and Education, 59*, 196-205.

Ward, D. S., Saunders, R., Felton, G. M., Williams, E., Eppings, J. N., & Pate, R. R. (2006). Implementation of a school environmental intervention to increase physical activity in high school girls. *Health Education Research, 21*, 896–910.

Winter, B., Breitenstein, C., Mooren, F. C., Voelker, K., Fobker, M., Lechtermann, A., . . . Knecht, S. (2007). High impact running improves learning. *Neurobiol Learn Mem, 87*(4), 597-609.

CHAPTER 7

Emotional Health

Designing Games for Emotional Health

Ralph Vacca, *New York University, New York, New York, U.S., ralph.vacca@nyu.edu*
Meagan Bromley, *New York University, New York, New York, U.S., meagan.bromley@nyu.edu*
Jakob Leyrer, *University of Vienna, Vienna, Austria, jakob.leyrer@univie.ac.at*
Manuel Sprung, *University of Vienna, Vienna, Austria, manuel.sprung@univie.ac.at*
Bruce Homer, *City University of New York, New York, New York, U.S., bhomer@gc.cuny.edu*

Key Summary Points

1. There is a growing understanding of key skills that can help individuals better manage emotions to improve well-being, such as emotional understanding, executive functioning, and emotion regulation skills.

2. In promoting emotional health, games can operate at the low-order brain training level (e.g., drill-and-skill), as well as the higher order meaning-making level.

3. Emotional health is broad, and efficacious approaches to skills development in emotional health are highly contextual, taking into account expected outcomes, environmental context, and individual psychometric conditions.

Key Terms

Emotions
Emotional health
Emotional regulation
Emotional intelligence
Emotional understanding
Self-regulation
Executive functioning
Mental health

Introduction

It is not often we think about emotional health. Physical health, yes. We have heard of mental health. But what do we mean by emotional health? Furthermore, what are we referring to when we talk about games for emotional health?

In this chapter we ask: can games help us develop specific skills that can in turn improve our emotional health? If so, what are the best practices for designing and using games to develop such skills?

Defining emotional health

First off, we should define what we mean by emotional health. In short, it means different things to different people, but for the purposes of this chapter, we are defining emotional health as how we manage our emotional responses in interacting with the world around us that partly contributes to our overall well-being.

While some use the term mental health interchangeably with emotional health, there is a key distinction worth making. Mental health refers to a general state of well-being that allows us to cope with the normal stresses of life and make a contribution to one's community (WHO, 2004). Emotional health refers specifically to the positive and negative affect resulting from life events that contributes to our overall mental and physical health (Hendrie et al., 2006).

One can conceptualize emotional health along a continuum of poor to excellent, much like our physical health. A common misconception is that "good" emotional health would resemble an individual that is always happy or stress-free. This is not the case, however. Research in positive psychology, among other research, has attempted to look at emotional health as falling within a particular positivity ratio which examines the ratio of "positive" and "negative" emotions that make up one's affectivity (Watson, Clark, & Carey, 1988). In other words, good emotional health merely suggests that an individual has the ability to manage their emotional responses in ways that contribute positively to their overall sense of well-being, rather than an absence of "negative" emotions. For instance, they may have the capacity to assume different perspectives, or relax their bodies to better manage stress responses, or simply bounce back faster from highly stressful experiences. On the other hand, at the heart of poor emotional health is severe difficulty in responding to environmental demands in ways that do not hamper one's physical and mental health. Often such challenges coincide with emotion disorders or traumatic experiences that have shaped the way we emotionally respond to stimuli such as stressful situations or relationship demands.

Games and emotional health

When thinking about how to design games to promote emotional health, a common question often emerges. What skills are we really teaching and can they actually be learned? In other words, what are we really teaching when we teach individuals to more effectively manage their emotions, and can games help teach these skills?

First off, it is important to note that there exists a well-established and rather large field of psychotherapeutic interventions dedicated to improving mental and emotional health, which primarily rely on in-person interactions. For instance there is Cognitive Behavioral Therapy (CBT), Emotional Processing Therapy, Rational Emotive Behavior Therapy (REBT), Dialectical Behavior Therapy (DBT), and dozens of others, all varying on how the interaction between therapist and client occurs. Many of these interventions have been fairly successful in addressing some of more prominent emotional health challenges such as managing depression and coping with anxiety (Aldao, Nolen-Hoeksema, & Schweizer, 2010; Ellard, Fairholme, Boisseau, Farchione, & Barlow, 2010; Fava & Tomba, 2009).

One core challenge with such interventions is access. According to the World Mental Health Surveys of the World Health Organization (WHO), one in three people in the U.S. suffer from a mental disorder in their lifetime (Kessler et al., 2009), but only a portion of those people receive treatment, ranging from 26% to 60% for mild and severe mental disorders respectively. Many of these disorders have a significant emotional health component (Aldao et al., 2010). Taking into consideration large diversity in the population and treatment quality, one other major challenge is attrition and low adherence (Thompson & McCabe, 2012), meaning individuals may not stick to treatment protocols and recommendations.

Some are seeing games as one tool that can, and already has, made headway in addressing these challenges, among others. Games can increase accessibility to populations that may not be able to gain access to traditional interventions, and they often provide high levels of repeated engagement with exercises that can improve or match traditional intervention outcomes (e.g., Tate, Haritatos, & Cole, 2009). Furthermore, games provide a new avenue for emotional health, allowing individuals that may not be diagnosed with disorders access to tools that may empower them to improve their emotional health or overcome emotional health challenges.

Why should we care about emotional health?

According to the WHO (2004), at any point in time, there are an estimated 450 million people in the world who are afflicted by some sort of mental, neurological, or behavioral problem. Furthermore, there are increasing numbers of individuals that are undiagnosed or have emotional health challenges that are not disorders, yet still compromise their overall well-being.

About this Chapter

The increasing popularity and role of mobile technology and games in daily life continues to present new opportunities in the emotional health space. There are two key questions framing this chapter. First, can games help us develop specific skills that can in turn improve our emotional health? Second, are there best practices for designing and using games to develop such skills?

Case Study One: *EmoJump*, A Game Targeting Emotional Understanding Skills

EmoJump is a computer game being developed by the games4resilience lab at the University of Vienna to enhance children's understanding of external causes of emotions, belief-based emotions, and mixed emotions. It is designed as a "forced-speed" jump and run game. In every level the player is shown several cartoons, where he or she has to decipher the emotional state of a specific character using only story-based visuals or lines of dialogue in the scene. Faces communicate emotions very effectively and the training focuses on emotion understanding beyond facial recognition, so the faces of game characters are not shown. Thus, the player has to understand the situation the cartoon depicts and hold in his or her mind which emotion one would feel in that particular situation.

After watching the cartoon, the player enters the "forced speed" jump and run sequence where he or she encounters "coins" with faces expressing one of four basic emotions (happy, sad, fear, anger) and is tasked with collecting the appropriate coins that correspond to the situation depicted in the cartoon. This sequence continues through several rounds of cartoons, providing the player with level feedback and trophies that can be earned for high scores.

In line with Pons and Harris' (2000) Test of Emotional Comprehension, the game's level design is aligned with levels of emotion, ranging from a surface level understanding of emotions to higher-order thinking used to regulate emotional responses. Using story-based challenges as described above, early levels focus on understanding external causes of emotions and identifying internal processes (e.g., interpretations) that form belief-based emotions. The challenge of collecting the correct coin to correspond with an emotion is situated through the point of view of the main character, causing players to not only analyze a situation, but also to engage in a task requiring perspective-taking, a component of theory of mind. Later levels deal with mixed emotions and different possible interpretations of a situation or associated thoughts. As a result, the task of collecting coins to correspond to the appropriate emotion requires holding multiple, often conflicting, emotions in mind and collecting more than one target item while completing the "forced speed" run sequence.

Given that the ability to comprehend emotional states and their contexts is crucial for successful engagement in highly social environments, the game targets these skills. As emotional understanding is also a prerequisite to successfully engage in emotion regulation (Jacob et al., 2011) the designers wanted to target deficits in emotion understanding first before teaching emotion regulation strategies.

Key Frameworks

Before designing any game that seeks to improve individual emotional health it is important to understand two things. First, scientific research in the area of human emotion continues to grow each year, bringing with it new insights into how we generate and manage our emotions. This means it is extra important to be up to date on the latest research around the specific approach you may be integrating into your designs. Second, there are many existing perspectives on how to improve emotional health, which means one major task (even more than usual) for designers is to understand how the learning context, expected outcomes, and learner profiles may lend itself to a specific approach. In this section, we will briefly describe a few key approaches taken to improving emotional health that may serve as the focal point of a game-based intervention.

Emotional understanding

A precursor to any discussion on managing emotions often assumes individuals possess some degree of emotional understanding. For example, our ability to label emotions using specific language (e.g., anger), identify related facial expressions (e.g., smiling), and understand how belief systems influence our emotions, are all examples of skills underlying emotional understanding (Garner, 1999). Sometimes referred to as emotional knowledge, or as a subset of emotional intelligence (Nelis, Quoidbach, Mikolajczak, & Hansenne, 2009), emotional understanding is all about making sense of information to better understand our own and others' emotional states. Deficits in emotional understanding can be found in a range of psychopathologies and problem behaviors (Southam-Gerow, 2002), and knowledge of facial expressions and labels is a major predictor of academic achievement (Izard et al., 2001). Interventions focusing on emotional understanding often target children, but have also included adolescent and adult populations.

Inherent aspects of many games such as multiple sensory representations (i.e., visual, auditory) and narratives that provide a context for decision-making, have been used to tackle emotional-understanding skills. See Case Study One for an in-depth example that is situated in this emotional understanding focus.

Executive functioning

The term executive functioning (EF) is broad and can be an amorphous concept to get across, if you are not well versed in psychological theories of cognitive systems. In short, the idea is that there exists a set of cognitive processes (i.e., brain functioning) that controls our ability to deal with novel situations— situations where we do not just automatically respond without thought. In dealing with these novel situations, EF helps us inhibit our responses, or resolve conflicting thoughts on how best to respond (e.g., going on a first date). As you can imagine, these cognitive processes include quite a few things such as directing our attention, self-monitoring, planning, organizing, remembering and inhibiting impulsivity (Tang, Yang, Leve, & Harold, 2012).

So what does this have to do with emotional health? Simply put, EF is essential to our ability to resolve conflict between competing emotions or tendencies in how we respond to something (Botvinick, Braver, Barch, Carter, & Cohen, 2001; Rothbart, 2011). Research has shown that deficits in components of EF are strongly associated with various negative outcomes across one's lifespan, such as behavior problems, aggression, antisocial behavior, inattention, attention deficit hyperactivity disorder (ADHD), problems with peers, school failure, depression, and substance abuse during childhood and adolescence (Eigsti et al., 2006; Floyd & Kirby, 2001; Ivanov, Schulz, London, & Newcorn, 2008; Perner, Kain, & Barchfeld, 2002; Riggs, Blair, & Greenberg, 2004). On the flipside, higher levels of EF are associated with better perspective-taking skills, self esteem, relationship success, as well as positive social, emotional, behavioral, economic, and physical health outcomes (Blair & Peters, 2003; Carlson & Moses, 2001; Moffitt et al., 2011).

Games present interesting opportunities in EF training, in that repetition and escalating difficulty often serve as key design patterns found in training interventions targeting EF skills. In other words, cognitive processes are modified through repeated exercise before moving on to more challenging exercises that push related cognitive processes (e.g., memorization, paying attention to changing instructions). See Case Study Three for an example that illustrates a game-based approach to executive functioning training for emotional health.

Emotion regulation

So far we have covered emotional understanding and executive functioning, as they relate to emotional health, yet perhaps the most direct approach found in emotional health interventions is to focus on emotion regulation—the use of specific strategies to manage one's own emotional response to varying situations. One useful model to conceptualize emotion regulation is the Emotion Regulation Process Model (Gross & Barrett, 2011), illustrated in Figure 1, which outlines five strategies we can use to influence our eventual emotional response.

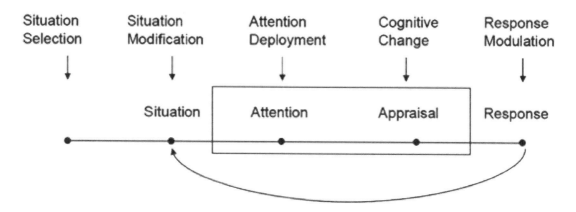

Figure 1. Emotion Regulation Model. Adapted from Gross & Barrett (2011).

The ability to effectively use such strategies is commonly referred to as emotion regulation skills, because these skills regulate the nature, frequency, and duration of one's own emotions (Gross & Muñoz, 1995). Two emotion regulation strategies commonly focused on are attentional deployment and cognitive change—more commonly referred to as cognitive appraisal. Attentional deployment skills refer to our ability to direct our attention to specific aspects of a situation to modulate our emotional response. Cognitive appraisal skills refers to our ability to re-interpret stimuli in different ways to in turn manage our emotional response.

Games for emotion regulation training can provide valuable decision-making and feedback experiences situated in contexts that largely influence the relevance of specific strategies. In other words, games allow players to experience the results of using specific strategies within specific contexts in ways in-person role-playing exercises may be unable to do. Furthermore, games provide interesting opportunities for using in-game data collected to aid in post-game reflection as well as monitoring changes in players.

Additional perspectives

There are several other approaches that may be relevant for game designers. Designers interested in working in conjunction with in-person therapy or leveraging specific therapeutic exercises may want to explore therapeutic frameworks that attempt to work across different diagnosed disorders. For instance, the Unified Protocol (UP) seeks to work across diagnosed disorders seeking to provide a more holistic approach that entails: 1) increasing emotional awareness, 2) supporting flexibility in appraisals, 3) identifying and preventing emotional avoidance, and 4) situational exposure to emotion cues (Ellard et al., 2010).

Lastly, but certainly not least, is a social approach where human-to-human interaction is the key focus. Research has shown that social interactions are closely linked to emotional health (Umberson & Montez, 2010) and there may be opportunities for designing social games situated in this focus.

Each of these approaches has a hefty body of literature that is worth diving into for more details. In the next section, we will consider what the psychological, game studies, and design research say about creating games to support the development of different skills linked to emotional health. In short, if enhancing emotional health is the goal, then how can we better design games or use them within interventions?

Case Study Two: *Leela*, A Commercial Game Targeting Mindfulness

In terms of emotion regulation training, mindfulness is one approach that has become increasingly popular. Typically when one hears mindfulness they imagine an individual in meditation or chanting. From an emotion regulation perspective, mindfulness is commonly defined as the process of directing attention on the present in a non-judgmental way (Kabat-Zinn, 2003) and incorporates emotion regulation strategies such as attentional deployment and cognitive reappraisal. In fact, emerging research in neuropsychology has shown that mindfulness can have profound emotional health benefits in managing anxiety, depression, pain, and psycho-regulatory activity (Chiesa, Calati, & Serretti, 2011). While traditionally mindfulness has been taught through in-person or audio-guided meditation, emerging technology incorporating physical interaction has expanded our possible approaches to developing such emotion regulation skills.

Deepak Chopra's *Leela* (N-Fusion Interactive, 2011) is a game for the Microsoft Xbox 360/Kinect that combines traditional relaxation with meditation techniques to cultivate mindfulness. The unique aspect of the game is the use of the Kinect platform, which allows players to use their body and movements to interact with the game in ways standard game controllers cannot enable. For instance, the "chakra" mini-games that are at the heart of the game make use of embodied game interactions such as twisting one's body, swinging one's arms, and controlling one's rate of breathing. Each of these mechanics is tied to traditional game mechanics such as win/lose states, escalating challenges, mastery sequences, and various feedback mechanisms.

The embodied approach—where you use your body—taken by *Leela* addresses one core limitation of many games designed to provide aspects of emotion regulation training, which is to involve the body in addition to our cognitive processes (Vacca, 2013). Research suggests that regulatory effort involving body-mind states and not just a cognitive focus can promote long-term engagement in that over time physiological involvement can relieve stress associated with engaging in self-control (Tang & Posner, 2009). Some key challenges in *Leela* and other game-based approaches that rely on promoting a "relaxed state" is balancing this goal with the tension that often comes with competitive win/loss mechanics incorporated into games (Sweetser & Wyeth, 2005). In addition, embodied learning experiences that require focusing on internal activity (e.g., shifting focus away from a wandering mind) often instead have to focus on external activity (e.g., breathing and gestures) (Mizen, 2009) to take advantage of commercial sensor technology, although that may quickly change in the coming years.

Key Findings

In the past few years, a number of research studies have suggested compelling directions for teaching skills related to emotional health through games, from a variety of different fields and with varying approaches.

Executive functioning

There have been several interesting findings on the use of games to improve executive functioning (EF) skills. As mentioned earlier, EF skills such as planning, inhibiting behavior, and remembering can also influence our ability to manage emotional responses.

In designing interventions targeting EF skills, repetition and escalating levels of challenges have been found to be effective (Diamond & Lee, 2011). For instance, the game-based intervention *Play Attention*, which targets learners with ADHD to train attention skills and improve memory, makes extensive use of repetition and varying difficulty levels, and has been found to improve performance on tasks requiring attentional control (Unique Logic and Technology, 2011). While the game does not directly target emotional health outcomes, the EF skills that are targeted, such as inhibiting impulsivity and shifting attention, could have implications for emotional health training. Other examples include the *Cogmed* program, which has been used with individuals who have ADHD and Autism as a means of improving working memory and by extension, attentional control (Klingberg et. al., 2005). For the most part, interventions focusing on executive functioning have largely targeted children, where research has shown that wider effects can be achieved (Wass, Scerif, & Johnson, 2012).

Lastly, interventions focusing on executive functions have been found to be more effective when the focus is broader so as to include emotional and social development (Diamond & Lee, 2011), in addition to physical engagement requiring body movement and awareness (Tang & Posner, 2009). In other words, games that make use of emerging physical gaming platforms such as the Nintendo Wii and Microsoft Kinect, may also be able to augment existing EF training approaches through physical engagement.

Emotion regulation

Interventions targeting emotion regulation skills—the use of emotion regulation strategies to better manage emotional responses—have been found to be more effective when designed with certain criteria in mind.

One such criterion has to do with the kind of strategies targeted. As you can recall from our earlier discussion on emotion regulation, particular strategies for response come earlier in the emotion regulation model. Research has shown that such strategies—often referred to as antecedent strategies—are generally more effective in managing emotional responses than inhibiting an emotional response generated (Goldin, McRae, Ramel, & Gross, 2008). For example, researchers from the University of Auckland designed a game called *SPARX* to help young people learn such antecedent strategies to deal with feeling down, depressed, or stressed using methods from Cognitive Behavioral Therapy (CBT).

Results from research by Merry et al. (2012) indicate that the game was as effective as standard care for adolescents and significantly reduced depression, anxiety, feelings of hopelessness, and improved quality of life. This game provides the player a first-person experience where he or she engages in mini-games that present challenges and prompt the player to make decisions and then receive feedback.

Another criterion is situational context in which strategies are learned. Research has shown that emotion regulation strategies are context dependent and training interventions should reflect the importance of such situational context. For instance, researchers have found differences in the effectiveness of different strategies based on the strength (i.e., magnitude) of the affect (e.g., anger) (McRae, Misra, Prasad, Pereira, & Gross, 2012). Games such as *Bravemind* from USC's Institute for Creative Technologies situates the use of strategies such as inhibition within situational reenactments so as to significantly improve the emotional health of individuals with post-traumatic stress disorder (PTSD) (USC ICT, 2013).

Lastly, there is increasing interest in expanding emotion regulation training to include physiological awareness. For example, researchers in Spain designed a video game to increase emotional and impulsivity self-control for individuals struggling with Bulimia Nervosa, which incorporates a motion-tracking suit equipped with various sensors. Results show that players saw improved abilities (Fagundo et al., 2013).

There are additional findings emerging from a variety of fields that overlap with findings in interventions to improve emotional health. Such findings include research in spacing or optimal repetition patterns, embodied cognition (how our body helps us think), and ambient computing (how our environment influences our thoughts and behavior).

Assessment Considerations

In understanding whether games can truly change skills associated with emotional health, it seems logical that we understand how emotions constantly change over time. How we can actually measure emotions, however, is an evolving and highly contextual endeavor. Emotional reactivity can be measured biologically, using *fMRI* to capture brain activity through changes in blood flow, heart rate and nerve activity via vagal tone monitoring, and facial muscle electrical activity through EMG (electromyography) measurements, to name a few. These measures can be combined and interpreted in different ways based on what you are interested in understanding and the context of the research (Cole, Martin & Dennis 2004).

In the clinical space, the Test of Emotion Comprehension has been developed by Pons & Harris (2000) as a useful tool for measuring children's understanding of emotion. The test is particularly useful for revealing hidden emotions that may be difficult for children to articulate depending on their self-awareness and level of development. The test consists of nine levels of emotion, spanning surface level understanding and emotion identification, to higher order emotional functioning. The children must determine whether emotions are real using false belief tasks that test a child's understanding of another person's emotions by attributing behaviors in given scenarios to how a character is feeling (Pons & Harris, 2000). This test can serve as a blueprint for mapping different levels of emotional comprehension onto game mechanics and levels, as will be discussed in the later case study of *EmoJump* (see Case Study One).

There are a few methods for measuring and assessing player emotion skills and behavior in games. Among these methods are:

1. **Observation:** Often conclusions about a player's emotional experience can be reached through simple observations by a researcher, either in person or via video recordings. Researchers and designers may use checklists of emotional responses, including expressions such as smiles and frowns to determine the emotional climate of the play session and specific responses to notable in-game actions and events. A drawback of this method is the issue of subjectivity among observers. People's observations and perception of the emotional climate of a given experience will vary and this can create inconsistency as well as problems establishing inter-rater reliability for the data collected.

2. **Player self-report:** Researchers can conduct emotional evaluations of players before, during, and after gameplay sessions. Typically, this involves a player responding to a series of questions posed by the researcher, or pointing to a visual cue to indicate the emotion he or she is feeling. Many game systems can actually embed this assessment within the play experience by having the player answer a quick question with a controller or gestural interaction, before moving onto the next segment in the game.

3. **Think-alouds:** Guided think-aloud methods require players to verbalize their internal thoughts and feelings to determine the effects of a game's design and the overall experience on the player's emotional state. Researchers moderate and guide the talk aloud. Information gathered from this method can also help designers and researchers learn more about strategies a player may engage in to address his or her emotional responses.

4. **Biometrics:** Biometrics are physiological measures of heart rate, respiration, skin galvanic response, eye tracking, postural movement, facial EMG and even brain activity via *fMRI*, which can help to determine a player's emotional states. Physical responses from a player's body allow researchers to chart when a player is in a heightened positive or negative emotional state, and at which point they are able to recover from it. In addition, there is increasing use of brain sensor interfaces (e.g., reading brain waves to control in-game elements) that designers can use for assessment that can be linked to neuroscience frameworks such as Davidson's (1999; 2012) emotional styles that outlines specific neural circuits underlying specific emotional response patterns.

5. **In-game data collection:** This growing field of research uses in-game actions in the form of clicks, level completions, and failures, and a number of other important in-game decisions, and aligns the resulting data with behavioral measures, such as biometric measures as described above, or data from psychological rating scales like the BASC, Behavior Assessment System for Children, which may include self-reports or teacher reports of behavior (Reynolds & Kamphaus, 2013). Analysis of the patterns in the game can reveal emotional regulation strategies and key moments for further evaluation.

Future Needs

Simply put, there is a growing consensus that emotion regulation skills in particular, are highly contextual and interventions must consider context as a design priority. For instance, particular strategies to improve emotional health that might serve high-poverty populations may not serve those with terminal illness. As such, game designers need to truly understand the situational contexts, as well as the psychometric contexts of their populations to design interventions that are helpful and not irrelevant or in worst case, harmful. Along the same lines with situational context, are limitations of one's target population, so as to consider a strengths-based focus rather than a deficit-based perspective. In other words, in particular contexts it may serve learners better to focus on leveraging skills that come easy to them, rather than build up skills that "fall short." Furthermore, there is a growing need to go beyond cognitive-only approaches and adopt mind/body approaches that incorporate embodied experiences such as the integration of physical sensors in gameplay. The increased ubiquity of new sensor technology will likely present needs around frameworks that connect in-game behaviors with target emotional health outcomes. Lastly, there is greater need for cross-disciplinary collaboration that can combine practical and theoretical knowledge to address specific populations. For instance, early childhood educators, counselors, and game designers can benefit from more formal collaborative spaces where they can share their practical and theoretical knowledge to improve relevant skills influencing emotional health.

Case Study Three:
Space Ranger Alien Quest, A Game Targeting Executive Functioning

Space Ranger Alien Quest is an action video game developed through an international collaboration among New York University's CREATE lab, CUNY's CHILD lab, the games4resilience lab at the University of Vienna, and the University of Applied Sciences Technikum Wien. Researchers in this consortium are currently investigating the alignment of game performance with executive functioning (EF) (a clear set of cognitive skills tied to self-regulation), with the intention of implementing the game as an intervention to train children and improve health and academic outcomes in the near future. The game has been designed to focus on shifting between mental sets of information while also incorporating design features known to influence emotional response. Research on games such as *Space Ranger Alien Quest* seeks to fulfill a need to assess individuals' self-regulation skills while also testing the capability of a specific game mechanic (e.g., sorting items based on new rule sets) to improve a specific cognitive strategy (e.g., mental set shifting).

The game, designed for children between the ages of seven and eleven, puts players in the role of a space ranger who must take care of aliens by giving them food and drinks. Specific aliens that appear on the screen have very specific needs, however the aliens are incredibly fickle and live on a strange planet with an unstable environment that is always changing. Players have to keep up with an ever-changing series of rule hierarchies and changes to advance through levels. For example, red aliens may be hungry and need food given to them at the beginning of a level, but then change their minds a series of times due to environmental changes like rapid sunsets and sunrises, strange storms or bolts of lightning appearing on-screen. Actions in the game are largely driven by empathic goals in which players are caregivers and emotionally driven feedback from the characters. The narrative, character design, and visual design of the interface are based on emotional design research on how the role of color, lighting and character design in games can induce positive states in players (Bura, 2008, Knez & Niedenthal, 2008, Um, Plass, Hayward, & Homer, 2012). Lastly, a player's success is measured in terms of the aliens' moods and his or her ability to make the aliens happy.

Thus far, validation research and a training study have been completed, and show promising results. Preliminary results have found that the game produces a similar range of scores to those achieved on established measures of EF in clinical settings (e.g., card sorting tasks, spatial attention tasks) and that children who play the game over a period of time show improved skills in comparison to those who are not exposed to the intervention (Bromley, et. al. 2013; Sprung, et. al., 2013). Additionally, children enjoyed playing the game and were motivated to pursue more difficult levels featuring complex rule structures with more rapid environmental changes and actions. Further studies unpacking the differences in behaviors resulting from an emotional response and cognitive skill development are planned for the future. Implications of these findings suggest that children's ability to self-regulate may benefit from playing video games that are specifically designed to address such cognitive activities.

Best Practices

The following design principles should be considered when creating games to build skills targeting emotional health based on the current frameworks and findings.

1. **Provide a situational context when providing training around emotion regulation strategies:** Environmental influences and social conditions can significantly influence the utility of specific strategies in the learner's real-world situations and needs.

2. **Provide opportunities for repeated practice over time:** While for younger populations it may be easier to develop emotion regulation and understanding skills, for adult populations it may require additional engagement to re-learn certain behaviors patterns.

3. **A narrow focus on implementing a specific strategy can lead to more rigorous, efficacious, and engaging gaming experiences:** Whether your focus is on attentional control, how to re-appraise body image, or emotional states that drive behaviors, keeping a narrow focus allows for diversification of application contexts and increasing levels of complexity.

4. **Consider focusing on strengths as much as focusing on needs:** At times our ability to respond in emotionally healthy ways to challenging life events relies on our use of specific strengths rather than building up what may be considered deficiencies.

5. **Where possible incorporate embodied experiences:** We often forget emotions are closely linked to our physical states. Gaming experiences that allow us to engage in embodied experiences can help us tap a broader spectrum of awareness and regulatory techniques (e.g., breathing deeply, focusing on a sensation).

Resources

Games

Beating the Blues (http://www.beatingtheblues.co.uk/)
Braingame Brian: Toward an Executive Function Training Program with
    Game Elements for Children with ADHD and Cognitive Control Problems
    (http://www.gamingandtraining.nl/beschrijving-braingame-brian/)
Deepak Chopra's Leela (http://www.thq.com/us/deepakchpoprasleela/360)
Lumosity Lab Brain Games & Brain Training (http://www.lumosity.com/)
Mindbloom (http://www.mindbloom.com/)
Mood Gym (https://moodgym.anu.edu.au/welcome)
MoodHacker by ORCAs (http://www.orcasinc.com/products/moodhacker/)
Play Attention (http://www.playattention.com/)
Playmancer (http://www.playmancer.eu/)
RAGE-Control: A Game to Build Emotional Strength
Re-Mission (http://www.re-mission.net/)
SuperBetter (https://www.superbetter.com/)

Books

Davidson, R.J. & Begley, S. (2013). *The Emotional Life of Your Brain: How Its Unique Patterns Affect the Way You Think, Feel, and Live—and How You Can Change Them.* New York, NY: Penguin Group.

Fogg, B.J. (2003). *Persuasive Technology: Using Computers to Change What We Think and Do.* San Francisco, CA: Morgan Kaufmann Publishers.

Games for Health Journal

Hanna, H. (2013). *The Sharp Solution: A Brain-Based Approach for Optimal Performance.* Hoboken, N.J.: John Wiley & Sons, Inc.

Ledoux, J. (1996) *Emotional Brain: The Mysterious Underpinnings of Emotional Life.* New York, NY: Simon and Schuster.

Rogers, S. (2010). *Level Up!: The Guide to Great Video Game Design.* West Sussex, United Kingdom: John Wiley & Sons, Inc.

Reports

Institute for the Future (2012). Innovations in Games: Better Health and Healthcare, Convened by the Office of the National Coordinator for Health IT and the White House Office of Science and Technology Policy.

Lieberman, D. (2009). Designing Serious Games for Learning and Health in Informal and Formal Settings. In U. Ritterfeld, M. Cody, & P. Vorderer (Eds.), *Serious Games: Mechanisms and Effects.* New York: Routledge

Primack, B.A., Carroll, M.V., McNamara, M., Klem, M.L., King, B., Rich, M. Chan, C.W. & Nayak, S, (2012). Role of Video Games in Improving Health-Related Outcomes: A Systematic Review, *American Journal of Preventative Medicine, 42*(6); 630-8.

Robert Wood Johnson Foundation (2011). Advancing the Field of Health Games: A Progress Report on Health Games Research, RWJF Program Results Progress Report.

Researchers

Richie Davidson, Center for Investigating Healthy Minds at the Waisman Center, University of Wisconsin, Madison (http://www.investigatinghealthyminds.org/)

Steve Cole and team at HopeLab (http://www.hopelab.org/)

Joseph LeDoux, Center for Neural Science at NYU (http://www.cns.nyu.edu/)

Manuel Sprung, Games4Resilience Lab at University of Vienna (http://www.manuelsprung.at/en/)

Ben Sawyer, Digitalmill (http://www.dmill.com/)

Nick Yee, Ubisoft (http://www.nickyee.com/)

Albert "Skip" Rizzo, Institute for Creative Technologies, USC (http://ict.usc.edu/)

Katherine Isbister, Game Innovation Lab, NYU (http://gil.poly.edu/people/)

Research Labs

Center for Investigating Healthy Minds Lab at University of Wisconsin, Madison (http://www.investigatinghealthyminds.org/)

Games4Resilience Lab at University of Vienna (http://www.manuelsprung.at/en/)

CREATE Lab at New York University (http://create.nyu.edu/)

Emotion Regulation Lab at Hunter College City University of New York (http://urban.hunter.cuny.edu/~tdennis/index.html)

Institute for Creative Technologies at University of Southern California (http://ict.usc.edu/))

References

Aldao, A., Nolen-Hoeksema, S., & Schweizer, S. (2010). Emotion-regulation strategies across psychopathology: A meta-analytic review. *Clinical Psychology Review, 30*(2), 217–37. doi:10.1016/j.cpr.2009.11.004

Blair, C., & Peters, R. (2003). Physiological and neurocognitive correlates of adaptive behavior in preschool among children in Head Start. *Developmental Neuropsychology, 24*(1), 479–97. doi:10.1207/S15326942DN2401_04

Bromley, M., Homer, B., Sprung, M., Hayward, E., Leyrer, J., Hoffman, A., Scharl, J., Puhringer, S., Was, V., & Bellmore, J. (2013). Can an action video game measure executive functioning? The validation of a game designed to assess EF skills. Paper presented at the Sixth Annual Subway Summit on Cognition and Education Research, New York, NY.

Botvinick, M., Braver, T., & Barch, D. (2001). Conflict monitoring and cognitive control. *Psychological ..., 108*(3), 624–652. doi:10.1037//0033-295X.I08.3.624

Bura, S. (2008). Emotion engineering: A scientific approach for understanding game appeal. Gamasutra. Retrieved December 12, 2012 from: http://www.gamasutra.com/view/feature/3738/emotion_engineering_a_scientific_.php

Carlson, S. M., & Moses, L. J. (2001). Individual differences in inhibitory control and children's theory of mind. *Child Development, 72*(4), 1032–1053. doi:10.1111/1467-8624.00333

Chiesa, A., Calati, R., & Serretti, A. (2011). Does mindfulness training improve cognitive abilities? A systematic review of neuropsychological findings. *Clinical Psychology Review, 31*(3), 449-64.

Cole, P.M., Martin, S.E., & Dennis, T.A. (2004). Emotion regulation as a scientific construct: Challenges and directions for child development research. *Child Development, 75*, 317-333.

Davidson, RJ, & Begley, S. (2012). *The emotional life of your brain: How its unique patterns affect the way you think, feel, and live—and how you can change them.* New York, NY: Hudson Street Press.

Davidson, R, & Irwin, W. (1999). The functional neuroanatomy of emotion and affective style. *Trends in cognitive sciences, 3*(1), 11–21. Retrieved from http://www.ncbi.nlm.nih.gov/pubmed/10234222

Diamond, A., & Lee, K. (2011). Interventions shown to aid executive function development in children 4–12 years old. Science. 333(6045), 959–964.

Eigsti, I.-M., Zayas, V., Mischel, W., Shoda, Y., Ayduk, O., Dadlani, M. B., … Casey, B. J. (2006). Predicting cognitive control from preschool to late adolescence and young adulthood. *Psychological Science, 17*(6), 478–84. doi:10.1111/j.1467-9280.2006.01732.x

Ellard, K. K., Fairholme, C. P., Boisseau, C. L., Farchione, T. J., & Barlow, D. H. (2010). Unified protocol for the transdiagnostic treatment of emotional disorders: Protocol development and initial outcome data. *Cognitive and Behavioral Practice, 17*(1), 88–101. doi:10.1016/j.cbpra.2009.06.002

Fagundo, A. B., Santamaria, J.J., Forcano, L., Giner-Bartolome, C., Jimenez-Murcia, S., Sanchez, I., &

Fava, G. a, & Tomba, E. (2009). Increasing psychological well-being and resilience by psychotherapeutic methods. *Journal of Personality, 77*(6), 1903–34. doi:10.1111/j.1467-6494.2009.00604.x

Floyd, R. G., & Kirby, E. a. (2001). Psychometric properties of measures of behavioral inhibition with preschool-age children: Implications for assessment of children at risk for ADHD. *Journal of Attention Disorders, 5*(2), 79–91. doi:10.1177/108705470100500202

Garner, P. (1999). Continuity in emotion knowledge from preschool to middle-childhood and relation to emotion socialization. *Motivation and Emotion, 23*(4). Retrieved from http://link.springer.com/article/10.1023/A:1021386725399

Goldin, P., McRae, K., Ramel, W., & Gross, J. (2008). The neural bases of emotion regulation: reappraisal and suppression of negative emotion. Biological Psychiatry, 63(6), 577–586. Retrieved from http://www.ncbi.nlm.nih.gov/pmc/articles/PMC2483789/

Gross, J.J. & Munoz, R.F. (1995). Emotion regulation and mental health. *Clinical Psychology: Science and Practice*, 2, 151-164.

Gross, J. J., & Barrett, L. F. (2011). Emotion generation and emotion regulation: One or two depends on your point of view. *Emotion Review*, 3, 8-16.

Hendrie, H. C., Albert, M. S., Butters, M. a, Gao, S., Knopman, D. S., Launer, L. J., … Wagster, M. V. (2006). The NIH cognitive and emotional health project. Report of the critical evaluation study committee. *Alzheimer's & Dementia : The Journal of the Alzheimer's Association, 2*(1), 12–32. doi:10.1016/j.jalz.2005.11.004

Ivanov, I., Schulz, K. P., London, E. D., & Newcorn, J. H. (2008). Inhibitory control deficits in childhood and risk for substance use disorders: a review. *The American Journal of Drug and Alcohol Abuse, 34*(3), 239–58. doi:10.1080/00952990802013334

Izard, C., Fine, S., Schultz, D., Mostow, a., Ackerman, B., & Youngstrom, E. (2001). Emotion knowledge as a predictor of social behavior and academic competence in children at risk. *Psychological Science, 12*(1), 18–23. doi:10.1111/1467-9280.00304

Jacob, M., Thomassin, K., Morelen, D., & Suveg, C. (2011). Emotion regulation in childhood anxiety.

Kabat-Zinn, J. (2003), Mindfulness-Based Interventions in Context: Past, Present, and Future. *Clinical Psychology: Science and Practice*, 10: 144–156.

Kessler, R. C., Aguilar-Gaxiola, S., Alonso, J., Chatterji, S., Lee, S., Ormel, J., & Wang, P. S. (2009). The global burden of mental disorders: An update from the WHO World Mental Health (WMH) Surveys. *Epidemiology Psychiatry Society, 18*(1), 23-33.

Klingberg, T., Fernell, E., Olesen, P., Johnson, M., Gustafsson, P., Dahlström, K., Gillberg, C.G.,

Knez, I., & Niedenthal, S. (2008). Lighting in digital game worlds: Effects on affect and play performance. *Cyberpsychology & Behavior*, 11, 129–137.

Kohn, R., Saxena, S., Levav, I., & Saraceno, B. (2004). The treatment gap in mental health care. *Bulletin of the World Health Organization*, 82, 858-866.

Lieberman, D. A. (2009). Designing serious games for learning and health in informal and formal settings. *Serious games: Mechanisms and effects*, 117-130.

McRae, K., Misra, S., Prasad, A. K., Pereira, S. C., & Gross, J. J. (2012). Bottom-up and top-down emotion generation: implications for emotion regulation. *Social Cognitive and Affective Neuroscience, 7*(3), 253–62. doi:10.1093/scan/nsq103

Merry, S. N., Stasiak, K., Shepherd, M., Frampton, C., Fleming, T., & Lucassen, M. F. G. (2012). The effectiveness of SPARX, a computerised self help intervention for adolescents seeking help for depression: randomised controlled non-inferiority trial. *BMJ*, 344, e2598-e2598.

Mizen, R. (2009). The embodied mind. *The Journal of analytical psychology, 54*(2), 253–72.

Moffitt, T. E., Arseneault, L., Belsky, D., Dickson, N., Hancox, R. J., Harrington, H., … Caspi, A. (2011). A gradient of childhood self-control predicts health, wealth, and public safety. *Proceedings of the National Academy of Sciences of the United States of America, 108*(7), 2693–8. doi:10.1073/pnas.1010076108

Nelis, D., Quoidbach, J., Mikolajczak, M., & Hansenne, M. (2009). Increasing emotional intelligence: (How) is it possible? *Personality and Individual Differences, 47*(1), 36–41. doi:10.1016/j.paid.2009.01.046

N-Fusion Interactive, C. P. (2011). *Deepak Chopra's Leela*. Agoura Hills, CA: THQ Inc.

Norman, D. A. (2002). Emotion and design: Attractive things work better. *Interactions Magazine, 9*(4), 36 42.

Perner, J., Kain, W., & Barchfeld, P. (2002). Executive control and higher-order theory of mind in children at risk of ADHD. *Infant and Child Development*, 158, 141–158. doi:10.1002/icd.

Pons, F., & Harris, P. L. (2000). *Test of Emotion Comprehension-TEC*. Oxford, UK: Oxford University Press.

Primack, B. a, Carroll, M. V, McNamara, M., Klem, M. Lou, King, B., Rich, M., ... Nayak, S. (2012). Role of video games in improving health-related outcomes: a systematic review. *American Journal of Preventive Medicine, 42*(6), 630–8. doi:10.1016/j.amepre.2012.02.023

Reynolds, C.R., & Kamphaus, R.W. (1992). BASC: Behavior Assessment System for Children manual. Circle Pines, MN: American Guidance Service.

Riggs, N., Blair, C., & Greenberg, M. (2004). Concurrent and 2-year longitudinal relations between executive function and the behavior of 1st and 2nd grade children. *Child Neuropsychology,* (February 2014), 37–41. Retrieved from http://www.tandfonline.com/doi/abs/10.1076/chin.9.4.267.23513

Southam-Gerow, M. A., & Kendall, P. C. (2002). Emotion regulation and understanding: Implications for child psychopathology and therapy. *Clinical Psychology Review, 22*(2), 189-222.

Sprung, M., Leyrer, J., Bromley, M., Homer, B., Hofmann, A., Scharl, J., Was, V., Bellmore, I., Pühringer, S., Kuczwara, J., Hayward., E., & Plass, J. (2013, August). Space Ranger Alien Quest: A video game to assess and promote executive functioning skills. Poster presented at the Annual Convention of the American Psychological Association. Honolulu, HI, USA.

Sweetser, P. & Wyeth, P. (2005) GameFlow: A model for evaluating player enjoyment in games. *ACM Computers in Entertainment, 3*(3), 1-24.

Tang, Y.-Y., Yang, L., Leve, L. D., & Harold, G. T. (2012). Improving executive function and its neurobiological mechanisms through a mindfulness-based intervention: Advances within the field of developmental neuroscience. *Child Development Perspectives, 6*(4), n/a–n/a. doi:10.1111/j.1750-8606.2012.00250.x

Tang, Y.-Y., & Posner, M. I. (2009). Attention training and attention state training. *Trends in cognitive sciences, 13*(5), 222–7.

Tate, R., Haritatos, J., & Cole, S. (2009). HopeLab's approach to *Re-Mission. International Journal of Learning and Media, 1*(1), 29–35. doi:10.1162/ijlm.2009.0003

Thompson, L., & McCabe, R. (2012). The effect of clinician-patient alliance and communication on treatment adherence in mental health care: a systematic review. *BMC Psychiatry, 12,* 87. doi:10.1186/1471-244X-12-87

Tuckman, B. W., & Hinkle, J. S. (1986). An experimental study of the physical and psychological effects of aerobic exercise on schoolchildren. *Health Psychology : Official Journal of the Division of Health Psychology, American Psychological Association, 5*(3), 197–207. Retrieved from http://www.ncbi.nlm.nih.gov/pubmed/3743529

Umberson, D., & Montez, J. (2010). Social relationships and health: A flashpoint for health policy. *Journal of Health and Social Behavior, 51,* 1–16. doi:10.1177/0022146510383501.Social

Um, E., Plass, J. L., Hayward, E. O., & Homer, B. D. (2012). Emotional design in multimedia learning. *Journal of Educational Psychology, 104*(2), 485.

Unique Logic and Technology (2011). *PlayAttention.* Retrieved from http://www.playattention.com

USC ICT (2013) *Bravemind.* A project from the USC Institute for Creative Technologies. Retrieved from: http://medvr.ict.usc.edu/projects/bravemind/

Vacca, R. (2013). Leela: Taking the mind-body journey. Proceedings of *DiGRA: DeFragging Game Studies,* pp. 198-199. Atlanta, Georgia.

Wass, S. V., Scerif, G., & Johnson, M. H. (2012). Training attentional control and working memory – Is younger, better? *Developmental Review, 32*(4), 360–387. doi:10.1016/j.dr.2012.07.001

Watson, D., Clark, L. a, & Carey, G. (1988). Positive and negative affectivity and their relation to anxiety and depressive disorders. *Journal of Abnormal Psychology, 97*(3), 346–53. Retrieved from http://www.ncbi.nlm.nih.gov/pubmed/3192830

WHO. Mental health. World Health Organization (WHO) 2004. Retrieved from: http://www.who.int/mental_health/en.

CHAPTER 8

Ethics

Designing and Using Games to Teach Ethics and Ethical Thinking

Karen Schrier, *Marist College, Poughkeepsie, New York, U.S., Kschrier@gmail.com*

Key Summary Points

1. Instead of focusing only on how games can teach specific values, we may also want to think about how they could teach skills associated with ethical thinking.

2. There are a number of frameworks and case studies that suggest the potential of ethics practice through games, but few of them have been empirically tested or assessed.

3. Some best practices include making consequences and feedback on choices clear, allowing more time for players to form relationships with characters in the game, and using authentic scenarios and contexts. These should be further tested.

Key Terms

Ethics
Morals
Values
Ethical thinking
Empathy
Ethical reasoning
Ethical reflection
Ethically notable games
Ethics education

Introduction

Often when people hear the terms "ethics" and "games" in the same sentence, they initially think of violence, addiction, online bullying, sexism, and racism in games, and the like. They may be worried games such as *Grand Theft Auto* or *Call of Duty* are teaching their kids negative values; that their teenager is getting harassed by others in the real-time chats of *Counterstrike*; or, they are concerned their students are spending more time playing games rather than being socially, educationally, or civically engaged. This chapter is **not** about these issues, though they may be valid concerns.

Rather, this chapter instead asks: can games also help us learn how to practice ethics and ethical thinking? If so, what does the research say about this? Are there best practices for designing and using games to teach ethics?

Defining ethics, morals and values

But first, what do I mean by ethics? There are many different definitions of ethics and morals, which often get conflated. Typically, morals refer to "universal truths, or public rules or principles" (Tierney, 1994, p. ix), or agreed-upon, more general guidelines. Ethics, on the other hand, usually are referred to as a more individual, active way of handling morals, an "individual's response to social morality in terms of reflective engagement, valuation, and choice" (Tierney, 1994, p. ix). Likewise, Sicart defines ethics as the practice of making choices and moral judgments to achieve a good human life (Sicart, 2005). The term "values" is also typically found alongside "ethics" and "morals" and are usually the output of one's ethics and morals—these are the principles or guidelines that define what matters to a person, organization or society. For a cross-cultural study of values, see Hofstede (2001) and Schwartz & Bilsky (1990). For more about types of values, see Schwartz (1994).

Some educators and designers reading this chapter may be looking for advice on how to teach kids positive values through games, or to use games to teach kids how to act and behave ethically, and to know right from wrong. The best practices listed at the end of this chapter, as well as the list of resources, may be useful to help you better design games for this purpose. The next section suggests some possible difficulties in using games to teach values.

From ethics to ethical thinking

Some researchers (Schrier & Kinzer, 2009; Schrier, 2010) argue that it could be problematic to design games that focus on teaching kids the so-called right way to behave without teaching the underlying principles or skills needed to determine what is ethical or appropriate. In other words, educators, mentors, and parents need to help kids build the skills and thought processes they need to learn to know how to determine the right or ethical way to act. One issue is that ethics may change from context to context. What is appropriate in one online forum may be very different from what is proper on a playground or a family function. Some of those differences may be obvious, while others may be nuanced, and require cultural awareness, interpersonal skills, empathy, and respect for others. These skills, therefore, would be more beneficial to teach, rather than a list of the rules to be followed in each context.

What may be more beneficial to teach through games is ethical thinking (Schrier & Kinzer, 2009; Schrier, 2010). Ethical thinking is not just about following some agreed-upon code of ethics, or the existence of one right way to do things or how to act. Rather, it is about being able to think critically about the questions and moments in one's life, and judging the right thing to do in a given context, space, or culture. Regardless of whether a person is offline or online, in a classroom or at work, with their family or strangers, in another country or their own backyard, that individual needs to be able to reason, reflect, empathize and gather information to judge how to best behave, act, share or choose. A game, therefore, should focus on teaching the skills associated with ethical thinking rather than merely posit which behaviors or concepts are right or wrong.

Why should we be ethical thinkers?

It may be obvious why we should become ethical thinkers. As we more regularly traverse other cultures in our globally interconnected world, we may also become more frequently challenged with knowing how to behave appropriately. Moreover, Kereluik et al. (2013) identify ethical thinking and ethical awareness as a key component of 21st century learning (2013). In their framework, ethical/emotional awareness contributes to the "Humanistic Knowledge (to Value)" hub, with "Foundational Knowledge" and "Meta Knowledge" as the other hubs (Kereluik et al., 2013). They explain that, "Ethical awareness included…the ability to imagine oneself in someone else's position and feel with that individual as well as the ability to engage in ethical decision making" (Kereluik et al., 2013, p. 5). For example, we need to be able to identify, address, and assuage bullying in new contexts, both virtual and real. Social conundrums, such as global warming, sustainability, poverty, educational inequalities, and access to healthcare are complex and require people to weigh multiple perspectives, evaluate consequences, and be system thinkers (Schrier, 2014). Finally, teaching ethical thinking is not just about helping students address ethical problems or negative values. We also all need to become more engaged ethical thinkers to find new ways to communicate, empathize, give, and accept support, connection, camaraderie, and care across distance, time, culture, and contexts.

Why games for ethical thinking?

Yet ethics as a practice—or as a subject even—is rarely taught or addressed in the K-12 classroom (Schrier & Kinzer, 2009). Games could be one additional way to formally or informally introduce and support ethical thinking skills practice, inside or outside of the classroom. In the preface to her edited book, *Ethics and Games: Teaching Values through Play,* Schrier (2010) notes that there are several characteristics of games, such as the ability to take on new identities and the ability to experience the consequences of one's choices and iterate on those consequences, which may make games particularly amenable to ethical exploration and practice (Schrier, 2010). Further research should consider the potential additional benefits to learning and practicing ethical thinking skills within gaming environments.

About this chapter

There are many concerns related to the domain of ethics and games. Some people are concerned with the modes of game production, distribution and marketing, and the ethical considerations of developing and selling games. Others are interested in how games, as they are both an art form and medium, express the creator's values, and how this may potentially influence or interact with one's audience. These all may be relevant topics that could be discussed and reflected upon as part of a classroom exercise on games. For example, a conversation on the harassment of a female game creator of *Depression Quest* on Steam's Greenlight could help initiate broader discussions of gender, ethnicity, and race in the media, microaggressions and violence, class and privilege, and/or online harassment (see more at Smith, 2013). While this chapter cannot cover all of the possible topics associated with ethics and games, educators, and designers should be aware of the many lenses through which we can use and play games to help us consider ethical issues and better understand humanity.

While there are many worthy ethical issues related to gaming, the rest of the chapter focuses mainly on the design and use of games to support ethical thinking skills and ethical reflection, instead of just the specific ethical topics that games may generate. In other words, how can we better design games or use them in our classrooms, if teaching ethics is one of our goals?

Case Study One: Ethics and Media Research Labs

There are a number of research labs and centers that are dedicated to the study of ethics, values and games. Looking at their latest research questions and findings is a good first step in this problem space.

PetLab (Prototyping, Evaluation, and Teaching and Learning Lab), Parsons The New School and Games for Change

This lab, led by Colleen Macklin, John Sharp, and Karen Sideman, is housed at Parsons The New School, and co-directed by the Games for Change organization. PetLab creates and tests games related to education, public interest, and civic engagement. Projects include *Re:Activism*, *Play It Forward*, and *Red Cross Games for Disaster Preparedness*.

Values@Play and Tiltfactor

Values@Play is a research initiative, set of game tools, and curriculum developed by researchers seeking ways to help designers incorporate values into their creation of games. For example, the Values@Play curriculum has been used to teach values conscious design (Belman et al., 2011; Belman & Flanagan, 2010). Principal investigators and directors include Mary Flanagan, who runs the Tiltfactor Lab at Dartmouth, and Helen Nissenbaum of New York University. One of the key outputs is the *Grow-A-Game* series, which is a deck of cards aimed at helping designers create games that prioritize values.

Good Play and The Good Project

The Good Project, originally initiated by Mihaly Csikszentmihalyi, William Damon, and Howard Gardner, is a research effort aimed at understanding how we create responsible and caring young citizens in a digital age. A component of this is the Good Play project (part of Harvard's Project Zero), which looks at how youth handle ethical issues in digital spaces, such as games. Good Play is funded by the MacArthur foundation and has collaborated with Henry Jenkins at USC to create a curriculum to encourage reflection on the ethical aspects of digital media, such as Facebook and online games. Their reports also may be especially useful for learning about the teen and young adult space. See more at http://www.thegoodproject.org/good-play/good-play-project/ and http://www.thegoodproject.org/good-play/developing-minds-digital-media/publications/.

Play Innovation Lab

The Play Innovation Lab is directed by Karen Schrier and focuses on creating digital and analog games that support social change, empathy, and ethical reflection. The lab, which is housed at Marist College and launched in 2014, is currently researching the use and design of games to teach ethics, issues of gender and sexuality in games, crowdsourcing and games, and methodologies for reducing online bullying and harassment in games. Relevant papers on ethics and games include Schrier & Kinzer (2009), Schrier (2011), Schrier (2012), Schrier (2014), and a forthcoming paper on the Ethics Practice and Implementation Categorization (EPIC) Framework.

Key Frameworks

There are a number of theoretical frameworks and perspectives that describe the intersection of games and ethics. In this section, I will briefly describe a few key perspectives, which include:

1. **Sicart (2009, 2013):** Sicart, in his book *Ethics and Computer Games* (2009) views games as being "designed ethical objects" (Sicart, 2009). He argues that games do not just feature ethical choices as part of their gameplay, but are also ethical systems themselves. They are products of, played by, and discussed by human beings. Additionally, those game players, game designers, and game commentators are ethical agents, embedded in complex social, historical, ethical and cultural systems (Sicart, 2009). Sicart also wrote a follow-up book, *Beyond Choices: The Design of Ethical Gameplay* (2013), which considers more deeply the design of games for ethics. He uses a variety of games as case studies, including Anna Antropy's *Dys4ia, Spec Ops: The Line,* and *Fallout New Vegas* as case studies.

2. **Zagal (2009, 2011):** Zagal (2009, 2011) describes a framework for evaluating "ethically notable" (Zagal, 2011) games. He explains that while not all games directly enable moral reflection and reasoning, those that do are ethically notable games. In Zagal's framework, he investigates whether a game's dilemmas are actually moral and whether there is consistency in how the ethical structure of the game is treated.

3. **In Schrier's doctoral dissertation (2011),** she develops a framework for conceptualizing and assessing ethical thinking in games, particularly role-playing video games. She constructs a model that includes four categories of ethical thinking skill and thought processes: 1) reflection, 2) information gathering, 3) reasoning, and 4) empathy. Her model also includes several "drivers" or underlying motivators, such as "personal ethics," "game status" and "relationship building," which interact with the four categories of ethical thinking to affect how people think through ethical decisions in role-playing video games (see Figure 1).

4. **The Values at Play (VAP) methodology:** Flanagan & Nissenbaum (2007) describe the Values at Play (VAP) methodology (2007), which is a game methodology that articulates how to incorporate social themes and values into one's game design. The VAP consists of three parts: 1) the discovery phase, where designers consider which are the relevant values to include, 2) the translation phase, which involves translating those values into design patterns, mechanics, and gameplay, and 3) the verification phase, which involves testing the game to make sure that the values expressed through the game are what was intended. Flanagan & Nussbaum describe the framework in their book, *Values at Play in Digital Games* (2014). For more information about the VAP, see Flanagan et al. (2005, 2007) and the Values at Play Team (2007).

5. **Ethics Practice and Implementation Categorization (EPIC) Framework:** Schrier (2014) created an in-progress ethics game categorization framework (EPIC) for using games for ethics education. This framework describes different categories of using games for teaching ethics, ethical thinking, and ethical reflection, and cites recent games as examples. The purpose of the EPIC framework is to help teachers find and use appropriate games for teaching ethics in the classroom. For instance, the framework's "Mood" category was defined as "Games that primarily convey emotion … in ways that could help us see new perspectives on humanity" (Schrier, 2014) and uses as examples *Dear Esther and Gone Home*. These are games that could be used in a lesson about how the emotional tone and mood of a game interact with one's empathy for a character's experience. Another category, "Choice," refers to games "with clear ethical choices and decision-making, which have differing effects on the game play," (Schrier, 2014) and consequences for one's game experience. The "Choice" category includes as examples games such as *The Walking Dead, The Stanley Parable,* and *Papers, Please.* These are games that could be incorporated into a lesson about weighing and making ethical choices and reflecting on the consequences of those decisions.

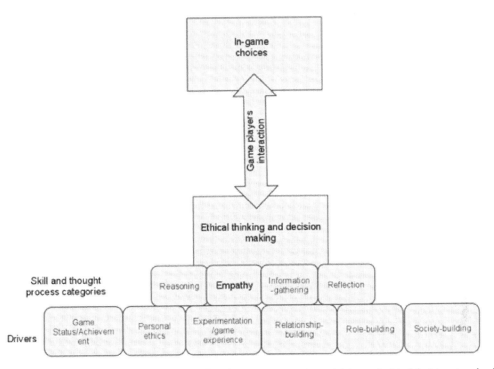

Figure 1. Framework of ethical thinking skills and thought process categories and drivers of ethical decisions in role-playing video games.

There are many other nascent frameworks that deal with ethical issues in games. Other frameworks that may be worth considering include:

1. **Consalvo's analysis of cheating in games and its implications for gameplay and game design (2005, 2007).** She looks at what it means when players use cheat codes, share information in forums, ignore established rules, hack systems, or read through walk-throughs. Her perspective asserts that players actively change and interact with game rules and systems (Consalvo, 2005).

2. **Freier & Saulnier's (2011) framework** for looking at ethical thinking skills through the lens of the moral and social development of children and adolescents (Freier & Saulnier, 2011).

3. **Bogost's (2007) approach to persuasive games**, in which games make arguments about its own meaning through the ways in which they are played. This is different from other types of media because games express meaning through rules and interactions with those rules (procedurally), and not just through the interplay of text and/or images (Bogost, 2007).

4. **Stevenson's (2011) framework,** which classifies and critiques ethics games to recommend ways to make games more ethically engaging.

In addition, when teaching ethics through games, it may be useful to identify an approach to ethics. There are a number of different perspectives on how to define ethics, what constitutes ethics, and how we arrive at ethical (i.e., appropriate or inappropriate, good or bad, or right or wrong) behavior, attitudes, or actions. The following list includes a number of the more commonly used approaches to ethics and ethics education. A good introductory text to these frameworks is Shafer-Landau (2010), *The Fundamentals of Ethics* (2nd Edition). These include:

1. **Virtue ethics:** Virtue ethics focuses on one's character and its virtues in helping to decide and assess the ethics of a situation. For example, what one's actions or behavior reveals about one's character, and the intention of one's actions, all factor into whether the behavior was ethical. The major thinkers related to this are Aristotle and Plato, though since then there have been many others. (For more information, see *Nicomachean Ethics* by Aristotle, Plato's *Republic*, St. Thomas Aquinas, David Hume, and Alasdair MacIntyre).
2. **Hedonism:** Hedonism focuses on the pursuit of pleasure above all others, and that people have the right to seek as much pleasure as possible, as it is the highest good to attain. The major thinkers related to this are Aristippus of Cyrene, Epicurus, and Michel Onfray.
3. **Deontology:** This framework emphasizes adherence to rules, regulations, duties, and other's rights. Kantian ethics is one sub-type. The core of Kantian ethics is the categorical imperative. Other major thinkers who were influenced by Immanuel Kant include Jorge Habermas and Jacques Lacan.
4. **Utilitarianism:** Utilitarianism emphasizes utility, or the best-case scenario that can be achieved by maximizing pleasure or goodness and reducing suffering. The greatest happiness for the greatest number of people is the typical axiom. John Stuart Mill and Jeremy Bentham are the key thinkers.
5. **Feminist ethics:** This is an approach to ethics that attempts to consider more diverse perspectives on ethics, such as including women viewpoints and female experiences on what is moral or appropriate behavior. For example, typically less credence was given to feminine traits, such as emotion, sharing, or connection, when evaluating the ethics of a situation, whereas typically masculine traits such as independence, dominance and autonomy were given more weight. Key thinkers are Mary Wollstonecraft and Elizabeth Cady Stanton.
6. **Ethics of care:** The ethics of care focuses on how empathy and compassion relate to ethics and ethical behavior. The major thinkers are Carol Gilligan and Nel Noddings.

Case Study Two: *Fable III*

Fable III is a role-playing video game developed by Lionhead Studios and published by Microsoft/Xbox. It is the third in the Fable series of games, where a player inhabits the imaginary world of Albion, a medieval-flavored game set in 1800s London. In *Fable III*, players take on the role of a prince or princess, who must go on quests to save Albion from a coming darkness. Along the way, players need to approach ethical choices, such as whether to sacrifice their friend or a number of villagers; or make decisions for Albion, such as whether to build a brothel or orphanage in a town. The choices have consequences for the game player and the game world. For example, if a player builds the orphanage, s/he can go visit the orphanage later in the game. If a player builds the brothel instead, s/he may see homeless non-playing character (NPC) kids and the surrounding town may look darker and more economically depressed.

Schrier (2011) investigated the skills and thought processes players used when working through the ethical scenarios in *Fable III*. To do this, she randomly assigned twenty males to play *Fable III*, with half assigned to play as a male avatar, and half assigned as a female avatar. She also randomly assigned ten males to a control condition, which included written versions of the ethical scenarios in *Fable III*.

Based on this, she found that game players did practice many ethical thinking skills in *Fable III*. She identified and categorized the ethical thinking skills and thought processes used, and labeled 35 distinct skills (e.g., interpreting evidence, weighing pros and cons) and 20 distinct thought processes (e.g., prioritizing people's feelings over any other reason).

Other overall findings were that participants used empathy-related skills more frequently with in-game characters, after they had time to play the game and build relationships with them. There were few gender differences in how people made ethical decisions or ethical skills and thought processes used, unless gender was a specific aspect of an ethical question.

In general, participants did not practice ethical thinking very differently between the written and game scenarios, however, participants used systems thinking more frequently in the game scenarios. Also, game participants seemed to empathize with other's perspectives more frequently than control condition participants, in an additional non-*Fable* related ethical scenario that was read to them, which was outside of the game.

Key Findings

In just the past few years, there have been a number of research studies that have suggested compelling directions for teaching ethics through games. Here are a few:

1. **Hodhod, Cairns, & Kudenko (2011)** created an interactive story game, AEINS, to teach character education.
2. **Fitzgerald & Groff (2011)** tested two games in a grade school in Cambridge, Massachusetts: *Diplomacy* and *Civilization IV: Colonization*, to understand how these games may teach ethics from a moral and cognitive development perspective.
3. **Koo & Seider's (2010)** investigated how video games can support prosocial learning.
4. **Belman & Flanagan's (2010)** research from the Values@Play project has suggested a connection between empathy and games.
5. **Simkins & Simkins (2008)** looked at role-playing games and their support of ethical reasoning skills. They determined four categories of features related to ethical reasoning, including mirroring, social context, effecting change, and having significant decisions. Their research is useful in thinking about the reasoning component of ethical thinking, and how it emerges during gameplay.
6. **Schrier, Diamond, & Langendoen (2010)** describe the process of creating a game, *Mission U.S.: For Crown or Colony*. They designed one part of the game to motivate ethical decisions surrounding testimonials on the Boston Massacre, and anecdotal findings suggested that empathy-related skills and thought processes were employed by players in the game, though this has not been studied empirically yet (Schrier et al., 2010). For more information, see Case Study One in Chapter Four.

A number of researchers have also looked at large-scale role-playing games to evaluate the potential of them to encourage ethical practice. For example, Svelch (2010) and Melenson (2011) each analyzed the ethical situations in games for their authenticity and complexity. They separately concluded that the morality meters in games, such as the karma point system in *Fallout III,* and the renegade/paragon system in the *Mass Effect* series, do not encourage the practice of ethics. Instead, they appear to motivate players to maximize the amount of "goodness" or "badness" achieved in the game, as if it is just another attribute for their avatar, like agility, strength, or happiness (Svelch, 2010).

Schrier (2011) investigated *Fable III,* a role-playing game, to identify, evaluate, and analyze the types of ethical thinking skills practiced in the game, versus written scenarios based on the game. Her findings are described in greater detail in the case study (see Case Study Two). Moreover, results from Schrier's (2012) study of *Fable III* and avatar gender found that the gender of one's avatar may affect how participants think through ethical scenarios, but only if it was a salient part of a scenario (all participants were male, playing as either male or female avatars). The results also suggested that players were more likely to make different ethical decisions based on their avatar's gender in the beginning of the game experience, when participants were not as fully immersed in their role. In addition, despite whether participants made so-called "good" or "bad" decisions, they still practiced a variety of ethical thinking skills, and there were no avatar gender differences found. Schrier (2014) also showed, using *Fable III*, how games could be windows into ethical thinking around sustainability and environmental questions, by showing how (through a game) people can think through and prioritize environmental concerns as opposed to other issues.

Assessment Considerations

How do we know if we are becoming more engaged ethical thinkers? How do we assess the ethics of one's behaviors, actions, or thoughts, particularly when there is debate about what it means to be ethical or how we arrive at this, in any context, let alone in games? One of the key challenges in assessing ethics games is that we do not yet have clear, vetted, universal assessment techniques. This is not surprising, since every ethical moment or situation is different, and there is no objective checklist for how people should act, behave, share, or feel. A few studies have sought to assess a game's efficacy in supporting the practice of ethical thinking and ethics. These include researchers who used:

1. **Mixed methods,** such as a "talk aloud" and discourse analysis, and the creation of a coding scheme and identification and comparison of skills and thought processes applied on scenarios, before and after the game, or between a control and experimental group (Schrier, 2011, 2012, 2014).
2. **A pre- and post-game activity,** such as a Paul Revere image, which was used in assessing historical and ethical thinking in *Mission U.S.: For Crown or Colony* (Schrier et al., 2010). (See more in Case Study One in Chapter Four.)
3. **Textual analysis,** such as those conducted by Zagal (2011), Svelch (2010), and Melenson (2011).
4. **Design research,** in which the process of design serves as a type of formative assessment, such as those designs conducted by Barab et al. (2011) on *River of Justice* and Macklin (2010) on *Re: Activism.*
5. **Focus groups or case studies,** such as those conducted by Fitzgerald & Groff (2011).
6. **Ethnographic approaches,** such as those done by Consalvo (2007).
7. **Designer reflection,** in which the designer interrogates and reflects on his or her design, as in the case of Brathwaite & Sharp (2010) and Brathwaite (now Romero's) *Train.*

Future Needs

There are still many gaps in the research, namely, further empirical research and assessment to understand the short- and long-term effectiveness of games to support the practice of ethical thinking. While hopefully this chapter has suggested the potential of games as a site for ethical exploration, reflection, and practice, more investigation is necessary to fully understand the factors that affect ethical thinking in games, such as how specific game elements affect, limit, and motivate ethical thinking.

Case Study Three: Bioware

Bioware, a game studio, is known for creating role-playing video games that feature ethical choices and scenarios, such as the *Mass Effect, Dragon Age,* and *Knights of the Old Republic* series. These games may be useful to play and use for educational purposes to better understand and reflect on how the designers created the game's "ethical system," ethics game mechanics, and ethics meters. For instance, in Bioware's games, the choices a player may have consequences in the game's world, and they may affect one's social standing, play options, story, and/or relationships in the game. Depending on one's actions, one's avatar may have levels or resources that go up or down, which in turn may affect their abilities and/or story options in the game.

In Bioware's *Mass Effect* series, for example, you create a character named Commander Shephard and lead him or her to make choices that will help keep peace in the galaxy and potentially protect the human race. Throughout a series of science fiction adventures, you, as Shephard, make choices on how to interact with alien races and other human beings, and build a team of allies to support you on your quest to save the universe. You can make choices and pick dialogue options—you can act polite and by the book, or act rebellious and above the law. Depending on how you act, you may end up more on the "paragon" or "renegade" side, respectively, or even somewhere in the middle, which may lead to new dialogue and gameplay options being unlocked or blocked, and differences in how non-playing characters (NPCs) treat you.

Similarly, in the *Dragon Age* series, you play as a character that is a Grey Warden (an order of warriors) in a fantasy setting. You need to form alliances with NPCs to help unite the world and go on quests to stop, and ultimately kill, an archdemon. As part of this game, you select from a list of dialogue options. Depending on how you relate to the NPCs, they will have differential levels of loyalty and friendship. As with *Mass Effect,* your choices have an effect on your gameplay and standing in the game world. In *Dragon Age,* however, it is sometimes less clear how dialogue options or actions map to the game's nuanced and complex morality system. The paragon/renegade distinction in *Mass Effect* is much more clear-cut and players can continually check to see where their avatar ranks in this moral system. Likewise, Bioware's *Knights of the Old Republic* game series also includes morality systems and is based on the Star Wars universe, such as the Jedi Knight versus Sith dichotomy.

Educators and designers may want to use Bioware's games, and the principles behind their games, in the classroom, or to inspire their own activities or games. Although the games are for mature game players, educators may be able to use or modify specific scenes or dialogue from the games. For example, a teacher could show a brief interaction between Shephard and another character, and invite students to discuss how they would respond to the situation. Another potential classroom activity is to discuss as a class how Bioware designers approached the challenge of representing ethical thinking in *Dragon Age,* including unpacking its moral system and game mechanics.

Best Practices

The following design principles should be considered when creating games to teach ethical thinking, based on a survey of the current frameworks and findings. These include:

1. **Players should be exposed to alternative perspectives.** Adolescents, for example, who are exposed to opposing views on social topics show improvement in argumentation skill (Kuhn, 2008; Kuhn et al., 2008).

2. **Players should be able to deliberate with others.** Players who had the opportunity to deliberate and debate topics with others were better able to improve argumentation skill (Kuhn, 2008; Kuhn et al., 2008). Further research should consider whether these need to be real people, or if virtual characters are sufficient.

3. **Players should be able to make choices.** The participants need to have an element of agency in making decisions.

4. **The choices should be relatable.** Players are more deeply engaged in practicing thinking skills with choices that are personally meaningful and relatable.

5. **The game's context should be personally meaningful and authentic.** The context surrounding any choices, as well as the choice itself, should be genuine and meaningful. By making the opposing views and choices authentic, participants are potentially more apt to bring in their own views and think through the problem as they would outside of the game, as well as use and apply what they learn and practice in the game.

6. **Any consequences should be appropriate.** Players are more motivated to apply thinking skills to dilemmas if the consequences to their choices are appropriate, relevant and authentic; and they are aware of the consequences.

7. **Players need time to develop relationships with their avatar and with other characters to build empathy for them**. Players may need time in the game to develop relationships with any NPCs to be able to better empathize with their points of view (Schrier, 2012). Players also may need more time to fully identify with their avatar to be able to think through ethical decisions more deeply, particularly if they feel, at first, that their avatar does not represent them. Embodying a different avatar gender than their own gender, for example, may make participants feel that their avatar does not represent them, at least initially, when playing a game. This appears to decrease over time as the participant has more opportunities to behave as him or herself in the game.

Resources

Research Labs

Berkman Center for Internet and Society

Engagement Game Lab

GoodPlay Project

MIT Center for Civic Media

PETLab

Play Innovation Lab

Tiltfactor

Values@Play

Related Researchers

Mia Consalvo

Jim Diamond

Mary Flanagan

Eric Gordon

Carrie Heeter

Helen Nissenbaum

Doris Rusch

Karen Schrier

David Simkins

Jose Zagal

Books, Blogs, Websites, and Reports

Anna Anthropy (http://auntiepixelante.com/?page_id=2142)

Bogost, I. (2011). How to Do Things With Games. Minneapolis, MN: University of Minnesota Press.

Bogost, I. (2007). Persuasive Games. Cambridge, MA: MIT Press.

Bogost, I. (2006). Unit Operations. Cambridge, MA: MIT Press.

Brown, H. (2008). Videogames and Education: Humanistic Approaches to an Emergent Art Form. M.E. Sharpe.

Campbell, H.A. & Grieve, G.P. (2014). Playing with Religion in Digital Games. Bloomington, IN: Indiana University Press.

Consalvo, M. (2007). Cheating. Cambridge, MA: MIT Press.

Feldman, F. (2006). Pleasure and the Good Life: Concerning the Nature, Varieties, and Plausibility of Hedonism. New York: Oxford University Press.

Flanagan, M. (2009). Critical Play: Radical Game Design. Cambridge, MA: MIT Press.

Galloway, A. (2006). Gaming: Essays on Algorithmic Culture. Minneapolis, MN: University of Minnesota Press.

Gardner, H., Csikszentmihalyi, M., & Damon, W. (2001). Good Work: When excellence and ethics meet. New York: Basic Books.

Gee, J. (2005). Why Video Games are Good for Your Soul. Common Ground.

Lenhart, A. (2008). Teens, Videogames, and Civics. Pew Internet.

Jenkins, H. et al. (2006). Confronting the Challenges of Participatory Culture. MacArthur Whitepaper.

Kahne, J. (2009). The Civic Potential Of Videogames. MacArthur Series.

Mattie Brice (http://www.mattiebrice.com/)

Project Horseshoe (http://www.projecthorseshoe.com/)

Russell, D., (Ed.). (2013). The Cambridge Companion to Virtue Ethics. New York: Cambridge University Press.

Schreiber, I., Seifert, C., Pineda, C., Preston, J., Hughes, L., Cash, S., & Robertson, T. Choosing between right and right: Creating meaningful ethical dilemmas in games. Project Horseshoe Whitepaper. http://www.projecthorseshoe.com/reports/ph09/ph09r3.htm

Schrier, K. (2012). Avatar gender and ethical thinking in Fable III. Bulletin of Science, Technology, and Society, 32, 375-383.

Schrier, K. & Gibson, D. (Eds.) (2010). Ethics and Game Design: Teaching Values through Play. IGI Global.

Schrier, K. & Gibson, D. (Eds.) (2011). Designing Games for Ethics: Models, Techniques, and Frameworks. IGI Global.

Sicart, M. (2009). Ethics and Computer Games. Cambridge, MA: MIT Press.

Sicart, M. (2013). Beyond Choices: The Design of Ethical Gameplay.

Wark, M. (2007). Gamer Theory. Cambridge, MA: Harvard University Press.

Well Played 1.0 and the Well Played series. ETC Press.

Values@Play website and papers (www.valuesatplay.com) and (http://www.valuesatplay.org/wp-content/uploads/2007/09/vap-chifinal06sub.pdf)

Games

While any game, arguably, can be useful to understanding teaching ethics through games, these games may be particularly relevant:

AEINS by Rania Hodhod, Paul Cairns and Daniel Kudenko

Akrasia

Airport Security

Awesome Upstanders

Bastion

Bioshock series

Buffalo

Cart Life

Darfur is Dying

Dear Esther

Deus Ex

Deus Ex: Human Revolution

Diplomacy

Dragon Age Series

Dys4ia

EthicsGame by Catharyn A. Baird

Everyday the Same Dream

Fable Series

Fallout 3

Fallout: New Vegas

Gone Home

Grand Theft Auto series

Grow-A-Game by Values@Play

Heavy Rain

Howling Dogs

Hush

Ico

Knights of the Old Republic

LA Noire

Layoff

Lim

Madrid Game

Mass Effect series

McDonald's Game

Mirror's Edge

Mission US series

Oblivion

Papers, Please

Paralect

Passage

Parenthood

Peacemaker

pOnd

Portal/Portal 2

Quandary Game by Learning Game Network

Re:Activism by PETLab

Red Dead Redemption

River of Justice by Sasha Barab, Tyler Dodge, Edward Gentry, Asmalina Saleh, Patrick Pettyjohn

Seeds by Nahil Sharkasi

September 12

Spec Ops: The Line

Super Columbine Massacre RPG

Sweatshop

Skyrim

The Arab-Israeli Conflict and *First Wind*, by Sharman Siebenthal Adams and Jeremiah Holden

The Shooting at Sandy Hook

The Stanley Parable

The Suffering

The Walking Dead Season One/Two

The Yawhg

Train by Brenda Brathwaite/Romero

Triad

Unmanned

Way

References

Belman, J., & Flanagan, M. (2010). Designing games to foster empathy. *Cognitive Technology, 14*(2), 5-15.

Belman, J., Nissenbaum, H., Flanagan, M., & Diamond, J. (2011, January). Grow-A-Game: a tool for values conscious design and analysis of digital games. Proceedings of DiGRA 2011 Conference: Think Design Play. Hilversum: The Netherlands, 14-17.

Bogost, I. (2007). *Persuasive games: The expressive power of videogames.* Cambridge, MA: MIT Press.

Brathwaite, B. & Sharp, J. (2010). The mechanic is the message: A post mortem in progress. In K. Schrier & D. Gibson (Eds.), *Ethics and Game Design: Teaching Values through Play* (pp. 311-329). Hershey, PA: IGI Global.

Consalvo, M. (2005). Rule sets, cheating, and magic circles: Studying games and ethics. *International Review of Information Ethics. 4*(2), 7-12.

Consalvo, M. (2007). *Cheating: Gaining advantage in videogames.* Cambridge, MA: MIT Press.

FitzGerald, R. & Groff, J. (2011). Leveraging video games for moral development in education: A practitioner's reflection. In K. Schrier & D. Gibson (Eds.), *Designing Games for Ethics: Models, Techniques and Frameworks.* (pp. 234-273). Hershey, PA: IGI Global.

Flanagan, M., & Nissenbaum, H. (2007). A game design methodology to incorporate social activist games. CHI, April–May.

Flanagan, M., Nissenbaum, H., Belman, J., & Diamond, J. (2007). A method for discovering values in digital games. Situated Play DiGRA 07 Conference Proceedings, Tokyo.

Freier, N. & Saulnier, E. (2011). The new backyard: Social and moral development in virtual worlds. In K. Schrier & D. Gibson (Eds.), *Designing Games for Ethics: Models, Techniques and Frameworks.* (pp. 179-192). Hershey, PA: IGI Global.

Hodhod, R., Cairns, P. & Kudenko, D. (2011). Fostering character education with games and interactive story generation. In K. Schrier & D. Gibson (Eds.), *Designing Games for Ethics: Models, Techniques and Frameworks.* (pp. 208-233). Hershey, PA: IGI Global.

Hofstede, G. (2001). Culture's consequences: Comparing values, behaviors, institutions, and organizations across nations. Thousand Oaks, CA: Sage Publications, Inc.

Kereluik, K., Mishra, P., Fahnoe, C., & Terry, L. (2013). What knowledge is of most worth: Teacher knowledge for 21st century learning. *Journal of Digital Learning in Teacher Education, 29*(4), 127-140.

Koo, G., & Seider, S. (2010) Video Games for Prosocial Learning. In K. Schrier & D. Gibson (Eds.), *Ethics and Game Design: Teaching Values through Play* (pp. 16-33). Hershey, PA: IGI Global.

Kuhn, D. (2008). Adolescent thinking. In R. Lerner & L. Steinberg (Eds.), *Handbook of Adolescence.* Hoboken NJ: Wiley.

Kuhn, D., Goh, W., Iordanou, K., & Shaenfield, D. (2008). Arguing on the computer: A microgenetic study of developing argument skills in a computer-supported environment. *Child Development. 79*(5). 1310-28.

Macklin, C. (2010). Reacting to *Re:Activism*: A case study in the ethics of design. In K. Schrier & D. Gibson (Eds.), *Ethics and Game Design: Teaching Values through Play* (pp. 274-290). Hershey, PA: IGI Global.

Melenson, J. (2011). The axis of good and evil. In K. Schrier & D. Gibson (Eds.), *Designing Games for Ethics: Models, Techniques and Frameworks.* (pp. 57-71). Hershey, PA: IGI Global.

Schrier, K. (2010). Preface. In K. Schrier & D. Gibson (Eds.), Ethics and Game Design: Teaching Values through Play. Hershey, PA: IGI Global.

Schrier, K. (2011). *An Investigation of Ethical Thinking in Role-Playing Video Games: A Case of* Fable III. Doctoral dissertation.

Schrier, K. (2011). Preface. In K. Schrier & D. Gibson (Eds.), *Designing Games for Ethics: Models, Techniques and Frameworks*. (pp. 57-71). Hershey, PA: IGI Global.

Schrier, K. (2012). Avatar gender and ethical thinking in *Fable III. Bulletin of Science, Technology, and Society, 32*, 375-383.

Schrier, K., & Kinzer, C. (2009). Using digital games to develop ethical teachers. In D. Gibson, & Y. Baek (Eds.), *Digital Simulations for Improving Education: Learning through Artificial Teaching Environments* (pp. 308-333). Hershey, PA: IGI Global.

Schrier, K., Diamond, J., & Langendoen, D. (2010). Using Mission US: For crown or colony? To develop historical empathy and nurture ethical thinking. In K. Schrier & D. Gibson (Eds.), *Ethics and Game Design: Teaching Values through Play* (pp. 255-273). Hershey, PA: IGI Global.

Schwartz, S. H. (1994), Are there universal aspects in the structure and contents of human values? *Journal of Social Issues, 50*: 19–45.

Schwartz, S. & Bilsky, W. (1990). Toward a theory of the universal content and structure of values: Extensions and cross-cultural replications. *Journal of Personality and Social Psychology, Vol 58*(5), May 1990, 878-891.

Shafer-Landau, R. (2010). *The fundamentals of ethics*. New York: Oxford University Press.

Sicart, M. (2005). The ethics of computer game design. Paper presented at DiGRA conference, Simon Fraser University, Vancouver.

Sicart, M. (2009). *Ethics and computer games*. Cambridge: MIT Press.

Sicart, M. (2013). *Beyond choices. The design of ethical gameplay*. Cambridge: The MIT Press

Simkins, D., & Steinkuehler, C. (2008). Critical ethical reasoning and role-play. *Games and Culture, 3*, 333-355.

Siyahhan, S., Barab, S. & James, C. (2011). Ethics of identity play in virtual spaces. *Journal of Interactive Learning Research, 22*(1), 111-138.

Smith, C. (2013). Depression Quest dev faces harassment after Steam submission. *The Escapist Magazine*. Accessed at: http://www.escapistmagazine.com/news/view/130525-Depression-Quest-Dev-Faces-Harassment-after-Steam-Submission

Stevenson, J. (2011). A framework for classification and criticism of ethical games. In K. Schrier & D. Gibson (Eds.), *Designing Games for Ethics: Models, Techniques and Frameworks*. (pp. 36-55). Hershey, PA: IGI Global.

Svelch, J. (2010). The good, the bad, and the player: The challenges to moral engagement in single-player avatar-based video games. In K. Schrier & D. Gibson (Eds.), *Ethics and Game Design: Teaching Values through Play* (pp. 52-68). Hershey, PA: IGI Global.

Tierney, N. L. (1994). Imagination and ethical ideals: Prospects for a unified philosophical and psychological understanding. Albany: State University of New York Press.

Zagal, J. (2013). *The videogame ethics reader*. San Diego, CA: Cognella.

Zagal, J. P. (2009). Ethically notable videogames; Moral dilemmas and gameplay. In Proceedings of the 2009 DiGRA conference (pp. 1-9) London, England: Digital Games Research Association. Retrieved from http://www.digra.org/dl/db/09287.13336.pdf

Zagal, J. P. (2011). Ethical reasoning and reflection as supported by single-player videogames. In K. Schrier & D. Gibson (Eds.), *Designing Games for Ethics: Models, Techniques and Frameworks* (pp. 19-35). Hershey, PA: IGI Global.

CHAPTER 9

Critical Thinking, 21st Century, and Creativity Skills

Teaching 21st Century, Executive-Functioning, and Creativity Skills with Popular Video Games and Apps

Randy Kulman, *LearningWorks for Kids, PeaceDale, Rhode Island, U.S.,*
randy@learningworksforkids.com
Teresa Slobuski, *Dr. Martin Luther King, Jr. Library, San Jose State University, San Jose, California,*
U.S., Teresa.Slobuski@sjsu.edu
Roy Seitsinger, *Westerly Public Schools, Westerly, Rhode Island, U.S.,*
rseitsinger@westerly.k12.ri.us

Key Summary Points

 21st century skills, including flexible thinking, collaborative communication skills, executive function and critical thinking skills, and digital literacy, will be necessary for education and jobs in the future.

 Video games and apps are an extremely powerful tool for teaching 21st century skills due to game mechanics that build in learning principles and their highly engaging nature.

 Games such as *Minecraft*, *Portal 2*, and a variety of casual video games have been demonstrated to teach skills, such as problem solving, processing efficiency, cognitive flexibility, and the 21st century skill of digital literacy.

Key Terms

21st century skills
Executive functioning
Creativity skills
Digital literacy
Common core state standards
Long-form games
Short-form games

Introduction

The skills needed for success in the future will go far beyond the content conventionally taught in U.S. schools. Success, today, and tomorrow, will require 21st century skills such as creativity, collaboration, executive functioning, and digital literacy (Trilling & Fadel, 2009). No longer will simple rote learning, memorization of facts, or training for traditional manufacturing, service, or agricultural jobs be adequate to prepare students for life and work in the future (*21st Century Skills and the Workplace, Microsoft, Pearson Report 2013*). Instead, 21st century skills defined by the capacity to think flexibly and innovatively (creativity); the aptitude to communicate with colleagues both face to face and digitally (collaboration); capability in planning, self-management, organization, time management, and critical thinking (executive functions); and the knowledge of how to use electronic media and tools (digital literacy) will become the core proficiencies for future success. The use of video games and apps has potential for encouraging the practice of creativity, collaboration, executive functions, and digital literacy.

Employers around the globe are looking for 21st century skills in their new hires to help them adjust to information-focused jobs that require problem solving, teamwork, the capacity to identify relevant facts, and organizational, planning, and efficiency skills. In 1990 the U.S. Department of Labor's Secretary's Commission on Achieving Necessary Skills report indicated that a variety of functional skills are needed to be successful at the modern workplace such as, resource management, social interaction, human and technology interaction, and affective skills (Kane, Berryman, Goslin & Meltzer, 1990). Educators, meanwhile, are rethinking how best to prepare children to meet these workforce needs by incorporating digital technologies and collaboration in the classroom.

In the U.S., the latest national education standards, the Common Core State Standards (CCSS) (National Governors Association Center for Best Practices (NGA Center) & Council of Chief State School Officers (CCSSO), 2010), attempt to meet these market demands by encouraging many of these skills along with more traditional academic content. Although concepts such as "teaching the whole child" and going beyond the fundamentals are not new in educational research, CCSS's national predecessor policy, No Child Left Behind (NCLB) (U.S. Department of Education, 2013), limited these educational aims through mandatory testing, which requires teachers to focus on content alone. For many educators, NCLB is seen as a stumbling block to teaching 21st century skills (Schoen & Fusarelli, 2008; Noddings, 2005). CCSS, however, integrates many 21st century skills through its standards on college and career readiness such as creativity, collaboration, and digital-technology use. Thus, as CCSS becomes integrated into classroom curricula, teachers have an opportunity to expand their teaching of these skills and many are finding that video games are one method to supplement the teaching of these skills.

In this chapter, we will consider 21st century skills as imperative to success during and after school. Rather than competing with the curriculum, 21st century skills can and should be integrated into the student experience. One of the more powerful ways of building 21st century skills is through the use of digital games and technologies, whether the content focus is on 21st century skills or not.

Key Frameworks

What are 21st century skills?

21st century skills are defined by the Partnership for 21st Century Skills (2009) as having three components:

1. **Learning and innovation skills,** which include creative thinking and problem solving and communication and collaboration. These skills are crucial to working in a group, developing new ideas, and analyzing and evaluating information.

2. **Life and career skills,** which encompass skills such as flexibility and adaptability; initiative and self-directed social and cross-cultural skills; productivity and accountability skills; and leadership and responsibility skills, many of which can also be described by the term executive functions. Executive functions are defined as brain-based cognitive skills that support self-management and critical thinking. Executive functions are based primarily in the prefrontal cortex of our brains and orchestrate various brain functions that integrate a person's perceptions, experiences, cognitions, and memories toward goal-directed behavior. These are identified by many experts as the key to academic and vocational success in the 21st century (Brown, 2013; Barkley, 2012). Executive functions include a set of related skills that help prioritize, regulate, and orchestrate an individual's thoughts and behaviors.

3. **Digital literacy skills,** which include understanding about digital information; being able to access information effectively; evaluating, analyzing, and using media; and being able to apply technology effectively. Proficiencies in being able to create media use technology for research, and competencies in using a variety of electronic forms of communication and networking tools are core digital literacy skills (Partnership for 21st Century Skills, 2009).

What are the Common Core State Standards?

The Common Core State Standards (CCSS) define the educational content and expectations of performance of students at all levels. The CCSS were developed with the recognition of the global nature of competition for jobs and the expectation of what workers need to know and be able to do. To prepare students for an increasingly competitive workforce, the CCSS are "staircased" in increasing complexity to guide students toward full readiness for college and career. To date 45 states, the District of Columbia, 4 territories, and the Department of Defense schools have adopted the CCSS based on these observations.

In drafting the CCSS, the Council of Chief State School Officers (CCSSO) and the National Governors Association Center for Best Practices (NGA Center) worked with a variety of stakeholders to develop standards that reflect the skills and experience necessary for American children to succeed in college and their careers. Not only does the CCSS cover what content is necessary for students to succeed, but it also recognizes the importance of a variety of 21st century skills throughout the standards. For example, the introduction to the CCSS for "English Language Arts & Literacy in History/Social

Studies, Science, and Technical Subjects" states that students who are college- and career-ready are able to "demonstrate independence," "respond to the varying demands of audience, task, purpose and discipline," "use technology and digital media strategically and capably," and "come to understand other perspectives and cultures" (NGA Center & CCSSO, 2010, p. 7), each of which is intimately tied to one or more 21st century skills. Throughout the standards there is additional emphasis on building students' ability with "flexible communication and collaboration," NGA Center & CCSSO, 2010, p. 8) a large piece of the 21st century skill puzzle. By using video games to teach skills such as collaboration and creativity teachers are able to provide students an opportunity not only to develop those skills, but also to increase their digital literacy skills.

Selecting Case Studies

Games are a particularly powerful tool for teaching 21st century skills because their reach extends beyond the classroom. Children ages eight to 18 spend an average of seven hours and 38 minutes per day using digital media (Rideout, Foehr, & Roberts, 2010), strongly suggesting that they are more than willing to play games and apps on their own as a part of homework or to pursue their own interests. Teachers are increasingly turning to a variety of types of games for their teaching. One of the common observations described by teachers who use games in the classroom is the level and sophistication of engaged discussion that takes place among classmates that leads to additional learning and insights (Cornally, 2012).

Selecting video games that can target specific skills and engender the type of engagement that encourages learning that goes beyond the classroom is one of the keys to game-based learning of 21st century skills. Both long- and short-form games can be implemented in the classroom to aid in teaching 21st century skills. Long-form games, which are more open-ended and may take place over many hours at home and school, can be used as a teaching tool. Examination of two long-form games, *Minecraft* and *Portal 2,* demonstrates how these types of games are being implemented in classrooms. Short-form games can be played within a single class period, and multiple games can be combined in a suite.

Case Study One: *Minecraft*

Minecraft is one of the most recognized and widely played games in the United States and counts 45 million people as having registered for the games (MinecraftEdu.com, n.d.). *Minecraft* is becoming a widely used game in many classrooms around the world due to the flexibility, ease of entry of the game, and mass appeal. *Minecraft* is an open-world game without specific goal. It has two major modes: survival, which requires players to acquire resources, maintain their health, and survive the night, and creative, which focuses on designing, constructing, and creating large projects. In addition to the standard version of *Minecraft* available through the developer, teachers have modified the game for better applicability in the classroom. Minecraftedu.com, developed by Joel Levin, a computer teacher, provides teachers with access to a customized *Minecraft* modification designed specifically for classroom use and has been used by more than 250,000 students to date (MinecraftEdu.com, n.d.).

While *Minecraft* does not contain specific curricula designed to teach 21st century skills, many of the classroom-based *Minecraft* projects are described as practicing executive-functioning, creativity, and collaboration skills (Levin, 2013) Rather than seeing *Minecraft* as being used for its 21st century skill building alone, Levin notes that many of the examples of *Minecraft* used in the classroom start off by being content driven and cover diverse topics such as Roman history, Newtonian physics, or mathematics. He described how the lesson plans generally start by focusing on a more traditional classroom objective such as understanding gravity, but that through playing *Minecraft* students frequently use a variety of 21st century skills such as innovation, creativity, and cognitive flexibility. Levin (2013) describes how student assignments often involve the division of tasks and time-management and collaboration skills. Learning how to access knowledge outside of the game to answer questions involves digital literacy skills. The skill of creativity is another necessary and important component of the world construction that takes place in *Minecraft*.

The use of *Minecraft* as an afterschool program is being planned at the Central Falls School District in Rhode Island by Michael St. Jean, the assistant superintendent of Central Falls Schools. St. Jean, who has written extensively about the powerful nature of *Minecraft* from his perspective as an educator and as the parent of a 13-year old-son who has embraced the game, describes *Minecraft*'s utility for teaching 21st century and problem-solving skills. He describes how the employment of *Minecraft* in the classroom is useful in teaching 21st century skills and the common core curriculum. He suggests that because the common core curriculum is based in part on project-based learning, *Minecraft* is an excellent opportunity for creativity, making and fixing mistakes, and conceptual understanding of materials. St. Jean also suggests that the computer skills necessary for becoming an expert at *Minecraft*, such as coding and modding, powerfully reinforce the digital literacy component of 21st century skills (St. Jean, 2013)

St. Jean further describes how *Minecraft* can be a great tool for teaching life and executive-functioning skills. He recounts that his son has announced that he wants being engineer or an architect and now notices the designs of buildings and is fascinated with books on historical architecture as a direct result of playing *Minecraft*. After seeing a similar potential after using *Minecraft* in a national competition on how to make a better future, a school in Sweden has added playing *Minecraft* as part of their compulsory curriculum. One teacher from the school stated that the students use *Minecraft* to "learn about city planning, environmental issues, getting things done, and even how to plan for the future" (Gee, 2013). Through the process of building *Minecraft* structures, students can learn skills and develop interests that will be important in meeting the needs of our collective future.

Key Findings

Video games, technology, and 21st century skills

Playing and using video games and technology can be strongly related to the development of 21st century skills. Gee (2007) identifies 36 "learning principles" that are built into good video games that can be leveraged as effective teaching tools. Many of Gee's learning principles, such as the active, critical learning principle; the multiple routes principle, and the probing principle parallel 21st century skills. Other studies describe how video games are excellent tools for teaching problem solving (Shaffer, 2006), strategic thinking (Adachi & Willoughby, 2013), cognitive flexibility (Green et al., 2012), and executive functions (Kulman et al., 2011). A comprehensive review of game-based learning found that video games could impact positively on problem-solving skills, motivation, and engagement, all of which support using these digital tools in teaching 21st century skills (NFER, 2013).

The use and mastery of technology as crucial for 21st century skills becomes evident as educators begin to define the components of these skills. Far more than simple digital literacy, engagement with video games, apps, and interactive digital media requires collaboration, critical thinking, adaptability, creativity, and decision-making skills. While primarily citing the use of the Internet and productivity tools, many educators now make the argument that video games can also be readily adapted for the teaching, development, and improvement of 21st century skills.

As 21st century skills are more deeply explored, many connections can be seen between the use of video games and digital technologies and the development of these important capacities. For example, many video games and digital technologies require learning and innovation skills such as critical thinking and problem solving, communicating and collaboration, and creativity and innovation for the user to be successful. Additionally, they do so in a manner in which high levels of motivation and sustained attention and effort are devoted to developing these skills. By capturing the attention of the users, these games are able to teach many of these skills through successful gameplay.

Many games require an array of problem solving, thinking, and planning skills such as *The Legend of Zelda* or the *Civilization* series. In *Legend of Zelda: Twilight Princess*, an action adventure game, players must learn to use planning skills when they buy items at shops and stock up on bombs and arrows to survive difficult dungeons to come. *Civilization*, a series of turn-based strategy games, requires players to choose where to place their energy in building new structures, improving existing ones, moving units, initiating negotiations, etc. to advance their civilizations' growth. Games such as *Legend of Zelda* and *Civilization* make players into critical thinkers by encouraging successful gamers to think many steps ahead.

Video games are increasingly integrating communication and collaboration as key components of play. Communication can be key to survival and a requirement for maximum success in massive multiplayer online role playing games (MMORPGs). In *World of Warcraft,* thousands of players stage raids to defeat particularly difficult dungeon challenges, which can include as many as 40 individuals working to defeat the same boss. Without advanced communication skills, collaborations of that size would not be possible in or out of the game world.

Creativity and innovation can frequently be seen in open video game platforms such as Scratch, a suite of interactive media creation tools from MIT or *Crayon Physics*, a puzzle game that requires users to create drawings that have realistic physics applied to solve the level. In addition to using creativity and innovation in gameplay, many gamers further practice using these skills in a variety of activities inspired by their play. Some gamers may continue to engage with a game by creating a website, contributing to a wiki, or participating in forums. Some games, particularly PC games, allow users to augment the game through a process known as modding. By writing their own parts of computer programs, gamers can develop custom maps, create a different interface, or visualize information otherwise unavailable to augment their gaming experience (Kow & Nardi, 2009; Brown, 2008). Modding allows gamers to be creative by altering a game as they see fit.

Life and career skills require the capacities for self-management, goal setting, decision-making, and adaptability. Although these skills are not often formally taught in the classroom, they remain important markers for success both in academics and in the workforce. By providing situational practice of these skills, many video games can benefit players outside of the game world.

By their very nature, video games and digital technologies require flexible thinking as problem-solving strategies change from one level to another. For example, in *Angry Birds*, structures are made from a variety of materials such as wood and metal, with unique layouts requiring the player to dramatically change strategies. An inflexible mind may attempt to break through metal as one can with wood structures, but will ultimately be unsuccessful in completing the level. Recognizing the differences between various situations and adapting play techniques accordingly is key to winning in Angry Birds and mirrors the flexibility required for adapting to real life situations.

Working independently and setting goals to maximize productivity are important parts of many complex video games. In the *Metal Gear Solid*, an action adventure stealth game, players normally move through the game attempting to attract minimal attention while completing their quests. The player, however, can determine what that means in a given situation, whether it means sneaking past to avoid being seen or killing guards as quickly as possible. Newer releases of the series have recognized the fun and challenging nature of "self rule" in the games and now provide additional achievements for different types of play, for example completing the game without killing enemies by choosing to tranquilize or avoid them instead.

Leadership and responsibility skills are noteworthy in many MMO games. These games often include guild or party structures where players work together to better everyone's play experience. To manage resources and be successful in play with larger groups, one or more players must take on a leadership role. Additionally, by agreeing to play in a party or be part of a guild, players agree to be responsible for holding their weight for the team. This may be in the form of collecting resources to prepare for a large battle or keeping an eye on other players during battle. Reeves (2008) conducted a study in which it was found that playing *World of Warcraft* was very useful for developing leadership skills such as visioning, sense-making, relating, and inventing that are crucial to business. Given the number of elements an advanced *World of Warcraft* player needs to balance, it is unsurprising to see those skills transfer into the real world.

Digital literacy skills are core requirements for expertise with video games and use of other digital media. As video gamers are digital in nature, any time spent playing can help increase a gamer's digital literacy skills and comfort with digital technologies. Gaming can additionally inspire players to interact with various digital technologies to support, augment, or share their gaming experience.

In many families, the expert at learning how to use a new cell phone, connect the cable box, or get the Internet back online is the video gamer. A multi-system gamer can be equally comfortable using a computer, console, or mobile device for their gameplay. Besides using the devices for actual play, a gamer may be responsible for setting up the hardware and/or software of the systems to start playing. Although knowing how to properly connect a new computer may not seem like an impressive feat, as digital technologies continue to be more integrated into our everyday experience, comfort with setting up and troubleshooting new technologies is an essential part to basic digital literacy.

Outside of active gameplay, many avid gamers are continuing to develop their digital literacy skills in affinity groups. Affinity groups are defined by Gee (2004) as places of informal learning where "newbies and masters and everyone else" (p. 85) all interact around their common interest, which could be a video game, television show, novel, etc. These affinity groups allow fans from diverse backgrounds to come together and discuss, learn, and share about their interest. Communities like this can not only feed into the social skills of an individual, but also help to increase ease of digital technology use. Learning to leverage the learning experiences occurring in these affinity groups will be key to harnessing the full educational potential of video games (Steinkuehler, 2004).

Earlier in Internet history, gamer interaction may have been limited to searches for cheat codes or walkthroughs to assist in completing difficult or tedious elements of gameplay. Today, increasing numbers of gamers are creating original content to share with the world including wiki editing, forum participation, and making "let's play" videos to demonstrate how they play their favorite video games.

This original content can then be used by fellow gamers and may inspire them to create their own original content. By participating in an ever-growing digital culture of gaming, gamers not only learn how to use technology to play games, but also learn how to use it to communicate with others, express themselves, and otherwise navigate the digital landscape.

Innovation, life and career, and digital literacy skills are vitally important for future jobs and must be incorporated into education in the 21st century. There is a wealth of research (Galinsky, 2010; Goldberg, 2001) showing that mastering 21st century skills, defined more broadly with terms such as "executive-functioning skills" (Diamond, 2007) and "learning skills" (McClelland, 2007), can be more important for academic learning than direct teaching of the same academic subjects. Many studies indicate that learning critical-thinking skills and creativity at a young age results in greater future academic achievement than if those same students were taught with a traditional curriculum (Willoughby et al., 2012; Diamond, 2012). The research shows that some of the time and energy devoted to instructing students in math and language skills would be better spent in teaching 21st century executive functioning, critical thinking, and creativity skills. Additionally, teaching academic and problem solving skills through the use of video games and other digital media has been repeatedly demonstrated (Clarfield & Stoner, 2005; Ota & DuPaul, 2002) to be a more powerful and engaging learning tool than what is used in the traditional classroom.

Case Study Two: *Portal 2*

Another commercial video game gaining adoption in classrooms for a variety of uses is Valve Corporation's *Portal 2*. Unlike *Minecraft*, normal play in *Portal 2* has clearly-defined goals for the players. Throughout the game, players are presented with rooms that require players to solve the puzzle to move forward. These puzzles generally involve use of the portal gun, a gun-like apparatus that creates portals between various wall/floor/ceiling surfaces, as well as other items in the environment, and require cunning and creativity to be successful. The game has garnered attention from educators not only for the innovative gameplay, but also for the robust puzzle maker, which furthers the possibilities for educational use by allowing individuals to design custom levels. Additional support for educators interested in using Portal 2 can be found through the *Steam for Schools Teach with Portals* program (*Teach with Portals*, 2013).

As essentially a puzzle game, *Portal 2* requires players to meet each puzzle with sharp critical thinking skills, creativity, and cognitive flexibility. As players move through campaign gameplay, an increasing number of elements become necessary for puzzle solving, such as propulsion gel, turret attackers, and a thermal discouragement beam. Players must use the knowledge they have gained from previous puzzles as these elements are reused throughout the levels while remaining flexible enough to recognize new opportunities. In addition to single-player mode, *Portal 2* also features a cooperative-campaign mode in which two players must coordinate their actions and resources to successfully complete more complicated puzzles than they experienced in a single player. Throughout both the campaign modes players continuously practice many 21st century skills while enjoying the immersive environment of *Portal 2*.

The Perpetual Testing Initiative, a post-release DLC (downloadable content) for *Portal 2*, has further expanded the educational potential of *Portal 2*. The DLC includes a puzzle maker, which allows gamers to build their own puzzles using all of the *Portal 2* elements. *Portal 2*'s level editor has provided an opportunity for deeper levels of learning using *Portal 2*'s framework by allowing teachers and students to develop levels and challenges using the *Portal* framework. Many of the puzzles built for educational purposes have a content-specific focus, such as teaching a lesson about physics. The nature of the game, however, will always require players to think critically and creatively to solve the puzzle. In addition to creating levels for one's own enjoyment, the Perpetual Testing Initiative allows players to share their creations with others, which allows the spread of educational uses of *Portal 2*.

Due to the ease of entry into puzzle making with *Portal 2*'s Perpetual Testing Initiative, teachers quickly appropriated the game for educational use. Recognizing the educational potential, the Valve Corporation created an educational game distribution unit, Steam for Schools, and began promoting the educational use of *Portal 2* through *Teach with Portals*. On the *Teach with Portals* website, instructors can see example lesson plans and communicate with other educators through the forum and wiki. The website provides *Portal 2*-using instructors with a space of their own where they can form an affinity group to discuss and share how they teach with *Portal 2*. Additionally, *Steam for Schools* provides free and cheap game access for teachers to use in their class (Teach with *Portals*, 2013), which helps lower one of the largest barriers to using commercial games.

Assessment Considerations

Given the impending changes to educational needs, how to properly assess 21st century skills are at the forefront of many educators' minds. As these are skills of practice rather than content knowledge, they can be difficult to quantify or measure reliably. Given the time required to accurately administer and grade assessments of these skills, mass adoption of any one assessment is unlikely due to problems in scaling. In the future, video games could be used as a means to assess 21st century skills. By requiring use of these skills to successfully complete a particular level or challenge, the game may serve as both the teacher and assessor of these skills. Currently, *River City*, an educational game designed for middle school science, is a working example of simultaneous teaching and assessing (Silva, 2009). The best methods of reporting to integrate into varied classroom experiences, however, are still relatively early in development.

While educators wait for technology to catch up, a variety of standardized tests already exist that can be used to measure students' 21st century skills. Several tests attempt to measure more than one of the 21st century skills defined earlier in this chapter. For example, the College Work Readiness Assessment

(CWRA) is a 90-minute exam intended to test how students manage a real-world dilemma, however it is not focused on individual student achievements, but is a tool for class or school improvement (Silva, 2009). The International Society for Technology in Education (ISTE) has developed a series of standards for students that include all of the previously discussed 21st century skills (ISTE, 2012). Although primarily for an undergraduate student audience, the Association of American Colleges and Universities (AAC&U) VALUE rubrics can be useful for examining a variety of skills. Rubrics that cover 21st century skills from AAC&U include: creative thinking, oral communication, written communication, critical thinking, and problem solving (AAC&U, 2014). The iSkills test combines critical thinking with technology by requiring test takers to perform scenario-based tasks using information provided in a digital format (Educational Testing Service, 2014).

This chapter cannot provide a comprehensive listing, but a variety of tests or rubrics are widely available that attempt to measure specific elements within the umbrella of 21st century skills, including (in no particular order): Torrance Tests of Creative Thinking (TTCT) (Scholastic Testing Service, 2013), California Critical Thinking Skills Test (CCTST) (Insight Assessment, 2013), Cornell Critical Thinking Tests (Critical Thinking Co., 2014), and Watson-Glaser Critical Thinking Test (Pearson Education, 2012).

Given the difficulty and cost of assessing many 21st century skills on a large scale, institutions or individual teachers may choose to develop their own criteria for measuring these skills. Creating rubrics for project assessment that include measurement of 21st century skills is one method to help students recognize the importance of 21st century skills in their success and allow teachers to understand where their students are on work/life skills. Checklists, learning contracts, or student reflections are additional methods for teachers to assess 21st century skills and emphasize the importance of their development in these areas to students. Each of these methods are quite time consuming, however, and with increasingly poor teacher to student ratios in many of our school systems, the feasibility for complete assessment of these skills in the majority of classrooms is minimal (Greenstein, 2012).

Future Plans

Research into the impact of game-based learning and behavior modification is in its infancy, and its potential is only just now being realized. Both long-form and short-form games can have their place in the classroom, but questions remain regarding how to maximize their usefulness. Researchers will need to answer questions such as, "How long should children play games?" "How can they best be integrated into a classroom curriculum?" "Are there limits to what can be transferred via game-based learning?" and more before the mass adoption of games can occur in K-12 classrooms. Furthermore, researchers need to further investigate the measurement of 21st century skills, especially as they relate to gameplay, to maximize efficiency in this arena.

Whether at school or at work individuals need to have the necessary 21st century skills to contribute and succeed. Creating new classroom strategies that support growth in creativity, collaboration, executive functioning, and digital literacy is the charge of parents, educators, and specialized student support staff.

Digital tools and gaming will be a prominent feature as schools reshape the methods and means of classroom instruction and use standards-based reforms to articulate curriculum and instruction in the 21st century. The ubiquitous nature of cloud-based smart tools allows schools to set aside the physical limitations of place, time, textbooks, and learning labs in favor of anywhere/anytime learning strategies, which creates opportunities for game-based learning as homework, during the bus ride to school, and as collaborative efforts from the comfort of a student's home. These types of strategies will enhance the acquisition of content and the growth of critical thinking skills, ultimately increasing the capacity of individuals and entire systems in the name of effective learning experiences. The myriad technological and content-specific curricula that embed gaming opportunities allow learning through gaming to become a permanent, possibly even dominant, component of building skills and knowledge.

Case Study Three: Short-Form Games

Given the demands of achieving the common core standards in the classroom, it can be difficult to have the dozens, if not hundreds of hours needed to use a game such as *Minecraft* or *Portal 2* to teach 21st century and executive function skills in a 50-minute class period. Fortunately, many short-form or casual games can be powerful tools for the practice and acquisition of these skills. Short-form games can have the advantage of being more targeted toward the development of a particular skill (Squire, 2008) and for being useful over the course of one-to-two classroom sessions. The Cooney Foundation strongly encourages schools to consider the use of short-form games for classroom teaching, as "collections of short-form games can be particularly attractive to schools because they have the ability to fit well into the current K-12 classroom structure and are easier to align to standards" (Richards et al., 2013).

Emerging research (Kulman et al., 2011; Klingberg, 2010; Baniqued et al., 2013) suggests that the targeted use of short-form games such as *Bloxorz, Silversphere*, and *Blobber* can improve skills such as problem solving, processing efficiency, working memory, and cognitive flexibility. While there are limited classroom studies, pilot research (Kulman et al., 2012) suggests a number of strategies for using casual, short-form games for classroom teaching of 21st century and executive skills. These strategies include:

1. Engaging in warm-up activities that practice and discuss the importance of the skill to be used in the game;
2. Demonstrating identification and reflection upon the skill through modeling the first part of the game for the class;
3. Encouraging teamwork and collaboration to overcome frustration of getting stuck on challenging levels;
4. Setting specific and achievable goals for gameplay rather than simply playing for a specified amount of time; and
5. Supporting engaging, high-level connection and generalization activities at the conclusion of gameplay.

There are many advantages to using short-form games for teaching 21st century skills in the classroom. Because they are shorter, more defined, and less immersive, students will have the time and inclination to discuss their strategies and thinking processes while using these games. The large number of available games facilitates them being more readily tailored toward teaching specific skills. Due to the variety of short-form games, they are more readily modifiable for an individual student's interest and skill levels. Short-form games can be completed in a classroom period, and because most of them are freely available on the Internet or as apps on a tablet device, they can be practiced outside of the classroom as "homework." Once a number of short-form games are identified as practicing the same skill, others can be assigned as homework to reinforce and generalize the skills. This type of repetition with different games has been demonstrated to improve the transfer of game-based skills to the real world (Mackey et al., 2011).

Best Practices

Successfully utilizing games and apps in the classroom to teach 21st century, executive functioning, and creativity skills requires that educators familiarize themselves with some of the basic literature on game-based learning. It is also necessary that games and apps be integrated into classroom goals so there is a clear rationale for the use of these technologies. While teachers do not have to be experts in playing the individual games, they should have some knowledge about game mechanics and how a particular game can be used to practice a skill. Perhaps more important is teacher knowledge that helps to generalize game-based learning into effective classroom learning. While classroom use of video games and apps is in earliest stages, there are a number of promising tools to help teachers select appropriate games, have a curriculum for using those games, and connect these games to larger academic and learning goals.

Resources

Research Labs

The Education Arcade
GlassLab
Partnership for 21st Century Skills (P21)

Researchers

Eric Klopfer
Scot Osterweil
Jennifer Grogg
Jason Haas
James Paul Gee

Websites

The Learning Games Network (LGN) (http://www.learninggamesnetwork.org/)
LearningWorks for Kids (LWK)(www.learningworksforkids.com)
Common Sense Media (www.commonsensemedia.org)
Graphite (by Common Sense Media) (http://www.graphite.org/)
The Partnership for 21st Century Skills (http://www.p21.org/)
Teach with Portals (http://www.teachwithportals.com/)
MinecraftEdu (http://minecraftedu.com)

Games

Angry Birds
Blobber
Bloxorz
Civilization
Crayon Physics (http://www.crayonphysics.com/)
Legend of Zelda: Twilight Princess
Metal Gear Solid
Mincecraft (https://minecraft.net/)
Portal 2 (http://www.thinkwithportals.com/)
Silversphere
World of Warcraft

References

Adachi, P., & Willoughby, T. (2013). More than just fun and games: The longitudinal relationships between strategic video games, self-reported problem solving skills, and academic grades. *Journal of Youth and Adolescence, 42*(7), 1041-1052.

Association of American Colleges and Universities (AAC&U). (2014). *VALUE: Valid Assessment of Learning in Undergraduate Education*. Retrieved from http://www.aacu.org/value/rubrics/.

Baniqued, P., DeSouza, S., Hyunkyu, L., Severson, J., Voss,M., Salthouse, T., Chandramallika, B., and Kramer, A. (2013). Selling points: *What cognitive abilities are tapped by casual video games? Acta Psychologica, 142,* 74–86.

Barkley, R. A. (2012). *Executive functions: What they are, how they work, and why they evolved.* New York, NY: Guilford Press.

Brown, H. J. (2008). Modding, education, and art. In *Videogames and education* (pp. 155-170). New York: ME Sharpe.

Brown, T. E. (2013). *A new understanding of ADHD in children and adults executive function impairments.* New York, NY: Routledge.

Clarfield, J., & Stoner, G. (2005). The effects of computerized reading instruction on the academic performance of students identified with ADHD. *School Psychology Review, 34*(2), 246-254.

Cornally, S. (2012, November 30). Video games in the stem classroom. Edutopia. Retrieved September 2013, from http://www.edutopia.org/blog/video-games-in-STEM-classroom-shawn-cornally.

Critical Thinking Co. (2014) *Cornell Critical Thinking Tests*. Retrieved from http://www.criticalthinking.com/cornell-critical-thinking-tests.html.

Diamond, A. (2012). Activities and programs that improve children's executive functions. *Current Directions in Psychological Science, 21*(5), 335-341.

Diamond, A., Barnett, S. W., Thomas, J., Munro, S. (2007). Preschool program improves cognitive control. *Science, 318*(5855), 1387-1388.

Educational Testing Service. (2014) The iSkills™ Assessment. Retrieved from https://www.ets.org/iskills/about.

Galinsky, E. (2010). *Mind in the making: The seven essential life skills every child needs.* New York, NY: Harper Collins.

Gee, J. P. (2004). *Situated language and learning: A critique of traditional schooling.* New York, NY: Routledge.

Gee, J. P. (2007). *What video games have to teach us about learning and literacy* (2nd ed.). New York, NY: Palgrave Macmillan.

Gee, O. (2013). Swedish school makes Minecraft a must. *The Local.* Retrieved September 2013, from http://www.thelocal.se/45514/20130109/#.UPPklGdZO2q.

Goldberg, E. (2001). *The executive brain: Frontal lobes and the civilized mind.* New York, NY: The Oxford University Press.

Green, C. S., Sugarman, M. A., Medford, K., Klobusicky, E., & Bavelier, D. (2012). The effect of action video game experience on task-switching. *Computers in Human Behavior, 28*(3), 984-994.

Greenstein, L. (2012) Beyond the core: Assessing authentic 21st century skills. *Principal Leadership, 13*(4), 36-42.

Insight Assessment. (2013) *California Critical Thinking Skills Test (CCTST).* Retrieved from http://www.insightassessment.com/Products/Products-Summary/Critical-Thinking-Skills-Tests/California-Critical-Thinking-Skills-Test-CCTST.

International Society for Technology in Education. (2012) ISTE and the ISTE Standards. Retrieved January 2014 from http://www.iste.org/standards.

Kane, M., Berryman, S., Goslin, D., & Meltzer, A. (1990). *The Secretary's Commission on Achieving Necessary Skills: Identifying and describing the skills required by work.* United States Department of Labor. Retrieved September 2013, from http://wdr.doleta.gov/SCANS/idsrw/idsrw.pdf.

Kow, Y.M. & Nardi, B. (2009) Culture and creativity: World of Warcraft modding in China and the US. In W. S. Brainbridge (Ed.), *Online Worlds : Convergence of the real and the virtual* (pp. 21-42). London, UK: Springer-Verlag.

Kulman, I., Stoner, G., Ruffolo, L., Marshall, S., Slater, J., Dyl, A., and Cheng, A. (2010). Teaching executive functions, self-management, and values through popular video-game play. In Schrier, K. and Gibson, D. (Eds), *Designing games for ethics: Models, techniques and frameworks.* Hershey PA: IGI Global.

Mackey, A. P., Hill, S. S., Stone, S. I., & Bunge, S. A. (2011). Differential effects of reasoning and speed training in children. *Developmental Science, 14*(3), 582–590.

McClelland, M. M., Cameron, C. E., Connor, C .M., Farris, C .L., Jewkes, A. M., Morrison, F. J. (2007). Links between behavioral regulation and preschoolers' literacy, vocabulary, and math skills. *Developmental Psychology, 43*, 947-959.

TeacherGaming, LLC. (n.d.) *MinecraftEdu.com: Bringing Minecraft to the classroom.* Retrieved September 2013, from http://minecraftedu.com/.

National Governors Association Center for Best Practices & Council of Chief State School Officers. (2010). *Common core state standards: English language arts standards.* Retrieved September 2013, from http://www.corestandards.org/the-standard.

Noddings, N. (2005). What does it mean to educate the WHOLE CHILD? *Educational Leadership 63*(1), 8-13.

Ota, K. R., & DuPaul, G. J. (2002). Task engagement and mathematics performance in children with attention-deficit hyperactivity disorder: Effects of supplemental computer instruction. *School Psychology Quarterly, 17*(3), 242-257.

Pearson education. (2012) *Watson-Glaser Critical Thinking Test.* Retrieved from http://www.thinkwatson.com/assessments/watson-glaser.

Perrotta, C., Featherstone, G., Aston, H., & Houghton, E. (2013). *Game-based learning: Latest evidence and future directions* (NFER Research Programme: Innovation in Education). Slough, Berkshire: National Foundation for Educational Research.

Reeves, B., Malone, T. W., & O'Driscoll, T. (2008). Leadership's online labs. *Harvard Business Review.* Retrieved September 13, 2013, from http://sm.avito.nl/wp-content/uploads/2013/02/Reeves-B.-T.-Malone-T.W.-O%E2%80%99Driscole-2008-Leadership%E2%80%99s-online-labs-Harvard-business-review-vol.-86-no.-5.pdf.

Rideout, V. J., Foehr, U. G., & Roberts, D. F. (2010, January). Generation M2: Media in the lives of 8- to 18-Year-Olds. *The Henry J. Kaiser Family Foundation.* Retrieved September 27, 2013, from http://kaiserfamilyfoundation.files.wordpress.com/2013/04/8010.pdf.

Schoen, L. & Fusarelli, L. D. (2008). Innovation, NCLB, and the fear factor: The challenge of leading 21st-century schools in an era of accountability. *Educational Policy, 22*(1), 181-203.

Scholastic Testing Service (STS). (2013) *Torrance Tests of Creative Thinking (TTCT).* Retrieved from http://www.ststesting.com/ngifted.html.

Shaffer, D.W. (2006). *How computer games help children learn.* New York, NY: Palgrave Macmillan.

Silva, E. (2009). Measuring skills for 21st-century learning. *Phi Delta Kappan, 90*(9),630-634.

Squire, K. (2008). Open-ended video games: A model for developing learning for the interactive age. In Katie Salen (Ed.), *The ecology of games: Connecting youth, games, and learning* (pp. 167-198). Cambridge, MA: MIT Press.

St. Jean, M. (2013, February 10). 21st century skills, gamification, and Minecraft. *Think (Ed + Tech).* Retrieved September 2013, from http://thinkedtech.blogspot.com/2013/02/21st-century-skills-gamification-and_10.html?q=21st+century+skills

Steinkuehler, C. A. (2004). Learning in massively multiplayer online games. In *Proceedings of the 6th international conference on learning sciences* (pp. 521-528). International Society of the Learning Sciences.

Valve Corporation. (2013). *Teach with portals.* Retrieved September 2013, from http://www.teachwithportals.com/.

The Partnership for 21st Century Skills. (n.d.). Retrieved September 13, 2013, from http://www.p21.org/.

Trilling, B., & Fadel, C. (2009). *21st century skills: learning for life in our times.* San Francisco, CA: Jossey-Bass.

U.S. Department of Education. (2013). *No child left behind.* Retrieved from http://www2.ed.gov/nclb/landing.jhtml

Thoughtful learning. (n.d) *What are 21st century skills?* Retrieved September 13, 2013, from http://www.thoughtfullearning.com/resources/what-are-21st-century-skills.

Willoughby, M., Wirth, R. J., & Blair, C. (2012). Executive function in early childhood: Longitudinal measurement invariance and developmental change. *Psychological Assessment, 24*(2), 418-431.

SECTION TWO

Design Considerations

CHAPTER 10

Methods of Design

An Overview of Game Design Techniques

Katrin Becker, *Mink Hollow Media and Mount Royal University, Calgary, Alberta, Canada,*
becker.minkhollow@gmail.com
Jim Parker, *University of Calgary and Mink Hollow Media, Calgary, Alberta, Canada,*
parker@minkhollow.ca

Key Summary Points

1 The design of games for learning requires knowledge of game design and of instructional design. One cannot merely be layer on top of the other.

2 A learning game must be designed to meet pre-specified learning objectives.

3 Games have specific characteristics that require specific design skills: they are entertaining as well as instructional, interactive, visually appealing, and often replayable.

Key Terms

Edutainment
Design
Models
Instructional design
Playtesting
Rapid prototyping
Instructional objectives

Introduction

Design is an applied endeavor: to design something one must have extensive knowledge of the thing being designed. Design is also a complex activity and while each design discipline shares some aspect with most other design disciplines, each also has important distinctions. It is simply not possible to be an expert designer in the general sense. Knowing how to design children's clothing or buildings does not qualify one to design theater sets or costumes, although that knowledge may well help in some situations. While digital games arguably share elements with other kinds of digital objects as well as with traditional games (such as board and card games), neither software designers nor traditional game designers are necessarily equipped to design digital games, although, just as in the previous example, that knowledge may well help.

To complicate matters further, designing a game for learning is not simply a matter of designing a game and adding some learning elements. Designing games for learning is a goal-driven activity. When we design a game for learning, we obviously have some learning goal in mind, such as learning about Mendelian genetics, for example.

Most design disciplines have various models or theories intended to help in the design process, and several of the ones for designing games are presented in this chapter. Simply knowing a design model, however, is usually insufficient preparation unless you also have experience actually building that thing, or at the very least using it. Becoming skilled at design always requires hands-on experience. When designing games for learning, this means that designers must play games as well as design them.

Finally, games for learning combine at least two distinct design disciplines: game design and instructional design, and some kinds of games also include aspects of simulation, which necessitates the involvement of a third design discipline, namely simulation design (Becker & Parker, 2011). The approaches taken for each can be very different so combining them is not straightforward, as will be seen. This chapter will examine some of the issues facing designers of games for learning and will highlight and discuss several models currently used to design these games.

Designing a game

The design of a digital game involves at least two design disciplines: game design and software design (i.e., knowledge of programming, the design of computer algorithms, and simulation design) and while many design models can be found for software (Budgen, 2003), far fewer exist for game design. Salen & Zimmerman's (2004) *Rules of Play* and Fullerton's *Game Design Workshop* (2008) approach the game design process, but do not include a concise design model. According to Fullerton, games are formal systems that include a variety of elements, including, but not limited to: objectives, procedures, rules, resources, boundaries, conflicts, and dramatic elements.

In addition to being games, digital games are also software systems, and are made up of computer algorithms. Therefore, we would expect a game design model to include some elements of software design.

Designing instruction

Instructional design is the practice of designing and creating instructional interventions and the development of models and frameworks to support the process of instructional design is common. Even those who advocate for the most structured approaches will admit that such models are often best suited as a support system for practitioners new to the field. Many experts still do make use of these models, but when they do, they often use them as rough guides, rather than prescriptions (Kenny, Zhang, Schwier, & Campbell, 2005).

In instructional design, there are well-known models that promote a fairly linear approach to design, such as Gagné's Nine Events of Instruction (Gagné, Briggs, & Wager, 1992), while others suggest more of an iterative approach (Dick, Carey, & Carey, 2001), and still others advocate an agile one (Piskurich, 2000). Briefly, Gagné's Nine Events of Instruction are: 1) Gaining Attention, 2) Informing Learners of the Objective, 3) Stimulating Recall, 4) Presenting the Stimulus, 5) Providing Learning Guidance, 6) Eliciting Performance, 7) Providing Feedback, 8) Assessing Performance, and 9) Enhancing Retention and Transfer. Many instructional design models have similar elements and the well-known ADDIE template (see Figure 1) that often forms the basis for these models (Molenda, 2003) still serves as a reasonable common denominator for all. The acronym became popular much later than the process itself (Branson, Rayner, & Cox, 1975) and in spite of being overly simplified, it remains a very popular model in professional training and should in some form be included in any design framework intended to support the design of a game for learning.

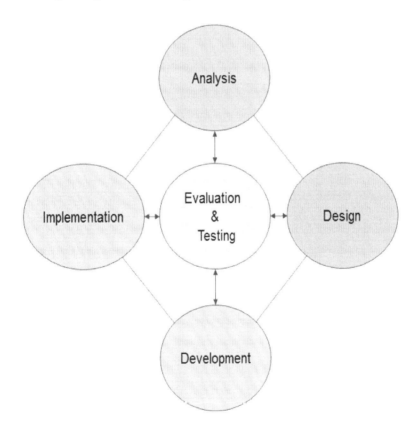

Figure 1. The ADDIE Instructional Design Model

The five parts of the ADDIE model are outlined below:

1. **Analysis**: The process for defining desired outcomes.
2. **Design:** The process of determining how desired outcomes are to be accomplished based on supporting system(s) needed, required resources, timetable, and budget.
3. **Development:** The process of establishing requisite system(s) and acquiring needed resources to attain desired outcomes.
4. **Implementation:** The process of implementing design and development plans within the real-world environment.
5. **Evaluation:** The process of measuring the effectiveness and efficiency of the implemented system and using collected data as opportunities for improvement in closing gaps between actual and desired outcomes.

What's important in a game for learning?

Serious games are games designed for purposes other than, or in addition to entertainment. Serious games, of which educational games are a subset, are distinct from traditional entertainment games in a number of ways, and these differences influence design. For instance, in a traditional game the key question is "Is it fun?" Fun is an ill-defined characteristic and is hard to design for, but it is a key motivator in the purchase and evaluation of a game. In an educational game fun is important too, but instead of relating to game sales, it concerns the delivery of the learning goals. An educational game that is fun will be played voluntarily and for a longer time, allowing longer exposure to the educational material being presented.

The set of learning objectives is lacking in a traditional game, but must be first and foremost present in an educational one. They must guide the design by providing an initial framework within which the game is played. For example, a game that teaches about sea life is likely to take place on a beach or under water. The learning objectives also provide a set of underlying assumptions that cannot be violated. The previously mentioned game about sea life must portray an accurate representation of the facts with respect to the organisms seen within the game. We can play fast and loose with other aspects of the game, though: players might be able to breathe the underwater or use hypothetical vehicles. Table 1 provides a summary of the key differences between commercial games and serious games.

Table 1. Commercial vs. Serious Games

Differences	Commercial Game Design	Serious Game Design
Concept Catalyst	Core Amusement	Performance or Knowledge Gap
Key Question	Is it fun?	Does it meet learning objectives?
Focus	Player Experience (the "how")	Content / Message (the "what")
Content / Method	Method is primary (content may be irrelevant)	Method secondary to content (game as receptacle?)
Vantage Point	Entertainment and Software Engineering	Special Interest Group (SIG) (e.g., medicine, military, social change)
Fidelity	Self-consistent, otherwise irrelevant	Faithfulness to message essential
Credentials	Industry	SIG (and industry)

Learning game design—what do we need?

Instructional designers say all we need is instructional design (Gunter, Kenny, & Vick, 2006); game designers say all we need is game design—even Gee implies this (Gee, 2003). The ongoing battle between these two groups, while softening, is still evident in the literature. Instructional designers claim that game designers suck all the learning out of games and game designers claim the other side is to blame: that instructional designers suck all the fun out of games (McDowell, Cannon-Bowers, & Prensky, 2005). There is truth to all four claims:

1. **"Instructional Design (ID) is all we need."** There is a well-researched body of knowledge in ID on what works and how to design instruction (Ely & Plomp, 1996).
2. **"Game design is all we need."** Many commercial games already do an excellent job of teaching players what they need to know to win the game (Becker, 2008b).
3. **"Game designers suck all the learning out of games."** Game designers without experience in education make educational games that are hollow—they end up taking their current favorite game and effectively "skinning" it with an educational veneer ("edufication") (Becker, 2008a).
4. **"Instructional designers suck all the fun out of games."** Instructional designers without game experience also skin, but they do it the other way around—they wrap a game around some instruction. Edutainment could be gamification at its worst. (Van Eck, 2011).

The solution is the development of approaches that are a true synergy of both instructional design and of game design (see Figure 2).

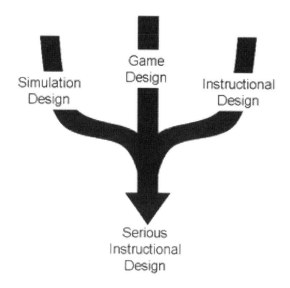

Figure 2. Serious instructional design (ID)

Case Study One: *Pavlov's Dog*

As a good example of an educational game, consider *Pavlov's Dog*. This game is quite clear about the educational objectives: to answer the questions "What's a conditioned reflex?", "What's a stimulus?", and "How can you learn a conditioned reflex?" The game's object is to train Pavlov's dog to respond to a signal that it will associate with being fed, just as in the scientific tale.

When the game begins, a cartoon dog is seen sleeping beside a food dish. On the left of the screen are food items that can be dragged into the dish using the mouse, such as bananas, drumsticks, and hot dogs. Along the bottom of the screen are icons representing three things that can make a sound: a horn, a drum, and a bell. The player needs to condition the dog to one of the sounds by clicking on a sound maker, thereby playing a relevant sound and waking the dog. Then, the player must quickly drag a food item into the dish. The dog will not eat the bananas, but gobbles up any of the other items, then goes back to sleep. After three repetitions of this process, the sound will result in the dog waking up and salivating without the food being present. When this occurs, the player wins, and the dog appears holding a diploma. The other sounds simply wake the dog. Feeding the dog without the sound has no effect, other than perhaps making the dog fat.

The game has a selection of educational material associated with it, about conditioned responses, Pavlov himself, and the Nobel Prize that Pavlov won in 1904. The art is cartoon style, which is appropriate, and the sounds are simple and to the point. There is no music. A key to this style of game is to focus on one educational issue, which this game does well.

Key Frameworks

There is a dearth of design models for educational game design. Instead, what is most commonly found are guidelines or design issues, which amount to things that should be kept in mind while designing such a game. These can be useful, but assume that one already knows how to design a game, and that an educational game is a game with extra conditions and content.

For example, Aldrich (2004) suggested four important criteria to be considered when designing educational simulations:

1. Scenarios must be authentic and relevant.
2. Scenarios should be compelling for the students. For example, student age and background must be considered.
3. Scenarios should offer many choices.
4. Scenarios should be replayable. The implication is that there will be some degree of variation or randomness in the decisions that the game makes.

One can see how to use these ideas in an educational game at the design level, but they are guidelines to use while designing, not a design strategy per se. There are too many of these guidelines to list all of them, but some are fundamental. If the game is to be used in a classroom then it is obviously a good idea to take into account that environment, and to ask teachers for their input. Kirriemuir (2005) did just that, and summarized the following requirements based on speaking with teachers:

1. The game should come with classroom plans and examples, preferably tested by teachers. Teachers work very hard and have little time to try to figure out how to use a game in a classroom, especially if the designers have not provided assistance.
2. The game should be able to be started at a point useful to the teacher. Daily lessons can begin in many different ways and can end in random places. Teachers need to be able to pick up where they left off. They also need to be able to assign homework or in-class tasks.
3. Games should be "light," in that long expositions, videos, and narrations should be kept to a minimum or removed altogether.
4. The game must be accurate in the process and facts it conveys, and should avoid political or scientific controversy. A game can remove the uninteresting parts of a simulation if they are not essential. For example, time can be speeded up.

In fact, Kirriemuir was discussing how to use pre-existing games (called commercial off-the-shelf games) in a classroom, but the rules can apply to a game being designed for the purpose. The guidelines are those that any instructional designer would probably know, and so a key lesson is to include instructional designers on the development team at an early stage—at the very beginning, if possible.

Four Frameworks

Chris Crawford's Game Design Model

One of the earliest game design models published is that of Chris Crawford, a game designer perhaps best known for his game *Balance of Power* (1985). In his 1982 book, *The Art of Computer Game Design* (Crawford), he outlines seven main phases in the design process:

1. Choosing a goal and a topic (Objective and premise)
2. Research and preparation
3. Design phase
    a. Input output structure (Interface)
    b. Game structure (gameplay and game mechanics)
    c. Program structure
    d. Evaluation of the design
4. Pre-programming phase
5. Programming phase
6. Playtesting phase
7. Post-mortem

This process was created in the context of entertainment games and acknowledges the fact that a game is a program (or a system of programs) and is useful for initiating the process of designing a game for learning.

Game Design by Brainstorming

Jesse Schell is a game designer and researcher who has developed a framework described in detail in his book, *The Art of Game Design: A Book of Lenses* (2008). Schell's approach involves examining games from various perspectives, such as the theme, characters, player's experience, aesthetics, and technology used. As a supplement, Schell created a deck of cards printed with questions intended to help designers remember the principles associated with the lenses.

There are also other decks of cards designed to help people brainstorm their game designs, such as Titlfactor's *Grow-A-Game* cards, available in three variations: Apprentice, Classic, and Expert (Belman, Nissenbaum, Flanagan, & Diamond, 2011). This deck consists of 86 cards containing words and phrases intended to help designers create game concepts that include oral, social, and political values. The Design for Playful Impact research program at the Utrecht School of the Arts has taken the concept of brainstorming cards to another level by turning their brainstorming cards into an actual game, where players play as game designers who follow the instructions given to them on the cards to produce game concepts and designs (Zaman, et al., 2012).

Rapid iterative prototyping

The term rapid prototyping originally referred to the techniques used to build models or examples of physical objects, like machine parts, buildings, and devices. Software developers, who created prototypes of software modules that are part of a larger system, also used this process. Rapid prototyping has the advantage of providing a visible, if non-functional, object that can be evaluated to see whether it is what the designers and users have in mind. This method was extended using typical software development methods to become rapid application development (RAD), a scheme that abandons significant advanced planning and begins projects by building rough prototypes, then refining them by interleaving stages of design and prototyping. The final prototype ends up being the product.

A computer game certainly has a software component, but is a more complex object than merely a computer program. A game is more like a motion picture or television program, requiring technical expertise, but also writers, artists, musicians, and designers. RAD only works for an educational game if a creative team first outlines possible directions of the game, using the learning objectives as guidelines. A small set of initial prototypes are developed, which are largely non-functional game units, but with including art and sound in the proposed style, and basic interactions to take the evaluators from game scenario to game scenario. We can think of these prototypes as instantiations of the high concept design for each of the proposals.

It is essential that each of these prototypes begin with considerations based on the learning objectives. Games generally begin with a set of ideas drawn for the designer's experience, similar, one would imagine, to the process a novelist or scriptwriter would use in their work. An educational game must begin by including the material to be taught as an integral component or theme. Imagine that the goal is to expose the students to the consequences of Newton's Law: $F=ma$. This particular learning objective does not limit the creativity of the game designer because there is a vast collection of interesting objects in the real world that interact using this rule. Games based on teaching about Newton's Law could include: ball games, including snooker; car and racing games; spacecraft; canons and games involving ballistics; and a host of other design concepts. A second aspect of the design is that the game should expose the learning objective (the underlying physical law in this case) instead of hiding it. Most games use Newtonian physics, but do not show the player explicitly what is happening. Collisions, for example, take place in games and are examples of this physical law, but do not show the player how it works or how to control it. Control is a key part of the learning experience.

The team evaluates the prototypes and selects one for development. At this point, a more detailed design document is prepared, and as this happens, more game prototypes are constructed and tested. At all times a playable version of the game is kept available for evaluation. Some parts of the game are more complete than others, of course, and it is important to realize that the fact that parts are advanced while others should not affect the basic design. The developers must be prepared to discard working parts of the game if they become obsolete by virtue of design changes. In fact, this is one disadvantage of this scheme is that sometimes work is done that needs to be discarded.

Evaluation of the prototypes is done at multiple levels:

1. **As software:** Does the game software work as intended?
2. **As learning:** Are the objectives embodied in the games and are they effective?
3. **As art:** Is the visual and auditory style consistent and effective?
4. **As a game:** Is it entertaining and fun to play?

The game testing process must evaluate all of these things and the results should be used to improve the next version.

Serious Instructional Design Model

Games and instruction are often designed from different starting points. Because there is often a need for accuracy in the models used for educational games it is necessary to examine design approaches in simulation as well as games and instruction. Simulation design includes elements that address approaches to data collection as well as data validation. Games are often built up from a single core idea—some experience, activity, or idea the designer finds interesting. Simulations, on the other hand are typically built to answer some sort of "what if?" question or to create some sort of environment that can be explored or experienced. Finally, instruction is designed from the starting point of some identified performance gap or a gap in understanding. Each field has its approaches to design and no single approach is likely to be able to account for the complexity of designing something that is, in essence, all three. The Serious Instructional Design Model was created as a synergy of all three. This model combines Chris Crawford's game design (Crawford, 1982); Zeigler's simulation design (Zeigler, 1976); and Rothwell & Kazana's instructional design models (Rothwell & Kazanas, 1998) to produce a new design model that is a blend of the important elements of each.

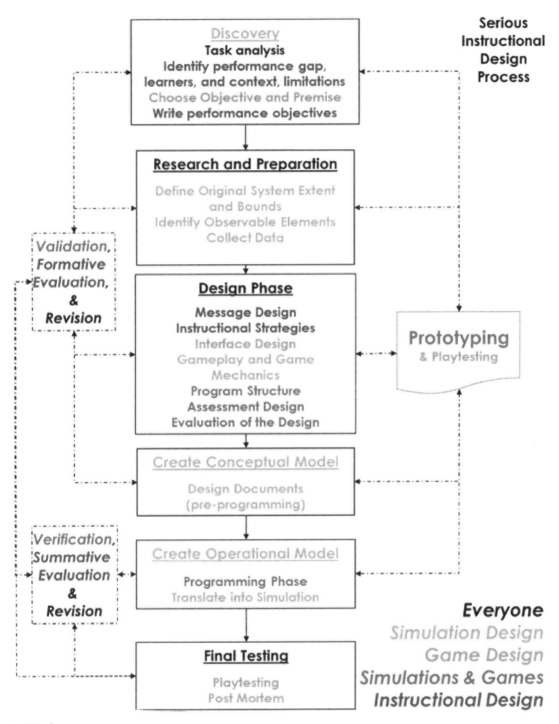

© K.Becker 2013

Figure 3. A schematic of The Serious Instruction Design Model.

The following are the components of The Serious Instructional Design Model:

1. **The discovery phase**: This is the initial phase of the process and includes all the usual needs analysis, and high-level outlines that will be needed later on. Since the game being design is the instructional strategy, it is possible that the bulk of the instructional needs analysis was completed before we even got to the point of knowing we wanted to make a game.

2. **Research and preparation:** This combines simulation-style data gathering, as well as deciding which details will need to be accurate and which can be omitted or even transformed.

3. **The design phase:** This is where the simulation or game will take shape. It is important at this phase to maintain connections between the overarching goals, which are instructional, and the simulation details or gameplay. Although it is not necessary for every aspect of the simulation or game to further the instructional objectives, it is necessary that they coincide often enough to ensure that the time spent in the simulation or game is time well spent.

4. **Creation of a conceptual model:** This is not normally part of an instructional design model but it does have a counterpart in game design, namely the first playables and proofs of concept. This is effectively the last stage where it will be feasible to back up for major revisions if problems are detected. The outcome of this phase will be the detailed design document and it should incorporate both the design elements of the simulation or game and the checkpoints needed to ensure that this solution has a reasonable likelihood of delivering on its instructional objectives.

5. **Playtesting:** Although the final phase is the only one that explicitly lists playtesting, it is highly recommended that playtesting be performed as early and as often as possible. The full educational potential of the game may not be testable in the early stages, but its playability can be, and that is crucial.

Case Study Two: *Fission Impossible*

The game *Fission Impossible* is an example of a less successful educational game than *Pavlov's Dog*. The game is intended to explain the basic concepts behind nuclear fission. Fission is a process that takes place at the atomic level. Essentially, large atoms such as Uranium are struck very hard by a subatomic particle called a neutron. The Uranium atom breaks apart, releasing energy, some new elements, and some more neutrons. These new neutrons strike more Uranium atoms, which also break apart, thus creating a chain reaction if enough Uranium atoms are in close proximity. A type of Uranium dubbed U-235 will do this, whereas U-238 will not.

In the game, the opening screen shows a U-235 atom (a green sphere) within a semi-circle of black circular objects, which turn out to be U-238 atoms, below which we see an orange sphere that represents a neutron. Immediately the neutron begins to drop off of the screen, and the play must use the arrow keys to guide it to strike the U-235 atom. This is hard to do, as some force seems to be pulling the neutron to the bottom of the screen. If the neutron goes outside of a circle of fixed radius centered at the U-235 atom, the game restarts. This circle is invisible until the neutron leaves it, so it is a very frustrating process: the player must fight the invisible force using arrow keys, not go outside the invisible circle, and hit the green sphere. When the player finally succeeds, there is a brief animation of spheres moving about, but nothing like what one would expect from a chain reaction; more like bubbles, really. Now the player is in level 2. There are now even more black U-238 atoms protecting the target, but otherwise no change.

Educationally, the game does not really reflect the physics of the situation. There is no chain reaction, no breaking apart of the U-235 into components, and the U-238 does not protect the U-235 from impact as it does in the game. As a game it is exceptionally frustrating. At the beginning, the neutron falls off of the screen five to six times before a typical player figures out how to prevent it. They then guide the neutron outside of the invisible circle many times and hit the U-238 many more times before figuring out the puzzle. At level two, the puzzle is harder, and when they inevitably fail that task the game starts over at level one; which makes the game tedious. The game cannot be started at a teacher-specified location, making it harder for a teacher to use effectively. The art is simple and clear, but the music is banal and repetitive, encouraging the player to turn the sound off. There is a pop-up window giving science information, but it is confusing and incomplete. Moreover, the learning objectives are not met by this game's design. A player can get through it (eventually) without reading anything or learning anything.

Key Findings

The design of a game for learning requires a synergy of multiple design disciplines: instructional design, simulation design, and game design. These design approaches cannot simply be layered upon one another, but instead must be combined to form a new approach that reflects a true synergy. That there is no single approach that is generally accepted reflects two key facts about learning game design. The first is that design generally is as much an art as it is engineering or science, and the moment a box is drawn around it as a process and rules are created, a limit is defined concerning what can be done. In other words, certain ideas and games are likely to be excluded by a restrictive design process, in other words. The earlier the formal design method begins in the process, the more possibilities will be discarded.

The second fact to consider is that games for learning should be designed with a learning model in mind, and modern instructional theories are still not complete. Indeed, there are disagreements between them that should be resolved. A game design process should collaborate in many specific ways with an ID model. Formal design processes help novices much more than experts, and so it would seem to be valuable to integrate a specific ID model with a learning game design so that novices have a place to begin. As experience is gathered, an expert will pick and choose among methods as being more or less relevant for a specific task.

As an example, consider the RETAIN model (Gunter, Kenny, & Vick, 2007) for game design. This has been devised specifically using Gagné's Nine Events of Instruction (Gagné, Briggs, & Wager, 1992) and follows it very closely by providing essentially one step for each event (see Table 2).

Table 2. A comparison of Gagne's Nine Events of Instruction and the RETAIN model.

	Gagné, Briggs, & Wager (1992)	Gunter, Kenny, & Vick (2007)
1	Gain attention	Game focus/Hook describes the essence of the game and provide an entry point for play.
2	Describe the goal	Didactic focus defines the subject matter to be taught and provide an entry point for instruction.
3	Stimulate recall of prior knowledge	Provide references to beyond-the-object reference sources that inform the pedagogic content development for the game.
4	Present the material to be learned	Game progression describes the individual game units (this process also has nine stages)
5	Provide guidance for learning	Define the critical path for gameplay and didactic resolution
6	Elicit performance practice	Define pedagogic elements to be used
7	Provide informative feedback	Describe how formative feedback will be distributed during each unit of gameplay.
8	Assess performance test, if the lesson has been learned. Also sometimes gives general progress information.	Describe how summative feedback will be distributed during each unit of gameplay and at the conclusion.
9	Enhance retention and transfer	Describe how replay will be encouraging to assist in retention and to remediate shortcomings.

In the RETAIN model, the game design steps described are in lock step with the ID model and this provides a very specific and detailed plan for someone starting out on a new design. After some years of experience, the designer would almost certainly use a large variety of ID models and find ways to incorporate the game design principles learned into the new (perhaps one-time-only) scheme.

Assessment Considerations

Educational research

An educational game can only be considered a success if it assists in communicating the target facts and processes to the student. The design cannot really be assessed independently from the implementation, as with any other educational experience. Fortunately, the field of educational research is well developed and includes multiple methodologies for examining everything from individual elements of a lesson to complete curricula.

People often ask for proof of a game's effectiveness if it is to be used for learning, especially in a formal setting. It is possible to use many of the commonly use research methods, such as pre- and post-testing, case studies, and surveys. If the design of a game for learning needs to be a mix of multiple design approaches, so must the evaluation of a game for learning also include methodologies specifically tailored to games for learning. A recent examination by Mayer et al. (2013) suggests that often those proposing to use a game for learning already have their own procedures and preferences for evaluations, which in some cases may even be mandatory (Mayer et al., 2013). There are some common elements that should be included in any examination of a game's effectiveness. These include:

1. Demographic information about the players and context.
2. The players' prior experience and knowledge.
3. Measures of in-game performance, whether collected within the game itself, or externally via observations or data collection.
4. Aspects of the gameplay itself (which is explained further in the next section).
5. Player satisfaction.
6. First order learning, which is short-term, usually measured on an individual player basis, and usually involves self-reported and measured changes in knowledge, attitudes, skills, or behavior.
7. Second order learning, which is longer-term, and can be self-reported, as well as measured changes in the larger group or organization.

Unfortunately, as in almost all research that attempts to measure the effectiveness of an instructional intervention, it is rarely possible to create the kinds of controlled conditions necessary for conclusive results.

Playtesting

Playtesting is fundamental to the development process in the game industry generally. The goal is to find out whether the game is fun to play, what parts are not fun, what parts are hard or confusing, and whether the players are generally pleased with the result. The process varies from developer to developer, but essentially involves watching typical players interact with the game. A small set of people in the correct demographic group for the game are recruited, are given the game and its instructions, and then told to start playing. Video recordings are often made of these play sessions for later analysis, and the game itself if often instrumented to record player actions, speeds, and strategies. Sometimes a questionnaire or interview is done after a play session, but it is important not to guide the players in advance of play or the responses might not be useful.

A playtesting session can be done as soon as a playable game exists, which should be early in the process, and playtesting should be repeated regularly. After each session the results should be examined to see if there are any problems in the design, and those should be repaired and tested in the next sessions. The idea is not to collect statistics but to gather impressions. The concept of "fun" has eluded definition, so playtesting enables the design to see whether actual players find the game entertaining, and where they have failed. Fun is hard to define, but most people know when they are having it.

For an educational game, playtesting is done to determine whether the target audience will be engaged with the game. If they are not, then the educational objectives will be missed. Fun, rather than being the opposite of learning, may well be the human's natural reaction to discovering something new. The playtest should indicate the places within the game where players have difficulties, and also those places that are most enjoyable. Both can be used to improve the next iteration. There is a variety of guides on how to conduct a play test to be found on the Internet and some quite valuable books on the subject (e.g., Schultz).

Future Needs

Many of the design methods describe here do not provide access to most issues important to a game designer, which includes matters of theme, play, and narrative. These are most frequently described vaguely as "describe the essence of the game," but in fact game design as a specific discipline concerns itself primarily with those things. Schell's design scheme considers those matters as a specific issue, and he does so as a more or less random juxtaposition of objects and activities. For example, there may be some game themes and mechanics that are better in the context of a game to teach history, and those may be different themes and mechanics than what would be used to teach physics. It would be useful to know how mechanics and other aspects of games influence learning. A computer game can keep track of everything a user (player) does. A very important feature of a game designed for learning is to provide feedback and an essential part of research into these games is an assessment of their effectiveness. We need more work on the automatic evaluation of games based on collected data and on determining exactly what feedback is best for the player.

Best Practices

It is critical when designing a game for learning to specifically consider the instructional objectives. As a key side issue, it is probably important for these objectives to be given to the game designers rather than for the designers to come up with them. These seem like obvious statements, but are all too frequently overlooked or underestimated. The objectives must be kept in mind when examining playable versions of a game. It is very easy to get caught up in the compelling aspects of a game and not pay sufficient attention to the original goals. The fact that games are compelling is why we want to use them, but design time is wasted if they do not help teach what is wanted.

If measurements are important, decide what measures of success will be used before the game is designed. A good scientific experiment always does this, of course, but it also means that you can do a better job of building in ways to collect data to support the evaluation. Games can generate a lot of data. It is important to be selective.

A complete game may teach many aspects of a subject, but each specific scenario or level should focus on just one of two things. Keep the situation, rules, and scoring system simple, or the learning objectives will be confused with the game objectives. Doing this makes evaluation and feedback possible and allows players to make a logical progression through the material.

Game designers know how players play games and how to engage them. Players rarely read game instructions, so create a tutorial level that clearly describes the scenario and the game rules and mechanics, and at a level that can be understood by the intended audience. Listen to game design experts with respect to player behaviors. For example, a good game can be replayed many times. A game designer knows how to do that, and if an educational game gets replayed then learning is reinforced.

Highly interactive games are better than ones that are not. For example, games based on questions and answers (e.g., Jeopardy style) are relatively passive and are nor really much better than a Q&A session in a classroom. Games that allow players to discover things are a more realistic presentation and require action on the part of the player.

The actions performed by the player in the game should be related to those used in the activity to be learned. For instance, some games have pop-up questions during play for the learner to answer. This never happens in real life. It is better if the questions are integrated into the game so that the player answers then because the answer is required by the play. An equation may need to be solved because the answer helps in navigation, for example, and not just because it is a math game.

Resources

Related Researchers

Katrin Becker

Simon Egenfeldt-Nielsen

Mary Flanagan

Tracy Fullerton

James Paul Gee

Carrie Heeter

Clark N. Quinn

Katie Salen

David W. Schaffer

Kurt Squire

Books

Adams, E., & Rollings, A. (2010). Fundamentals of Game Design (2nd ed.). Berkeley, CA: New Riders.

Becker, K., & Parker, J. R. (2011). The Guide to Computer Simulations and Games: Wiley.

Brathwaite, B., & Schreiber, I. (2012). *Breaking into the game industry : advice for a successful career from those who have done it.* Boston, Mass.: Course Technology, Cengage Learning.

Crawford, C. (1982). The Art of Computer Game Design (Kindle ed.): Amazon Digital Services, Inc.

Fullerton, T., Swain, C., & Hoffman, S. (2008). Game Design Workshop : A Playcentric Approach to Creating Innovative Games (2nd ed.). Boston: Elsevier Morgan Kaufmann.

Koster, R. (2004). Theory of Fun for Game Design. Scottsdale, AZ: Paraglyph Press

Quinn, C. N. (2005). Engaging Learning: Designing e-Learning Simulation Games: John Wiley & Sons Canada, Ltd.

Salen, K., & Zimmerman, E. (2006). The Game Design Reader: A Rules of Play Anthology. Cambridge, Mass.: MIT Press.

Schell, J. (2008). The Art Of Game Design : A Book of Lenses. Amsterdam ; Boston: Elsevier/Morgan Kaufmann.

Reports & Papers

Pinelle, D., Wong, N., & Stach, T. (2008). Heuristic evaluation for games: Usability principle for video game design. Paper presented at the The 26th ACM Conference on Human Factors in Computing Systems (CHI '06).

Games, Game Engines, Design Tools

Construct 2 (www.scirra.com)

Fission Impossible (game to teach basic principles of fission reactions) (http://www.wonderville.ca/asset/fission-impossible)

GameMaker (engine)

Pavlov's Dog (game to teach basics of classical conditioning) (http://www.nobelprize.org/educational/medicine/pavlov/)

Processing (programming language)

Unity (engine)

UDK (Unreal Development Kit)

Game Seeds (brainstorming card game)

Grow-A-Game (brainstorming cards)

References

Aldrich, C. (2004). *Simulations and the future of learning.* San Francisco, CA: Pfeiffer.

Becker, K. (2008a). Design paradox: Instructional game design. Paper presented at the CNIE Conference 2008, "Reaching New Heights: Learning Innovation."

Becker, K. (2008b). Video game pedagogy: Good games = good pedagogy. In C. T. Miller (Ed.), *Games: Their Purpose and Potential in Education* (in press) New York: Springer Publishing.

Becker, K., & Parker, J. R. (2011). *The guide to computer simulations and games.* Wiley.

Belman, J., Nissenbaum, H., Flanagan, M., & Diamond, J. (2011). *Grow-A-Game:* A tool for values conscious design and analysis of digital games.

Branson, R. K., Rayner, G. T., & Cox, J. L. (1975). Interservice procedures for instructional systems development: Executive summary and model (Contract Number N-61339-73-C-0150 ed.). Ft. Benning, Georgia: Center for Educational Technology at Florida State University for the U.S. Army Combat Arms Training Board.

Budgen, D. (2003). *Software design (2nd ed.).* New York: Addison-Wesley.

Crawford, C. (1982). *The art of computer game design.* Available from http://www.vancouver.wsu.edu/fac/peabody/game-book/Coverpage.html

Dick, W., Carey, L., & Carey, J. O. (2001). *The systematic design of instruction (5th ed.).* New York: Longman.

Ely, D. P., & Plomp, T. (1996). *Classic writings on instructional technology.* Englewood, Colo.: Libraries Unlimited.

Fullerton, T., Swain, C., & Hoffman, S. (2008). *Game design workshop: A playcentric approach to creating innovative games (2nd ed.).* Boston: Elsevier Morgan Kaufmann.

Gagné, R. M., Briggs, L. J., & Wager, W. W. (1992). *Principles of instructional design (4th ed.).* Fort Worth, Tex.: Harcourt Brace Jovanovich College Publishers.

Gee, J. P. (2003). *What video games have to teach us about learning and literacy (1st ed.).* New York: Palgrave Macmillan.

Gunter, G., Kenny, R., & Vick, E. (2006, April 6-8, 2006). A case for formal design paradigm for serious games. Paper presented at the CODE—Human Systems; Digital Bodies, Miami University, Oxford, Ohio.

Gunter, G., Kenny, R., & Vick, E. (2007). Taking educational games seriously: using the RETAIN model to design endogenous fantasy into standalone educational games. *Educational Technology Research and Development.* December 2008, Volume 56, Issue 5-6, pp 511-537.

Kenny, R. F., Zhang, Z., Schwier, R. A., & Campbell, K. (2005). A review of what instructional designers do: Questions answered and questions not asked. *Canadian Journal of Learning and Technology, 31*(1), 9-26.

Kirriemuir, John (2005). A survey of COTS games used in education, presented at the Serious Games Summit/ Game Developers Conference, San Francisco.

Mayer, I., Bekebrede, G., Harteveld, C., Warmelink, H., Zhou, Q., Ruijven, T., et al. (2013). The research and evaluation of serious games: Toward a comprehensive methodology. *British Journal of Educational Technology.*

McDowell, P., Cannon-Bowers, J. A., & Prensky, M. (2005). The role of pedagogy and educational design in serious games, Serious Games Summit. Arlington, VA.

Molenda, M. (2003). In search of the elusive ADDIE Model. *Performance Improvement.*

Piskurich, G. M. (2000). *Rapid instructional design: learning ID fast and right.* San Francisco, Calif.: Jossey-Bass.

Rothwell, W. J., & Kazanas, H. C. (1998). *Mastering the instructional design process: a systematic approach (2nd ed.).* San Francisco, Calif.: Jossey-Bass.

Salen, K., & Zimmerman, E. (2004). *Rules of play: game design fundamentals.* Cambridge, Mass.: MIT Press.

Schell, J. (2008). *The art of game design: a book of lenses.* Boston: Elsevier/Morgan Kaufmann.

Schultz, Charles and Bryant, Robert. (2012). *Game testing: All in one (2nd. ed.).* Dulles, VA: Mercury Learning and Information.

Van Eck, R. (Producer). (2011, Mar 10, 2011) The gaming of educational transformation TEDxManitoba. YouTube Video retrieved from http://youtu.be/khJDLo0oMX4

Zaman, B., Poels, Y., Sulmon, N., Annema, J.-H., Verstraete, M., Cornillie, F., et al. (2012). Concepts and mechanics for educational mini-games a human-centered conceptual design approach involving adolescent learners and domain experts. *International Journal On Advances in Intelligent Systems, 5*(3 and 4), 567-576.

Zeigler, B. P. (1976). *Theory of modeling and simulation.* New York: Wiley.

CHAPTER 11

Audience

Designing for the Audience: Past Practices and Inclusive Considerations

Gabriela T. Richard, *University of Pennsylvania, Philadelphia, Pennsylvania, U.S., gric@upenn.edu*

Key Summary Points

1. Most research on designing for the audience centers on understanding personality, pleasure preferences, or player motivations. Structural and dramatic elements are integral to driving motivation and constructing game pleasures.

2. The physical and cognitive abilities of players should also be important when considering your audience.

3. Design should be inclusive in ways that look beyond demographics and assumed differences (such as gender differences). Particular attention should be paid to increasing diversity in representation, and decreasing bias and harassment in play.

4. Design should consider how to limit player avoidance of game or learning mechanics (through cheating or exploiting) and should craft ways to vary how players use game affordances and solve problems.

Key Terms

STEM

User research

Motivation

Game structure

Inclusive design

Race

Sexuality

Ability

Audience

Player types

Pleasure

Representation

Gender

Ethnicity

Identity

Introduction

In Fullerton's (2005) *Game Design Workshop: A Playcentric Approach to Creating Innovative Games,* she reminds us that the role of a game designer, before anything else, is to be an advocate for the player—the audience (Fullerton, 2008). Making the audience central to the design process can be difficult, however, especially when there are multiple demands during production and development, and multiple perspectives on the design team.

> The interesting and challenging thing about game development teams is the sheer breadth of types of people who work on them. From the hardcore computer scientists, who might be designing the AI or graphic displays, to the talented illustrators and animators who bring the characters to life, to the money-minded executives and business managers who deliver the game to its players, the range of personalities is Incredible… A big part of [a game designer's job]… is to serve as a sort of universal translator, making sure that all of these different groups are, in fact, working on the same game… Games are fragile systems, and each element is inextricably linked to the others, so a change in one variable can send disruptive ripples throughout. (Fullerton, 2008, pp. 6-7)

We often discuss game design from the perspective of the experiences we are creating and not from the perspective of the audience. As Fullerton points out, however, while it can be easy to get caught up with new graphics and features, the balance of all of these features into a solidly playable system is what actually excites and hooks players.

Game designers ask players to engage in Huizinga's "magic circle," where game rules create opportunities for play within the safety of constraints; players can perform actions and see things from perspectives they are normally unable to do in the confines of the "real world" (Salen & Zimmerman, 2003). The kinds of actions afforded in the circle are especially powerful from an educational perspective because learners can take on roles, simulate experiences, and interact with and view phenomena that would be difficult otherwise (e.g., Gee, 2004; Squire, 2011).

As we think about education and learners, some of the challenges faced by commercial games when it comes to designing for audiences become especially important to consider. The next section will expand on this further as we examine the prevailing theories and perspectives around designing for the audience.

Case Study One: *Gone Home* as an English Text (Written by Paul Darvasi)

Gone Home is a first-person exploration game that was used as a text in three senior high school English classes at Royal St. Georges' College, an all-boys independent school in Toronto, Canada. Fifty-seven students played the game and then carried out relevant activities and responses over the course of a two-week unit. Prior to starting the unit, players were sent redemption codes that allowed them to load the game to their laptops. Students played independently and progressed at their own pace.

Set in 1995, *Gone Home* is an interactive and non-linear narrative that develops through the player's exploration of a family home. Players reconstruct the family drama by piecing together documents, artifacts and personal possessions they find around the old mansion. The central story revolves around a teenage girl's adolescent romance and coming out story, while her father struggles with his past and a failed writing career, and her hardworking mother negotiates the temptations of an extramarital affair.

The game substitutes a traditional English text and was implemented without modification. Both its content and functionality make it a relevant selection for classroom use. Unlike many long-form games with a narrative focus, *Gone Home* can be easily played in less than three hours, has low hardware requirements, and has a user-friendly interface. The game does away with levels, points and achievements, which make for a smooth and non-competitive gameplay experience. It is also scrubbed of gratuitous sex and violence, but retains an "edge" by virtue of the house's gloomy and haunting atmosphere. Its focus on character development through environmental storytelling naturally lends itself to a consideration of the setting, characters, perspectives and non-linear narrative structure—concepts relevant to any secondary school literature class. Its reliance on an assortment of realistic and diverse documents and objects such as *X-Files* videos, graffiti-covered lockers, and journal pages also expose students to a wide range of written voices and forms.

Guided activities and response strategies include:

1. **A written "annotation" of a single room in the game.** A combination of screenshots and notes were employed to unpack the first room they entered, which acquainted students with all the main characters, basic gameplay functions and let them practice taking in-game screenshots.
2. **Individual tracking assignments.** Students selected topics to track and were tasked to take relevant notes and screenshots as they played. Tracking topics included gathering information on specific characters, identifying and researching objects endemic to 1995, finding and contextualizing intertextual references to other video games, and the copious allusions to the Riot Girl movement. Some kept notes as they played, others opted to play through once and take notes during a second run.
3. **A study of tone and mood**
4. **Written reviews of the game**
5. **Group presentations**

These directed activities encouraged purposeful and deliberate exploration, without restricting player agency. After the gameplay phase, players were grouped together according to their tracking assignments and collaborated on presentations that were delivered to the rest of the class. Finally, they read examples of game reviews, and then wrote their own which they then published in gaming websites such as Metacritic, Gamespot, and IGN. The game's developers added an optional in-game commentary a week before the unit was launched and many students played the game a second time with the commentary switched on, which provided valuable insights that enhanced their reviews and presentations.

Most players seemed engaged and invested throughout. They remained focused during in-class play, and many offered unsolicited comments about enjoying the experience. Some students remarked that the game was not for them or that they found the graphics subpar. Discussions led to questions of the characters' motives and the realism of the game, and students traded knowledge about the whereabouts of certain spaces and items. One high performing student, who does not play video games outside of school, noted he enjoyed the experience and found it easier to remember narrative details than he did when reading a story or novel. The reviews showed critical thought on storyline, gameplay and production values, and the quality of their final products were generally high, perhaps because they were destined for public consumption. The final presentations were informative, engaging, and visually appealing and collectively addressed most narrative elements of the game. *Gone Home* could easily be implemented in any high school English class with access to laptops and/or desktop computer.

Key Frameworks

When designing for an audience, one of the key elements to take into consideration is how to make them connect emotionally and engage with the game (Fullerton, 2008). This means different things to different players, and not everyone will engage with games similarly. In fact, some game designers and scholars have proposed that there are different player types, who have different intentions and pleasures that motivate them.

Player types and personalities

Bartle (1996), credited with creating the first multiuser dungeon (MUD) and online games, categorized MUD players as ascribing to one of four player types: achievers, explorers, socializers and killers. A personality test was created based on his work and his theory has been updated for virtual worlds and contemporary multiplayer games (though the updated taxonomy has not been widely cited or used). Bartle's original taxonomy was based on hundreds of forum posts in response to the question of what people wanted out of a MUD. He stated that there were 15 key respondents and about 15 complementary ones, made up of the top players of one popular MUD who helped shaped his theory. He found that each player leaned a bit toward each of the subgroups, but was primarily characterized by one.

1. **Achievers** are primarily concerned with achieving the goals of the game and they enjoy challenge.
2. **Explorers** are concerned with getting to know as much as they can about the world, sometimes beyond the play space and into the actual system and its structural makeup. They enjoy discovering the world and its boundaries.
3. **Socializers** like to use the game's communication system and interact with other players, as part of their play. They enjoy how other players can contribute to their experiences of the game.
4. **Killers** are interested in "acting on other players" in ways that are mostly understood as harmful but can also "appear helpful" (Bartle, 1996, Interest Graph Section, para. 8). They are often players who want to "demonstrate their superiority over" (Bartle, 1996, Interest Graph Section, para. 8) other human beings and desire showing off their knowledge and skills against real people instead of non-playable characters (NPCs).

Bartle proposed that a stable MUD, or game space, was designed to keep all player types in equilibrium. He felt it was the job of designers and administrators (or, these days, community managers) to think through how the system was designed and maintained in striking this balance.

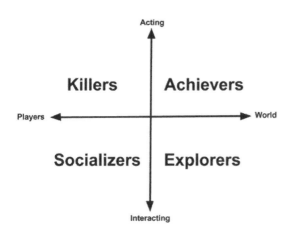

Figure 1. Graph of how Bartle's four player types cover a space.

Figure 1 shows a graph of Bartle's four player types and how they cover a space. The vertical axis represents acting on or interacting with, and the horizontal axis represents players or the world. To interpret the player type, one would locate its position on the axis. For example, Achievers act on the world (hence its position between acting and world) whereas Socializers interact with other players, Explorers interact with the world, and Killers act on other players.

On the other hand, Yee (2006) raised the concern that Bartle's Taxonomy of Player Types, while widely cited, had not been put to the test. For example, he questioned whether the four player types were truly independent from one another. Players may have different motivations to take on different characteristics at different times and with different games; in these cases, types would be fluid and not fixed. Fullerton (2008) argues that Callois' (2001) seminal *Man, Play and Games* brings focus to the kinds of pleasures that different game types imbue for players. For example, most strategy games, whether they be board-base games (such as *Chess*), turn-based digital strategy games (such as *Civilization*), or real-time strategy games (such as *Starcraft*), have rule-based and competitive elements, emphasizing certain kinds of play. These kinds of games would not only embody different kinds of playful experiences, they would also be differentially appealing to players.

Vandenberghe (2012), a creative director at Ubisoft, presented on the *Five Domains of Play* during the 2012 Game Developer Conference. He proposed that psychology's big five personality traits could easily and accurately predict a player's game choices and that each of the five personality traits (openness, conscientiousness, extroversion, agreeableness, and neuroticism) is related to the motivations that drive behavior and choices in general, which also includes games. In other words, each personality trait maps well to what he coins are the five domains of play:

1. **Novelty:** The newness of the experience.
2. **Challenge:** The amount of effort or self-control the player is expected to use.
3. **Stimulation:** The engagement of the play experience.
4. **Harmony:** The relation of the rules to social and player-to-player accord in game.
5. **Threat:** The presence and strength of negative emotional triggers.

Vandenberghe urged designers to "appeal to both ends of each facet," (Vandenberghe, 2012) believing that each player mapped onto the domains of play differently. He recognized, however, that while we cannot always design for everyone, he encouraged designers to think about personality and play style, beyond the demographics (and assumptions) that are often used. Vandenberghe's work connects theories of personality with theories of motivation, but some researchers have looked more exclusively at what motivates players to play in different complex gaming environments. In fact, he and his colleagues contend that the Big Five model of personality traits does "an excellent job of predicting taste... [and] relates to the acquisition phase of game engagement... [as well as] points the way for the reasons why people will quit playing" (Brink et al., 2013, p. 1). They have conceded that, while the Big Five predicts which games people are likely to gravitate toward, it does not predict behavior well once engaged, and that theories of motivation do a much better job.

Vandenberghe and his collaborators juxtapose their work to that of Ryan, Rigby, & Przybylski (2006) who, along with Yee (2006), argue that motivation to play is fluid and highly dependent on context. Ryan et al. (2006) and Yee (2006) also focus on understanding player motivations, as opposed to personalities or player types.

Player Motivations

Ryan et al. (2006) focuses on the role that self-motivation and determination played in human behavior—including playing games— which stemmed from Ryan and Deci's Self-Determination Theory of Motivation (Ryan & Deci, 2000). They proposed that individuals' motivations to play video games could be accounted for by how well the game is able to satisfy basic psychological needs. These basic needs were:

1. **Competence:** How much the game and its associated tasks allow for a sense of accomplishment or mastery.
2. **Autonomy:** How much the game provides choice over tasks and goals, and sustains the ability to feel a sense of control, as opposed to being controlled by feedback.
3. **Relatedness**: How much the game allows for being connected or related with others.

Rigby & Ryan (2007) expanded on this theory by creating the player experience of needs satisfaction (PENS) applied model and methodology. They felt that the PENS model needed to be thoughtfully applied to the game mechanics (controls and rules), the gameplay (activity in the game) and player narrative (uncovering of elements related to the character over time). To optimize on player competence, games should give players the opportunity to apply and demonstrate mastery, provide positive, yet relevant feedback as well as an overarching sense of continual success for sustained enjoyment. There should further be a sense of player agency, which combines competence and autonomy, by allowing players "who they will be...and when, where and how they take action" (Rigby & Ryan, 2007, p.12). To create a sense of autonomy, games should allow, as much as possible, opportunities for players to act, through interactive elements (such as NPCs and items) and ways to meaningfully interact with them (through talking to characters or collecting items). Relatedness can often be achieved through optimizing the kinds of social interactions available online. While these social interactions can be different in shape and form (i.e., interacting in short matches in a first-person shooter is very different from sustained, long-term teamwork in Massively Multiplayer Online Role-Playing Games), allowing for player contact and relationship building is important to satisfaction of player needs with games.

In analyzing Massively Multiplayer Online Role-Playing Games (MMORPGs), Yee (2006) found that play motivations do not suppress each other; in other words, players can have a range of emotions that influences what they play and how they play. He found that there were three key overarching motivation components that could be described:

1. **The achievement component:** This is made up of advancement (the desire to gain power, or achieve symbols of status or wealth), mechanics (interest in analyzing the underlying rules of a system for optimization), and competition (the desire to challenge and compete with others).
2. **The social component:** This is composed of socializing (the desire to chat, make friends and help others), relationships (interest in forming bonds with others), and teamwork (feeling satisfaction from collaborating with others toward a group effort).
3. **The immersive component:** This involves discovery (finding hidden or unknown things that others might not find), role-playing (creating an interesting and complex persona, which often involved interacting with other players), customization (creating unique looks for one's character), and escapism (using the game or virtual space to escape reality).

While he discovered some gender differences, with males exhibiting higher achievement motivations and females having higher relationship building motivations, he found that this was more correlated with age than gender. Specifically, he found that older players were less likely to be achievement oriented, but that female players also tended to be older than male players (Yee, 2008). Also, male and female players were equal in their social motivations, but socialized differently, hence why only the subcomponent of relationship building was significantly different across gender. However, more important that gender and age differences were his findings around the variability of why players play MMORPGs leading him to conclude that "this variation suggests that one reason why MMOs are so popular may be that there are many subgames embedded within a larger system" (Yee, 2008, pp. 89).

Radoff, author of *Game On* (2011), sought to simplify the work of Yee and Bartle by making them applicable to any game genre. He felt that two axes could be used to define the environment the player is in: the horizontal axis represents the number of players involved in gameplay and the vertical axis represents how the player is informed they are winning in the form of motivation. For example, quantitative feedback or rewards could include leaderboards and points, whereas qualitative feedback or rewards would be stories or emotional-based cues. Depending on the play environment, and number of players, different motivational elements would emerge. This framework, however, has mainly been applied to creating gamified (or game inspired) contexts outside of games as opposed to within them. In many ways, it breaks down what works well in digital games (e.g., badges, virtual goods) to apply them to other contexts to stimulate motivation, rather than mapped onto gameplay in digital games. Radoff's work is a good segue into understanding game pleasures and emotion.

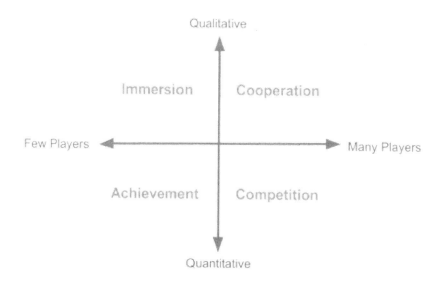

Figure 2. Radoff's Model of Player Motivation

Game Pleasures and Emotion

Schell (2008), professor and CEO of Schell Games, a game design company, proposes that we often look to demographics to get at what groups find pleasurable. As Lazzaro (2008), president of XEODesign, a player experience design consultancy, contends, however, designing for demographics can limit an audience, specifically if there are gender assumptions. Instead of demographics, Lazzaro has proposed designing for core game pleasures.

Game designer Marc LeBlanc created a taxonomy of eight primary game pleasures. He focused on several kinds of experiences that elicit pleasure:

1. **Sensation:** pleasures that involve the senses and sensations, like seeing something beautiful and hearing something pleasurable. These are often delivered through game aesthetics.
2. **Fantasy:** pleasures that involve imagination and experiencing yourself as someone or with other attributes.
3. **Narrative:** pleasures of experiencing a narrative unfolding through play.
4. **Challenge:** pleasures of solving problems through play.
5. **Fellowship:** pleasures of friendship, cooperation, and community achieved through gameplay.
6. **Discovery:** pleasures of discovering new things through gameplay, which can include exploring a game environment or finding out a new strategy or exploit.
7. **Expression:** pleasures of creating something or expressing oneself through gameplay or through game affordances (i.e., creating a level someone else can play, or creating outfits for your character).
8. **Submission:** the pleasure of entering the fantasy space ("magic circle") of a game and leaving the real world behind.

Taxonomies are not without criticism. The biggest critique is whether they are exhaustive enough. Schell (2008) contends that LeBlanc and Bartle's taxonomies have gaps, which could "gloss over subtle pleasures that might be easily missed" (p. 111). He adds the following additional pleasures to LeBlanc's Taxonomy, which he states may not cover all of the variety of pleasures derived from human experience:

1. **Anticipation:** The pleasure of knowing something is forthcoming.
2. **Delight in another's misfortune:** This pleasure is often experienced when someone who has been unjust gets what was coming to them.
3. **Gift giving**: The pleasure of giving a gift and making someone happy by doing so.
4. **Humor:** The pleasure of something funny.
5. **Possibility:** The pleasure of being able to choose from many options.
6. **Pride in accomplishment:** The pleasure of satisfaction in having achieved something.
7. **Purification:** The pleasure of clearing or cleaning something out (such as clearing the board or killing all of the enemies).
8. **Surprise:** The pleasure of revelation or astonishment.
9. **Thrill:** The pleasure of experiencing terror while safe and secure.
10. **Triumph over adversity:** The pleasure of accomplishing something difficult or with many obstacles.
11. **Wonder:** The pleasure of amazement.

Both of these taxonomies raise issues about whether they could ever cover all of the possible pleasures human beings have come to find enjoyable and motivating. Through extensive interviews and observations of hardcore, casual and non-gamers, Lazzaro (2004) found that there are four keys to unlocking player emotions. Not all players like the same kinds of things but overall "players play to experience these body sensations that result from and drive their actions" (p. 7). According to Lazzaro, top-selling games utilize at least three of the four keys. Each key is a reason people play, and combining each of the keys makes for a "deeply enjoyable game for a wide market" (p. 3). The following are Lazzaro's four keys:

1. **Hard fun:** This refers to creating opportunities for the player to overcome obstacles and to pursue a goal. Challenge focuses attention, creates emotions such as frustration and inspires creativity in developing and applying strategy. Players are often rewarded with feedback and they often use Hard Fun to test their skills and feel accomplishment.
2. **Easy fun:** This refers to maintaining player focus with player attention instead of a winning condition. This is often achieved through "ambiguity, incompleteness and detail" (Lazzaro, 2004, p. 4) as well as rich stimuli (like intricate landscapes or enticing rhythms), which encourage players to explore and immerse themselves.
3. **Altered states (updated to "serious fun"):** This involves creating opportunities for players to experience different emotions, senses and interactions. Players can escape from reality or experience relief from their thoughts or feelings.
4. **The people factor (updated to "people fun"):** This involves allowing players to use games for social experiences, including competition, teamwork, social bonding, and personal recognition.

Structuring Play

So far, we have discussed the motivational or pleasurable capacities of games, without necessarily thinking concretely about the structural and dramatic elements that create them. Fullerton (2008) suggests that there are five interrelated elements that are key to engaging the player: challenge, play, premise, character, and story.

1. **Challenge:** Challenge is an important element in creating the tension they must resolve through gameplay, which is often highly motivating when designed well. We have to balance how great or small the challenge may be, as frustration or lack of engagement can occur when challenges are too large or too small, respectively.
2. **Play:** According to Fullerton, "play itself is not a game [but] the more rigid systems of games can provide opportunities for players to use imagination, fantasy, inspiration, social skills, or other more free-form types of interaction to achieve objectives within the game space, to play within the game, as well as to engage the challenges it offers" (Fullerton, 2008, p. 34). How rigid or free form the play space is designed is important for engagement, because different players will approach its affordances and constraints differently.
3. **Premise:** The premise of the game gives context to the rest of the elements because it sets the backdrop, the environment, and the roles of the players and characters.

4. **Characters:** Characters "are the agents through which dramatic stories are told" (p. 40) but they can also provide players "vessels" through which to experience situations, conflicts or live vicariously through.

5. **Story:** Unlike the premise of a game, stories tend to unfold during gameplay, and not all games contain a story. Special thought should go into how the story works with the intentions of the game and how it unfolds.

Concerned that designers tended to focus on pleasure and motivation more than capacity, Brathwaite & Schreiber (2008) proposed six key areas to take into account when targeting your audience: reading ability, learning curve, cognitive ability, learning style, physical ability, as well as tactile desires. While tactile desires do not necessarily highlight capacities, they are often overlooked as part of the appeal. As a result, they highlight the importance of marketing and packaging in encouraging play.

1. **Reading ability:** Brathwaite & Schreiber (2008) caution designers not to overestimate the reading abilities of children, and even some young and older adults. Using auditory feedback, even if included with text, will help those with reading difficulties or limitations.

2. **Learning curve:** They encourage designers to think about how game controllers and in-game attributes relate to perceived learning curves because individuals often "dismiss things before they try" them (p. 149). When designing peripheral devices and in-game feedback, like health meters and heads-up displays, think about accessibility. Design for common references, like existing controllers, or feedback systems, while also thinking about how you would translate those elements for a novice so they are not overwhelming.

3. **Cognitive ability:** When designing for different audiences, think about the kind of cognitive challenge present, and whether it would be capable or interesting for that target age group's cognitive ability. For example, some games are rather complex and difficult for young children, while others do not provide the kind of mental challenge certain advanced players might find stimulating.

4. **Learning style:** Citing the work of Graner Ray (2004), Brathwaite & Schreiber (2008) contend that men and women gravitate to different learning styles (though this is up for debate, as will be discussed later).

5. **Physical ability:** Thinking about the physical abilities of an audience is also crucial. Designing controllers that are too large for some users, or designing games that require absolute precision with a mouse may limit who can play your game. When designing, there should be some thought into whether, how and why you are limiting your audience through the physical requirements of your game.

6. **Tactile desires:** Brathwaite & Schreiber (2008) also point out that the tactile affordances of your game, from the packaging, to the artwork, send strong signals to your audience about its quality and emotional attributes.

Case Study Two: *Jewish Time Jump: New York* (Written by Owen Gottlieb)

Jewish Time Jump: New York is a mobile placed-based augmented reality game and simulation in the form of a situated documentary. It is designed to act as a learning intervention, not only to engage learners and spark their curiosity in exploring content knowledge in modern Jewish history, but also to deepen their historical thinking and their civic participation, and in so doing, seek a means by which a short-term intervention might have a longer-term effect on learner engagement with modern Jewish history. The Jewish social justice concern of *Tikkun Olam*, or healing the world, is realized in the game through centering on civic engagement in a pluralist democracy. The game's design is concerned with presenting engrossing historical narratives in which players investigate multiple, conflicting perspectives and they come to explore the constructed nature of historical narrative. They learn about issues based advocacy and organizing, as well as citizen journalism and political power structures in an historical context.

Jewish Time Jump: New York works to push the boundaries of the genre of situated documentary (Mathews & Squire, 2010) in terms of production, game mechanics, and narrative devices. The player's geographic place is directly related to the game theme, events, and setting. The game "augments" reality, so while standing in Washington Square Park, or the buildings nearby. Players receive images based on their GPS location—images from over 100 years earlier—giving a place-based experience of the historical narrative.

In this game and interactive story, players travel back in time to take on the role of reporters working for the fictional *Jewish Time Jump Gazette*. They are tasked with bringing a story back to their editor that was "lost in time." They "travel" back to 1909 in Washington Square Park in Greenwich Village, New York, where they land on the eve of The Uprising of 20,000, a garment workers' strike, led in large part by a number of young Jewish women were among those who led 20,000 shirtwaist workers out into the streets. It remains the largest women-led strike in U.S. History.

The uprising occurred two years before the devastating Triangle Shirtwaist Factory Fire. The Uprising also occurs eleven years before women have the right to vote. Players gather perspectives from digital characters with opposing views, receive items such as digital reproductions of original Yiddish newspapers with a translation feature, and track down elements of their story, trying to complete their quests before time runs out. They face obstacles such as being mistaken for strikers by local shtarkers, who were thugs hired by owners as strikebreakers, and who often attacked the women.

The project that would become *Jewish Time Jump* originated in the desire to bring advances in contemporary research in games for learning to bear on Jewish education. Jim Mathews' *Dow Day* (Mathews & Squire, 2010) served as the jumping off point. *Dow Day*, which takes place on the campus of the University Madison-Wisconsin, is a mobile, augmented reality situated documentary in which players act as reporters during the 1967 student protests against Dow Chemical, who was recruiting on campus. They meet digital characters of protesters, administrators, and police and are fed stills, videos, and historic artifacts from 1967. For the development of *Jewish Time Jump: New York*, this investigator formed, and led a New York based team of historians, archivists, digital graphic and video artists, and game designers. The New York team also collaborated with Mathews, David Gagnon, and the ARIS Team at the University Wisconsin-Madison.

ARIS, or the Augmented Reality and Interactive Storytelling platform is an open source platform, based out of the University of Wisconsin-Madison, and the inheritor of an early project at MIT. *Dow Day* had been ported to ARIS, and to this day, ARIS remains the only open source, readily available technology for GPS, location-based game-design available for mobile devices. *ARIS* runs on iOS (iPhone and iPad). *ARIS* allows for interactive storytelling and triggers events by GPS location. At the same time, the platform itself has constraints, and so the model of *Dow Day*, which was already running on *ARIS*, was used as a basis for the initial kinds of gameplay that could be devised. While development on *ARIS* was done over the course of *Jewish Time Jump,* the initial design work had to begin from the then-current constraints of *ARIS*. *ARIS* remains in development and *Jewish Time Jump* remains in iterative design. *Jewish Time Jump*'s development has contributed to the *ARIS* platform in a number of ways, including the addition of haptics (vibration scripts), and a variety of new design-editor tools including universal location controls.

Implications for the game are potentially broad, including a variety of player-audiences both inside and outside formal and informal Jewish and secular social studies education settings. For the purposes of the research study, and the focus of design, the initial target audience was fifth to eighth graders and their families,primarily in Reform Hebrew supplementary schools. This choice was to attempt to address a population of Jewish learners with high attrition from secondary schools. Could an intervention potentially impact attrition numbers? The researcher is still working on answering this research question, and understanding how the game may address attrition from formal and informal Jewish education settings. Initial results suggest that numerous design elements can contribute to deepening engagement in perspective-taking, and historical investigation with an emphasis on civic participation in a pluralist democracy, informed by a player's religio-ethnic-communal perspective.

Key Findings

In summary, these frameworks explore and highlight the importance of designing for the variability in personalities, pleasures, motivations, and abilities. These frameworks make a strong case for 1) embedding content within reachable, yet challenging goals, with strong feedback and mastery ability, 2) allowing for delightful and unexpected experiences that could not necessarily be achieved in the real world in the same way, 3) allowing for meaningful interaction with others, in variable ways, and 4) being aware of the accessibility of the designed space, as well as the variability of the audience for which it is being designed.

Learning and audience

In recent times, there has been a bit of a debate about whether commercial and serious games can benefit learning, with several studies on the subject (for example, see Connolly, Boyle, MacArthur, Hainey & Boyle, 2012; McClarty, Orr, Frey, Dolan, Vassileva, & McVay, 2012; Shute & Ke, 2012; Wouters, vanNimwegen, vanOostendorp & vanderSpek, 2013; Young et al., 2012) The most compelling evidence seems to state that games designed for learning (i.e., serious games) are significantly beneficial for learning and retention over traditional instruction, though are not significantly motivating (see Wouters et al., 2013).

The research on learning with digital games has often focused on the motivational and learning properties of games. As such, most of what we know about effective learning with games focuses less on learning styles and more on their multisensory potential (in other words, how effective game mechanics, attributes or design elements aid in learning, motivation or engagement). This may be in part because the research on learning styles has mostly remained inconclusive (Pashler, McDaniel, Rohrer, & Bjork, 2008).

Wounters et al. (2013) suggest that effective learning with serious games needs to 1) be supplemented with other instructional methods, 2) incorporate multiple training sessions, and 3) allow learners/players to work in groups. Their findings are very similar to findings involving other learning technologies, particularly computer-assisted instruction. Wounters et al. (2013) also offer that one reason games may not have been found more motivating than traditional instruction may have been competing outcomes such as "learning versus playing or freedom versus control" (p.13). They cite that the world of instructional design and game design are still in the process of alignment.

Koster (2005) outlines that learning can be problematic, particularly because learners look for shortcuts (or cheats). Cheating, however, does not allow us to fully understand a concept, and is often reflective of problems in the design. Cheating can involve using codes to easily gain money or experience, or downloading modded weapons or armor developed by others so that you can gain an unfair advantage. Exploiting the game, on the other hand, involves very experienced play. It involves finding work-arounds not intended by the developers, which can put certain players at an advantage when used. Someone who has mastered and explored the game system is better able to do this. Koster points out that human beings often want to get better at things and one way to do this is to make things more predictable and easier by exploiting (i.e., taking unintended shortcuts or racking up experience beating weaker opponents). As designers, however, we do not want players/learners to circumvent the challenges we have put in place.

Koster (2005) recommends that the game system can be successfully designed to minimize cheating and exploitation, as well as enhance learning. He recommends incorporating the following elements:

1. **Preparation:** Allowing a player to prepare before a given challenge with choices that can affect their chances of success (i.e., allow them to practice in advance, or heal before facing a strong opponent).
2. **A sense of space:** Create this through the landscape, and players.
3. **A solid core mechanic:** Create an intrinsically interesting rule sets.
4. **A range of challenges:** Vary the challenges they encounter in interesting ways.
5. **A range of abilities required to solve the encounter:** Provide multiple kinds of tools with multiple abilities. In many games, these abilities unfold over time as you play. Koster (2004) provides the example of checkers, where you learn to force the player to make moves that work against her over time, but not the first time you play.
6. **Skill required in using the abilities:** Vary the kinds of elements or tools a player has during play. Different resources and how they are applied can lead to success or failure, and skills develop over time as they learn to apply resources differently.

To ideally make a game a constructive learning experience, it should include:

1. **A variable feedback system:** A player should receive feedback on their performance and ways to improve it.
2. **Ways to deal with the mastery problem:** Finding ways to tailor the game to the player's level of experience. High-level players will not learn anything new from easy experiences and will end up exploiting; inexperienced players cannot learn from games that are too difficult.
3. **Failure should be part of the learning experience:** While Gee (2004) points out that games lower the consequences of failure, Koster (2004) feels that there should be an opportunity cost. You are more likely to learn if you are forced to prepare differently after a failed task.

Creating opportunity costs for failure can take many forms and does not have to involve losing it all. In fact, most contemporary games allow players to start near a particularly difficult part of the game (instead of going all the way back to an earlier or incredibly far point in the game). As Lazzaro (2004) points out, frustration can inspire focus and creativity, but it has to be effectively designed to do so. We do not want learners to abandon the objective, but we want them to understand there is an opportunity cost to not completing the experience as intended. We should try to scaffold that in the form of a learning-oriented goal or activity.

A further and fundamental consideration when designing games for learning is how formal or informal educational content is presented to the learner. "Learning mechanics are patterns of behavior or building blocks of learner interactivity, which may be a single action or a set of interrelated actions that form the essential learning activity that is repeated throughout a game" (Plass, Homer, Kinzer, Frye, & Perlin, 2011, p. 3). In designing for learning, Plass et al. (2011) make the case that learning mechanics must further be intrinsically and meaningfully connected with game mechanics. They argue that the learning mechanic must be grounded in the learning sciences or learning theory.

Learning mechanics describe which kinds of functions and scaffolds are needed in the environment, though not the actual game mechanics involved, which can vary by game design. An example of an ineffective learning mechanic would involve interrupting a racing or shooting game with popup "educational" questions before play could continue (Plass et. al., 2011). An example of an effective learning mechanic might be having a learner select or integrate related objects, though how they select or integrate them through game mechanics could vary by game or interface. For instance, a learner could drag one object onto the other, such as in a simple matching game, or break objects apart and put them back together again in new and meaningful ways, such as in *Minecraft*. The goal of the activity and the game type employed should reflect the learning outcomes desired (i.e., learning related objects or categories versus learning properties of objects that could make new objects).

Designing for inclusive learning

For many years, games were designed for demographics, which often meant designing for stereotypes and assumptions of what people liked according to their gender (Lazzaro, 2008). Female players who enjoyed playing what was considered male-themed games were often not researched or marketed to because they were thought of as "oddities" (Taylor, 2008). Some felt, however, it was important to create a market and design for female play precisely because it would help to create more common ground and encourage development for female interests (Cassel & Jenkins, 1998).

Contemporary research suggests that females and males enjoy more in common in games (Lazzaro, 2008). In fact, recent studies have found that once females are given equal chances to train, gender differences decline and skill sets that often put inexperienced female players at a disadvantage level out (see Feng et al., 2007; Jensen & deCassel, 2011; Vermeulen et al., 2011). For a full review on the evolution of this literature, see Richard (2013a).

Research highlights that more is going on than differences in assumed gender preferences. Recent events and research suggests that females experience a significant amount of harassment online. In fact, they are three times more likely to experience harassment when using voice chat to play online (Kuznekoff & Rose, 2013). Harassment and gender discrimination can play a large role in discouraging females from playing and participating equally in gaming and learning opportunities from games (Richard, 2013c; Richard & Hoadley, 2013).

Less has been studied regarding ethnicity and race. Studies have found that ethnic minorities do not have the same access to high tech computer equipment as Whites (DiSalvo & Bruckman, 2010) and that they are more likely to experience racial harassment when playing online (Nakamura, 2009; Gray, 2012; Richard, 2013c). Studies have found that ethnic minorities can be profiled by the way they speak or by their avatars. Studies have also found that players want to have the opportunity to play as their ethnicity, and minorities are not always allowed to choose avatars that look like them (Kafai et. al. 2010).

Shaw's studies (2012a; 2012b) have found that LGBTQ (Lesbian, Gay, Bisexual, Transgender, and Queer), gamers (also known as "gaymers") are more concerned about finding places where they can express their experiences, than the lack of LGBTQ characters. She attributes this in part to the need to find safe spaces from bigotry, as well as anxiety over exploiting gay identity.

Overall, research demonstrates that marginalized gamers, who are overwhelmingly female, minority, and LGBTQ, are more likely to be negatively affected by exclusionary practices in game spaces (Gray, 2012; Kuznekoff & Rose, 2013; Richard, 2013c; Richard, 2013d; Shaw, 2012a; Shaw, 2012b), which affects their ability to identify with gaming (Richard, 2013d; Richard & Hoadley, 2013; Shaw, 2012a; Shaw, 2012b), develop confidence in their skills (Richard, 2013d; Richard & Hoadley, 2013), and ultimately learn from games (Richard, 2013c; Richard, 2013d; Richard & Hoadley, 2013).

Research shows that the absence of female and ethnic minority characters in games makes female and ethnic minority players feel they do not belong and reinforces others feeling they do not belong (Lee & Park, 2011; Behm-Morawitz & Mastro, 2009). Further, research shows that stereotypes of ethnic minorities and sexualized female characters make female and minority players feel less confident in their abilities, and reinforce stereotypes that are negative in general (Dill & Burgess, 2013; Miller & Summers, 2007).

Richard (2013d) conducted a mixed-methods study of game players and online communities where she looked at players' gender, ethnicity, sexuality (among other demographics), gaming identification, and gaming sense of ability. She found that female and ethnic minority players were more vulnerable to stereotype threat (stress caused by negative stereotypes aimed at your gender or ethnic group), which would affect their performance and confidence with games and learning from games.

Specifically, through her three-year ethnography, which involved playing and participating in online and offline console and PC gaming, she found that harassment was a persistent and prevalent gatekeeping activity that marginalized female and ethnic minority play and participation in the space. Females were more likely to be harassed, though ethnic minorities (specifically, African Americans and Latinos) also experienced harassment around ethnic characteristics, when they were easy to discern, typically through "linguistic profiling" (Gray, 2012) or through profile stalking (i.e., the act of looking up another player's profile to figure out their gender, cultural background, or sexuality (Richard, 2013c)). Richard (2013d) further found that a female-supportive (yet co-ed) community reduced stereotype threat vulnerability for females, as well as increased confidence across gender (Richard, 2013d; Richard & Hoadley, 2013). Her data showed support that harassment and negative stereotypes in games could affect players differently (specifically females and ethnic minorities). When designing games for learning, stereotype threat is particularly important because it can affect how people perform on learning tasks along with long-term identification with that potential learning medium.

Assessment Considerations

There is not necessarily one way to understand player experience, but prevailing methods have used quantitative measures (typically through surveys), qualitative measures (typically through interviews or ethnography), or a combination of both. Survey measures can come in various forms and depend on what is being measured. When investigators are interested in how a specific game might affect player or learner outcomes, they may be applied concurrently (or at some point during game play), or retrospectively, involving reflecting upon game play. Some survey measures are more interested in overall characteristics of players or their views on their overall experiences, so measuring how one particular game affects them may not be as important as players' sense of how certain games or experiences around games shape them or motivate them.

Many survey measures, however, as well as interviews and related measures (e.g., think alouds), are considered subjective, because individuals have to reflect on their conscious meaning making around their experiences. Survey measures, interviews, and similar reflective measures are useful in understanding player experiences, especially when point of view is important. When measuring social experiences around play, for example, point of view and personal experience may be important.

Particularly when dealing with survey data, issues of validity and reliability are important. Validity issues concern whether an instrument is measuring what it is intended to, while reliability issues concern whether the instrument remains dependable over time. Yee's critique of both Bartle's player types (2006) and the Big Five personality traits (2005) highlight issues of validity. For example, Yee (2005) makes the case that there's actually a large amount of inter-correlation among the Big Five factors (except for neuroticism), demonstrating that they are not truly independently measuring discrete parts of our personality. Similar critiques of independence have been made about Bartle's player types, as discussed earlier.

Ethnographic methods have been used extensively in research on virtual worlds and online games (particularly massively multiplayer ones) to understand player experience in socially complex game spaces. Boellstorff, Nardi, Pearce, and Taylor (2012), who have all conducted large-scale ethnographies on player experiences in these kinds of spaces, have written an extensive and thorough guide to online ethnographic methods. Typically, researchers take on the role of participant and observer, taking in and participating in play practices, as well as cultural practices. Analysis is still highly negotiated through the individual researchers' experiences and perspectives, but ethnography, like many rich qualitative methods, can often offer great insights into social interactions, particularly when wanting to understand contexts of play and meaning making, as well as where and how play or learning may be different for different groups of players, due to context or differential experiences.

There are also measures that are considered less subjective, such as those that use eye tracking, galvanic skin response (GSR), functional magnetic resonance imaging *(fMRI)*, Electroencephalography (EEG), and facial or body expressions. Some of these seemingly objective measures, however, are still subject to interpretation, and may measure physiological or emotional responses to stimuli, but not necessarily learning outcomes in personal accounts or reflections on experience. Other forms of objective measures can involve implicit response tests, such as the implicit association test, where individuals rapidly respond to stimuli in a way that gets at underlying biases or associations.

Increasingly, scholars have argued for "stealth assessment" (Shute, 2011), or embedded and responsive assessment measures in games, so that games can be tailored for individual needs (e.g., Shute, 2011). For example, a game could vary its difficulty, provide just-in-time help, or offer dynamic feedback. It could also provide the teacher or instructor with feedback to help tailor instruction to students in other ways. Individual tailoring, however, may be complicated by collaborative, cooperative, or other kinds of multi-configurational play or learning. Furthermore, complex kinds of social experiences may be lost on these kinds of quantitative measures. Also increasingly, studies have relied on blending multiple methods to provide both detailed outcome measures (e.g., performance or learning outcomes), along with detailed case studies, interviews, or ethnographies, to give nuance and richness to the findings.

Future Needs

We are still uncovering which factors may derive motivations or pleasures from players, as well as the ways that social interactions and expectations influence and shape play. Researchers are starting to uncover and explore the relationships between large-scale interactions and individual experiences in context to further understand learning outcomes. As we start to learn more about who is playing, how much, and in what ways, especially in the ways that they play, learn and engage as compared to others with different backgrounds, pleasures, motivations and experiences, we will understand further about additional design consideration for addressing diverse players.

Case Study Three: *PlayForward: Elm City Stories* (Written by Sabrina Haskell Culyba)

PlayForward: Elm City Stories is a behavior change game developed in 2012 for Yale University's play2PREVENT lab by Schell Games, in collaboration with Digitalmill. The goal of PlayForward is to reduce players' risky behavior, thus reducing their exposure to HIV. It is a single-player, tablet-based game whose target audience includes at-risk young teens. It was designed for initial use in a clinical trial whose participants were located in the New Haven, Connecticut area.

PlayForward engages players with topics of risky behavior, including substance abuse, sex, and social pressure. The gameplay features story scenarios modeled after potential real-life situations, and minigames on developing strategies for navigating peer pressure, evaluating the riskiness of peers, identifying and sharing facts in a social setting, and decision making. The game also promotes future orientation, allowing players to create a profile based on their life aspirations like career, health, and family.

Because the game openly addresses serious and highly personal topics, it was important for the content to feel authentic to players. Early in the project, the play2PREVENT team forged a relationship with an afterschool program in the New Haven area with a representative group of teens from the target demographic. As the Schell Games development team was remote and had little firsthand experience with at-risk teens, the information and artifacts from this representative group were instrumental in shaping the authentic feel of the game. The participants in these activities were generally in the targeted age range of 11-14, though at times slightly younger and older teens were included to get a broader perspective. The information included:

1. In-depth interviews, which probed the teens' perceptions of risky behaviors, as well as their attitudes of the future. This information provided high-level direction on the types of scenarios and themes that would resonate with the demographic.
2. A hands-on "My Life" project, which asked the teens to map out a vision of their next ten years, giving insight into what they did (and did not) already think about in terms of their own future.
3. A open-ended storytelling activity, which prompted the teens to comment on a concept drawing of a crowded party scene. They were asked to describe what they thought was going on with each character, what had happened earlier, and what might happen later. This activity revealed how they evaluated social situations and the kinds of real-world stories they perceived going on around them.
4. A photo feedback project, which provided the teens with disposable cameras and asked them to photograph their life, including their homes, bedrooms, friends, clothes, as well as aspirational items like adult role models, dream homes, and dream cars. These images became guides for character and set designs, and informed the options available in the game for the player's profile.

5. Story review focus tests, which verbally led the teens through the game's stories, asking questions like "Do you know someone this has happened to?" or "What might happen next?" These helped shape the game's narratives to keep them relevant to the target demographic.

6. Line-by-line dialogue reviews prompted the teens to suggest rewrites of dialogue lines to sound more like something they or their friends might say. It became clear that word choice was particularly important for creating an authentic feel for peer pressure or sexual situations.

7. Art reviews of characters and scenes invited the teens to comment on details such as clothing styles and room layouts, to make sure the game's visuals felt familiar to the teens' real world lives.

8. An on-site visit by the development team allowed members of the Schell Games development team to see the New Haven community sites and observe a focus group in person.

Best Practices

Based on the survey of literature, the following design principles should be considered when thinking about the audience:

1. **Consider the learners' ability:** The abilities of learners should always been considered. Effective design for an audience is dependent on the audience's ability (physical and cognitive) to engage with the game.

2. **Consider the player diversity, in backgrounds as well as preferences:** Players have a variety of personalities, learning and emotional preferences. While we cannot address all players' preferences with one game, and research is inconclusive on whether learning styles are applicable, we can structure games that are complex enough to appeal to a variety of pleasures and learning activities.

3. **Allow for the core features of successful games:** Successful games create opportunities for immersion, achievement, interaction and socialization.

4. **Have strong feedback:** Players should have the opportunity for comprehensive and variable feedback that responds to their skill level and ways to improve it.

5. **Allow for responsiveness through design:** Games should tailor to the player's level of experience for optimal learning, and failure should have fair setbacks that require someone to learn from them.

6. **Provide diversity in representation:** Games should feature a variety of characters of different genders, sexualities, races, and ethnicities with varying abilities that are not stereotyped. Research shows that more diversity lowers people's negative stereotypes of others and increases players' own sense of ability.

7. **Create structures so that harmful behavior is minimized:** Harassment should be monitored and enforced in games, whether this is through the developers, educators or community administrators. Studies continue to show that harassment alienates ethnic minorities, females, and LGBT players. This kind of harassment does not just make players distance themselves from gaming, but from the skills and opportunities offered through gaming, like tech-savvy identity building. Also, they are put at significant disadvantage when it comes to learning from games.

8. **Accommodate learning in contexts where the game is played**: When designing for classroom learning, how to accommodate teachers' abilities to play and master the games should be considered, along with how they can monitor and support classroom management.

Resources

Books and Articles

Bartle, R. (1996). "Hearts, clubs, diamonds, spades: Players who suit MUDs." *Journal of Virtual Environments, 1*(1). Retrieved July 8, 2013 from http://www.mud.co.uk/richard/hcds.htm

Brathwaite, B., & Schreiber, I. (2009). *Challenges for game designers*. Boston, MA: Course Technology/Cengage Learning.

Fullerton, T. (2008). *Game design workshop: A playcentric approach to creating innovative games*. Burlington, MA: Morgan Kaufman.

Gee, J.P. (2004). *What video games have to teach us about learning and literacy*. New York: Palgrave.

Kafai, Y. B., Heeter, C., Denner, J., & Sun, J. Y. (2008). *Beyond Barbie and Mortal Kombat: New perspectives on gender and computer games*. Cambridge, MA: MIT Press.

Koster, R. (2005). *A theory of fun for game design*. Scottsdale, AZ: Paragylph Press.

Lazzaro, N. (2004). *Why we play games: Four keys to more emotion without story* (XEODesign, Inc). White Paper. Retrieved from: http://www.xeodesign.com/xeodesign_whyweplaygames.pdfhttp://www.xeodesign.com/xeodesign_whyweplaygames.pdf

Radoff, J. (2011). *Game on: energize your business with social media games*. Indianapolis: Wiley.

Richard, G. T. (2013b). "Designing games that foster equity and inclusion: Encouraging equitable social experiences across gender and ethnicity in online games." In G. Christou, E. L. Law, D. Geerts, L. E. Nacke & P. Zaphiris (Eds.) *Proceedings of the CHI'2013 Workshop: Designing and Evaluating Sociability in Online Video Games*. Retrieved from: http://www.scribd.com/doc/136417975/Proceedings-of-the-CHI-2013-Workshop-on-Designing-and-Evaluating-Sociability-in-Online-Video-Games

Richard, G.T. & Hoadley, C.M. (2013). "Investigating a supportive online gaming community as a means of reducing stereotype threat vulnerability across gender." In *Proceedings of Games, Learning & Society 9.0*. ETC Press.

Ryan, R. M., Rigby, C. S., & Przybylski, A. (2006). "The motivational pull of video games: A self-determination theory approach." *Motivation and emotion, 30*(4), 344-360.

Schell, J. (2008). *The art of game design: A book of lenses*. Boca Raton, FL: CRC Press.

Yee, N. (2006). "Motivations for play in online games." *CyberPsychology & Behavior, 9*(6), 772-775.

Games

Dow Day

Jewish Time Jump

Gone Home

References

Bartle, R. (1996). Hearts, clubs, diamonds, spades: Players who suit MUDs. Journal of Virtual Environments, 1(1). Retrieved July 8, 2013 from http://www.mud.co.uk/richard/hcds.htm

Behm-Morawitz, E. & Mastro, D. (2009). The effects of the sexualization of female video game characters on gender stereotyping and female self-concept. *Sex Roles*, 61, 808–823.

Boellstorff, T., Nardi, B., Pearce, C. & Taylor, T.L. (2012). *Ethnography and virtual worlds: A handbook of method.* Princeton University Press.

Brathwaite, B., & Schreiber, I. (2009). *Challenges for game designers.* Boston, MA: Course Technology/Cengage Learning.

Brink, K., Fowers, T., Long, T., Bura, S., Hiwiller, Z. & Vandenberghe, J. (2013). *Group report: Psychology for game designers* (Fat Labs, Inc.). White Paper. Retrieved from: http://www.projecthorseshoe.com/reports/ph13/Project_Horseshoe_2013_report_section_8.pdf

Callois, R. (2001). *Man, ply and games.* University of Illinois Press. (Original work published in 1961).

Caperton, I. H. (2012). *Learning to make games for impact: Cultivating innovative manufacturing skills for the digital economy.* Retrieved from: http://gamesandimpact.org/wp-content/uploads/2012/09/Idit-WhitehouseConv-Feb2012-1.pdfhttp://gamesandimpact.org/wp-content/uploads/2012/09/Idit-WhitehouseConv-Feb2012-1.pdf

Connolly, T. M., Boyle, E. A., MacArthur, E., Hainey, T., & Boyle, J. (2012). A systematic literature review of empirical evidence on computer games and serious games. *Computers & Education*, 59(2): 661–686.

Dill, K. E., & Burgess, M. C. (2013). Influence of Black Masculinity Game Exemplars on Social Judgments. *Simulation & Gaming*, 44(4), 562-585.

DiSalvo, B. & Bruckman, A. (2010). Race and gender in play practices: young African American males. In *Proceedings of the Fifth International Conference on the Foundations of Digital Games* (pp. 56-63). ACM Press.

Gee, J.P. (2004). *What video games have to teach us about learning and literacy.* New York: Palgrave.

Gray, K. L. (2012). Intersecting oppressions and online communities: Examining the experiences of women of color in Xbox Live. *Information, Communication & Society*, 15(3), 411-428.

Feng, J., Spence, I., & Pratt, J. (2007). Playing an action video game reduces gender differences in spatial cognition. *Psychological Science*, 18(10): 850-855.

Jensen, J. & de Castell, S. (2011). Girls@Play: An ethnographic study of gender and digital gameplay. *Feminist Media Studies*, 11(2), 167-179.

Fullerton, T. (2008). *Game design workshop: A playcentric approach to creating innovative games.* Burlington, MA: Morgan Kaufman.

Kafai, Y. B., Cook, M. S., & Fields, D. A. (2010). Blacks deserve bodies too!: Design and discussion about diversity and race in a tween virtual world. *Games and Culture*, 5(1), 43-63.

Koster, R. (2005). *A theory of fun for game design.* Scottsdale, AZ: Paragylph Press.

Kuznekoff, J. H., & Rose, L. M. (2013). Communication in multiplayer gaming: Examining player responses to gender cues. *New Media & Society*, 15(4), 541-556.

Lazzaro, N. (2004). *Why we play games: Four keys to more emotion without story* (XEODesign, Inc). White Paper. Retrieved from: http://www.xeodesign.com/xeodesign_whyweplaygames.pdf

Lazzaro, N. (2008). Are boy games even necessary? In Y.B. Kafai, C. Heeter, J. Denner & J.Y. Sun (Eds.) *Beyond Barbie and Mortal Kombat: New perspectives on gender and gaming* (pp. 198-215). Cambridge, MA: MIT Press.

Lee, J. R. & Park, S. G. (2011) Whose *Second Life* is this? How avatar-based racial cues shape ethno-racial minorities' perception of virtual worlds. *Cyberpsychology, Behavior & Social Networking, 14*(11): 637-642.

Mathews, J. M., & Squire, K. D. (2010). Augmented reality gaming and game design as a new literacy practice. In *Media Literacy: New Agendas in Communication* (pp. 209–232). University of Texas at Austin: Routledge

McClarty, K. L., Orr, A., Frey, P. M., Dolan, R. P., Vassileva, V., & McVay, A. (2012). *A Literature Review of Gaming in Education* (Research Report), Upper Saddle River, New Jersey: Pearson.

Miller, M. K., & Summers, A. (2007). Gender differences in video game characters' roles, appearances, and attire as portrayed in video game magazines. *Sex roles, 57*(9-10), 733-742.

Pashler, H., McDaniel, M., Rohrer, D. & Bjork, R. (2008). Learning styles concepts and evidence. *Psychological science in the public interest, 9*(3), 105-119.

Plass, J. L., Homer, B. D., Kinzer, C., Frye, J., & Perlin, K. (2011). *Learning mechanics and assessment mechanics for games for learning* (Games 4 Learning Institute, New York University). White Paper. Retrieved from: http://steinhardtapps.es.its.nyu.edu/create/classes/2505/reading/Plass%20et%20al%20LAMechanics%202505.pdf

Radoff, J. (2011). *Game on: Energize your business with social media games*. Indianapolis: Wiley.

Richard, G.T. (2013a). Gender and game play: Research and future directions. In B. Bigl & S. Stoppe (Eds.): *Playing with Virtuality, Theories and Methods of Computer Game Studies,* Frankfurt: Peter Lang.

Richard, G. T. (2013b). Designing games that foster equity and inclusion: Encouraging equitable social experiences across gender and ethnicity in online games. In G. Christou, E. L. Law, D. Geerts, L. E. Nacke & P. Zaphiris (Eds.) *Proceedings of the CHI'2013 Workshop: Designing and Evaluating Sociability in Online Video Games.* Retrieved from: http://www.scribd.com/doc/136417975/Proceedings-of-the-CHI-2013-Workshop-on-Designing-and-Evaluating-Sociability-in-Online-Video-Games

Richard, G.T. (2013c, Aug). The interplay between gender and ethnic harassment in game culture and its implications for play and learning. Paper presented at *the 6th Digital Games Research Association (DiGRA) Conference: Defragging Game Studies.* Georgia Institute of Technology, Atlanta, GA, USA.

Richard, G. T. (2013d). *Understanding gender, context and video game culture for the development of equitable digital games and learning environments* (Doctoral Dissertation). New York University, New York, NY, USA.

Richard, G.T. & Hoadley, C.M. (2013). Investigating a supportive online gaming community as a means of reducing stereotype threat vulnerability across gender. In *Proceedings of Games, Learning & Society 9.0.* ETC Press.

Rigby, S. & Ryan, R.M. (2007). *The player experience of need satisfaction (PENS): An applied model and methodology for understanding key components of the player experience* (Immersyve, Inc). White Paper. Retrieved from: http://www.immersyve.com/downloads/research-and-white-papers/PENS_Sept07.pdf

Ryan, R. M., & Deci, E. L. (2000). Self-determination theory and the facilitation of intrinsic motivation, social development, and well-being. *American psychologist, 55*(1), 68-78.

Ryan, R. M., Rigby, C. S., & Przybylski, A. (2006). The motivational pull of video games: A self-determination theory approach. *Motivation and emotion, 30*(4), 344-360.

Salen, K. & Zimmerman, E. (2003). *Rules of play: Game design fundamentals*. Cambridge, MA: MIT Press.

Schell, J. (2008). *The art of game design: A book of lenses*. Boca Raton, FL: CRC Press.

Shaw, A. (2012a). Talking to gaymers: Questioning identity, community and media representation. *Westminster Papers, 9* (1): 67-89.

Shaw, A. (2012b). Do you identify as a gamer? Gender, race, sexuality and gamer identity. *New Media & Society, 14*(1), 28-44.

Shute, V. J. (2011). Stealth assessment in computer-based games to support learning. *Computer games and instruction, 55*(2), 503-524.

Shute, V. J., & Ke, F. (2012). Games, learning, and assessment. In D. Ifenthaler, D. Eseryel & X. Ge (Eds.), *Assessment in Game-Based Learning* (pp. 43-58). New York: Springer.

Squire, K. (2011). Video games and learning: *Teaching and participatory culture in the digital age.* New York: Teachers College Press.

Sunden, J. & Sveningsson, M. (2012). *Gender and sexuality in online game cultures.* New York, NY: Routledge.

Vermeulen, L., Loy, J.V., De Grove, F. & Courtois, C. (2011). You are what you play? A quantitative study into game design preferences across gender and their interaction with gaming habits. In *Proceedings of the 5th International Digital Games Research Association Conference.* DiGRA.

Wouters, P., van Nimwegen, C., van Oostendorp, H., & van der Spek, E. D. (2013). A meta-analysis of the cognitive and motivational effects of serious games. *Journal of Educational Psychology, 105*(2), 249.

Vandenberghe, J. (2012, March). The 5 domains of play. Paper presented at the *Game Developers Conference 2012.* San Francisco, CA, USA. Retrieved from: http://www.darklorde.com/2012/03/the-5-domains-of-play-slides/

Yee, N. (2005, March). Hidden agenda: What do personality trait assessments really assess [web log post]. Retrieved from http://www.nickyee.com/ponder/big5.html

Yee, N. (2006). Motivations for play in online games. *CyberPsychology & Behavior, 9*(6), 772-775.

Yee, N. (2008). Maps of digital desires: Exploring the topography of gender and play in online games. In Y. B. Kafai, C. Heeter, J. Denner & J.Y. Sun (Eds.) *Beyond Barbie and Mortal Kombat: Perspectives on Gender and Gaming* (pp. 83-96). Cambridge, MA: MIT Press.

Young, M. F., Slota, S., Cutter, A. B., Jalette, G., Mullin, G., Lai, B., Simeoni, Z., Tran, M. & Yukhymenko, M. (2012). Our princess is in another castle: A review of trends in serious gaming for education. *Review of Educational Research, 82*(1), 61-89.

CHAPTER 12

Goals

Developing Goals and Objectives
for Gameplay and Learning

Charlotte Lærke Weitze, *Aalborg University, Copenhagen, Denmark, cw@learning.learning.aau.dk*

Key Summary Points

1   When designing learning games consider how the learning goals can interact with the game goals and how both should be addressed through the game mechanics used in the game.

2   Let the design of the progress toward the game goals make it necessary to engage with the intended learning goals as the player/student works her way through the game.

3   The design of the challenges, rules and feedback are important when implementing and aligning the learning goals with the game goals.

Key Terms

Game goals
Learning goals
Alignment of goals
Design of feedback
Goals in learning and games
Implementing learning

Introduction

"It is a delicate dance between art and science, between instructional design and game design, and between play and guided discovery" (Hirumi, Appelman, Rieber, & Eck, 2010, p. 37).

This chapter introduces goals in games and then potential differences between learning goals and goals in games, as well as the difficulties that may occur when implementing learning goals in games.

What are goals?

To design game goals for a learning game, we should begin by looking at the characteristics of goals and how they are traditionally used in games.

Goals are objectives that a person or a system desires to achieve (Oxford Dictionaries, 2014). In a game, a goal is what we strive for (e.g., goals can be to kill the dragon and rescue the princess). Goals are fundamental to games; they determine what the player has to do to win the game, and give the player a sense of accomplishment and progression. Goals are what a player reaches for in the game and they are traditionally quantifiable, meaning that the goals are entities that can be measured, depending on which goals we use. By making measurable goals, it is possible to tell when the goals are reached. The player will typically know if she has reached the goal through feedback in the game. For example, this feedback can be communicated using trophies, badges, points or unlocked new challenges and goals.

By adding a goal we can make a game out of casual activity. For instance, we can change "doing homework" to a game by stating "the person who finishes her homework first gets to choose what movie to see in the cinema." The goals are often central to the structure of the game, which means that goals are used to purposefully guide the player through the game, as they are the focal point of the player's desire in the game. A useful practice in designing goals is not just having one end goal, but a series of sub-goals that help guide the player. For example, when a player is working her way through the *Rayman Legends* game, she is guided by sub-goals. Examples of sub-goals in one of the challenges are catching fireflies and hearts giving her points and trophies when escaping from and fighting the boss monster, freeing different figures in the game on the way to complete one of the many levels. Here, you can regard the fireflies and hearts as small sub-goals, the aim of escaping and fighting the current boss monster as another sub-goal, the objective of freeing other figures as a sub-goals and the aim of completing the current level as a sub-goal. The overall goal of the game is to complete all the levels and become a hero. In this way all the sub-goals helps to gradually lead her toward the end-goal and also gives her a feeling of progress, thereby keeping her engaged in the overall experience (Fullerton, 2008; Ferrara, 2012).

Goals in a game can set the tone in a game and can also be adjusted to generate particular behaviors, actions, and feelings in a game (Fullerton, 2008). For example, in *Rayman Legends* the goals in the game will make the player run, jump, and stop. It can foster feelings (e.g., fear of the monster or joy of achieving the goal and defeating the monster). When it comes to what you want to achieve in a game you can aim to reach your goal, but you can also have it as your aim or goal to avoid a threat. For example, if you look at a scene in *Plants vs. Zombies*, the aim is not to be eaten by zombies, so your aim in the game is to avoid the threat of the zombies. The goal is to survive the hordes of zombies and kill enough of them within a certain timeframe; thus, the goal is to avoid the zombie attack.

Once we define the goal(s) of a game, we need to develop rules for how to reach this goal, and which obstacles or challenges are necessary to overcome to reach the goal. For example, in *Plants vs. Zombies* if you want to reach the goal of the next level by keeping the specific zombies out of your house at the current level, you have to plant enough flowers to save up for buying weapons, as well as to choose the right weapons and be strategic in the order and timing of using your protective weapons to be able to survive. Once a game's end-goal is reached, it means the player has won, and he must find a new game with new goals. In a way, winning causes a sort of "death" in the game experience (Koster, 2005).

How are goals in a game different from goals in learning?

There have been examples of games where the learning goals and game tasks are implemented separately, and the learner is rewarded with a small game or puzzle that is entirely separate from the learning objectives of the experience. For instance, a game could involve solving a math problem and then getting to play a short racing game as the reward (Ratan & Ritterfeld, 2009). This approach is traditionally called chocolate covered broccoli, because it hides what is supposed to be "not fun" or unappetizing under something delicious, such as games, while not making a connection between the learning and the fun in the game.

But how do learning goals and game goals differ? The basic difference between the learning goal and the game goal is that the learning goal is the knowledge and intellectual abilities we want the student to learn in the game, whereas the game goal is the actual goal the student/player is striving for in the game. But it will depend on the game how this difference is constructed and how close they come to each other. In some games, the learning goal is not the target game goal, but a means to reach the game goal. For instance, in the game *Citizen Science*, an adventure game that teaches scientific literacy and limnology (the study of freshwater lakes) to schoolchildren, the player's game goal is to restore a polluted lake, Lake Mendota. Through the play of the game, the learner/player gathers information and knowledge to build arguments that can convince people with influence in the game and change the life in the lake. In this way, the game goal is different, but related to, the learning goal. The learning goals enhance scientific literacy and knowledge about limnology, and this practice becomes the sub-goals that are necessary to achieve the larger game goal, which is to restore the polluted lake in the game. By focusing on the ecological needs of Lake Mendota, as well as its surrounding community, the game, through its goals, achieves its learning goals as well (e.g., the understanding and practice real-world issues and scientific practices). Thus, when designing learning games, we need to consider how the learning goals can interact with the game goals, and how the game mechanics support these goals. Game mechanics are what you can do in the game—the combination of actions with rules that produces the game or gameplay (Iuppa & Borst, 2010). For example in *Citizen Science* the designers succeeded in letting the learning goals (e.g., understanding and practice of limnology and how you can work toward saving a polluted lake) interact with the game goal (e.g., saving the polluted lake). The game mechanics support the goals since the rules, possibilities, and challenges in the game are constructed in a way such that the player/learner has to gain knowledge to experience and practice how they can work toward saving a polluted lake (through the non-playing characters (NPCs) in the game). The learning goals, game goals, and the content should be structured in a way that allows for a progressive comprehension of the content of the game (Annetta, 2010). Gee also describes this as "fish tanks" (Gee, 2007). A way to implement the learning goals is to be creating small simplified eco-systems or fish tanks in the game, starting out with a simplified model of a complex system, making it possible for the learner to interact with the system, and getting to know it little by little, and then letting the game add a bit more complexity along the way ending up with the learner having understood the complexity of the whole system and how it interacts.

The challenges of designing games with respect to learning goals

One of the difficulties about designing according to the learning goals is that the learning goals might not be easy to incorporate into the play of a game. In a learning game, the learning goals are essential. In other words, the learning goals are what are to be experienced, considered, practiced, and reflected upon. Teaching successfully through a learning game will only happen if we succeed in aligning our learning goals and game goals in the game in a way that both addresses the curriculum and keeps the fun of playing a game. This can be challenging, but when the process of learning and achieving competence is designed in a way that is fun in and of itself it can be done (Koster, 2005).

In the development and use of a game for learning in the classroom, it is important to ensure possibilities for implementation of the learning goals in a measureable and controlled way in the game, meaning that when you develop and implement a learning goal you should at the same time consider how this learning goal can be measured and aligned with assessment to be able to evaluate when the learner has reached the learning goal (Hirumi et al., 2010). Thus, considering how the learning goals are implemented in the game enhances the possibility of useful evaluations of learning, such as whether the particular parts of the curriculum were achieved through the play of the game in class as well as the extent to which the games were effective in helping the students learn (Institute of Play, 2014a).

Another challenge is that instructional designers, educators, and game designers construct goals differently. The instructional designer or educator aims to develop a game that helps the students reach the learning objectives. She has the expertise to choose and plan which content and learning activities will support the different learning processes that traditionally lead to the students reaching the learning goals. The game designer, on the other hand, knows how to design the gameplay and the different game elements, such as game mechanics, navigation, interaction, and levels, and how to make everything come together for a fun and interesting experience for the player (Iuppa & Borst, 2010). So where the teacher traditionally is focused on the learning, the game designer has his focus on how to make everything an interesting and coherent experience. The resulting game must be a balance between the aims of these two perspectives.

Case Study One: *Piano Dustbuster*

The *Piano Dustbuster* game from JoyTunes is an example of how piano teaching can work in a game experience. This game teaches children how to play piano, giving them the opportunity to train using their own real piano, using a stealth recording of what you play at the piano and letting the played tones influence the game. In this way there is a seamless integration between what is played on the piano and what is happening in the game. This is an innovative and intuitive way to introduce piano playing to children, which can be used by the children alone or as a supplement to actual piano lessons.

In the game you can choose to play many different songs and they are divided into different popular styles and levels of difficulty. Earning points and stars in the game provide an assessment of your progress. The game is divided between a rehearsal mode and a concert mode. In the rehearsal mode, an old lady in the game tries to sweep away the dust and the player has to help her by hitting the keys on her own piano at the right moment when the different speck of dust hits the piano keys in the game. This interaction will create the melodies played with the correct tones in the correct order at the correct time. The rehearsal mode provides more help than the concert mode; for example, it stops if you miss a tone. In the concert mode you are still sweeping dust and accompanied by an orchestra or a band. This accompanying feature is motivating because it sounds nice, like an entire band when you playing. Though the game will not be able to replace the piano teacher it is a motivating and engaging way of getting to know how to play different tunes. The game's gameplay is "composed" of traditional game elements (Weitze & Ørngreen, 2011), such as:

1. **Action stage:** There is a story with an old lady sweeping dust of the piano keys. And the *stage* in the game is not only inside the game but also "outside" at the real piano.
2. **A goal:** To be able to play a song without mistakes in the right tempo.
3. **Rules:** You have to hit the right keys at the right moment.
4. **Choice:** You can choose what songs you want to play and what style.
5. **Challenge:** You can progress through the different songs with ascending levels of difficulty.
6. **Feedback:** Different kinds of feedback are given, including:
    a. Short-term, as you are at once informed if you have played the right piano key.
    b. Long-term, as you are told how well you performed in different categories (number of right notes, accuracy).

A reward also can be considered as a kind of feedback, as the reward is that you get to play with a "real band" in the game after having practiced. You can also achieve stars when everything works out well for you. This game is a good example of how you can design a game by making it a supplementary motivational tool for learning.

Key Frameworks

In this section, I will cover the two concepts *ludus* (game-like structured goals) and *paidia* (play-like player-led goals), the design of game goals, the design of learning goals and how to align learning goals with game goals.

Clear and measurable goals are often what make a game differ from more ambiguous play activities (Salen & Zimmerman, 2004). This is indeed true for many traditional as well as learning games and is one way to categorize and characterize games. Prensky (2001) has divided learning games into a number of categories showing how different kinds of content, learning activities and subject matters are possible to implement in the different kinds of categories of games. We also have to consider that this way of matching subject matters and game categories when choosing style and shape of the game also to a large degree will dependent on the designer's imagination and innovative talent.

These design choices will influence how the goals in the game are designed. One framework that can be used for revealing characteristics of the game, making it clearer how to design goals, involves placing the games on the axis between the concepts *ludus* and *paidia* (Caillois, 2001). *Ludus* refers to a game that is more goal-oriented with structured rules and objectives. An example of this is *Dragonbox* (2014). *Dragonbox* is a math game teaching children a range of math rules (for example a + 0 = a) in an intuitive way. Here, the subject matter in itself is very rule-based and to reach the sub-goals in the game, the player is both guided as well as discover all the different rules and procedures by exploring the game. On the other hand, *paidia* is a more open-ended kind of playing that involves fantasy, creativity, and improvisation. The goals in *ludus* are structured, specific and measurable and it takes effort and acquisition of skills to reach them. In *paidia*, the goals are more flexible, implicit, changeable, and player-led, like playing in a sandbox. For example, in *Minecraft Creative Mode* (2014) players set their own goals, create their own worlds, and their goals may change as their designs evolve or if they are inspired by the materials or by other players in the game-world (Murphy Chertoff, Guerrero, & Moffitt, 2013). Teachers also use Minecraft in Creative Mode as a learning game where the teachers create the goals and rules according to the subject matter, which moves *Minecraft* toward the *ludus* pole. These different kinds of goals offer different kinds of possibilities for both subject matters as well as for pedagogies when designing games. The possibilities for letting the students decide for their own learning goals in the *paidia* end of the spectrum will for instance harmonize well with social constructivist pedagogies.

Table 1. The spectrum of *ludus* and *paidia*

	Ludus	**Paidia**
	←——————————————————————————→	
Characteristics of goals	Structured, specific and measurable	Flexible, implicit, changeable and player-led
Game examples	*Dragonbox*	*Minecraft Creative Mode*

Designing game goals

There are a number of methods to use when designing learning games, but when it comes specifically to establish game goals there are not many frameworks—game goals are typically part of the whole game design. Schell (2008) has outlined the qualities that goals should have in the game to make them appropriate and well balanced. The four most important qualities for goals are as follows:

1. Goals should be concrete in a way that makes it clear for the player what the ultimate goal is for the game. If there are a series of goals, these should also be understandable.
2. The goals should be challenging but achievable, letting the player feel that he will be able to reach the goals, so he does not give up.
3. The goal(s) should be designed in a way that both makes the player look forward to the achieving the goal, as well as enjoying having reached the goal. If you have placed the goal after the right level of challenge the goal will be rewarding in itself.
4. You also have to balance the goals in your game in the short- and long-term, and let them relate to each other in a meaningful way (Schell, 2008).

Goals are powerful in games since it is common to use the goals as an indirect control in games. For example, if you have a path splitting in two in a game, you cannot predict which direction the player will take, as she has her freedom to make her own choices. But, if you give the player a goal (e.g., find a new weapon to kill the dragon) and you give a hint about the new weapon being on the left side, then the player most likely will choose the left direction. When you have designed goals that make the player care for the game by wanting to achieve these goals, then you can sculpt the game world around these goals, since the player traditionally will choose to follow the paths that lead toward the goals (Schell, 2008).

Goals or objectives can also be used to help categorize games (Fullerton, 2008). This list of different kind of game goals in different categories of games is for commercial games, but may inspire us for developing game goals in learning games.

1. **Capture:** In capture games the goal is to destroy something that belongs to the opponent and at the same time avoiding being killed or captured. An example of this is *Chess*.
2. **Chase:** In a chase game the goal for player is to elude her opponent if she is chased, or to catch her opponent.
3. **Race:** In a race game, the player's goal is to reach a goal before the other players—the goal being either conceptual or physical in time. It will often be a mix of strategy and chance that determines who wins the race.
4. **Alignment:** In an alignment game, the goal is to arrange the objects in the game in a certain spatial configuration or create conceptual alignment. Examples of this are *Tic-tac-toe* or *Tetris*.
5. **Rescue or escape:** In a rescue game, the goal is to bring a unit in the game in safety. An example of this is *Mario Brothers*.

6. **Forbidden act:** In this kind of game the goal is to break the rules or do wrong moves, such as *Twister*, for example. These games are traditionally not digital games.

7. **Construction games:** In the game the goal is to build, manage and maintain objects. This can for example be *SimCity* or *Minecraft*.

8. **Exploration games:** In exploration games the goal for the player often is to explore the game areas and at the same time collect treasures and solve puzzles.

9. **Solution:** The goals in these games are to solve puzzles more accurately or before the opponents.

10. **Outwit:** The goal in outwit games is to use your knowledge to win over your opponent, for example *Trivial Pursuit*.

If we are using a list such as the above for inspiration when creating game goals in learning games we should be careful not just to create commercial games with learning implemented superficially in the gameplay, but instead reflect on how we can use the different kinds of goals, and also reflect on the quality, integrity and relevance of the goals in a creative way (Belman & Flanagan, 2009). One example of a non-commercial game use of goals can be experienced in the game *Hush* (2007). This serious game evokes a story about a personal experience of a complex historical situation from Rwanda and focuses on a singular, personal experience as a solitary approach to the topic of genocide (Bogost, 2014). *Hush* is created with inspiration from the Values at Play/Tiltfactor Lab's *Grow-A-Game-Cards* (2014). In *Hush* you are a mother and the goal is that you must calm your baby by singing a lullaby (tapping with the right rhythm at the right key). The story takes place during war, and if the mother fails to keep her child from crying, they will be discovered and killed. This is an example of a very different use of goals in a game. The *Grow-A-Game-Cards* are a deck of cards used to inspire game design that incorporate values into play. There are four card categories: challenges, games, values, and verbs. The game designer takes a random card from each category and then uses the combination of cards for a brainstorm on the design of a new game. In the *Grow-A-Game-Cards* (2014) the goals are implicit, in the sense that the goals are to be found in all the different games in the game category. For example if you get the game card, *Go*, the card will tell you, "one player uses black stones, the other white stones. In turns the players "capture" as much territory as possible on a grid lined board." This could be interpreted as a version of a goal from Fullerton's (2008) "capture" category above. When playing or designing with the *Grow-A-Game-Cards*, three card categories, and the specific card, might be:

1. Value: family
2. Challenge: social inequality
3. Verb: wandering

The deck challenges the user to create a game that encompasses the four cards in an innovative way. In a learning game, it would be relevant to use the game goals as a means to make the learning situated in the sense that some of the game goals can be used to make the game relevant compared to where this learning could take place in the real world. For example, we could design a math game that takes place in a shop, where the shop owner has to keep account with how much he is buying and selling on a daily basis. A goal in this imaginary game may be to earn more than the storeowner next door, and use this as a way to learn basic addition and subtraction. So, when designing game goals it is important to be creative and consider how the game goals can relate to the learning experience.

Designing learning goals

There are a number of methods to use to establish learning goals. In this section I will describe a framework for designing learning consequences for setting learning goals, and then explain characteristics of how learning goals can be defined and designed. Next, I will describe six levels of understanding when mastering the learning goals, and then conclude with an explanation of how to design a progression when implementing the learning goals.

Framework for learning design

Setting the learning goals is a part of the entire design for learning, that is, how you plan to carry out the teaching and learning (Laurillard, 2012). Learning goals are a tool that can be used by the teacher and students to improve teaching and learning, and they should be clear, relevant, realistic and meaningful. Clear learning goals will make it easier for the student to evaluate her own learning process and work. When choosing your learning goals, these goals should be seen in the context of the learning conditions, the setting of the teaching, the educational content, the learning processes and the need for evaluation of the learning all parts of Hiim & Hippe (1997) framework for learning design. All of these elements are intertwined and should all be considered when designing a learning game. Though we aim to design the learning goals in the game, it is also important to consider the following (Hiim & Hippe, 1997):

1. **Learning conditions:** This is the users' prerequisite for learning. What prior knowledge can the learner already be expected to have, or what knowledge does she need to have to be able to reach the learning goals and be a successful learner in the game?
2. **Setting of the learning:** The setting of the game is important, but we also have to be aware of time available and other contextual conditions to meet the learning goals from the curriculum.
3. **Learning goals:** This includes a list of the learning goals, short-term and long-term, to be achieved in the game. It is a highly motivating factor if the students are allowed to be a part of choosing their own learning goals to make them meaningful for the students. These goals can traditionally be seen as a contract between the student and the teacher, that is what they both aim at respectively teaching and learning.
4. **Learning content:** This answers the question: What specific learning content should we choose to make the student able to reach the learning goals?
5. **Learning process:** The learning processes are supported by all the learning activities that we design to make the student reach the learning goals. These activities are determined by the subject matter, but also to a great extent to which pedagogical approaches and learning theories we want to use in the game. The learning theories can be based on behaviorism, cognitive science, social constructivism, constructionism (Dede, 2008; Wu, Hsiao, Wu, Lin,

& Huang, 2012) or experiential learning (Kolb, 1984). Many recent evaluations on research projects evaluating the efficiency of learning games emphasize that we should make a clear standpoint about which learning theory we use when designing games, since this will help in our later ability to measure the effectiveness of the game in helping to reach the learning outcomes (Wu et al., 2012).

6. **Evaluation/assessment:** The point is that we also need to design for evaluation and assessment of whether our learner has reached the learning goal and the growth and mastery we have aimed for in the game. These six points of attention are important to consider when we design our learning game, since this will help ensure that the learner reaches the learning goal.

When designing the learning in the game, the learning goals are what we are aiming for, but the pedagogical approaches will vary depending on the subject matter. If, for example, the learning goal is learning the alphabet, this involves understanding the abstract relationship between symbol and sound, and part of the learning process will involve repetition and memorization, but also reflection and evaluation. On the other hand, acquisition of social skills, for example, will acquire another set of skills, competencies, and attitudes. As in more traditional learning processes outside games, we always have to consider what the student should learn before choosing how she will learn it in a learning game (Kirriemuir & McFarlane, 2006), and thus what kind of learning activities will help the student to achieve the learning goals.

Definition and design of learning goals

The learning goals traditionally capture the three areas: knowledge, skills, and attitudes (Hiim & Hippe, 1997), though some taxonomies prefer to define the third area as competencies (Winterton, Delamare-Le Deist, & Stringfellow, 2006). The knowledge goals describe which knowledge and intellectual abilities the students should learn (Hiim & Hippe, 1997). The skills have a more practical nature and encompass what the student can do with her knowledge and how she can demonstrate her knowledge. The attitudes are learning goals encompassing feelings, attitudes and values (Hiim & Hippe, 1997). Competence is interpreted in many ways but can be interpreted as learning goals covering a combination of the theoretical knowledge and the practical skills (Winterton et al., 2006).

We should aim to design clear learning goals to make it easy for the student to comprehend what she should learn and to make the learning goals easy to evaluate after the learning process for the teacher. One way this is done is by making the goals observable, so we can see if the student masters the learning goal. This is often obtained by applying action verbs in the formulation of the learning objectives. An example of this is, "after playing [a specific game], the student should be able to [recognize/ demonstrate/ calculate/ decide/ evaluate/ formulate] [a fact, concept, topic, theme, task, activity, or skill] (Hiim & Hippe, 1997). A way to start formulation learning goals is to end the sentence: "After playing [this game] you should be able to [blank]."

A commonly used taxonomy of cognitive complexity was developed by Bloom (1956). In the slightly revised version (Anderson & Krathwohl, 2001, p. 67-68), the model describes six levels of understanding and mastering the learning goals, formulated as the students thinking according to the cognitive levels of complexity. The ascending levels are: remembering, understanding, applying, analyzing, evaluating and creating. Designing the learning objectives with these different cognitive levels in mind will give an overview of how and at which level we expect our students to be able to master the learning goals, and these levels will also help making the learning goals more simple to measure when we evaluate what has been learned in the game and at what level of cognitive rigor (Hess, Jones, Carlock & Walkup, 2009). When studying a subject such as human rights, the specification of the cognitive levels when designing the learning goals will make it possible to measure if the student only is able to remember basic human rights or if she is able to apply and use human rights concepts for analyzing complex social situations.

Progression in the choice of learning objectives in the game

When designing learning goals you should also be aware of the progression in the learning to make the goals attainable. Learning progressions within a content area begin at the novice level with the core concepts and skills as the learning goals; these core concepts and skills are considered fundamental. To progress through a content area to reach the learning goal, every learner needs to master these core competencies. For example, you could say that the student must learn and master the rules and procedures within each learning topic to achieve the learning goal (Dreyfuss, 2001). This is one of the things that successful computer games do very well. As the student has acquired the knowledge or the learning goals in the novice level, the rules and skills are integrated into each other, and you can begin to let the student get to know more complex relationships within the current topic, higher learning goals as in Bloom's taxonomy of cognitive complexity. In education, it is important to take the student's zone of proximal development into account (Vygotsky, according to Santrock, 2008). This zone is located between the student's actual level of development and the potential development. You need to support and scaffold the implementation of the learning goals and slowly begin to "remove the scaffolding" until the student is able to work on his own at the current level of competence. This should be followed by the next level in the new zone of proximal development, and in this way he will progress in an expanding cycle, reaching new learning goals progressively.

Aligning game goals with learning goals

There are a number of different methodologies for aligning game goals with learning goals. I will start by describing the *Q Design Pack for Games and Learning*, then Whitton's recommendations for implementing learning in games, then The Smiley Model, which explains how the game elements in this model relates to the learning goals.

One methodology for aligning game goals with learning goals is by the Institute of Play and described in their book, *Q Design Pack for Games and Learning*. This book explains that, "All effective classroom games are designed with specific learning goals in mind. Before you can design games focused on specific learning goals, you need to learn about game design" (Institute of Play 1, 2014, p. 11). Learning goals and game goals can be aligned by providing a practice space for goal-oriented challenges. For example, in the game *Dragonbox* (2014), the student/player is provided with a practice space in which she can gradually move through the challenges, explores and solve the puzzles reaching the game goals and learning goals of each level.

The *Q Design Packs* offer a framework to develop learning games and within this frame it is central to help align game goals with learning goals (Institute of Play 1, 2014; Salen, Torres, Wolozin, Rufo-Tepper, & Shapiro, 2011). To align game goals with learning goals, we first generate ideas with the learning goal in mind, while also considering how to assess these goals during and after gameplay. This is based on backward planning, which means knowing your students learning goals, and the final assessment before planning the individual lessons and activities (Wiggins & McTighe, according to Institute of Play 1, 2014). This is followed by an elaboration of the game design comprising an overall mission with an overall game goal and several quests with sub-goals on the way to the end goal. At the Institute of Play, the students have used this framework for making their own learning games.

Whitton, in *Learning with Digital Games* (2009), states that for a learning game to be a successful learning tool, it should be designed in a way that ensues that the game goals support the learning goals. Whitton suggests creating a list that describes the intended learning goals, followed by a description of the traditional learning activities that would lead to the student achieving these learning goals. Then, this should be followed by a process of deciding which learning activities can be modified or embedded within a game, as things we can do in the game. Whitton does not directly mention the role of the game goals in this design process.

There are many attempts to design frameworks for educational game design (Winn, 2008; Staalduinen & Freitas, 2011). The Smiley-Model is a game design model describing how to design engaging learning games (see Figure 1) (Weitze & Ørngreen, 2011). The model addresses how to design the learning and how to implement the learning elements into the game while at the same time always considering how to make the game motivating and engaging. The Smiley-Model uses the Hiim & Hippes (1997) learning design framework described above for the learning design (Weitze & Ørngreen, 2011).

In the Smiley-Model, the game goal is one of the six game elements you can use when you want to "set the learning design into play" (Weitze & Ørngreen, 2011). The five other game elements are: 1) action space, 2) rules, 3) choice, 4) challenge, and 5) feedback. All the game elements are intertwined and thus, the game goals are strongly related to the other game elements, when designing a learning game.

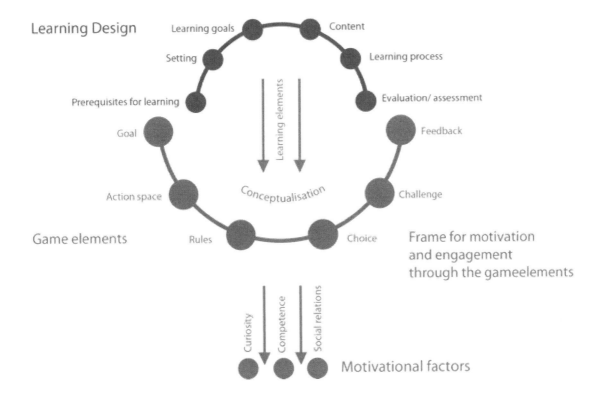

Figure 1. The Smiley Model. (Weitze & Ørngreen, 2011).

Because the game goal differs from the learning goal, we need to consider how we actually implement the learning objectives in the game. The game mechanics, or which actions can be taken in the game, what we can do, provide the structure to the game.

If all the game elements are intertwined, where are the learning goals found in a game? The "challenges" in a learning game should be encompassing the learning goals, the learning content, and the learning activities. For example, challenges can be, patterns you have to recognize, rules you have to learn, tasks that should be solved, and hand-eye coordination to be learned (Koster, 2005). The framing of the learning goals should determine which challenges are appropriate to include helping to meet the learning goals. For example, when playing a learning game the purpose is to attain the learning goal and to learn to master the action or to understand the pattern. By playing the game successfully, the learner will automatically show her competence when overcoming the challenges, since completing the game would require that she knows how to solve the problem. If the student/player finds it difficult to meet the challenge in the game, the game should provide feedback or scaffolding, breaking down the task into smaller game goals to support the player.

Koster (2005) suggests that challenges can be patterns or skills you have to learn, and similarly, Gee (2005) suggests that it is possible to use skills as strategies in games. Gee (2005) explains that you can design learning in a way that lets the learner practice a skill (this skill being part of the learning goals) as part of a strategy to accomplish the game goals she wants to accomplish. In this way, the learner will feel like the practicing process is part of a strategy to accomplish her game goal, removing the attention from the traditional boredom that occurs when practicing the same thing over and over again.

When implementing learning elements into the game and in this situation observing and designing the connection between the game goal and the other game elements in the Smiley-Model the player will make some "choices" in the game and the "rules" are determining when the game goals are reached or not reached. If the learning goals for example are to learn algebra in the *Dragonbox* game, the "rules" at the same time are a big part of the learning process since they are making the student/player reach the "learning goals" by letting her train "basic memorization" and even reflexes, by doing the same thing over and over if she does not succeed the first time. This learning will happen while the student is working her way through the game (Flanagan, Hash, & Isbister, 2010).

Moreover, the 6th game element "feedback" is crucial to let the student/player know if he has reached the goals and to assure that learning has occurred (Table 2). In fact, feedback in the game corresponds very well with the feedback that is needed when learning (Murphy et al., 2013). If "short-term feedback" in the game is given within one and a half seconds on the action taken (Wilms, 2011), research suggests that this will give the student/player the opportunity to experience the feeling of "learning by doing," meaning developing and learning as a result of first-hand experience (Chatfield, 2010; Kirriemuir & McFarlane, 2006). If the player does not fulfill the learning goal he should have "feedback." The "long-term feedback" given in a game should be more instructive and can provide guidance and strategic feedback (process-feedback) (has resemblance with formative feedback in learning) or give information on action/performance-based data (outcome-feedback), which then will lead the learner toward the learning goal (Sanchez, Cannon-Bowers, & Bowers, 2010) (For more details on feedback, see Murphy et al., 2013).

Table 1. Feedback on the sixth game element in the Smiley Model

Feedback		Characteristics
Short-term feedback		Within 1,5 seconds on the action taken, enables the experience of "learning by doing"
Long-term feedback	*Process feedback*	*Instructive, provides guidance and strategic feedback*
	Outcome feedback	*Performance-based data*

In the game development process and when the game is tested you have to alter, add and adjust the different game elements to improve the game and reach both the learning goals as well as the game goals (Schell, 2008).

Case Study Two: *Re-Mission 2*

Re-Mission 2 is a game for young people with cancer developed by HopeLab, a research and development nonprofit company. *Re-Mission 2* consists of six small games and the aim is to help young people with cancer fight their disease. The learning goals are to teach young people to stick to their treatments and shift attitudes about chemotherapy since these two elements are important parts of a successful treatment that helps to fight cancer. The game aims to motivate the players to stick to their treatments by boosting self-efficacy and building positive emotions in the players.

For children, a problem with cancer treatment is that it is a very rough treatment both physically and psychologically. The children sometimes feel more ill after their chemotherapy treatment, and therefore, at times it feels like they are hurting themselves more by sticking to the treatment. But this treatment will help them fight the disease, and therefore it is crucial that the children work with and not against the treatment. The knowledge about the disease and treatment is normally given by doctors as written information and is difficult for the children to understand and learn. The game has been developed by medical professionals, game developers, and young patients and has been designed so the children learn about what is going on inside their bodies when cancer attacks. The game also gives the children an idea of what power they have in defeating cancer.

The learning goals and game goals are aligned in *Re-Mission 2*. For example, the learning goals are:

1. That cancer can be defeated.
2. That you have different kinds of possibilities to take an active part in defeating cancer.
3. What is going on inside the body when cancer is attacking and how the different kinds of medical treatments work.
4. That the body has weapons and there are also medical weapons that can be used to fight cancer.
5. That there are different kinds of cancer cells more and less aggressive, so you have to attack them in different ways.

In the game, the player is put inside the human body to defeat cancer, being able to use weapons such as chemotherapy, antibiotics, and the body's natural defenses. The overall goal is to defeat cancer and there are different sub-goals inside each game.

In the game *Nanobot's Revenge* in *Re-Mission 2*, the mission and game goal is to defeat the Nuclear Tyrant and his forces. The player is the powerful microscopic robot Nanobot designed to blast away cancer and the mission is to prevent the cancer cells completing the tumor and stop the tumor from reaching the blood stream. The goal is thus concrete, achievable, and is designed in a way that makes the player look forward to achieving them. The game goals also give the player an opportunity to feel that he achieves competence, autonomy, and control when being able to defeat the Nuclear Tyrant because he is learning what it takes to kill the bad cells. There are nested goals in the game, since there are different kinds of challenges with enemy-cells to be defeated at the different levels in the game—all representing different kinds of cancer cells having different kinds of ways to build cancer and resist the players' attacks. The player, on the other hand, has different kinds of weapons with which to defeat the bad cells (e.g., chemo, radiation, antibiotics) and the rules in the game determines if you beat the Nuclear Tyrant and his forces (e.g., some of the bad cells can only be defeated with specific kinds of treatment). The sub-goals make it easier for the player to understand the game and experience small successes while managing the different challenges. The game is thus designed so the learning goals are implemented in an overall mission with an overall game goal and several sub-quests with sub-goals on the way to the end goal. By playing the game with progression toward the game goals, the player is learning what is going on in the body when cancer is attacking, experiencing that he has the power to use the different kind of treatments to fight the bad cells and is engaged with the intended learning goals while playing the game.

The research suggested that playing *Re-Mission* (the first *Re-Mission* game with a gameplay that resembles *Re-Mission 2*) significantly improved key behavioral and psychological factors associated with successful cancer treatment and that the game had an impact on the biological level as well (Kato, Cole, Bradlyn, & Pollock, 2008). The players showed a faster increase in self-efficacy and also showed a faster acquisition of cancer-related knowledge. The results indicate that *Re-Mission* successfully reached its learning goals through the game goals, giving a positive impact on the young peoples health behavior. Furthermore, another study showed that the fact that the young people with chronic illness was actually playing the game instead of just watching someone else playing the game is the main reason for the activation of the brain's positive motivation circuits, supporting earlier findings suggesting that *Re-Mission*'s effectiveness stems from its impact on individual emotional and motivational processes. The impact on the emotional processes leads to a shift in the young people's attitudes and emotions, which helps boost the players' adherence to the prescribed chemotherapy and antibiotic treatments (Cole, Yoo, Knutson, 2012). The *Re-Mission* games have thus successfully been able to align learning goals and game goals.

Key Findings

In this section, I discuss research on findings in game goals and describe Hirumi et al.'s (2010) experiences with implementing learning goals in the game.

Research findings on game goals

The game goals should be motivating, and this will happen if they arouse curiosity, and provide a sense of competence, autonomy, and control (Weitze & Ørngreen, 2011). If you give the player an opportunity to choose and adjust her own goals, research suggests that it will enhance feelings of freedom, autonomy and give her the possibility of targeting special interests (Deci & Ryan, 2000).

Game goals should be presented in a way that ensures that a structured flow of goals following and nested inside each other will pull you through the game. This means presenting a long-term goal or overall goal (e.g., rescue the princess and become a hero), and medium-term goal (e.g., kill level the dragon) and the short-term goals (e.g., collect jewels for the princess). These goals are nested such that the small goals help progress and guide the player toward the larger goals. Larger and smaller goals can be achieved throughout the game (Deterding, 2011). Splitting game goals into many small and large goals will help to provide a sense of having many small successes for the player (Chatfield, 2010). It is also important to link the goals to each other in a meaningful way so the game can be experienced as coherent (Schell, 2008).

Implementing learning goals in the game

Instructional designers may know little about game development and on the other hand game developers often may know little about training, education and instructional design. Therefore, it sometimes might be difficult to work together for the two professions, being able to use and realize the potentials of both game and learning (Hirumi et al., 2010; Iuppa & Borst, 2010).

Some of the differences for learning designers and game designers can be described like this: For game designers the goals and outcomes are important, but goals are only secondary to the gameplay itself (Koster, 2005). For the learning designers goals, outcomes are very important and have a high priority. The game designer will prioritize an engaging gameplay, perhaps sacrificing veracity and coherence. This might seem to be happening in the wrong order but in learning games the goals are not more important than an engaging gameplay. Instead the learning goals and game goals are more like "anchor points on intersecting continua" and not opposed concepts (Hirumi et al., 2010, p. 32).

On the other hand the learning game designer should not ignore the learning goals and it is important to choose appropriate educational strategies and plan for assessment in the game. Hirumi et al. (2010) suggest that the key lies in finding ways to incorporate gameplay into our objectives, and to design effective learning into gameplay design. If the game is not fun, a game designer will often try to find a way to solve that situation at once, without playing the same full attention to assure that the learning goal is met. The learning goals do not have to be represented explicitly in the game, but we can aim to align the desired learning outcomes with the game outcomes, and at the same time aim to facilitate learning and engagement (Hirumi et al., 2010).

Game designers and learning designers need to work together and understand each other's perspectives. The game designers will design challenges, quests, obstacles and puzzles at the same time deciding for the conditions for progress and mastery. The learning designers on the other hand can elaborate on the "Learning Task Maps," specifying the skills that will be needed to achieve the overall goal. The game and learning designers then move on to specifying the context, behavior, as well as the criteria for mastery of each challenge or skill. In a learning game, the evaluation and feedback in the game has to include evaluation of the learning goals. On the other hand, the learning designers have to learn and understand that evaluation has to be imbedded in the gameplay, and that this might change the traditional strategies and sequence of learning as well as some of the challenges and strategies in the game may go beyond traditional achievement of the learning goals.

What is actually learned in the game?

The aim is to design the game in a way that enables the player to reach the learning goal as well as the game goal. To do this, we should also consider the difference between the two (Staalduinen & Freitas, 2011, p.44):

1. What the player can learn in the game, that is, what the game's creator has intended in the design concerning learning goals.
2. The skills and topics the player must learn to be able to finish the game. This should partly be the same as what the player must learn in the game.
3. Things that the player actually has learned after playing the game.
4. Collateral learning: This is what the player learns in the game that was not directly intended or just was not connected directly to the subject matter.
5. "Cheats" or the things the player has learned in the game, often by taking short-cuts or exploring the game, but sometimes a consequence of this also is that the student skips over the intended learning in this process (Staalduinen & Freitas, 2011, p. 44).

No matter how thoroughly you plan your implementation of the learning goals and align them with the game goals, you need to playtest your game with real students to see if your intentions came through.

Assessment Considerations

In learning games assessment has an important role, since we want to be able to investigate if the student has achieved the learning objectives while playing the game. Feedback in a learning game is essential, since the possibility to give individual informative feedback to the student is one of the advantages of learning games. Games should be able to gather data from the learner and give direct, useful and relevant feedback, telling the student where he is in the learning process and where he should consider going next. We need to decide how the learning objectives will be measured in the game and how student performance will be evaluated to provide actionable and relevant feedback and support student self-reflection (Wilson, Bejar, Scalise, Templin, Wiliam, & Irribarra, 2012).

Likewise, a teacher needs to set the learning objectives, select content appropriate for reaching the learning objectives, design appropriate learning activities, and after having conducted these activities, observe and evaluate/assess the obtained learning of the students, followed by giving helpful feedback to the student afterward (Hiim & Hippe, 1997). The same type of process needs to be integrated into the game's design.

Evaluation should happen in the game as well as around the game. Staalduinen & Freitas (2011) distinguishes between three kinds of player assessment in games:

1. **Post-game assessment:** Here the teacher tests after the game with a written or oral test examining what the student has learned. This is not really a part of the game, but can be a good way to test if the teacher has used a commercial game for learning.
2. **Post-game debriefing or evaluation:** This kind of assessment is an evaluative talk between the students/players and the teacher about which experiences they have had in the game. (Staalduinen & Freitas, 2011).
3. **In-game feedback:** The game measures progress, achievement, and scores (long-term feedback), that is feedback on the player's actions in the game (Staalduinen & Freitas, 2011; Wilson, Bedwell, Lazzara, Salas, Burke, Estock, Orvis, & Conkey, 2009; Salen & Zimmerman, 2004).

Learning is situated inside learning games and therefore the assessment also can be designed to happen continuously within the narrative context of the game. This can both happen with short-term goals (e.g., by solving the puzzle and moving on in the game), and long-term goals (e.g., by solving all the challenges and reaching the final goal). Successful performance is therefore not necessarily communicated as it is in traditional teaching (e.g., giving marks), instead assessment in games is happening as part of the story through real (game) world consequences (e.g., you unlock new challenges, you move to another part of the world, you level-up when having solved one of the learning goals). In this kind of in-game assessment it is important to understand the difference between assessment in games and in traditional teaching and design in a way such that the learning goals also take the game context into account (Hirumi et al., 2010).

It is important that we create a supportive environment for learning (Wiliam, 2012). When we give feedback in games, we basically either tell the student if her current performance has reached the goal or has fallen short on the goal. Our wish is that the student's response is increased effort and aspiration toward the learning goals. If the feedback gives the learner a feeling that she might fail while many others has succeeded, she might be disengaged, deciding that it is better to be thought lazy than dumb, and thus she does not continue the progress toward the learning goal. Thus, to increase the likelihood of a productive student response you should:

1. Make the game a safe place to make mistakes.
2. Let the feedback effectively convey the idea that everyone can become smart. If the learner does not feel smart, then he is just not smart "yet."
3. Provide the learner with the support needed in a way that acknowledges that we do not all learn the same way, and that is okay.
4. Enable the student to focus on the comments and details of the feedback, and not on the scores.
5. Give useful feedback only focusing on the subjects that the learner can change.
6. Give feedback in a way that gives space and place for the learner to improve the results.

Future research

There is little research to be found on how to align the learning goals with the game goals, therefore the field of learning games can benefit from further research in this area, since a number of studies confirm the importance of aligning the learning goals with what can be learned in the game (Gee, 2011; Wilson et al., 2009) and the need of frameworks for doing this (Akilli, 2007). There have been many pedagogical approaches when designing game-based learning (Wu, et al., 2012; Kebritchi & Hirumi, 2008), for example, behaviorism, cognitivist or constructivism. To be able to assess the variables in a successful learning game, we should define which learning theories are behind the design of the game, since this will give an opportunity to measure the pedagogical components, among these the learning goals, and later repeat the success in other learning games. Dede (2011) recommends establishing common research strategies and models for educational games to aim at making studies that complement each other in what and how they explore. One way to research how to better align learning goals with game goals is to observe and analyze the conditions of when learning games are successful at providing an effective learning environment for the students and then take the following into consideration: the pedagogical approach, the curriculum, the subject matter, the context, and the characteristics of the students, teachers in the learning situation in question, and mapping these variables that are in every learning situation (Dede, 2011). This will be a better way of researching instead of aiming at universal frameworks, which will work in every condition since no educational approach and no educational technology will be universally effective. Then, we might be able to take all the necessary parameters into consideration when aiming at embedding the leaning goals into the game's goals and game's mechanics.

Case Study Three: Research Labs

A number of research labs and centers are dedicated to the study of implementing learning into games and how to assess the learning in and around the game.

Glasslab at Institute of Play has developed *SimCityEdu* (2014) a *SimCity*-based learning tool that allows teachers to make use of the already provided lesson plans or to design their own lesson plans inside the game. In *SimCityEdu*, students can explore the simulations created in the city. For example, there is a challenge on how to bring the air pollution down, and at the same time keeping the employment up, letting the students experience the complex consequences of their choices within a complex system. In the game, the students can play the role of a mayor, responsible for the challenging work of addressing environmental impact, while at the same time balancing the employment needs and the happiness of the citizens in the city. In *SimCityEdu*, the students have individual learning experiences, and the game aims at improving the learning process by providing formative assessment of the learning goals. The teacher can access information about the students' ability to problem solve, read, and explain the relationships in complex systems.

Institute of Play has recently released a whitepaper on how to assess student learning by formative assessment as well as by using gameplay data, proposing a design approach that links the process of game design with the process of assessment design (Mislevy, Oranje, Bauer, Davier, & Hao, 2014). This paper describes some of the thoughts behind the continued elaboration of *SimCityEdu* and the work on developing standards for game-based assessment.

The *SimCityEdu* game is built so the teachers can create their own lesson plans encompassing learning goals, and teachers and students also have access to dashboards that give an overview. Glasslab has developed lesson plans for *SimCityEdu*, which teachers are free to use. For instance, one of the units in the physical science-based lessons is called "Power to the People." This unit deals with energy consumption, cost, and consequences and is designed for grades six through eight. This specific lesson ("Power to the People") lasts 5 days with 45-minute lessons, with the students studying fossil fuels, nuclear power, solar, and wind energy—all renewable energy sources. The students have to create an energy system grid in their city in the game to supply power to everything that they build. In the game they will experience that there are real-world consequences according to the choices they make in the game, giving them opportunities to reflect on these consequences. A teacher can see the learning goals that the students will be working with on all five days and there is also a list of essential questions that the students should be able to answer after playing the game. The assessment takes form as formative assessment, both 1) outside the game in the discussions in the class, as well as 2) inside the game, since to make some of the right choices in the game and move on in the game, the students have to understand part of the knowledge in the curriculum. But the teacher can also choose to use the designed 3) pre- and post-assessments in the game to get an idea (summative assessment) of what the students has learned in the game.

Best practices

The following is a list of best practices for aligning game and learning goals.

Game goals

1. **Goal qualities:** The goals should be concrete, achievable and designed in a way that makes the player look forward to achieving them.
2. **Sense of control:** The goal should provide a sense of competence, autonomy and control as well as arouse curiosity.
3. **Many small and large goals nested in the game:** Make a meaningful and structured flow of nested goals in the game, from short-term to long-term goals by letting the small goals help progressing and guiding the player to the larger goals. This will give an overview in the game and provide a feeling of many small successes.

Integrating game goals and learning goals

1. **Backward planning:** Designers need to know the student's learning goals and the method of assessment before planning the individual lessons, activities and game goals.
2. **Elaborate missions and quests:** Use the learning goals to determine the game design, which should comprise an overall mission with an overall game goal, and several sub-quests with sub-goals on the way to the end goal.
3. **Engagement with learning goals:** Let the progress toward the game goals necessitate engagement with the intended learning goals.
4. **Embed the learning activities in the game**: Let the learning activities be modified or embedded within the game.
5. **Challenges:** The challenges in a learning game comprise the learning goals, the content and the learning activities. When overcoming the challenges in the game, the learner will show her competence since this requires that she know how to solve the problem and attain the learning goal.
6. **Purpose of the challenge:** To reach the learning goal and to learn to master the action or to understand the pattern you have to recognize, skills or rules you have to learn, tasks that should be solved, and hand-eye coordination to be learned.
7. **Game goals and rules:** The rules should help determine if the game goals are reached or not reached.
8. **Connection between the learning process and rules:** The rules might be part of the learning process, helping to meet the learning goal. This can, for example, be designed in the game by letting the rules and goals invite the player to repeat or retry the task until the challenge is solved.
9. **Goals and feedback:** Feedback gives the student/player a possibility to know if he has reached the learning, as well as the game goals, thereby helping to ensure learning and transfer.

Resources

Books

Ferrara, J. (2012): *Playful design*. Rosenfeld.

Fullerton, T. (2008): *Game Design Workshop*. Morgan Kaufmann.

Gee, J.P. (2007): *What videogames have to teach us about learning and literacy*. Palgrave Macmillan.

Iuppa; N. & Borst, T. (2010): End-to-end Game Development, Creating Independent *Serious Games and simulations from start to finish*. Elsevier, Focal Press.

Koster, R., (2005): *A Theory of Fun for Game Design*. Paraglyph Press.

Salen, K. & Zimmerman, E. (2004) *Rules of play: Game design fundamentals*. Cambridge, MA: The MIT Press.

Games and Tools

Breakaway (www.breakawaygame.com)

Citizen Science (www.gameslearningsociety.org/project_citizen_science.php)

*Construct 2 (*www.scirra.com)

Dragonbox (www.dragonboxapp.com/index.html)

Gameglobe (www.gameglobe.com)

Game maker (www.yoyogames.com)

Gamesalad (www.gamesalad.com)

Games for change (www.gamesforchange.org/2011/02/breakaway-a-soccer-game-about-gender-violence/)

Grow-A-Game-Cards (valuesatplay.org/grow-a-game-overview) and (itunes.apple.com/us/app/grow-a-game/ id657244924?ls=1&mt=8)

Hush (valuesatplay.org/play-games)

Institute of Play (www.instituteofplay.org)

Kodu (www.kodugamelab.com)

Minecraft (minecraft.net)

MinecraftEdu.com (minecraftedu.com/wiki/index.php?title=Teaching_with_MinecraftEdu

Piano Dust Buster, Joy Tunes (www.joytunes.com/piano/)

Plants vs. Zombies (www.popcap.com/plants-vs-zombies-1)

Rayman Legends (rayman.ubi.com/legends/en-gb/home/)

Scratch (scratch.mit.edu)

SimcityEdu (www.instituteofplay.org/work/projects/simcityedu-games/)

Values at Play/ Tiltfactor (valuesatplay.org)

Unity (unity3d.com)

References

Akilli, Göknur. K. (2007). Games and simulations: a new approach in education? In David Gibson, Clark Aldrich, Prensky M (Eds.): *Games and Simulations in Online Learning: Research and Development Frameworks*, IGI Global.

Anderson, L. W., & Krathwohl, D. R. (Eds.). (2001). *A taxonomy for learning, teaching and assessing: A revision of Bloom's Taxonomy of educational objectives: Complete edition*, New York: Longman.

Annetta, L. (2010). The "I's" have it: A framework for serious educational game design. *Review of General Psychology 2010*, Vol. 14, No. 2, 105-112.

Belman, J. & Flanagan, M. (2009). Designing Games to Foster Empathy. Cognitive Technology. 14(2), 2009, pp. 5-15.

Bloom, B.S. & Krathwohl, D.R. (1956). Taxonomy of educational objectives: The classification of educational goals, by a committee of college and university examiners. *Handbook 1: Cognitive domain*. New York, Longmans.

Bogost, I. (2014). Persuasive games: Videogame vignette, *www.gamasutra.com* retrieved January 26th, 2014. http://www.gamasutra.com/view/feature/131942/persuasive_games_videogame_.php?print=1

Caillois, R. (2001). *Man, play and games*. Chicago: University of Illinois Press.

Chatfield, T. (2010). 7 ways games reward the brain. Ted talk, retrieved January 26th, 2014, (www.ted.com)

Cole, S.W., Yoo, D.J., Knutson, B. (2012). Interactivity and reward-related neural activation during a serious videogame, *PloS One*, Volume 7, issue 3, start page: e33909

Deci, E.L. & Ryan, R.M., (2000). Self-determination theory and the facilitation of intrinsic motivation, social development, and well-being, *American Psychologist*, Vol.55, No. 1, 68-78.

Dede, C. (2011). Developing a research agenda for educational games and simulations in Tobias, S. & Fletcher, JD. (Eds.): *Computer games and instruction*, Information Age Publishing Inc.

Deterding, S. (2011). Don't play games with me! Promises and pitfalls of gameful design, *web directions @media, London,* May 27, 2011. retrieved January 26th, 2014. at http://codingconduct.cc/1523514/Don-t-Play-Games-With-Me

Dreyfuss, H.L. (2001). Livet på nettet, translated by Ole Lindegård Henriksen from *On the Internet,* Hans Reitzels Forlag.

Ferrara, J. (2012). *Playful Design,* Rosenfeld.

Flanagan, M. Hash, C. & Isbister, K. (2010). *Designing games for learning: Insights from conversations with designers.* CHI 2010, Atlanta, Georgia, USA.

Freitas, S.d. and Oliver, M. (2006). How can exploratory learning with games and simulations within the curriculum be most effectively evaluated? *Computers & Education.* 46 (2006) 249–264, Elsevier.

Fullerton, T. (2008). *Game Design Workshop,* Morgan Kaufmann.

Gee, J.P. (2005). Learning by Design: good video games as learning machines, *E–Learning and Digital Media,* Volume 2, Number 1, 2005, p. 5-16, Symposium Journals.

Gee, J.P. (2011). Reflections on empirical evidence on games and learning in Tobias, S. & Fletcher, JD. (Eds.): *Computer games and instruction,* Information Age Publishing Inc.

Hess, K.K., Jones, B.S., Carlock, D., & Walkup, J.R. (2009). Blending the strengths of Bloom's Taxonomy and Webb's Depth of Knowledge to enhance classroom-level processes. *Online Submission, ERIC Number: ED517804.*

Hiim, H. & Hippe, E., (1997). Læring gennem oplevelse, forståelse og handling, Gyldendals uddannelse.

Hirumi, A., Appelman, B., Rieber, L., & Eck, R.V. (2010). Preparing Instructional Designers for Game-Based Learning: Part 1, *in TechTrends.* May/June 2010, Volume 54, Number 3.

Institute of Play 1 (2014). Q Design pack, Games and Learning, retrieved January 26th, 2014. http://www.instituteofplay.org/work/projects/q-design-packs/q-games-and-learning-design-pack/)

Institute of Play 2 (2014). Q Design Packs: Tools and methods to remix the Quest Schools model of game-like connected learning in your own school retrieved January 26th, 2014. http://www.instituteofplay.org/work/projects/q-design-packs/

Kato, P.M., Cole, S.W, Bradlyn, A.S., Pollock, B.H. (2008). A Video Game Improves Behavioral Outcomes in Adolescents and Young Adults With Cancer: A Randomized Trial, *Pediatrics,* Vol. 122 No. 2, August 1, 2008, pp. e305-e317.

Kebritchi, M & Hirumi, A. (2008). Examining the pedagogical foundations of modern educational computer games. *Computers & Education,* Volume 54, issue 4, pp.1729-1743, Elsevier.

Kirriemuir, J. & McFarlane, A. (2006). Literature review in games and learning, Report 8, Futurelab.

Kolb, D.A. (1984). Experiential learning: Experience as the source of learning and development. Prentice-Hall, Inc., Englewood Cliffs, N.J.

Koster, R., (2005). *A Theory of Fun for Game Design,* Paraglyph Press.

Laurillard, D. (2012). *Teaching as a design science: Building pedagogical patterns for learning and technology,* Routledge.

Macklin, C. & Sharp, J. (2013). "Freakin' hard": Game design and issue literacy in Steinkuehler et al. (eds.). *Games, Learning, and Society.* Cambridge: Cambridge University Press, pp. 381-402.

Malone, T.W. (1980). What makes things fun to learn? Heuristics for Designing Instructional Computer Games. Xerox Palo Alto *Research Center.*

Mislevy, R.J., Oranje, A., Bauer, M.I., Davier, A.v. & Hao, J. (2014). Psychometric considerations in game-based assessment. Institute of Play, CreateSpace Independent Publishing Platform; 1 edition (February 4, 2014).

Murphy, C., Chertoff, D., Guerrero, M. & Moffitt, K. (2013): Design better games! Flow motivation, & fun, Chapter 5 in *Design and Development of Training Games: Practical Guidelines from a Multi-Disciplinary Perspective,* Cambridge University Press. Retrieved January 26th, 2014. http://www.goodgamesbydesign.com/Files/Chapter5_Flow_Motivation_Fun_Final_WebVersion.pdf

Oxford Dictionaries. (2014). http://www.oxforddictionaries.com/

Prensky, M. (2001). *Digital game-based learning,* McGraw-Hill.

Ratan, R. & Ritterfeld, U., (2009). *Classifying serious games* in Ritterfeld, U. (Eds.) *Serious Games, Mechanics and Effects,* Routledge

Salen, K & Zimmerman, E. (2004). *Rules of play: Game design fundamentals,* The MIT Press.

Salen, K., Torres, R., Wolozin, L., Rufo-Tepper, R., & Shapiro, A. (2011). *Quest to Learn: Developing the school for digital kids.* MIT Press, from John D. and Catherine T. MacArthur Foundation Reports on Digital Media and Learning

Sanchez, A., Cannon-Bowers, J., & Bowers, C., (2010). Establishing a science of game based learning in Cannon-Bowers, J. & Bowers, C., (Eds.) *Serious Game Design and Development, Technologies for Training and Learning,* Information Science Reference.

Santrock, J. (2006). Cognitive and language development in *educational psychology,* McGraw Hill Higher Education.

Schell, J., (2008). *The art of game design,* Elsevier.

Staalduinen, J.P.v. & Freitas, S.d. (2011). A game-based learning framework: Linking game design and learning outcomes: in Khine, M.S. (Ed.): *Learning to Play: Exploring the Future of Education with Video Games,* Peter Lang Publishing Inc.

Wiliam, D. (2012). Feedback: Part of a system in *Feedback for Learning, Educational Leadership,* September 2012, Volume 70, Number 1, p. 30-34, Association of Supervision and Curriculum Development: http://www.ascd.org

Wilson, K.A., Bedwell, W.L., Lazzara, E.H., Salas, E., Burke, C.S., Estock, J.L., Orvis, K.L., & Conkey, C. (2009). Relationships between game attributes and learning outcomes review and research proposals, in *Simulation & Gaming,* Volume 40, Issue 2, pp.217-266.

Wilson, M., Bejar, I., Scalise, K., Templin, J., Wiliam, D. & Irribarra, D.T. (2012). Perspectives on Methodological Issues, Chapter 3 in Griffin, P. (Ed.): *Assessment and Teaching of 21st Century Skills,* Springer.

Whitton, N. (2009). *Learning with digital games: A practical guide to engaging students in higher education,* Routledge.

Winn, B. (2008). The design, play, and experience framework in *Handbook of research on effective electronic gaming in education,* Volume 3, pp. 1010-1024, IGI Global Hershey, PA.

Winterton, J., Delamare-Le Deist, F. & Stringfellow, E. (2006). Typology of knowledge, skills and competences: clarification of the concept and prototype, Office for Official Publications of the European Communities Luxembourg.

Wilms, I., Mogensen, J. (2011). Dissimilar outcomes of apparently similar procedures as a challenge to clinical neurorehabilitation and basic research: when the same is not the same. *NeuroRehabilitation.* Vol. 29(3), 221-227.

Weitze, C. & Ørngreen, R. (2012). Concept Model for designing engaging and motivating games for learning: The Smiley-model, Electronic proceedings in Meaningful Play Conference 2012, Cathegory: Innovation in Game Design, Michigan State University, retrieved January 26th, 2014. at: http://meaningfulplay.msu.edu/proceedings2012/mp2012submission148.pdf

Wu, W.H., Hsiao, H.C., Wu, P.L., Lin, C.H., Huang, S.H. (2012). Investigating the learning-theory foundations of game-based learning: a meta-analysis, *Journal of Computer Assisted Learning,* Volume 28, issue 3, pp. 265-279, Wiley Online Library.

CHAPTER 13

Playtesting and Iterative Design

The Most Important Process for Making Great Games

Ira Fay, *Hampshire College, Amherst, Massachusetts, U.S., ira@irafay.com*

Key Summary Points

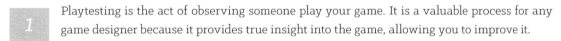

1   Playtesting is the act of observing someone play your game. It is a valuable process for any game designer because it provides true insight into the game, allowing you to improve it.

2   For learning games, playtesting also focuses on understanding if the player is actually learning anything from playing your game and ideally how well that knowledge is retained and/or transferred.

3   The iterative development process is a three-step loop (design, build, test) and playtesting is one of the three steps in that loop.

Key Terms

Playtesting
Iterative design
User testing
Design build test loop
Game development best practices
Playtesting for learning games

Introduction

Many people want to make a great game that engages players and provides educational impact, but how does one actually accomplish this goal? One process that can improve your chance of success is the iterative development process. This process is a repeating loop: first we design something, then we build it, and then we test it. Based on the results, we change our design and modify what we had built. Then we test the game again, modify the design based on the test, update the game accordingly, etc. To maximize quality, we strive to repeat these three steps (design-build-test) as many times as possible in the time available.

When we build something, it could be a very basic prototype (analog or digital), a specific feature in the game, or the final polish on a nearly finished game. At the start of development, the quality of our design is least certain, since we have not been able to test the game yet. If we spend a long time building the full game before testing, we will likely discover that our design needs to change and we have wasted a lot of time building unnecessary features. Therefore, especially near the beginning of development, it is best to build something small (such as a prototype), which can be tested quickly to confirm the design is on the right track.

When we talk about testing in the context of game development, we are really talking about playtesting. Playtesting is the act of observing someone play your game with the intention of understanding that player's experience. This is different than simply watching someone else play a game. While playtesting, we strive to truly understand what the player is thinking, feeling, and doing, and why. We then use that understanding to improve the game.

The ability to accurately and insightfully observe players is a skill that anyone can develop with practice. Every time you moderate a playtest, your observational skills will improve. Fortunately, we also have many tools available to support that effort, such as cameras or touch/click tracking software.

A playtest involves three people or groups:

1. Player
2. Moderator
3. Development team

The player plays the game while the moderator observes and takes notes. The moderator should attempt to track the player's actions (e.g., clicking, touching, choices), as well as more subtle things like pauses, points of confusion or excitement, or facial expressions. The goal of the playtest is to understand the player's actions and feelings, allowing the development team to improve the experience for other players in the future.

The moderator spends most of his or her time silently observing the player. Sometimes, the moderator may ask a question to understand what the player is thinking at a particular moment. If the player gets particularly stuck, the moderator may also choose to intervene, allowing the player to reach other areas of the game. To maximize the player's comfort and willingness to speak openly about the game, often the development team will also observe in a separate area, possibly via a one-way mirror or recordings afterward. Sometimes a member of the development team may serve as the moderator, but an unaffiliated person as the moderator may minimize bias and ensure that the player feels comfortable critiquing the game honestly.

At the earliest stages of development, when the game is still far from being finished, it is sometimes easy and efficient for a single person to be the player, the moderator, and a member of the development team! In a certain state of mind, a person can play a game while simultaneously observing themselves play the game, almost like an out-of-body experience. After the playtest, the person can write notes about the experience and share them with the team. Ideally, such notes will be analyzed, leading to improvements to the design and continued progress around the design-build-test loop.

For learning games, the playtesting process can be even more complicated. Not only are you trying to observe levels of fun and how effectively the player can control the game, but you are also trying to understand how much the player learns by playing the game. First you will need to identify what you want the player to learn. For simple concepts, such as a fact or piece of trivia, often this learning is relatively binary—they either know it or not. Whether the player learned the fact can be assessed through simple questions from the moderator, or through observation of in-game activities. For more complicated concepts, such as understanding complex system interactions or almost any topic beyond simple facts, you will likely need to follow up with players after they complete the game playing experience. Though playtesting is not a science, there are some processes that you can follow as a moderator and playtest designer to maximize your chances of gathering useful information that is as unbiased as possible.

In this chapter, I will discuss the iterative design loop (design-build-test), best practices in playtesting, and how designers of games for educational impact can modify their playtesting practices to support their specialized goals.

Case Study One: *Unearthed*

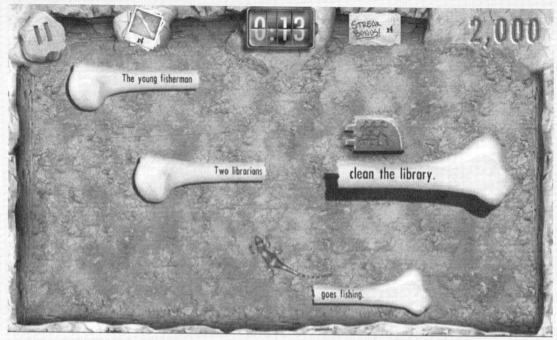

Figure 1: Sample screenshot of Unearthed.

Unearthed was designed to help middle school students learn grammar, and very specifically, subject-verb agreement. The team for *Unearthed* consisted of five or six experienced game developers, who have experience in engineering, art, production, design, audio, and quality assurance. The design goal of *Unearthed* was to help middle school students learn grammar, and very specifically, subject-verb agreement. Early in the design process I met with educational experts and middle school teachers, discovering how the subject is best taught in classrooms. Several people suggested the idea of half-sentence matching. Students would see half-sentences with subjects and half-sentences with verbs, and then need to match the sentences properly. With that, we had the core idea for our game. We created an early prototype and we quickly identified several questions:

1. What is the best way for students to connect two half sentences on a tablet device? Touch one, and then touch another? Touch and drag? Multitouch?
2. Should the full sentences make sense logically, or is it sufficient to accept gibberish sentences as long as the subject and verb agree?
3. Are students actually learning anything by playing the game?

As I mentioned above, whenever I playtest I strive to create questions in advance that are specific to my current design needs. I also create some general questions (likely quantitative) that I ask at every playtest, allowing the team to identify any trends that emerge. Finally, I also leave some room for the moderator to improvise questions as needed.

Below are some examples of the questions I asked at this stage of playtesting *Unearthed*. Remember that the moderator strives to answer these questions himself or herself, based on observation of the player. These questions can likely be answered through observation, but sometimes the moderator must ask the player a question to be more certain of the answer. Of course, when talking to someone who is playing a game, the player's brain is occupied and he or she may have difficulty playing the game and talking to you at the same. Therefore, if you must ask the player a question during gameplay, try to keep it short and easy to answer.

A. Does the player understand the goal of the game?
B. If so, how does the player naturally try to connect the half-sentences?
C. Does the player seem to understand the correct answers, or is the player often guessing at the right answer?
D. Does the player seem to improve over time?

Along with the sample questions for the moderator above, we also surveyed the player:

1. Demographic information (e.g., age, gender)
2. Rate the game on a scale of 1-5.
3. Rate the game on a scale of too easy/just right/too hard.
4. Name a few things that could be improved and a few things you liked. Any other comments?

Questions (A) and (B) focused on basic usability issues, while questions (C) and (D) focused on learning objectives. The (1) - (4) survey questions considered whether the player was having fun, though a better indication can be gauged by the moderator during the playtest by allowing the player to stop playing at any time, and seeing when the player stops. Fun and engagement can be inferred by how long the player continues to play.

As it turns out, regarding question (B), players tried to connect half-sentences in all three ways (touch-touch, touch-drag, multi-touch). Therefore, we changed the input detection code to support all three methods.

Regarding question (C), we noticed that many players were guessing very quickly. We had not implemented a major penalty for guessing, nor a reward for getting many right in a row. Therefore, since the game was timed to last 60 seconds, the optimal strategy for any player was to guess immediately, without taking the time to read the sentences at all. Based on our playtesting, we changed the scoring and messaging to strongly reward correct answers in a row, and we also penalized wrong answers.

For question (D), we did see some high scores increasing over time, but we cannot be sure if that was caused by actual learning, or if it was something else like a better understanding of the game controls. To get a clearer answer to this question, we would need to do a rigorous study.

Key Frameworks

I believe there is widespread consensus among professional game developers that iterative development is a wise process and that playtesting is a useful tool for designers to employ. Playtesting allows developers to understand how players will experience their game, leading to increased fun, sales, and a higher quality final product.

Therefore, instead of asking *if* we should playtest and iteratively develop, the more interesting question is *how* we effectively playtest and iteratively develop. Fortunately, with practice and care, we can improve our processes and our playtesting skills.

Particularly for learning games, it is important to be clear in your own mind (and your boss's mind!) that playtesting is not intended to be a scientific process from which you can publish statistically significant results. Playtesting is intended to be a tool for the development team, allowing the team to iteratively improve the game. While the moderator or playtest designer may attempt to assess whether the player has learned anything by playing the game, those results need not be scientific, they merely need to be useful enough to guide development. The time, effort, and cost required to create a well-designed and scientifically rigorous assessment study simply is not practical during most development cycles. Of course, if you have the time and money to do so, great! Such rigorous, scientific studies of learning games will help all developer in the long run. But for most of us, nonscientific playtesting can suffice.

As a quick introduction to moderating a playtest for those who are unfamiliar with it, I offer the following steps that I typically follow:

1. As moderator, work with the development team to craft the questions that you will try to answer in the playtest, based on the team's current stage of development. Early in development, the team might be wondering about basic game controls or the story hook. Later in development, the development team might want to know if level seven is taking within the desired 120-180 seconds to complete. Either way, create a list of questions that you will try to answer during the playtest.

2. After you have a list of questions, recruit players for the playtest. The players should ideally match the target demographic of the game, and have an appropriate level of experience with the game given the questions that are being asked. For example, if you are trying to understand the effectiveness of the tutorial, it would be best to test with players who have never played before. On the other hand, if you are trying to understand if the crafting system has sufficient depth to retain players for ten or more hours, playtest with experienced players.

3. Before the playtest session, create a script of events with approximate times. What do you want the player to do first? What questions will you try to answer during that time? What will the player do next? How long do you want to spend with each player? A typical playtest lasts 30-60 minutes, though it can vary widely based on your needs. Also, before

the playtest starts, it is wise to ensure your recording devices are working properly, if you intend to use them. I often prepare an online survey for the player to complete just after finishing the session.

4. At the beginning of your session with a player, remind the player that he or she can stop at any time. Not only is this ethical, it is also a very useful measure of engagement. If players want to stop at certain points of the game, such behavior provides a helpful clue to the development team. Also remind the player that the game is unfinished, and that you are testing the game, not the player. It is important to create an emotionally comfortable environment for the player so that he or she is more willing to give you honest feedback.

5. During the session, it is generally best to stay quiet and focus on observing the player. Ideally, you want the player to forget you are even present, allowing you to witness a more authentic game playing experience. If the player asks you a question, take note of it and answer at the end of the session.

6. Once the playtest session is done, finish any necessary notes to yourself while the events are still fresh in your mind. Give the player a survey, if desired. Prepare to welcome your next playtester.

The steps above provide a rough outline to moderating a playtest, but you should modify them as needed to match your preferences. As a note, there are many existing and comprehensive books on usability testing, which serve as a foundation for playtesting (please see the Resources section).

Case Study Two: *The Tomes*

The Tomes is a game designed to help middle school students learn vocabulary. After talking with educational experts, we learned that one important facet of long-term vocabulary retention is using and seeing the words in context, not merely using flash cards. Therefore, we considered a game design that supported this learning objective and encouraged students to read and use vocabulary in context. We settled on the idea of a choose-your-own-adventure game, with a graphic novel visual style.

We wanted the game to appeal equally to boys and girls, but due to the complexities of writing a work of interactive fiction, we decided to restrict players to a male protagonist. When we playtested the game, we gathered basic quantitative data from players in the form of a very simple survey, similar to the one listed above. Below are the results from the question, "How fun was the game? (1 = worst, 10 = best):"

Three boys, average 8.7
Three girls, average 4.8

While there were other variables and considerations, this result stood out. Even though the sample size is so small, the result is still useful.

When we saw that playtest result, we revisited the idea of giving the player a choice of protagonist gender. It would mean a bit of rewriting and rethinking the story, plus additional art assets, but we decided it was worth a try. This was a classic case of the design-build-test loop:

1. We designed a game with a male-only protagonist.
2. We built the original prototype with a male-only protagonist.
3. We playtested the prototype and gathered observations from real players.
4. We analyzed the results and decided to modify the design, adding the choice of protagonist gender.
5. We updated the game by allowing players to choose a protagonist gender.
6. We playtested the new version and gathered observations again.

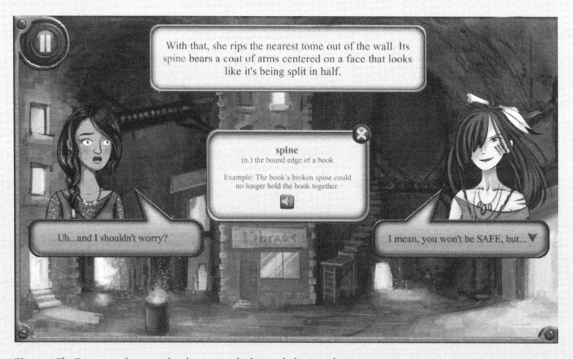

Figure 2: *The Tomes* sample screenshot, having touched a vocabulary word.

Below are the results we got when we playtested again with gender choice and the exact same survey question:

Three boys, average 9.0
Three girls, average 8.3
(Note: these were different playtesters from the previous version)

Touch next to your animal to move.
Moving costs energy.
Avoid predators and eat prey!

Of course, between the two versions, other things may have changed too. The art was more polished, the writing had improved, and ten other uncontrolled factors may have changed. At this point in development, we were reasonably sure that the gender choice had a positive impact, but either way, the average rating of fun increased for girls. We continued to track the numbers over the course of the project, and if we saw dips in the future we would try other experiments as well. As it turns out, the numbers stayed high and we kept the gender choice in the game.

Figure 3: Once one touch away from starting a game of *Food Web*.

Assessment Considerations

For playtesting

As mentioned above, playtesting does not often result in scientific, statistically significant results, which is fine. Instead, playtesting is intended to provide useful guidance and feedback to the development team. When assessing the effectiveness and value of your playtesting, consider the following questions:

1. **Are you playtesting with your target audience?** If your game is designed for sixth to eighth graders in the United States and you playtest with older kids, your data may not be as effective. While it can be useful to playtest with anyone at all, strive to playtest with your target audience.
2. **Are you reusing playtesters from session to session?** This may seem obvious, but sometimes there is a shortage of playtesters and you must reuse playtesters. In that case, any information you are trying to glean related to their first-time play experience may not be useful. Instead, focus on the more advanced aspects of the game with playtesters who have seen an earlier iteration.
3. **With similar methodology, do you see changes over time?** Ideally, you will establish a playtesting process early in your development cycle, which you can then use whenever you playtest. For example, you could ask the playtester to complete a survey, and then keep some of the questions consistent from session to session. Over time, you may see trends in the results that can inform design.

For iterative development

There are a variety of software development methodologies that strive to facilitate the iterative development process. For example, all the flavors of agile development are, at their core, trying to help teams employ iterative development. A thorough analysis of all iterative development methodologies is beyond the scope of this chapter, but here are some things to consider when thinking about your development process:

1. Is there effective communication flowing between members of the same discipline? Across disciplines? At different levels of seniority and management? Between client and publisher?
2. Does the team regularly reflect on its current process and strive to improve it?
3. Does everyone on the team remember the importance of the design-build-test loop, and act accordingly?
4. Is the schedule and budget reasonable to support the goals of the project? Since a precise schedule is very difficult to know at the beginning of the project, are all key stakeholders aware of the design-build-test loop?
5. Does the team playtest regularly?
6. Is it easy for anyone on the team to get a current version of the game and play it, even (especially!) in the middle of development?

Future Needs

There are many passionate people interested in improving educational systems and/or making fun games. The reality is that great teaching is quite difficult, making fun games is quite difficult, and doing both at the same time is even harder. As this aspect of the games industry continues to develop, veteran game developers need to partner with veteran teachers to craft experiences that take the best of both crafts.

A scientific study that demonstrates the value of playtesting and iterative development may be useful, but may not be necessary to show their effectiveness. Anyone who has ever made a game and moderated a playtest knows that playtesting is a valuable tool. Seeing in advance what your players think of your game is extremely beneficial.

Case Study Three: *Food Web*

At the time of this writing, I recently finished development on a science game designed to help middle school students learn about the food chain or food web. Specifically, the game strives to help students learn that predators eat prey and organisms need food to survive.

The game design was inherited from a different team and at the beginning of the project all the key stakeholders agreed on these four learning objectives:

1. A food web ecosystem exists.
2. Organisms have predators and preys.
3. Specific predator-prey relationships exist in a rainforest habitat. For example, fig seeds are eaten by Black Rail birds, which are eaten by South American Bushmaster Snakes, which are eaten by Southern Crested Caracara birds.
4. Organisms eat other organisms for energy.

As we were nearing the end of development, we had the opportunity to playtest. I created many questions for the moderator to strive to answer, based on the learning objectives and various lingering design questions. Here are a few example questions:

1. When players start the app for the very first time, do they touch the unlocked animal and then start the game, or do they get lost in the menu system?
2. Do first-time players understand that they need to touch next to their animal to move?
3. Do players quickly learn that predators will eat them?
4. Do players quickly learn that they need to eat prey?
5. Do players learn over time that they spend energy to move, and gain energy when eating prey?
6. Do players learn that there are some animals that are neither prey nor predators, and that those animals cannot be eaten?
7. Do players ever unlock a new animal by going to the Upgrade menu?
8. Do players realize that different animals have different predators and prey?
9. Do players notice the goals?
10. Do the goals drive player behavior in some way? (e.g., they notice they need to eat mosquitoes, so they change to an animal that eats mosquitoes?)
11. After a while, can players name any specific predator-prey relationships? (e.g., Agoutis eat Fig Seeds. Bushmaster Snakes eat Agoutis.)

As you can see, there are many questions here related to usability (e.g., Can players start the game?, Control their animal?, Notice goal messaging?, Go to the Upgrade menu?). There are also quite a few goals specifically related to the learning objectives. When an observant and caring moderator takes time to watch players play the game, the moderator will be able to answer questions like the ones above. Such answers will be able to inform design.

In this particular case, we got positive results related to the learning objectives. For example, we knew players were understanding predator-prey relationships and naming specific animals because we had videos of players saying the animal names and relationships. Fortunately, we also caught some lingering issues related to the first-time player experience. New players would get lost in an interactive food web, instead of getting into playing the game first. We improved messaging, removed superfluous buttons, and reduced the number of screens shown to a first-time player before she or he started playing, all based on the playtest feedback. While the game is still not perfect, the informal and nonscientific playtesting helped us make good design choices and improve the game during development.

Best Practices

When considering how to playtest, here are some guidelines to keep in mind:

1. **Test early, test often:** A playtest with a sample size of even one or two people is vastly superior to no playtesting at all. Also, the more frequently you playtest, the fewer things will have changed between playtests, which makes it easier to determine cause and effect.

2. **Create a good environment for observation:** The foundation of an effective playtest is carefully observing the player. Strive to create an environment where the moderator (and supporting tools such as cameras and/or click/touch tracking software) can do their job. For example, it is often better to observe a single player carefully, instead of many players simultaneously. In the many simultaneous players situation, you will get more survey data, but you will miss detailed observations of individual player actions. In the single player situation, you will be able to focus on everything the player does, which will allow you to better deduce what is happening inside that player's mind.

3. **Practice moderating playtests:** With practice, playtest moderators will get better at observing players, noticing subtle things, asking open-ended questions, staying patient, and taking good notes during and after the session. It is a skill that can be improved, so practice it.

4. **Create a good environment for feedback from the player:** A moderator can observe quite a few things, verbally and non-verbally, but it is very difficult to get at the player's thoughts. Often players will not be able to accurately communicate their own experiences. To attempt to understand a player's experiences more fully, moderators can ask direct questions to the player during or after gameplay. Cultivate a welcoming environment that exudes serious curiosity about the player's ideas is something that can be cultivated over time.

5. **Create quantitative questions that you can ask consistently throughout development:** The process will not be rigorously scientific, but you will have a few questions and answers that you can track, which will be useful for observing possible trends.

6. **Create qualitative questions as needed to support your current design questions:** If you take time before a playtest to think about your current design questions, it will be relatively easy to create questions to match. With a list of questions to answer, the moderator can help gather the information you need.

Resources

Brian Schrank (http://www.brianschrank.com/capstone/resources/Playtesting_reports_template.pdf).

Holly Gramazio, the lead game designer at Hide & Seek (http://hideandseek.net/2011/01/26/a-guide-to-playtesting-from-h-g-wells/).

Best Practices: Five Tips for Better Playtesting, by Vin St. John (http://gamasutra.com/view/feature/185258/best_practices_five_tips_for_.php). Notice in the comments that Vin responds to the first comment, presumably to a random person on the internet who he does not know, "We're constantly trying to improve our process, so if you have any criticisms or suggestions I would welcome them."

Finding Out What They Think: A Rough Primer To User Research, by Ben Lewis-Evans (http://www.gamasutra.com/view/feature/169069/finding_out_what_they_think_a_.php, http://www.gamasutra.com/view/feature/170332/finding_out_what_they_think_a_.php).

References

Brathwaite, B. & Schreiber, I. (2008). *Challenges for game designers: non-digital exercises for video game designers.* Cengage Learning.

Fay, I. (2011). Filtering feedback, in G. Costikyan & D. Davidson (Eds.) *Tabletop: Analog Game Design,* Pittsburgh: ETC Press.

Gramazio, H. (2011). *A guide to playtesting from H.G. Wells,* accessed at: http://hideandseek.net/2011/01/26/a-guide-to-playtesting-from-h-g-wells/

Krug, S. (2014). *Don't make me think. Third edition.* New Riders.

Lewis-Evans, B. (2012). Finding out what they think: A rough primer to user research, accessed at: http://www.gamasutra.com/view/feature/169069/finding_out_what_they_think_a_.php, http://www.gamasutra.com/view/feature/170332/finding_out_what_they_think_a_.php

Norman, D. (2002). *The design of everyday things.* Basic Books.

Ries, E. (2011). *The lean startup.* Crown Business.

Schell, J. (2008). *The art of game design: A book of lenses.* CRC Press.

Schrank, B. *Capstone winter quarter playtesting guide,* accessed at: http://www.brianschrank.com/capstone/resources/Playtesting_reports_template.pdf

St. John, V. (2013). Best practices: Five tips for better playtesting, http://gamasutra.com/view/feature/185258/best_practices_five_tips_for_.php

CHAPTER 14

Assessment

Assessing Video Games for Learning

David Simkins, *Rochester Institute of Technology, Rochester, New York, U.S.,*
www.davidsimkins.org, dwsigm@rit.edu

Key Summary Points

1. As we assess games for learning, we should create an inclusive environment that allows for a wide variety of methods.

2. As we publish on assessment, we should be forthright about our foundational assumptions, particularly our epistemologies. We should judge the contribution of assessments taking the stated foundational assumptions as given, but with an eye for improving methods and practices of assessment given those assumptions.

3. Design and development of learning games needs to similarly own their epistemology, design learning goals in keeping with them, and create experiences that conform closely to those epistemologies.

Key Terms

Assessment
Games
Learning games
Serious games
Epistemology
Methods

Introduction

The increased interest in the use of games for instruction in formal and informal learning spaces has led to an increased interest in assessment of learning games (Annetta, 2010; Clark, Tanner-Smith, Killingsworth & Bellamy, 2013). These assessments originate from many different fields, many of which have differing beliefs about what constitutes knowledge. These differences are indications of significant epistemological diversity within the field. That is, we do not all share the same premises about what it means to know, and therefore we do not all agree on what methods we should use to gain knowledge.

Epistemological diversity is not unique to the study of games and learning. It is a characteristic source of discussion and debate throughout education (Pallas, 2001). It is also present in the media studies and computer science divide within games studies. Having discussion around what it means to know is common in all academic fields, even in hard sciences such as physics where there are commonalities among most scientists about how one might consider something "known" within the field. Diversity of epistemologies is much greater within humanities, social science, and education. In education research, epistemology is a vexing issue because it not only relates to how we study learning, it relates to how we believe people learn in the first place. Epistemology is central to our inquiry on all levels, and differences among epistemological commitments lies at the center of what we believe we should do and expect from learning (Greeno, Collins, & Resnik, 1996). For reasons beyond the scope of this chapter, we cannot solve this problem by simply determining the correct epistemology. It is unlikely, perhaps impossible, which we will ever resolve all questions about what it means to know. If we accept that we will not simply resolve our differences, this chapter is an attempt to allow us to move forward together as a field. Given that we will not resolve epistemological differences, how should we go about sharing our research findings with each other and building useful understanding?

Three core questions stand out in assessment research, and regardless of the epistemological approach used, any study should first consider these three questions. The three include: 1) the game's learning goals, 2) the core mechanics/core gameplay, and 3) the out-of-game context of play. These are, in part, derived from central studies of games and leaning that form the foundation of the growing field (Clark, Tanner-Smith, Killingsworth & Bellamy, 2013; D'Angelo, Rutstein, Harris, Haertel, Bernard, & Borokhovski, 2013; Shute & Ventura, 2013) and from my own experience assessing video games for learning (Simkins & Steinkuehler, 2008; Simkins, Egert, & Decker, 2010; Steinkuehler et al., 2011). For many of us, the goal of sharing studies about assessment of games is to create better learning games. These three questions, collectively, address the core of that inquiry, and finding a way to work together toward finding helpful answers to these questions may help us to find a way to act as a field of study.

Question one: What are the learning goals?

Before making any other determinations about a study, it is helpful to identify the learning goals. For games developed for learning, these may be easy to determine. Hopefully the designers were prioritizing learning goals throughout their design and development process. Not all games, however, which show promise for learning are specifically designed for that purpose. Researchers must often examine the game's design and conduct prior or simultaneous research to identify the potential of a game as a tool for learning. For example, Squire's work on the *Civilization* series of games shows that some games created for entertainment may have excellent potential as learning games (Squire, 2011). In various studies with diverse populations, it is suggested as a useful tool for explaining alternate theories of historical process, explaining historical contingency, and offering a "modding" environment for creating scenarios for *Civilization* that highlight historical processes, environments, and facts.

Occasionally, even a game designed for learning may be effective in more areas than intended. What happens when a game about scientific hypothesis testing is also very good at developing scientific collaboration and communication skills among group members? Sometimes in the process of research we discover learning affordances we had not intended to test, opening opportunities for future inquiry. Researchers studying complex environments in the wild must often use a variety of research tools to identify potential learning affordances in an open-ended way. Ethnographic, grounded theory, and various qualitative and mixed methods inquiries that apply to research "in the wild" can be extremely helpful in identifying potential learning goals that could be used in conjunction with more targeted game assessments.

Question two:
What are the core game mechanics and other important aspects of play?

In any good learning game, the gameplay should be aligned closely with learning goals (South & Snow, 2012). If we are studying unintended learning goals, this may be a little more complex. Still, to assess a game, it helps to deeply understand the game. The amount of time we need to spend understanding a game may vary dramatically depending on the game itself. The simpler the game, the less time one needs to spend with it to understand what is really going on in play. Even simple games can have surprising affordances for learning, so it is helpful to have a deep understanding of the game's play.

SimCity provides one of the earliest examples of a game created for entertainment and studied for its potential learning content (Betz, 1995-6; Squire 2005). In the early versions of *SimCity*, the core mechanic was the placement of blocks representing areas zoned for a particular purpose. As a city planning game, the focus was on developing the infrastructure for a city, building it over time and balancing constraints and resources, such as money, pollution, and population growth. There was no single objective for *SimCity*; rather, it was a sandbox in which to explore the constraints and affordances of the tools provided. As a learning game, it was a good example of learning through exploration. To understand its play, however, we would need to have an understanding of how the constraints and affordances worked together to make a challenging environment for *SimCity* players, challenges that could be overcome, potentially providing a sense of accomplishment even when there were no explicit goals.

We would also benefit by understanding the cheating mechanisms built into the game—one could enter a code to give oneself more money, for example. I place cheat in quotes because though we may see this as an inappropriate way to play the game, the developers did not. The ability to "cheat" was provided to allow players to continue to have fun in the way they wish. Many early *SimCity* players believed cheating was cheating and would never use the ability to give themselves extra money. For others, it was a normal part of the practice, perhaps even a necessity for their play style. Because it is a sandbox game, it is up to the player to identify his or her own goals and create engaging play in the space provided. The ability to cheat or not cheat is a core aspect of its gameplay; it is not just coincidental to it.

In the *SimCity* example we can quickly identify the core mechanics of the game. Understanding the potential practices and cultures of play, however, may require us to play the game more extensively. Even after exploring the play in depth, we may also need to explore the culture around play, observing other's play and discussing play with others to get a wider sense of the varieties of play.

The goal of this second question is to understand the in-game context of the assessment. How we use this in-game context will depend on our methods of assessment. Researchers may also need to understand when and where to constrain the player's options to facilitate the study of learning, based on the target learning goals. For example, researchers may need to disable *SimCity*'s cheat commands if managing resources is central to the learning goals of a particular curriculum that uses the game as a tool for learning.

Question three: What is the out of game context?

The in-game context is not the only context relevant to learning. It is important to take account of the environment in which learning takes place. Often, the environment is a critical component for facilitating learning, though it can also have the effect of distracting players away from the learning goals. Some methodologies may require us to minimize this out of-game effect. Other methodologies focus on understanding the out-of-game effects, requiring us to see the gameplay within a more natural environment. The learning context is the out-of-game environment in which the game is played. In Gee's terminology (2012), everything in-game is the game, with a small "g." The context around play is part of the Game, with a big "G." That is, it is not only the physical environment around the game but also the virtual environment. Some companies that develop learning games are also developing social spaces around the games, sometimes called affinity spaces (Gee, 2012), which encourage the collaborative and social aspects of learning. A positive and constructive learning environment can be crucial to the achievement of learning objectives, and understanding or controlling context is a part of a complete assessment of a learning game.

When we talk about complex games, we really cannot understand the entire learning environment without being deeply steeped in the practices that surround the game. Such is the case with any large, multiplayer game environment. Looking at the learning that takes place in *Whyville* (Kafai & Fields, 2009) or *World of Warcraft* (Steinkuehler, 2007) both require intimate knowledge of the game's social structures and communities, not just what the players are doing on the screen. The games are just two examples of game contexts that are driven by community. They are influenced by designed structures that facilitate constructive community and where player self-organization creates opportunities for mentoring among players. This network of player interaction facilitates a player's access to information about expert play. While this development of networks to promote expert practice is player generated for many games, some games for learning are designed specifically to mirror established practices, such as Shaffer's epistemic games (2006), which leverage professional practices to create contextualized play.

We can see similar affinity spaces grow around games in ways that do not directly tie back to the game at all. In the work of Black (2008), Magnifico (2010), and Jenkins (2012) on fan fiction communities, we can see the development of literacy practices through participation in the writing, sharing, and commenting on fan fiction related to, but not specifically supported by the game. In situations where the game we are assessing contains "unsanctioned" or completely player-generated and operated content sites, it may be necessary to find expert informants to introduce the researchers to the player communities.

The entire context of a game can be described in terms of circles representing different spaces where players interact with games (see Figure 1). Researchers implementing assessment protocols need to be aware of each of them, though it may restrict assessment, or even player access, to a subset of the three. The innermost circle is the immediate physical context of the players playing the game while they are playing. The second is defined by the opportunities for interaction around the game built specifically by people with special authority over play, which could include researchers, instructors, game designers, or publishers. Whether moderated or unmoderated, these spaces are to some extent controlled by and the responsibility of non-players. The third circle is defined by the social interactions around the game by the community of game players—the students or players themselves. The power structure of these spaces is less formal, often with greatest influence by those players with the greatest social influence within the group.

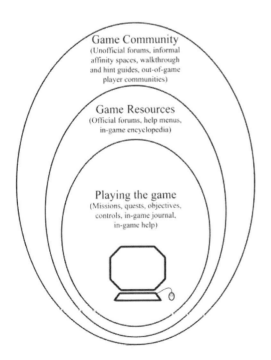

Figure 1: Game context

Identifying the circles is merely a heuristic, and the boundaries between them are not always clear-cut, but understanding that communities of practice around games are formed in several layers can help identify which environments the assessor needs to access to complete a full assessment of play. In identifying the circles, one can begin to determine where your players are playing and in what game-related activities they are participating. After which you can determine what access researchers, instructors, and designers can or should have to complete an assessment.

Case Study One: Dark Gold:
Analyzing Big Data Through Quantitative Stealth Assessment

As an outside researcher, it is not always possible to examine a massive data set. Fortunately, Sony Online allowed a select group of researchers to access much of the in-game transaction data for *Everquest 2* (Keegan, Ahmed, Williams, Srivastava & Contractor, 2011). The resulting data set allowed for in-depth queries about actual gameplay for hundreds of thousands of players carried out with minimal, if any, direct effect on the players' behavior. This level of authenticity is in line with the ideals of stealth assessment (Shute & Ventura, 2013).

To understand the study, the researchers needed to know a great deal about the game. For example, researchers needed to know that in *Everquest 2*, it was against the rules of the game to trade in-game items for out-of-game currency or goods. They also needed to know that the rule was commonly broken, and not merely by individuals, but by organized groups of players who would collect in game gold and goods and sell them. The gold and goods were traded online, but no in game money was transferred. Instead, the transaction was completed in game when first the receiving player completed an out-of-game real money transaction.

To complete the study, the researchers used existing research on massively multiplayer online games to identify opportunities within the game that could be compared to out of game examples. In this case, the researchers hypothesized that in-game "criminal organizations" will respond to game policing in ways analogous to how criminal organizations in our society as a whole respond to policing. The in-game "criminals" are gold farmers, who are only criminals by analogy because they do not break laws but they do break the end-user license agreement of the game they are playing. These data were compared to data from criminology research about how criminal organizations respond to the threat of enforcement. These responses to law enforcement included a variety of ways in which criminals learned and adapted to policing so that the impact of the enforcement was minimized.

The study investigated specific in-game behaviors and compared them with the out-of-game behaviors of criminal organizations—methods that included creating decentralized authority, and interacting through multiple tiers of operatives. To compare to out-of-game criminal organizations, the researchers found data with a similar scope: a longitudinal analysis of criminals and co-offenders collected through Project Cavier, a Canadian law enforcement task force.

While we can only assume the criminal's learning goals to be the avoidance of prosecution, such an assumption seems justified. Similarly, in-game gold farmers were assumed to be actively seeking to find ways to continue their efforts despite enforcement of in-game rules against selling in game items or characters for out-of-game money, established by the game's producers.

Even with a tremendous amount of in-game data at their disposal, any action occurring outside of the game was unavailable and needed to be inferred. The in-game markers of gold farming and information about the variety of interactions that occurred outside of game space were both influenced by qualitative research, such as that carried out by Dibbell (2006) on the Chinese gold farming industry.

The study purported to show that there was an analogy between the reaction of physical world criminals to increased enforcement and the reaction of virtual world rule breakers to enforcement of the rules by the game companies. If true, this opens the door to using in-game enforcement to learn about how to investigate and enforce out-of-game criminal syndicates. It could also, potentially, indicate that in game breach of rules may prepare one for out-of-game participation in criminal syndicates, much as some first person shooters have been allegedly used as training tools for terrorists (SAIC, 2007).

Key Frameworks

The focus of this chapter is on how to make sense of and use of assessments across the field, despite our variety of methods and underlying assumptions within the field. To bridge differences within the field, we need to communicate and be flexible in our understanding of what good studies will look like. A principled study will be conducted within a stated point of view, with clearly indicated assumptions and following through with data collection, analysis, and interpretation of results that are coherent with the assumptions. No study is perfect, and all data is at least somewhat limited or compromised. The process of critique helps our community develop better tools for analyzing and discussing games for learning, but such critique needs to be consistent with the stated assumptions of the study—internal to the epistemologies of the researchers, not external to them.

To understand better how to approach creating community across assumptions, the chapter has followed two divisions within the field. The first is of epistemology. That is, the way we believe people come to know and understand which, implicitly, also indicates what we believe to be the limits of human knowledge. The second is overall methodology. Both I break into heuristics that are a bit rough. Neither of them can completely encapsulate the differences or approaches within our community, but they should provide a general sense of the communities and breadth of the field.

The end of the chapter discusses uses three case studies to introduce different models for assessing learning within gameplay. Each is grounded in an epistemology and therefore uses methods that differ from the others.

Methods

The goal of this chapter is to help us learn from each other. Part of this process is learning how to better study games and learning. This does mean evaluating each other's methods; however, the focus of evaluation should not be to prove one method better than another, but to improve and refine each of the methodologies and approaches to which our community is committed.

Within the last few years there have seen several significant publications about the assessment of learning in video games (Annetta & Bronack, 2011; Ifenthaler, Eseryl, & Ge, 2012). Generally, the methods for assessing learning in games are the same as assessing learning anywhere, and any quality methods text should help establish good methodological practices. Mirroring educational assessment in general, assessment of learning games tends toward statistical analysis, conversation analysis, discourse analysis, pragmatist methodology, critical theoretical approaches, and ethnomethodology. Education research has a general preference toward case study, which lends to meta-analyses as well. There are also relevant ways to use ethnographic methodologies, particularly in work on large social games played outside of formal learning environments. In a dense, but extremely helpful discussion of the field of cognition and learning, Greeno, Collins, & Resnick (1996) break the field into three epistemological views: the behaviorist/empiricist view, the cognitivist/rationalist view, and the situative/pragmatist-sociohistoric view. While grouping approaches can raise as many questions as it answers, the categories they use succeed in showing the major differences within the larger field of learning.

Greeno et al. (1996) do a better job than we can here of fairly describing the field within each general approach. At the risk of oversimplification the three tend to fall into epistemological and ontological camps—the largely post-positivist behaviorist/empiricist approaches that focus on repeatable experiments in controlled environments. The largely post-structuralist cognitivist/rationalist view in which knowledge is understood only within an individual and often non-reproducible context. Thirdly, the language and practice theoretical situative/pragmatist-sociohistoric view, in knowledge is shared and constructed—understood collectively and not individually.

Whichever viewpoint one holds will be crucial in determining which methods are best pursued. Generally, behaviorist/empiricist epistemologies tend one toward quantitative measurement and statistical analysis. The differences within cognitivist/rationalist or situative/pragmatist-sociohistorical viewpoints depend, in part, on the locus of knowledge. When knowledge is maximally localized and sensitive to context, in depth qualitative analysis is likely required. When knowledge can be generalized to any significant degree, qualitative, quantitative, or mixed methods approaches may be useful.

Quantitative methods

Quantitative methodologies are those that focus on measuring. That is, collecting and analyzing data in such a way that it can be measured against other data. This almost always means collecting numerical data and analyzing it statistically.

The general goal of most quantitative assessments will be in isolating and reproducing verifiable results. To do this, it is important to identify learning goals that are themselves measurable. In other words, the researcher needs to be able to identify when the goal has been met. This is often discussed in terms of mastery, with identifiable conditions for mastery. Once mastery of the learning goal can be correctly identified, the researchers need to create a use of the game that can be studied for attainment of mastery. There is a growing interest in the use of games to show the attainment of mastery. In this chapter we are concerned with assessment of games, not games as an assessment tool, but these can sometimes go hand-in-hand because measuring the success of the game usually requires measuring student success within the game, to show that the player is improving through the use of the game as a learning intervention. To do this, it is important for the researcher to account for the role of play in a learning game. By understanding play, one can identify which indicators or behaviors on the part of the learner evince mastery, which suggest a lack of understanding, and which are distractors that could be misinterpreted by assessing researchers.

Though the intent is to create reproducible, verifiable knowledge, even in quantitative methods the learning context is important. Context affects outcomes, just as interventions affect outcomes. It may be desirable to create as neutral a learning environment as possible, allowing the assessment to be judged for its learning affordances without reference to outside influences. In many cases, however, a sterile learning environment may be counter-productive or misleading.

Table 1. Strengths and challenges in sample quantitative methods

	Strengths	Challenges
In-game instrumentation	Assesses player activity in-game. Time stamped and accurate, if implemented well.	Can be difficult to ascertain correct data to collec. Requires access to game code. Limited explanation of intent.
Pre/post-test	Relatively easy to create and implement. Can be targeted specifically to learning goals.	If not completed immediately before and after can potentially conflate results from other learning opportunities. If completed immediately before and after can suffer from participant exhaustion. Does nothing to help answer why an implementation works or fails only whether it seems to be beneficial. Takes time away from gameplay.
Eye/head tracking	Assesses what the player is attending to in game, not just what they are doing in game.	Equipment can be expensive. Can result in confusing data that shows attention but does not suggest reason for it.

While there are a variety of quantitative methods used in games assessment (see Table 1), the most common assessment method, for almost all quantitative learning and most mixed methods research, is a pre-test and a post-test. That is, using an assessment tool to measure what the student knows about the learning goals before the learning intervention, before playing the game, and what the student knows following the intervention. The gold standard for this is to use a normalized and validated research instrument, which is targeted specifically at the competencies addressed in the assessment's research questions. That is, we are looking to use tests that have been studied for their statistical reliability. That is, the questions (or other analysis tools) of the test(s) used as pre- and post- tests should be constructed so that an arbitrary selection of members of the target population of the study have the same chance of answering a question on the pre-test as on the correlate question on the post-test. While this gold standard is optimal, it can also be nearly impossible to achieve within a reasonably scoped study. This is primarily because each intervention we create has its own learning goals, often, but not always, designed to fill a niche in a particular region or state's curriculum. Each assessment needs to be keyed to the precise research questions of the assessment and the research questions are tied directly to the learning goals. It is therefore quite expensive to create normalized and validated instruments that address each research question for each study. Still, when a pre- and post-test is used, it is important to understand and account for the compromises in the testing tool and process. It is possible to use some testing tricks to approach normalization even when optimal normalization cannot be assured. If the number of participants is sufficiently high, the most effective way of handling a non-normalized and validated test can be to randomize questions between the pre- and post-test. If each question type is represented in each test, the questions can be distributed across the pre- and post-test within each population studied so that half of people within each group, randomly determined within the group, receive the first of two equivalent questions in the pre-test, and the other half receive the other question. In the post-test, these are switched. Unless the tests are handled by a relatively sophisticated online process, this too can be difficult to manage, and online tests that include logins are not entirely anonymous and can be therefore difficult to use without risking some threats to protecting human subjects. It is also important to watch human impact on the study, including such things as participant exhaustion. A participant is not as able to answer test questions before a long game and after a long game session. One can help with this problem by administering pre- and post-tests on different days than the intervention itself, but this also poses many challenges, some examples include the potential loss of participants because they cannot or choose not to participate in each day of the assessment, organizational difficulty orchestrating the assessment across multiple days, and the potential for confounding results due to other experiences the students have during the elapsed time. The level of normalization is a decision based on research scope and potential impact, and compromises should be minimized, but expected.

Within a lab, a researcher might also have access to other methods of taking quantitative data. Tracking eye or head movement during play can be easily interpreted quantitatively and the results are often reproducible (Gomes, Yassine, Worsley & Bilkstein, 2013). Other forms of identifying what is happening during observed data can also be used to identify the instances or duration of behaviors. This can include taking video, audio, or transcribed data and marking the data with identifying marks, or codes, which indicate data where something is happening that is interesting and potentially relevant to the researcher's research questions. In addition to coding data, other measures can be used to identify what is occurring. Time on task and recording how long a player is engaged in each activity within the game, are methods of directly and quantitatively collecting data related to gameplay. Time on task data collection is, essentially, recording the amount of time spent playing the game, often breaking play down into specific tasks and determining how much time is spent with each task. Methods such as this can provide a quantifiable measure of key behaviors that provide evidence of mastery (Bell, 2008).

The methods used are generally those that provide the greatest confidence of the learner's level of attainment of mastery. In explaining the limitations of the study, an account should be made of conditions that prevented true mirroring of interventions. These may include such factors as the use of similar but not identical classroom populations, limits in creating uniform content instruction, or potentially inconsistent levels of assistance given to students in performing in-game tasks. Given the realities of learning assessment, researchers cannot always control all variables, but a complete account helps future researchers to be aware of the limitations of the study.

Case Study Two: *Assessing Martha:* A mixed methods approach

The author was involved in mixed methods research on *Martha Madison's Marvelous Machines,* a learning game developed by Second Avenue Learning through a Small Business Innovation Research (SBIR) grant (Simkins, Egert & Decker, 2012). The game is a physics game targeted to teach the properties and uses of simple machines to middle school children, particularly middle school girls. This mixed methods approach used a combination of pre- and post-tests to show the effect of the intervention.

The study included three parts: a technical aptitude test, a Science, Technology, Engineering, and Mathematics (STEM) affinity test, and a content assessment targeted to the game's learning outcomes. The standardized technical aptitude test measured familiarity with web and PC applications. This test was given only during the pre-test and was used to determine if the population had the necessary skills to fully participate in the intervention without unintended effects due to unfamiliarity with the machines and controls. The STEM affinity test was derived from existing tests that show whether to what extent the participant sees STEM studies and STEM vocations as something in which they are capable and competent to engage. The content assessment tested the student's knowledge of the subject matter covered in the game and was adapted from standardized state assessments.

The pre- and post-tests were analyzed with typical statistical measures for test analysis, in this case one-tailed Wilcoxin signed-rank tests were used, given the sample size, controlled population, and types of questions. ANOVAs and t-tests are standard, when they are applicable.

In addition to pre- and post-tests, players were recorded playing the game and their in-game play was recorded. The in-game recording included a movie of each student's upper body as they played. This was matched with the in-game recording of their play, as their controlled characters moved through the game. The two video streams—in and out of game—were synchronized using pre-established markers as a beginning point for each. We did this by having the in-game characters perform a specific action that we recorded with the out of game camera by turning the camera on the screen. After the two streams were synchronized, we used Adobe Premiere to align the two videos into a single stream, side-by-side, for the purposes of data analysis. The side-by-side combined video was then coded using a pre-existing coding scheme.

Once the video was synchronized, researchers segmented the combined video into ten second chunks and codes were applied to each chunk. Using our pre-defined code set derived from similar research, researchers all coded one arbitrarily determined ten-minute section of video, recording all the codes that were applied to each ten-second segment. This created 60 coded segments (10 minutes = 600 seconds = 60 chunks). This short 10-minute subset was used to determine the inter-rater reliability. That is, to determine if there was sufficient uniformity among researchers to treat one researchers coding of a segment as equivalent to any other researchers. Once our inter-rater reliability target of 95% accuracy was achieved (difference among codes <= 0.05), researchers then coded the thirteen videos, again breaking the video into ten-second chunks for the purpose of coding. The videos had an average of 219 segments, which equates with 36.5 minutes (2190 seconds) of play. Each of the codes either applied (1) or did not apply (0) to the ten-second chunk, using criteria finalized during the inter-rater reliability process. The coding spreadsheet included each code as a column, and researchers added chunks as rows filling out which codes applied for each chunk (see Table 3). Codes were non-exclusive and independent. Each code could either apply or not apply to each chunk with no assumption of positive or negative causality between any two codes.

Table 3. Sample coding segment including 13 codes in ten-second increments.

	PRO	PEX	EXE	PAS	COO	STP	IMP	WGO	ALG	WEX	DSF	PUZ	REC
5:00	X		X								X		
5:10	X		X										
5:20			X										
5:30	X												
5:40			X									X	
5:50	X		X										
6:00	X												

The outcome of this coding method was a large bank of data that could be used to test statistical hypotheses, a form of mixed methods data collection. Since the video was maintained intact, areas of note could also be evaluated through traditional qualitative methods, such as discourse or conversation analysis.

These methods of coding produce anonymized collections of data that can be used to compare among participants playing the same game or between games, so long as any of the same codes are used. Since each code is independent from the others, the entire code set does not need to be identical, as each code stands alone as either applying or not applying to each ten seconds of video. It is not clear as yet, but it is likely important that the chunk size not vary between data sets, as the size of the chunk has an effect on the relative complexity of the data coded. Longer chunks are likely to have more codes relevant to each chunk.

Once the data set is established, it is possible to identify relative percentages of each code, showing trends within a given intervention. It is also possible to run statistical comparisons among the codes to determine if there are trends of codes over time, if some codes tend to correlate with others.

There are limits of what hypotheses can be tested with this data, depending on what exactly is coded. For example, since nothing coded particular speech patterns among players, such as turn taking, there would be no way to look for turn taking in the coded data. Many hypotheses are relevant to the data coded, however, and the coding process creates a data set that is largely agnostic to the kinds of analysis one might want to perform on the data.

Mixed methods

As one might expect, mixed methods approaches supplement quantitative data collection and analysis with qualitative data collection and analysis. Generally, the intent is to approach data collection from a few directions, using complementary methods to heighten the strengths and mitigate the weaknesses of each approach. This variety of approaches, called triangulation, is the most common approach for gaining confidence in mixed methods assessments. The intent of triangulation is to accept the inability to completely control or understand the environment and to try and overcome this limitation by showing the alignment or disjunction of results gleaned from multiple types of inquiry. On one level, triangulation, or the use of multiple methods in coordination, occurs in most data collection, even within purely quantitative or qualitative approaches. The key of mixed methods research is that quite different forms of collection are used, such as using ethnographic interview and qualitative discourse analysis alongside traditional statistical methods, or by interpreting qualitative data as quantitative data through a process of numerically evaluating qualitative data. The goal should be to increase one's understanding of the whole learning experience by combining several methods across the qualitative-quantitative divide, acknowledging and working to enhance benefits and mitigate limitations of each approach to more completely describe the learning taking place during and around gameplay.

Pre- and post-tests are staples of both quantitative and mixed methods assessments of learning. As part of a mixed methods assessment, the test can be combined easily with other methods to triangulate effect. Another common method is to create a close but more generalizable read of qualitative data by identifying specific activities during play, called coding, which can then be potentially understood through quantitative analysis. These codes may be based on "top-down," pre-determined rubrics, or they may be based on "bottom-up" codes developed by the researcher from ongoing research into games and learning. A top-down coding scheme is used when the researchers already know what information they are looking for in the study. Bottom-up coding schemes are more often used in exploratory studies, or in ongoing process of creating sets of codes that can be applied to data. These approaches are not necessarily mutually exclusive, and researchers may choose to make multiple "passes" through codes, using top-down codes to identify what they know they will be interested in, and using a bottom-up coding process to identify those activities they did not expect. This is time consuming, of course, but possible. It is also possible, especially in a new area of study, to use a bottom-up coding process on a substantial portion of the data to identify a set of desired codes, and then to use those codes in a top-down way to code the data.

Bottom-up coding schemes are often related to grounded theory approaches (Strauss, 1987; Glasser, 1992). In addition to grounded theory coding, thematic coding and clinical or standardized coding is common. Thematic codes identify tendencies or themes that recur in the coded data. Thematic codes are not justified exactly, but are designed by experts of phenomena, or in conjunction with expert insiders, to identify the interesting activities within a community practice. Standardized codes, including clinical codes, are systems of codes that have been used in previous studies and which have been given specific, normalized and reproducible definitions. All coding methods are also used to describe phenomenon in learning environments. While these coding schemes are not necessarily quantitative, they are compelling in part because they can be so easily converted into quantitative data, though quantitative interpretation of codes are not equally meaningful. The meaningfulness of this quantified qualitative data depends on the way the codes are determined and the quality and reproducibility of the coding scheme's results. As a result, clinical or standardized coding schemes are often produce the most meaningful and substantive quantitative data. There are several methods of achieving confidence in a coding system as a representation of quantitative as well as qualitative data. Central to them is the process of inter-rater reliability, which should be involved in all substantive coding processes. Developing inter-rater reliability involves testing the use of codes by multiple researchers coding the same content. These codes are then compared to determine that the coders are coding the same phenomenon the same way. To achieve parity of coding, researchers will need to engage in a process of learning and negotiating a uniform understanding of the precise meaning of each code within the group of researchers (Johnson, Penny, & Gordon, 2008). The somewhat arbitrary standard for acceptable inter-rater reliability is greater than 90% agreement when using a pairwise comparison of coded data. When comparing data between two coders, greater than 95% agreement is considered acceptable. The 95% agreement (>= 5% variance) is preferable in almost all studies.

As triangulation is generally central to mixed methods approaches, the qualitative and quantitative methods that are chosen are coordinated to complement each other. The key is to provide a convincing collection of data that can identify the successes and limitations of the learning environment and intervention. While more data may always seem better, it is important not to take data based on different initial premises and epistemologies and then interpret them as if they were coherent with each other. While pragmatist epistemologies may be able to interpret almost all methods as useful to an increased understanding of phenomenon, and could find useful comparisons among almost any sets of data, positivist empirical epistemologies would have use for most qualitative data, and most post-modern epistemologies would have little use for data claiming to be universal.

Qualitative methods

Qualitative methods involve collecting data on what people are doing within their context. This involves a very close read of the actions, speech, practices, and behaviors—words that may or may not mean the same things, depending on one's qualitative tradition. It is also important to qualitative researchers to provide a close read of the environment, social, cultural, and physical, and to provide, in analysis, an account of how these phenomena effect, correlate with or interact with each other. I use the term tradition here because multiple traditions exist within the same methodology. For our purposes here, tradition refers to one's qualitative research style. Methodologies relate to one's ontological and epistemological beliefs, which is "what is" and "how we can come to understand it," respectively.

Regardless of tradition or methodology, qualitative methods are used to tell the story of the intervention and the students' passage through it. In some traditions this storytelling is a metaphor, and the story is a description of what occurred. In other traditions, the researcher's role is quite literally to depict a story of what occurred through, for example, writing, film, or theater. In either case, the goal is to produce a substantive and knowledge-producing account.

Qualitative inquiry can be broken into two loose categories—ethnography and case study. Ethnography is the study of culture. It is an in depth, all-inclusive form of inquiry involving involvement in the practices of a culture, recording of field notes, and reporting out in a way that produces deep understanding of the target population. One major strand of ethnography follows Geertz (1973) methods for producing what he calls "thick description" of culture. Thick description is produced through a multi-layer account of many events that bring into analysis multiple perspectives, which are sensitive to and include within the description the role of as many contextual influences as possible. While much of quantitative analysis seeks to reduce the effect of outside influence from the description of the event, ethnographic analysis seeks to incorporate a rich and complete description of contextual influences into the description of the event. Whereas most quantitative analysis finds greatest utility in that which can be abstracted, qualitative analysis finds greatest utility in that which can be understood wholly only within a complex context.

In contrast to ethnography, case study is narrower in focus. Rather than studying culture as a whole, case study takes a narrower view, perhaps focusing on a single event, person, or group. Due to its narrower focus, case study is more often utilized in games assessment. There are ethnographies that focus on games and learning (Steinkuehler, 2004), but the focus on ethnography as a study of culture often precludes it from looking at a particular game as effective for learning. Assessment of the game for learning may be a part of the whole, but it is only a part of the whole.

Still, while ethnography is a larger enterprise, many qualitative case studies that study the efficacy of games make use of ethnographic methods to gain a rich understanding of what is occurring in and around gameplay. Ethnographic observation and interviews are methods used within many case studies.

Whether case study or ethnography, qualitative methods require the same three stages as all research—data collection, data analysis, and reporting. Data collection is dominated by traditional ethnographic methods, but analysis is varied in both ethnography and case study. Contemporary qualitative research in games and learning utilizes a variety of methods of analysis, including ethnomethodology (Garfinkle, 1967), conversation analysis (Sacks, 1992), discourse analysis (Gee, 2005), expert-novice study (Chase & Simon, 1973), narrative analysis (Bruner, 1990), and practice theory (Bourdieu, 1977). The diversity of methods is, in part, due to the descriptive nature of qualitative inquiry, and there is significant overlap and often non-distinctive lines between different approaches. The best methods will be those that help to make a case for the affordances and limitations of learning that takes place in play and helps others to create effective learning environments or games (see Table 2). The rigor of the method is reflected in the degree to which the data is included and interpreted fairly and completely within the complexity of its context. Its usefulness will be in the researchers ability to synthesize a meaningful narrative from that complex data such that the reader comes away with a deeper understanding of the subject of research, in this case the learning the occurred during play.

Table 2. Strengths and challenges in sample qualitative methods

	Strengths	Challenges
Ethnomethodology/ practice theory	Deep focus on practice can reveal ways in which learning turns into legitimate participation.	Time consuming. Focus on process and practice may be too restrictive for most games and learning assessments.
Conversation analysis	Reveals language as facilitation and constraint of activity. Identified meaning, norms, and action in text.	Requires focus on a small data set. Limited use of context.
Critical discourse analysis	Contextualizing text can expand understanding of language to understanding of practice.	Time consuming. Requires extensive understanding and engagement with context.
Expert-novice study	Can show process of how learners develop into experts. Can identify patterns in error as one develops understanding.	Requires a prior understanding of expertise in a practice.
Narrative analysis	Able to identify the conveyed reasons behind practice— the "why" of practice. Identifies ways that knowledge is shared.	Limited coherence between "objective" learning goals and the participant-focused assessment of meaning may limit use when specific learning goals are being studied, rather than the process of learning.
Ethnography (cultural, cognitive, etc.)	Thick description can provides deep understanding of phenomena.	Time consuming. Data collection and sifting and winnowing process of analysis places little or no value on research efficiency. Can treat culture as static rather than dynamic.

As with quantitative assessment, the qualitative researcher will need to attend to the central learning objectives of the game, and the assessment will hold the intervention to its ability to achieve these objectives. More than with quantitative research, however, qualitative research can identify previously unforeseen learning occurring within the phenomenon. This is in large part because qualitative research is concerned not with describing conformity to what was expected to happen, but to accurately describe what did happen. To do this it is important for the researcher to be able to be surprised, without necessarily trying to be surprised, by what occurs during observations, which allows for previously unexpected observations.

The greatest strength of qualitative research is in its ability to incorporate the effects of context and to explain the significance of context within learning. It is able to mark the process of learning over time while incorporating the context and to identify trends and changes within a single research participant. The cost of this is high in terms of time required for data collection and analysis. The time and amount of access required by qualitative researchers generally means that they follow a very limited number of participants. The method of describing learning process in qualitative inquiry is not seeking wide-scale verifiability and it would be impossible to recreate a learning environment exactly as it occurred in the qualitative analysis.

Case Study Three: Cognitive Ethnography of *Lineage*

Ethnographies are well-discussed, particularly within the field of anthropology. A rigorous, long-term ethnographic inquiry (Geertz, 1973; Malaby, 2003; Chen, 2012; Simkins, in press) may be the best possible approach to qualitative research, when time and access allows. Within educational research, researchers often lack either time or access to complete ethnographic inquiry, which requires months of intense participation within the community, but those that are completed can provide much needed insight into learning.

Conducting an ethnography requires a holistic approach to the understanding of culture. The social, cultural, and physical environment is explored from a contemporary and historical perspective. Analysis of observation involves a move between emic points of view, those from within the studied culture, and etic points of view, those from outside the culture, usually primarily focused on the perspective of the researcher.

One educational games ethnography was conducted by Steinkuehler (2004) over the course of two years, through interacting with a particular community of gamers who started together on *Lineage*, a massively multiplayer online game released by Korean company NC Soft. The community was on English speaking servers, and included participants from across the world as they played *Lineage*, and later moved on to *Lineage 2* and *World of Warcraft*.

Over the course of two years, Steinkuehler had the opportunity to play with a large variety of game players, learn specialist language around the game, and explore the specific practices that signify expert game playing. The work was largely analyzed through discourse analysis, and included a number of analytic tools including various kinds of expert-novice studies, studies of ethical play, cheating, ways of playing that mark one as an insider or outside to the core community of the game, and how one transitions from peripheral to central participant. A lot of time and energy is spent on understanding what it means to be full member of the practice, what it means for one's sense of being and identity as a leader, follower, and member of community.

Through this inquiry, a core group of practitioners became her core participants, and playing involved building trust and care relationships with her participants. Eventually, Steinkuehler became a community leader in her own right, having established herself as a trustworthy and valuable member of the community. This was not intended, nor particularly desirable for Steinkuehler as a researcher, but it did open doors to understanding all sides of the complex negotiations that underlie forming and maintaining a group of players within each of these games—each of which have particular challenges and affordances when it comes to developing meaningful connections between community members.

While tools of analysis vary widely, data collection is more uniform, and both are in ample evidence in Steinkuehler's ethnographic data. The first is an extensive record of observation of activities in and around play. The second is evolving interviews with key informants who can describe and explain the practices of the community, and help the researcher to interpret meaning of behaviors and patterns evident in observations. These interviews may be formal interview interactions where the researcher and participant are self-consciously engaging in an interview. It can also be informal interview interactions that occur during normal interactions in and around the games. As with almost any other modern research, each of the participants was aware that they were engaged in research, and each was identified by a pseudonym that protected them from potential social ramifications for what they might have said. The combination of interviews and observations allowed Steinkuehler to gain an in-depth understanding of these communities of practice as they played the three MMOs.

Best Practices

1. Identify the game's learning goals, both explicitly and implicitly.
2. Create assessment methods that maximize access to and understanding of data relevant to the learning goals. Ensure that the methods are compatible with researcher's epistemological commitments.
3. Assess the game using rigorous standards.
4. Report on your assessment, clearly identifying your epistemology, methods used, and learning goals assessed. Include a good description of the gameplay that shows the relevance of learning goals to the gameplay.

Resources

Epistemology and Methods

Cresswell, J. W. (2008). *Research Design: Qualitative, Quantitative, and Mixed Methods Approaches*. LosAngeles, CA: Sage Publications.

Greeno, J., Collins, A. M., & Resnick, L. (1996). *Cognition and Learning.* (pp. 15–46) In D. Berliner and R. Calfee (Eds.), *Handbook of Educational Psychology.* New York: Macmillan.

Levison, S. C. (1983). *Pragmatics.* Cambridge, UK: Cambridge University Press.

Assessment

Annetta, L. & Bronack, S. (2011). *Serious Educational Games Assessment: Practical Methods and Models for Educational Games, Simulations and Virtual Worlds*. Rotterdam, The Netherlands: Sense Publishers.

Shute, V. J. (2011). Stealth Assessment in Computer-Based Games to Support Learning. In S. Tobias & J. D. Fletcher (Eds.), Computer games and instruction (pp. 503–524). Charlotte, NC: Information Age.

Learning Game Design

Bogost, I. (2007). *Persuasive Games: The Expressive Power of Videogames.* Cambridge, MA: MIT Press.

Gee, J. P. (2007). *What Videogames Have to Teach us about Learning and Literacy.*New York: Palgrave MacMillan.

Salen, K., & Zimmerman, E. (2005). Game Design and Meaningful Play. In J. Raessens & J. Goldstein (Eds.), *Handbook of Computer Game Studies* (pp. 59–80). Cambridge, MA: MIT Press.

Squire, K. (2011). *Videogames and Learning: Teaching and Participatory Culture in the Digital Age.* New York: Teacher's College Press.

References

Annetta, L. & Bronack, S. (Eds) (2010). *Serious educational game assessment: Practical methods and models for educational games, simulations, and virtual worlds.* Boston, MA: Sense Publishers.

Bell, Ann (2008). *Game rubric: Assessing student learning in virtual simulations and serious games.* Downloaded on July 17, 2013 from http://www2.uwstout.edu/content/profdev/rubrics/gamerubric.html .

Betz, J. (1995-6). Computer games: Increase learning in an interactive multidisciplinary environment. *Journal of Educational Technology Systems.* 24(2), pp 195-205.

Black, R.W. (2008). *Adolescents and online fan fiction.* New York: Peter Lang.

Bourdieu, P. (1977). *Outline of a theory of practice.* Cambridge, MA: Cambridge University Press.

Bruner, J. (1990). *Acts of meaning.* Cambridge, MA: Harvard University Press.

Chase, W. G. & Simon, H. A. (1973). Perception in chess. *Cognitive Psychology.* 4, 55-81.

Chen, M. (2012). *Leet noobs: The life and death of an expert player group in World of Warcraft.* New York: Peter Lang.

Clark, D. B., Tanner-Smith, E. E., Killingsworth, S., & Bellamy, S. (2013). *Digital games for learning: A systematic review and meta-analysis.* Menlo Park, CA: SRI International.

Cresswell, J W. (2008). *Research design: Qualitative, quantitative, and mixed methods approaches.* LosAngeles, CA: Sage Publications.

D'Angelo, C., Rutstein, D., Harris, C., Haertel, G., Bernard, R., & Borokhovski, E. (2013). *Review of computer-based simulations for STEM learning in K-12 education.* Menlo Park, CA: SRI International.

Dibbell, J. (2006). *Play money: Or, how I quit my day job and made millions trading virtual loot.* New York: Basic Books.

Garfinkle, H. (1967).*Studies in ethnomethodology.* Englewood Cliffs, CA: Prentice Hall.

Gee, J. P. (2005). *An introduction to discourse analysis: Theory and method.* London: Routledge.

Gee, J. P. (2007). *What videogames have to teach us about learning and literacy.* New York: Palgrave MacMillan.

Gee, J. P. (2012). *Big "G" games.* Downloaded on July 17, 2013 from http://www.jamespaulgee.com/node/63 .

Geertz, C. (1973). Thick description: Toward an interpretive theory of culture. In *The Interpretation of Cultures: Selected Essays.* New York: Basic Books, 3-30.

Glaser, B. (1992). *Basics of grounded theory analysis.* Mill Valley, CA: Sociology Press.

Gomes, J. S., Yassine, M., Worsley, M. & Bilkstein, P. (2013). Eye tracking analysis of visual spatial engineering games.In the proceedings of *The Sixth Annual Conference on Educational Data Mining* (EDM 2013). Memphis, TN, July 6-9.

Greeno, J., Collins, A. M., & Resnick, L. (1996). Cognition and learning. (pp. 15–46) In D. Berliner and R. Calfee (Eds.), *Handbook of Educational Psychology.* New York: Macmillan.

Hammersley, M. & Atkinson, P. (1986). *Ethnography: Principles in practice (2nd ed.).* London· Routledge.

Ifenthaler, D., Eseryl, D., & Ge, X. (2012). *Assessment in Games based learning.* New York: Springer.

Jenkins, H. (2012). *Textual poachers: Television fans and participatory culture.* New York: Routledge.

Johnson, R. L., Penny, J. A., & Gordon, B. (2008). *Assessing performance: Designing, scoring, and validating performance tasks.* New York: The Guilford Press.

Kafai, Y. & Fields, D. (2009). Cheating in virtual worlds: Transgressive designs for learning. *On the horizon 17*(1), 12-20.

Keegan, B., M. Ahmad, J. Srivastava, D. Williams, N. Contractor (2011). Dark gold: Statistical properties of clandestine networks in massively multiplayer online games. *International Journal of Social Computing and Cyber-Physical Systems.*

Latour, B. (2004). Why has critique run out of steam? From matters of fact to matters of concern. *Critical Inquiry 30*(2),25-248.

Levison, S. C. (1983). *Pragmatics.* Cambridge, UK: Cambridge University Press.

Magnifico, A. (2010). Writing for whom? Cognition, motivation, and a writer's audience. *Educational psychologist 45*(3), 167-184.

Malaby, T. (2003). *Gambling life: Dealing with contingency in a Greek city.* Urbana, IL: University of Illinois Press.

Menand, L. (2001). *The metaphysical club.* New York: Farrar, Strauss, and Giroux.

Pallas, A. M. (2001). Preparing education doctoral students for epistemological diversity. *Educational Researcher 30*(5), pp 6-11.

Sacks, H. (1992). *Lectures on conversation, volumes I and II.* Oxford, England: Blackwell.

Science Applications International Corporation (SAIC) (2007). Games: A look at emerging trends, uses, threats and opportunities in influence activities. Downloaded from *ProPublica* on 2/20/2014. http://www.propublica.org/documents/item/889134-games

Shaffer, D. W. (2006). *How computer games help children learn.* New York: Palgrave Macmillan.

Shute, V. J. (2011). Stealth assessment in computer-based games to support learning. In S. Tobias & J. D. Fletcher (Eds.), *Computer games and instruction* (pp. 503–524). Charlotte, NC: Information Age.

Simkins, D. (in press). *The arts of LARP: Design, literacy, learning and community in Live Action Role Playing.* Jefferson, NC: McFarland Press.

Simkins, D., Egert, C., and Decker, A. (2012). Evaluating *Martha Madison:* Developing analytical tools for gauging the breadth of learning facilitated by STEM Games. In *Proceedings from the 2012 IEEE International Games Innovation Conference,* pp. 137-140. Rochester, NY, September 7-9, 2012.

Simkins, D. & Steinkuehler, C. (2008). Critical ethical reasoning & role play. *Games & Culture,* 3, 333-355.

Squire, K. (2011). *Videogames and learning: Teaching and participatory culture in the digital age.* New York: Teacher's College Press.

South, J. & Snow, B. (2012). Immersive game design: Aligning game mechanics with learning goals to maximize engagement and mastery. 18th Annual SLOAN Consortium International Conference on Online Learning, October 11-12.

Steinkuehler, C. A. (2004). *Learning in Massively Multiplayer Online games.* Downloaded on 11/1/2013 from http://citeseerx.ist.psu.edu/viewdoc/download?doi=10.1.1.105.626&rep=rep1&type=pdf

Steinkuehler, C. (2007). Massively multiplayer online gaming as a constellation of literacy practices. In B. E. Shelton & D. Wiley (Eds.), *The Design and Use of Simulation Computer Games in Education* (pp. 187-212). Rotterdam, The Netherlands: Sense Publishers.

Steinkuehler, C., King, E., Alagoz, E., Anton, G., Chu, S., Elmergreen, J., Fahser-Herro, D., Harris, S., Martin, C., Ochsner, A., Oh, Y., Owen, V. L., Simkins, D., Williams, C., & Zhang, B. (2011). Let me know when she stops talking: Using games for learning without colonizing play. In C. Steinkuehler, C. Martin, & A. Ochsner (Eds.), *Proceedings of the 7th Annual Games+Learning+ Society (GLS) Conference.* Pittsburgh PA: ETC Press.

Squire, K. (2005). Changing the game: What happens when videogames enter the classroom? *Innovate Journal of Online Education.* 1(6).

Squire, K. (2011). *Video games and learning: Teaching and participatory culture in the video age.* New York: Teacher's College Press.

Strauss, A. (1987). *Qualitative analysis for social scientists.* Cambridge, England: Cambridge University Press.